*Eighth Edition*

# PUBLIC RELATIONS PRACTICES

## MANAGERIAL CASE STUDIES AND PROBLEMS

### Allen H. Center, Fellow PRSA

*Distinguished Resident Lecturer*
*San Diego State University*
*Retired Vice-President, Public Relations, Motorola Inc.*

### Patrick Jackson, Fellow PRSA

*Editor, pr reporter*
*Senior Counsel & Partner, Jackson Jackson & Wagner*
*Former Adjunct Faculty, Boston University*

### Stacey Smith, APR, Fellow PRSA

*Senior Counsel and Partner, Jackson Jackson & Wagner*
*Former Adjunct Faculty, Antioch University,*
*University of New Hampshire*

### Frank R. Stansberry, APR, Fellow PRSA

*Instructor, Public Relations, University of Central Florida (Retired)*
*The Coca-Cola Company (Retired)*

Boston   Columbus   Indianapolis   New York   San Francisco   Upper Saddle River
Amsterdam   Cape Town   Dubai   London   Madrid   Milan   Munich   Paris   Montréal   Toronto
Delhi   Mexico City   São Paulo   Sydney   Hong Kong   Seoul   Singapore   Taipei   Tokyo

**Editor in Chief:** Stephanie Wall
**Director of Editorial Services:** Ashley Santora
**Editorial Project Manager:** Lynn M. Savino
**Editorial Assistant:** Jacob Garber
**Director of Marketing:** Maggie Moylan
**Executive Marketing Manager:** Anne Falhgren
**Marketing Assistant:** Gianna Sandri
**Senior Managing Editor:** Judy Leale
**Production Project Manager:** Thomas Benfatti
**Operations Specialist:** Thomas Benfatti
**Creative Art Director:** Jayne Conte
**Cover Designer:** Suzanne Duda
**Cover Photo:** Shutterstock
**Full-Service Project Management:** Jouve
**Composition:** Jouve
**Printer/Binder:** Courier Westford
**Cover Printer:** Moore Langen
**Text Font:** Times

Credits and acknowledgments borrowed from other sources and reproduced, with permission, in this textbook appear on the appropriate page within text.

**Library of Congress Cataloging-in-Publication Data**

Public relations practices: managerial case studies and problems / Allen H. Center ... [et al.]. — 8th ed.
   p. cm.
  Includes index.
  ISBN 978-0-13-312764-5
 1. Public relations—Case studies.  I. Center, Allen H.
  HM1221.P787 2014
  659.2—dc23

2012041110

4 5 6 7 8 9 10 V092 15 14

ISBN 10: 0-13-312764-8
ISBN 13: 978-0-13-312764-5

# This book is now and forever will be dedicated

*To Allen Center and Patrick Jackson, two of the most gifted and insightful practitioners of all time. May your vision and commitment to the profession of public relations be reflected for years to come through the students, teachers, and professionals you have educated and empowered. May those students, teachers, and professionals continue to find ways to share your vision of the fundamental importance of public relations' role in giving individuals a voice in decisions that affect their lives.*

## A TRIBUTE TO CENTER AND JACKSON

### Allen H. Center, APR, Fellow PRSA, Leader, Writer, Teacher, Inspiration

By Glen M. Broom, San Diego State University

Allen H. Center took early retirement as vice-president of Motorola in 1973 to write the first edition of *Public Relations Practices,* a management case studies book for advanced public relations students. Patrick Jackson joined Allen as coauthor beginning with the fourth edition, published in 1990.

Allen's public relations career began during World War II in the Southwest Pacific. For three years in Guadalcanal, New Guinea, and the Philippines, Corporal Center edited a daily newspaper for the 13th Air Force Fighter Command Headquarters.

That began a public relations career that spanned more than 60 years and included stops with Parker Pen, Motorola, Leo Burnett, and finally San Diego State University, where he taught part time as SDSU's first and only "Distinguished Resident Lecturer." He taught there until 1987.

In 1981, he received the PRSA's highest national honor—the Gold Anvil—for his contributions to advancing our field. In 1986 he was the second person to be inducted into the Arthur W. Page Society's Hall of Fame. (Page's son John was the first, and Scot Cutlip the third.)

Allen served as president of the Foundation for Public Relations Research and Education, now the Institute for Public Relations, 1973–1975. In 1977, he established and, with matching funds from the Motorola Foundation, endowed that organization's Pathfinder Award, which annually recognizes scholarly research in public relations. He and his wife, Nancy, also endowed the Allen H. Center Lectureship in Public Relations at San Diego State University.

In a lifetime of achievement, Allen Center was a true pathfinder who set the standards and aspirations for the emerging profession that he saw as his "calling." Until his death in November 2005 at age 93, he served as role model for generations of students and practitioners who shared his vision of the social value and nobility of purpose in building harmonious relationships.

### A Colleague Remembers Pat Jackson

*—Melvin L. Sharpe, APR, Fellow PRSA,*
*Professor & Coordinator PR, Department of*
*Journalism, Ball State University, Muncie, Indiana*

Pat inspired and encouraged us to think outside the box. He served as a beacon in a sea of professionals. Pat Jackson provided vision.

At a 1984 Schranz Lectureship at Ball State University, Pat challenged students and attending professionals to "lift their eyes above process and to concentrate on behavioral outcomes." The lecture is as fresh today as it was then. When the lecture was handed out in a recent conference where Patrick was speaking, he said, "Mel, have I been speaking on this need that long?" Of course he had, and he kept challenging professionals to think about behavioral outcomes and to apply behavioral knowledge to performance until his death.

So how do we pay tribute to a man who influenced a profession, influenced public relations education, influenced recognition of the importance of high ethical values, and who stood as a leader in the profession and education in every sense of the word?

The answer is simple.

It is the only answer we can have. We simply must not allow the torch that Pat carried as the result of his love and belief in the public relations profession to go out or to touch the ground. Pick it up. A thousand hands. Carry it forward. When we do so, we will adequately honor him and what he stood for in our profession. Pat built vision and that is what we must have.

We treasure his memory and the values for which he stood.

---

## Pat Jackson believed . . .

**Any profession exists only by public consent** and that public relations provides an overriding social benefit when people have a voice. His ideal was Jeffersonian democracy. Public relations becomes a true profession when it brings people in touch with organizations, ideas, and leaders. Every organization needs a person who can listen to what people are thinking and bring about harmonious relationships.

**Harmony is an outcome of public relations practiced over a long time.** On the way, there is room for conflict and conflict management. Harmony by itself, however, will not be effective unless it is part of a process of mutually beneficial behavior, such as buying products and coming to work. When real trust develops, it is a sign that we have done our job properly. Trust arises from only one thing, and that is consistency.

**Harmonious relationships—not just relations—fortified with trust require coauthorship.** It is the win–win idea, in contrast to the victory syndrome. An organization must become so close to its publics that its policies, products, and stands on issues reflect the thoughts of key publics. Don't, however, pander. Create enough understanding so they can participate in an organization's thinking. Then turn some of the decision-making authority over to publics.

It is the role of public relations to help managers understand that their **communications role is to transmit not only information but emotions and intuition.**

Pat believed in going the whole way on the hierarchy of effects **to seek changes in behavior.** He felt that unless we, as practitioners, could impact behavior, we weren't doing our job. That building awareness was only a preliminary step and that the profession would never be taken seriously in the C-suite until we could impact the bottom line and prove it through behavioral research.

*Otto Lerbinger, Professor Emeritus, Boston University, Boston, Massachusetts, written in* pr reporter, *April 2, 2001.*

---

*Note:* pr reporter *was the leading think piece in the field of public relations, edited for 25 years by Patrick Jackson.*

*Stacey Smith*

# BRIEF CONTENTS

# CONTENTS

# PREFACE

As case texts mature, more and more often individual cases take on the aura of classics. It becomes difficult to remove a case that so well defines a subject, classically illustrates the models and theories, or, in its success or failure, teaches so well. But then again, time goes on and new cases arise that teach the key principles and are definitive of our time. We call these "teachable moments."

The practical purpose of this text remains the same. We seek, with case studies and problems, to help future practitioners understand the principles of and become agile in applying effective two-way communications in a wide variety of situations likely to confront them and their employers.

## New to This Edition

- Fifteen new cases—almost half the book—including some of the most-talked-about events of the recent past
- Ten additional cases updated with new events to shed a different light or paired with similar events happening now in other organizations
- Contributions of cases from leading academics and practitioners, to add new voices and perspectives
- Social media elements added or considered in most cases
- More content—eliminating some nice-to-have visuals that are replaced by thoughtful commentary
- And most important: a Web site to access many retired cases from editions 1 through 7, or to discuss current and future cases. Go to www.prpractices.com.

## HOW THE BOOK IS ORGANIZED

1. *The first two chapters* describe the purposes of public relations and the manner in which the function deals with problems and opportunities.
2. The bulk of the book contains *real-life case studies* in eight chapters that are organized according to primary publics, such as employees and media, or major problems such as public issues, crisis management, and standards or ethics.
3. Each chapter has a *definitive introduction* providing insights that come to life in the cases that follow. Introductions vary in size and substance, tailored to the assumed knowledge of students. Employee relations, for instance, reflects that most students have had work experience of some kind, whereas crisis management contains elements most students will not yet have encountered.
4. Each chapter closes with a *case problem* or two for class discussion closely related to the thrust of the chapter.

We believe that there is enough variety to permit educators to select sections that fit the size of their classes and the structure of their courses—and enough provocation for lively classroom participation.

## THE AUTHORS AND THEIR APPROACH

Following the lead and style of Patrick Jackson from earlier editions, Frank and Stacey have updated the book to be an interesting read—one that keeps your attention but will cause you to think!

Frank R. Stansberry, APR, Fellow, PRSA, retired in 2006 as an instructor of public relations at the University of Central Florida. His career spanned 46 years of print journalism, agency, and corporate public relations, and, finally, education. A member of the Public Relations Society of America since 1971, he served the Society and the profession at every level—local, district, and national. He was inducted into the PRSA College of Fellows in 1997.

Stacey Smith, APR, Fellow, PRSA, has been practicing public relations for 32 years and is Senior Counsel & Partner at Jackson Jackson & Wagner. She worked side by side with Patrick Jackson until his passing in 2001. She has taught at both the graduate and undergraduate levels. She is a frequent public speaker on the subject of behavioral public relations and is the editor of *The Best of Pat Jackson in* pr reporter, a compendium of Jackson's writings, theories, and models published over his quarter century as editor of that publication.

The authors purposely chose to use a narrative description and avoided a set format for presenting each case. The real world does not come neatly packaged. The many teachers who regularly share their experiences with the text tell us they want students to gain experience in picking out the problem situation, delineating an environmental scan, and having to decide whether the solutions chosen were wise or flawed. Outlining the cases according to a formula denies them this most important learning from case studies.

Putting together a text of real-life case *studies,* contrasted with a collection of successful case *histories,* requires objective cooperation among the organizations represented, particularly when the subject, the scenario, or the conclusion is not laudatory. We are grateful for the information and illustrations supplied. We hope the cooperation pays off, and this text enables instruction to be better attuned to the pressing needs of employers and the profession.

### Contributors

Thanks to all those who contributed a variety of excellent cases to this edition. The various perspectives—geographical, academic, practitioner, specialty area—make this edition broader and stronger.

- Tiffany Derville Gallicano (Ph.D., University of Maryland) is an assistant professor of public relations at the University of Oregon. Social media and relationship management are her areas of specialization. She won the Jackson-Sharpe award for her research about ghost blogging, and she is a Page Legacy Scholar. Her experience includes work for a U.S. Senate campaign, two major public relations agencies, a nonprofit organization, and an educational institution. (Case 6-4: Marriott on the Move Cultivates Customer Relationships)
- With previous experience as a grassroots civil rights organizer and one of the founders of the Cambridge (Massachusetts) Women's Center, Bev Edwards, Temple, New Hampshire, chair of the Temple Energy Committee and coordinator, Monadnock Energy Resources Initiative, has led her town's energy committee in a multifaceted program of stunningly successful local energy conservation efforts. She is also coordinating a program to bring low-cost weatherizations and solar energy installations into New Hampshire's Monadnock region, using the community-building model of volunteer labor and "barn-raisers."(Case 4-4: Driving Community Behavior to Save Energy and the Environment)

- Deborah Silverman, Ph.D., APR, is an associate professor and associate chair of the Buffalo State College Communication Department. Her academic research focuses on the role of ethics in the public relations curriculum and service learning in the public relations classroom. She was a practitioner for more than 20 years before becoming a full-time professor of public relations. (Case 9-3: The Crash of Continental Connection Flight 3407; Case 9-4: The Case of BP)
- Paul Dusseault is a 25-year veteran of Fleishman-Hillard, one of the world's leading communications firms. He has directed strategic media and publicity initiatives for some of the agency's largest clients and currently heads the account team serving Aflac. As senior vice-president and senior partner, he leads the corporate practice group at Fleishman-Hillard's Atlanta office. He is a former newspaper reporter. He received a bachelor's degree in history from Loyola University in New Orleans. (Case 5-2: Aflac Gives Shareholders a Say on Pay)
- Robin Schell, APR, Fellow PRSA, is senior counsel and partner at Jackson Jackson & Wagner, a national public relations and management consulting firm. She specializes in strategic planning, behavioral public relations research, internal communications, crisis communications, and community relationship-building programs. She lectures on communications topics to client and professional associations across the country and has served as an adjunct professor at both the University of South Carolina and the University of New Hampshire. She is an accredited member of the PRSA and an active member of the College of Fellows. (Case 3-1: Southwest Airlines Takes on AirTran and Blends Employee Cultures)
- Dr. Shannon A. Bowen is a tenured associate professor at University of South Carolina. Bowen specializes in communication ethics, strategic communication management, issues management, dominant coalition decisions, public relations theory, organizational communication, social media and engagement, and the intersection of organizational culture with ethics. Bowen's Ph.D. (2000) is from the University of Maryland in communication (with the Grunigs) and business management (marketing). Her dissertation on the pharmaceutical industry, *A Theory of Ethical Issues Management: Contributions of Kantian Deontology to Public Relations' Ethics and Decision Making,* won the International Communication Association's (ICA) Public Relations Division Outstanding Dissertation Award for 2000–2002. Her master's degree, specializing in corporate crisis management, is from the University of South Carolina, and her bachelor's degree is from the University of North Carolina at Chapel Hill in both journalism (advertising) and sociology (quantitative methodology). (Case 10-1: Forest Laboratories and Celexa)
- Dr. Barb DeSanto, APR, Fellow PRSA, teaches and writes in the A.Q. Miller School of Journalism and Mass Communications at Kansas State University. DeSanto's research areas include public relations management, public relations curriculum development, and public relations management roles. DeSanto earned her doctorate from Oklahoma State University in 1995 and has recently published *Public Relations: A Managerial Perspective* with coauthor Dr. Danny Moss, University of Chester, United Kingdom. DeSanto is active in the Association for Education in Journalism and Mass Communication (AEJMC) and the Public Relations Society of America (PRSA). (Case 5-3: Money Smart Week®)
- Dr. Rachel Kovacs is an adjunct associate professor and teaches public relations and other communication courses at the College of Staten Island and John Jay College of Criminal Justice, City University of New York. Her areas of research specialization are international public relations, NGO activism, and corporate social responsibility. Dr. Kovacs has been an adviser to PRSA chapters at the University of Hartford and Bradley University

and directed Hartford's 2001 award-winning PRSSA entry in the national Bateman Competition. (Case 6-3: Johnson & Johnson Then and Now)

- Ken Plowman, associate professor, Brigham Young University, specializes in strategic communication and conflict resolution in public relations. He earned a doctorate in journalism from the University of Maryland and an MPA from George Washington University. He has spent 15 years in the field of public relations, the majority of that time on Capitol Hill. He is the author of over 40 publications and is a retired public affairs officer from the U.S. Army Reserve. (Case 7-1: Real Salt Lake Builds Stadium in Utah)
- James Fetig, APR, has practiced public relations in a variety of sectors including the U.S. military, the White House, Ketchum Public Relations, Lockheed Martin, the Raytheon Company, and the Georgia Institute of Technology. He is currently the chief communications officer for the Corporation for National and Community Service in Washington, D.C. (Case 3-3: How 100-Day Plans Work)
- Jonathan Slater, Ph.D., is an associate professor in SUNY Plattsburgh's Center for Communication and Journalism, where he leads the public relations program. His career includes work in public relations, advertising, economic development, and public television. Dr. Slater is a former Fellow of SUNY Plattsburgh's Institute for Ethics in Public Life. Dr. Slater received his Ph.D. from New York University's Steinhardt School. (Case 9-4: The Case of BP)

## And Finally, Ethics

We would like to stress the importance and necessity of combining all public relations actions with both personal and professional ethics in behavior. PRSA's Member Code of Ethics (see Chapter 10 for further discussion) deals with this combination. As the Code states: "The foundation of our value to our companies, clients, and those we serve is their ability to rely on our ethical and morally acceptable behavior."

Codes of ethics can be found not only on the PRSA Web site but on most all public relations associations' Web sites including those for the following organizations:

- PRSA—Public Relations Society of America
- NSRPA—National School Public Relations Association
- IPR—Institute for Public Relations
- Arthur W. Page Society
- IPRA—International Public Relations Association
- IABC—International Association of Business Communicators

The main principles adhered to include:

- Present fact-based content, with the obvious implication that you should tell the truth at all times.
- To be an objective advocate, providing timely and credible information and offering direct interaction with all expert sources.
- Making relevant and accurate information available to all interested parties, disclosing participation in online chat rooms and conferences, and correcting misinformation that appears online.
- Educating the public relations profession on best practices in the use of the Internet and new media.

# 1

# The Purposes
# of Public Relations

## PUBLIC RELATIONS IS AN APPLIED SCIENCE

However firm our grasp of the principles, the history, and the theories of any field, they are not useful to us unless we can apply them to actual cases. This statement is true for the entry-level recent graduate and the seasoned professional. The proof of competence is being able to handle cases successfully for employers or clients.

- The bottom line of public relations practice is in the results that come from putting theories and principles to work and in doing so in a way that benefits the organization issuing the paycheck *and* the society of which that organization is a part.

For this reason, the case study method of learning about public relations is an essential part of a practitioner's education. Case studies accurately model situations that organizations, managers, and public relations practitioners routinely face.

Though this book came into being primarily for use in the classroom—and includes practical exercises in each chapter suitable for students—it is also the major collection of carefully analyzed case studies for the field. Students can feel confident that they are using these cases right alongside seasoned veterans.

## PUBLIC RELATIONS IS A RESPONSIBILITY OF MANAGEMENT

Although everyone in an organization affects the organization's relationships with various publics, establishing public relations policies, goals, and activities is a managerial function. Public relations staffers are part of management.

In approaching the cases and problems presented in this book, an understanding of the meaning of *management* is essential. Here is a basic definition:

- *Management is getting things done with people.*

This statement means that managers work with and through others to carry out their assignments. Their job is not to do the work themselves but to guide and assist others in doing it. But there is another implication here that is related directly to public relations:

- *Management must be able to get the cooperation of people both inside and outside the organization in order to achieve the organization's objectives.*

Thus, *public relations managers* must become competent in both the internal and external aspects of management. For this reason, they are usually selected as much for their managerial abilities in leading a staff and counseling others in the organization as for their public relations skills. The cases and problems in this book will help you hone your skills in both areas.

- The term *public relations* is often confusing because it is frequently used inaccurately. Used correctly, *public relations* describes the *processes* of practice—the techniques, strategies, structures, and tactics of the field. As such, the term is analogous to *law, medicine, nursing,* and so on. Too often, *public relations* is also used to describe the *outcomes* of effective practice—so we hear of "good public relations." The proper term for the desired outcomes of public relations practice is public *relationships*. An organization with effective public relations will attain positive public relationships.

## THE FOCUS OF PUBLIC RELATIONS IS ON BEHAVIOR

When an organization invests resources in public relations, it expects that something will be different from before, or from what it would have been had the investment not been made. Examples of change might be:

- Improved purchases by, and relationships with, customers
- Better community relationships
- Active support from opinion leaders
- Reduced tension with watchdog agencies
- Greater employee loyalty or productivity
- More confidence in the value of a company's stock
- For a nonprofit agency, increased donations

If all public relations does is maintain the status quo, it is being used ineffectually. If it only changes the way people feel or think about the organization—or vice versa—it has not realized its full potential. Effective public relations elicits *mutually favorable behavior* from both the organization and its publics.

### Behavior May Be of Three Types

| Getting people to *do* something | Getting them *not* to do something | Winning their consent to *let the organization* do something |
|---|---|---|

Looked at from another perspective, the type of change sought may be to

1. *Motivate* new behavior,
2. *Reinforce* existing positive behavior, or
3. *Modify* negative behavior.

In studying the cases we present, ask yourself what is different about behaviors after the public relations activities have been carried out. If the answer is nothing, you must consider whether public relations has failed.

## ELEMENTS OF THE PUBLIC RELATIONS FUNCTION

In general, public relations is what public relations *does* (which is true of every field). The employer or client, by formulating objectives, and the practitioners, by accepting those objectives, define the function for that organization at that time. Historically, the function has evolved from *one-way information transfer,* to a *two-way concept* of sending messages and listening to feedback, to the present idea of an organization's *adjusting harmoniously* with the publics on which it depends.[1] Underpinning this perspective, however, are at least six activities that are basic and endemic to practice:

1. ***Research.***    The first step in any project is to gather intelligence in order to understand the variables in the case. What are key publics' opinions and attitudes? Who are the opinion leaders who matter? Which groups or persons are concerned enough to act?
2. ***Strategic planning.***    The situation and the data need to be formed into a strategy. Where are we now? How did we get here? Where do we want to be? How do we get there?
3. ***Counseling.***    Fellow managers must understand the plan and agree that it should be implemented. They may have a role in implementation and, at least, will need to explain it to their staffs.
4. ***Internal education.***    People in the organization need to be informed about the plan and their roles in it. Public relationships are not formed only by the executives or the public relations professionals, but far more by *everyone who interacts* with customers, employees, the community, stockholders, and all other publics.
5. ***Communication/action.***    The plan must be carried out. Messages or appeals are sent to the various publics involved; activities or actions are staged; feedback must be interpreted; and everyone must be kept informed as the project unfolds.
6. ***Evaluation.***    Another type of research—evaluation—charts effectiveness, or lack of it, and very likely will result in a new plan.

Chapter 2 reviews how this sequence is applied with a four-step model.

## PLANNING: MANAGEMENT BY OBJECTIVES

Effective organizations have a business plan made up of *long-range goals* for the future and *short-term objectives* attainable soon. The name commonly given to this type of plan is *management by objectives,* or *MBO.*[2]

Within the statement of goals and objectives, the role expected of public relations is usually stated in general terms. Public relations activities are tied to overall objectives, creating what is called the **management concept** or **public relations strategy**.

---

[1] For a thoughtful analysis of the evolving definition, see Scott M. Cutlip, Allen H. Center, and Glen M. Broom, *Effective Public Relations*, 8th ed. Upper Saddle River, NJ: Prentice Hall, 1999, Chapter 1.
[2] Courses in marketing and business methods are recommended for all students planning a career in public relations, whether in profit or nonprofit enterprises. Readers who want a detailed understanding of MBO should see Norman Nager and T. Harrell Allen, *Public Relations Management by Objectives*, Lanham, MD: University Press of America, September 1, 1991.

The public relations staff draws up a set of specific departmental goals and objectives. The staff members devise programs or campaigns, hire any needed outside talent, plan budgets, establish timetables, implement activities and communications, and evaluate results—all tied to the organization's overall business plan. This working process is called the **functional concept, or public relations tactics**.

One key to success in planning—observable in several cases in this book—is to anticipate problems and opportunities. This proactive, or preventive, approach is preferable to the reactive, after-the-fact approach because it lets you take the lead, rather than being forced to respond to others. Increasingly, this **issue anticipation** approach is becoming one of the major values public relations is expected to provide.

## WHAT COMES ACROSS IS VALUES

More than anything, what public relations activities communicate are the values and vision of the organization—for better or worse. These may be socially positive, acceptable values or questionable ones. But whatever the explicit message set forth, with it goes an implicit message of whether the organization really cares about people, the community, and the future, or is instead self-centered and concerned only with its immediate profits or success—or is possibly even antisocial.

The primary value public relations professionals promote inside organizations is the *open system*. An open system fosters a willingness to adjust and adapt to change, with management sensitive to all interactions in the environment. Such managers are available, listen well, and communicate forthrightly both within the organization and with external stakeholders.

In contrast is the *closed system* organization, where change is difficult. Managers cling to the status quo and seek to change an environment that does not favor the old ways. Usually they try to limit or tightly control the flow of information. In such organizations, public relations is often on the defensive, forced to put forth the view, "If only you knew us better, you'd agree with us."

Private enterprise, as a system, is often accused of being closed. Often it seems to insist its ways are inviolate. "Everything, everybody else, must change to our ways" is the value that sometimes comes across. Needless to say, this attitude limits effectiveness.

For public relations practitioners, the conflict between open and closed systems of management poses several important questions:

- Must an organization always go along with public opinion?
- When is it acceptable to advocate change in public opinion?

Many cases discussed here illuminate this conundrum.

## THE COMMON DENOMINATORS

In almost all successful programs or campaigns, seven common characteristics are evident:

1. Concern about social norms, group attitudes, and individual behavior
2. A strategy embodying specific objectives, selected audiences, careful timing, and cost controls
3. Actions that are consistent with the mission, vision, policies, standards, and personality of the organization represented

4. Emphasis on the use of **communications and participative activities to persuade,** rather than the use of coercion
5. Consideration of the ethical and legal implications and consequences
6. A method of assessing the outcome in terms of benefits and costs
7. Translation of this assessment into decisions for continuation, alteration, or termination of the program

## PROVEN MAXIMS THAT EVERY PRACTITIONER MUST KNOW

As the library of case studies and the experience of scholars and practitioners have grown, the practice has accumulated an inventory of maxims with a high degree of reliability. Many of them derive from timeworn adages applied to persuasion and the formation of public opinion. Here are some examples of these maxims[3].

1. An appeal to audience **self-interest** is most likely to be effective.
2. A **source of information** regarded as trustworthy, expert, or authoritative is most likely to be believed.
3. **Personal, face-to-face contact** is the most effective means of communication.
4. **Understanding a subject** is the first requisite for a communicator wishing to explain the subject to others.
5. **A suggested action or appeal,** as part of a message or coupled with it, is more likely to be accepted than a message by itself.
6. **Participation in, or awareness of, the decision process** increases the likelihood of acceptance.
7. **Personality needs and drives as well as peer group identity** affect the acceptance of messages and positions on issues.
8. **Degree of clarity, simplicity, and symbolism** has a direct and measurable effect on message acceptance.
9. **Explicitly stated messages** and appeals tend to produce more behavior or opinion change than explanations of concepts or theories.
10. **Major issues and events** cause wide swings in public opinion for brief periods. The degree of lasting change tends to diminish with the passage of time.
11. **Self-imposed censorship by the audience**—not paying attention or not feeling involved— can vary the degree of opinion or behavior change substantially.
12. **Subsequent events that reinforce the original stimulus** for opinion or behavior change will tend to increase the degree and durability of the change.
13. **Messages related to goals** are more readily acceptable than messages related to the steps and methods of attaining the goals.
14. **When a public is friendly in a controversial situation,** presenting only one side of the issue tends to be effective. If the audience is not friendly, or is likely to be receptive to both sides, presenting both sides tends to be more effective.

---

[3] The "maxims" offered here are, for the most part, simple restatements of tenets advanced as "laws" of public opinion by Hadley Cantril, "barriers to communication" described by Walter Lippmann, Roper's "hypothesis," and Gallup's "regulators of the absorption rate of new ideas." Students can develop some of their own "maxims" or "precedential guidelines" by relating such concepts as the diffusion process, the concentric circle theory, and the two-step flow of information to situations with public relations overtones in their lives or in the news.

15. In controversy, **opposing views seeking major change of opinion** tend to strengthen the positions held. Similarly, a strong threat to those positions tends to be less effective than a mild threat. A reliable assumption is that **people tend to resist change**.
16. When there is little to choose from between opposing views, a determining factor tends to be **the argument heard last**.
17. In a confusing situation involving opposing messages, people tend to **believe what they want to and hope for** rather than messages that strike discord.
18. **Sensitivity to public leadership** is heightened in times of crisis or controversy. At such times, people affirm or disapprove more forcefully and openly.

## GUIDELINES FROM BEHAVIORAL SCIENCE

Although there are few strict rules in psychology, sociology, or anthropology, the following are four well-proven concepts from these disciplines that can be applied to public relations.

### Four Rules from the Behavioral Sciences

1. The rule of ABUSE from sociology
   - People who *perceive* that they have been, or *might be,* abused by an organization, its policies, or actions cannot hear what it is trying to say to them until the abuse is eliminated or at least acknowledged.
2. The rule of PARTICIPATION from psychology
   - People will fully support only those ideas or programs they perceive they have had a voice in creating.
3. The rule of REWARDS from psychology
   - People will ultimately do only those things for which they feel rewarded.
4. The rule of CHEERLEADING from anthropology
   - Every successful organization of any type has at its core someone or several people we would today call cheerleaders, those who urge the members on to success.

## PROFESSIONALISM

Edward L. Bernays described a **profession** as "an art applied to a science in a manner that puts public interest ahead of personal gain."[4] The practice of public relations lays claim to professionalism on seven counts:

1. A codified body of knowledge and a growing bank of theoretical literature, precedents, and case studies
2. Insight into human behavior and the formation and movement of public opinion
3. Skill in the use of communications tools, social science technology, and persuasion to affect opinions, attitudes, and behavior
4. Academic training including the Ph.D., offered in colleges throughout the world, and professional development available through a multiplicity of professional societies
5. A formal code of ethics[5]

---

[4] Bernays, Edward L. *The Later Years: Public Relations Insights 1956–1986*. Rhinebeck. NY: H&M Publishers, 1986, p. 138.
[5] See PRSA's *Member Code of Ethics*, Chapter 10, pp. 365–366.

6. A service that is essential in contemporary society
7. Nobility of purpose in harmonizing private and public interests thus enabling individual self-determination and democratic societies to function

In the cases presented in this book, observe whether the practitioners involved are meeting these tests of professionalism—and whether application of or failure to observe these guidelines has an impact on their effectiveness.

Success

must be **CONFERRED** on us

by **OUTSIDERS** like

customers

opinion leaders

neighbors

elected officials

vendors

voters

prospective employees

coalitions

stakeholders

shareowners

Therefore, the bottom line for every organization is

to **BUILD RELATIONSHIPS**

that **EARN TRUST**

and **MOTIVATE SUPPORTIVE BEHAVIORS**

## References and Additional Readings

Awad, Joseph. *The Power of Public Relations*. New York: Praeger, 1985.

Baskin, Otis, Craig Aronoff, and Dan Lattimore. *Public Relations: The Profession and the Practice,* 4th ed. New York: McGraw-Hill Higher Education, 1996.

Bernays, Edward L. *Crystallizing Public Opinion*. New York: Liveright, 1961. This was the first book on the field when it appeared in 1923— and is still a good overview. *Public Relations*. Norman, OK: University of Oklahoma Press, 1952. *Engineering of Consent*. Norman, OK: University of Oklahoma Press, 1955.

Budd, John, Jr. "When Less Is More: Public Relations' Paradox of Growth," *Public Relations Quarterly* 35 (Spring 1990): 5–11.

Burson, Harold. "Beyond PR: Redefining the Role of Public Relations." Presented to the 29th Annual Distinguished Lecture of the Institute for Public Relations Research and Education, Inc., the Union League Club, New York, October 2, 1990.

Cutlip, Scott, Allen Center, and Glen Broom. *Effective Public Relations,* 8th ed. Upper Saddle River, NJ: Prentice Hall, 1999. Chapters 1–4.

Grunig, James, et al. *Excellence in Public Relations and Communications Management*. Mahwah, NJ: Lawrence Erlbaum Associates, 1992.

Grunig, James, David Dozier, and Larissa Grunig. *Manager's Guide to Excellence in Public Relations and Communications Management*.

Mahwah, NJ: Lawrence Erlbaum Associates, 1995.

Haynes, Colin. *A Guide to Successful Public Relations*. Glenview, IL: Scott-Foresman, 1989.

Hiebert, Ray Eldon. *Precision Public Relations*. New York: Addison-Wesley, 1988. Compendium of essays by public relations notables.

Jackson, Patrick. "Tomorrow's Public Relations." *Public Relations Journal* 41 (March 1985).

Lesly, Philip. *Lesly's Handbook of Public Relations and Communications,* 5th ed. Chicago, IL: NTC Business Books, 1998.

*pr reporter* Vol. 31 No. 38 (September 26, 1988). Deals editorially with acceptance yet insecurity of function; urges reenergizing through social compact and a professionwide management awareness program.

Wilcox, Dennis, et al. *Public Relations: Strategies and Tactics,* 6th ed. New York: Longman, 2000.

# How Public Relations Deals with Problems and Opportunities

## WHAT IS PUBLIC RELATIONS?

Here is a formal three-part definition of **public relations**:

1. Public relations is a condition common to every individual and organization in the human environment—whether or not they recognize or act upon the fact—that refers to their reputation and relationship with all other members of the environment.
2. Public relations is the systematized function that evaluates public attitudes and behaviors; harmonizes the goals, policies, and procedures of an individual or organization with the public interest; and executes a program of action to earn public understanding, acceptance, and supportive behavior.
3. Public relations is the full flowering of the democratic principle, in which every member of society is valued for himself or herself and has both a right and a duty to express an opinion on public issues, and in which policies are made on the basis of free exchange of those opinions. This result in public consent.

In other words,

- Public relations is something everyone has.
- Public relations fosters the improvement of public relationships through specific activities and policies.
- Public relations is the cornerstone of a democratic society.

## PROACTIVE AND REACTIVE APPROACHES

An organization or corporation is a group of people working together for a specific purpose. That purpose invariably involves gaining the confidence of other people who will buy the product or use the service, invest in the organization's stock (or donate funds to nonprofit entities), and support its positions on issues. In short, every organization exists in a societal or people-orientated environment, first and foremost. The late counselor Philip Lesly called this the *human climate*.

Because people form impressions and opinions of one another almost without thinking about it, every organization has a reputation, be it good or bad. Most likely, it will be good for some people and bad for others, depending on the perspective of those people and their particular interactions with the organization. As it does between persons, this reputation influences the ability of the organization to win friends, persuade others to do business with it, or be trusted in public matters.

- *The managerial challenge is whether something is consciously done to face the fact of reputation and relationships.*

When something is consciously done, the result is a public relations policy: recognition by management that positive relationships with key publics are essential to success. This management concept (see Chapter 1) is usually carried out by forming a public relations department and assigning it the responsibility of building and maintaining positive working relationships inside and outside the organization.

The approach the public relations department takes, however, is another challenge. Many companies—too many, some observers say—operate in a *reactive* mode. They wait for public criticism, emergencies, or bad publicity before they act. They are usually likened to firefighters who don't get going until there's a fire.

Because reputations are formed and re-formed in people's minds continuously, and because public issue debates are constantly taking shape, a more strategic approach is to be *proactive*. This approach is like fire prevention. It constantly looks for potential opportunities and problems. Proactive public relations practitioners will be ready to take advantage of opportunities when they arise and to prevent potential problems from flaring up.

## STRATEGY AND PLANNING MAKE THE DIFFERENCE

Given the unpredictable nature of our world, unexpected situations that require reactive responses will always arise. But just as promotions come to those who have worked hard for them, successful reactive responses are made by those who are prepared. The best preparation involves:

1. Understanding thoroughly your organization's or client's business, operations, culture, and goals;
2. Learning as much as possible about the publics on which the organization or client depends for success; and
3. Putting that understanding and knowledge together in a formal strategic plan.

With preparation, reactive responses will more likely fit better into the overall pattern of the public relations effort. Trouble comes when they do not fit—when what is put forward in response to customer complaints now contradicts what the company has been saying in publicity, publications, or advertising. The company is not speaking with One Clear Voice, and this "double-talk" raises questions about the accuracy of its statements and its trustworthiness.

In analyzing the cases in this book, you will not know as much about the subjects or organizations as you would want to if you were actually involved in the case. Nevertheless, it should be apparent in most cases whether the public relations response was based on a strategic plan or just a hunch or gut feeling. More than anything else, planning makes the difference between success and failure.

## PRELIMINARIES TO PLANNING

Many misunderstandings and poor public relationships occur because a legitimate inquiry is not promptly and properly answered by deed or word. Many others occur because responses are ill-timed, inaccurate, or altered by the interpretation given by a critic, or they are blown out of proportion by news media seeking sensational headlines.

Naturally, given a choice between spot reaction? and time for a thoroughly considered response, public relations practitioners would opt for the latter. Sometimes there is no choice: microphones are being thrust in your face, an idea is going viral, or a political figure is waiting impatiently in the reception area.

The substitute for a thoroughly considered response is a **strategic plan** that anticipates at least broad topics that are likely to arise. Specific problems that affect public opinion and relationships rarely exist in isolation. Each one is connected to larger matters of public concern. By considering these problems in advance, one often can deal with a problem before it arises. Mastering the planning process is an essential and basic skill of public relations. Such plans must take place within the context of the goals and culture of the organization, of course.

## THE PUBLIC RELATIONS PROCESS

In devising a program or campaign, practitioners follow a series of logical steps that overlap so that they constitute a continuous **four-step process** (often called the RACE model—*R*esearch, *A*nalysis, *C*ommunication, *E*valuation):

1. **Research,** which often includes formal research, to define clearly the specific problem or opportunity
2. **Analysis and planning** to devise and package a strategy
3. **Communication, action, and relationship building** to implement the strategy
4. **Evaluation** to determine results and to decide what, if anything, to do next or to do differently

### Step 1: Research

Public relations problems do not often come neatly bound with all the facts, nuances, and history carefully laid out. More likely, information and facts dribble in, some of it not seen until a critical moment in the course of events. Perceptions of what is going on, what is being experienced by stakeholders, run the gamut. It is the **practitioner's responsibility** to gather the facts and perceptions in order to build a plan that is both reasonable and effective. This is done through informal and formal research with internal and external stakeholders. A practitioner must look through the lens of every involved stakeholder group to determine how they view the situation and what their understanding is or perceptions are for their position or current behavior. These will guide the theoretical strategies used in planning and programming.

### Step 2: Analysis and Planning

Planning involves prioritizing stakeholder publics for the situation at hand. Time and budget will always influence what can be accomplished, so a practitioner must prioritize which publics are most critical to the current problem or opportunity. Setting specific, measurable goals and objectives for each public will guide strategies, as will specific activities and messages that are then developed as part of an overall plan. Budgets and timelines are set and assignments are made.

Frequently, thorough research will reveal a problem or problems that must be addressed before the planned program can continue or succeed. Taking remedial action to fix the problem is a necessary step at this point.

Setting appropriate goals is not easy. Far too many practitioners fail to set any goals at all for their activities or use vague, general words such as "improve" to define their goals. To ensure that the goals are strong enough to withstand scrutiny, a savvy practitioner will use the SMARTS acronym when setting goals for the program:

S = Specific: Is the goal direct and to the point?

M = Measurable: Is the outcome measurable?

A = Attainable: Is it possible to achieve this goal?

R = Realistic: Is it likely this goal will be met?

T = Time locked: How much time do you have? How much do you need?

S = Sufficient: If the goal is met, will you be where you need to be?

## Step 3: Communication, Action, and Relationship Building

At this point, implementation of the public relations plan as laid out in step 2 must be undertaken. It is important to review the plan and tweak it based on the continually changing situation and the progression of stakeholder perceptions and behaviors. It is equally important to remain focused on the overall goals and not be swayed by distractions or drawn away from the goals. Activities in this step will include many one-way and two-way communication tools. The diffusion process shows us that sending out information only builds awareness and interest; therefore, it is important to build in and implement relationship-building tools that involve two-way communication.[1]

## Step 4: Evaluation

A good public relations plan incorporates evaluation tools to determine how successful the plan has been in achieving the goals set forth. This evaluation should take place at two levels, or tiers: monitoring and measuring. The plan will include evaluation markers along the way to monitor as well help guide the plan as it is implemented. A plan that is constantly tweaked based on specific research is much more effective than one tweaked on gut instinct or management whims. The final evaluation—measurement—weighs the results of the program against the stated goals.

## WHAT GOOD MODELS AND THEORIES BRING TO THE TABLE

**A *theory* is the application of knowledge that has been verified and confirmed to consistently "work" in consistent situations.** In other words, *theory* comprises the principles and methods of public relations. Most introductory texts explain theoretical approaches and models as a way of getting to the practice of public relations.

Some healthy friction has always existed between theory and practice. Public relations, as a practice, did not begin with theory. It began with leaders such as Ivy Lee working on "gut

---

[1] For an in-depth look at the diffusion process, see "Diffusion of Innovations," by Everett M. Rogers, The Free Press, NY (1962) or "Diffusion Process" on Wikipedia.

instinct," while others, such as Edward L. Bernays, tried to apply behavioral science methods to reach what he called "the merger of public and private interests."[2]

Public relations education today continues this dichotomy. Some programs are "too theoretical" to be useful, critics say. On the other side, some programs do not use enough theory, relying instead on anecdotal evidence—war stories. In truth, most public relations programs try to balance theory with good practical examples—examples that prove a particular theoretical point.

Theory is useful and necessary for public relations education. Specifically:

- Theory validates good practice:
    1. Theory is not case specific, but can be generalized over a broad range of clients and issues.
    2. A theoretical background enables a practitioner to move easily between jobs, industries, and clients.
    3. Theory increases efficiency.
    4. The theoretical approach is cost-effective. Trial and error are expensive.
    5. The theoretical approach uses time effectively. Trial and error is time-consuming.
- Good theory helps move the practice of public relations into a profession. Good theory begets a body of knowledge that then facilitates the exchange of information necessary for a profession to sustain itself.
- Good theory, coupled with good research, helps the practitioner to chart a wise course. Good research enables the practitioner to define the status quo, explain the status quo, and predict what actions are necessary to extend or modify the status quo to create the behaviors needed to meet the program's goals.

As public relations continues to move "past communication to achieving behavioral outcomes," good theory will become the backbone of the new models.

## THE BEHAVIORAL PUBLIC RELATIONS MODEL

As first posited by Pat Jackson, behavior is the only outcome that truly counts. What stakeholder groups think or feel about an organization or product means very little unless they "behave" in such a way that makes a difference. This means motivating people to (1) do something, (2) not do something, or (3) let you do something. Jackson suggested that too many practitioners think of themselves as communicators. They believe that their objective is to transmit information, facts, and data, or move feelings, evaluating success by clips, attendance, "reach," and similar measurements. To all of these, knowledgeable employers or clients ask, "So what? What has changed because of this? Never mind what our publics are thinking; the question is what are they *doing?*"

The behavioral public relations model (see Figure 2.1) basically shifts the objective away from awareness as a goal to a behavioral response, and with it, the focus on thinking, strategizing, and planning. Practitioners ask, "What behaviors am I trying to motivate?" rather than "What information am I trying to communicate?"

A behavioral strategic planning model can be useful for deciding:

1. What **behaviors** must be motivated, reinforced, or modified to achieve the plan's goals? Beginning every project by making a list of desired behaviors gives the practitioner a

---

[2] Conversation with E. L. Bernays, 1989, Lake Buena Vista, FL.

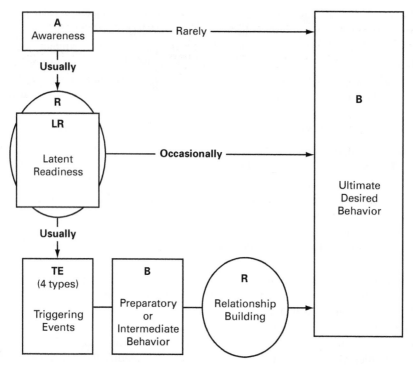

**FIGURE 2.1**   Behavioral Public Relations Model

specific guide for what he or she is trying to accomplish. This is the most important step toward engendering those behaviors instead of thinking at the outset about messages, media, or activities.

2. Which stakeholder groups or segments must exhibit these behaviors or could prevent achievement of the goals either by withholding the behaviors or by overt opposition?

3. Because people often do not go straight to the ultimate desired behaviors, what intermediate behaviors might they have to be led through?

4. Because groups do not usually act spontaneously, who are the opinion leaders in these groups and what special behaviors must be sought from them to stimulate group behavior?

## Understanding the Behavioral Public Relations Model

The first step of the behavioral public relations model is **awareness**. A person cannot act on something of which he or she is not aware, so creating awareness is the natural first step in creating the desired behavior. This is one area in which mass media and social media are useful.

### Social Media: A Magic Bullet?

There are a wide variety of tools in the practitioner's toolbox. Social media is the darling of the moment. Students who come out of school armed with a working knowledge of how to manage Facebook, Twitter, YouTube, and such are in high demand in organizations that believe these tools are critical to their awareness building. But one should not automatically assume that social media is the only tool necessary. GM just announced it was pulling its ads from Facebook because it felt that Facebook was ineffective in motivating potential car buyers. Research must first determine whether a stakeholder group uses and/or responds to social media activities. If not, or if the stakeholder group talks only to itself, then the tool is ineffective. Use the tools that best fit the ongoing behaviors of the audience you are trying to reach.

Publicity via mass media is an excellent tool in creating initial awareness, as is paid advertising. Creating a buzz via social media can extend awareness easily, quickly, and inexpensively.

However, according to the behavioral model, awareness rarely, if ever, leads to behavior change or the ultimate desired behavior. What it does is open a "file" in the mind of the stakeholder in which to store information and feelings about the subject. This process is called building *latent readiness.*

A person's propensity to develop a **latent desire to act** based on the newly acquired awareness is the second step of the model. Latent readiness can be positive or negative, depending on the information and influences that build over time. Before deciding to act, most people engage in a "social trial," asking friends and opinion leaders for their opinions. If these people who the stakeholder respects add to the information positively or negatively, that will influence the direction in which the stakeholder *might* behave. Core values can also influence latent readiness.

Stakeholders might carry around this awareness and latent readiness to act for a long, long time before doing something about the subject, or they may never act. What it takes to stimulate the behavior to happen is what Jackson calls the "triggering event."

A **triggering event** is an activity that motivates stakeholders to act on their latent readiness. It can be something that occurs naturally, such as a thunderstorm or the change of seasons. Election Day is the triggering event for a politician running for office. The largest commercial triggering event each year is the holiday season. Noon is a triggering event for most consumers—lunchtime. Or it can be a manufactured triggering event—something that an organization can control and release to stimulate behavior—such as a sale at a store, a layoff of employees, an open house, or a similar event.

Understanding triggering events is key to the behavioral public relations strategy. People are available to do, or are even ready to do, more than they actually do. Lack of time or money, other priorities, laziness, and a thousand other barriers inhibit them from undertaking the behavior spontaneously. Overcoming these barriers requires:

1. Constructing a triggering event that pushes the behavior into a priority position. For example, retailers hold sales to lure shoppers to buy goods they previously felt they could not afford or that were not a high priority.
2. Usurping naturally occurring triggering events in the lives of your stakeholders. For example, 40th birthdays start people thinking about their health.
3. Capitalizing on triggering events that randomly come along in the social environment. For example, "Sesame Street" tipped a revolution in early-childhood education.
4. Fending off triggering events launched by competitors and opponents or occurring in the environment.

Appealing to people to go straight from awareness to the ultimate behavior is usually futile. Most people work through intermediate behaviors before proceeding to the ultimate behavior. The focus of public relations efforts should be on leading people to intermediate behaviors and concentrating appeals there. Asking right off for the ultimate behavior is usually ineffective.

If the intermediate activity—perhaps a celebration, meeting, or event—puts the organization in direct contact with people, it is a prime time to build face-to-face relationships with stakeholders. The combination of attracting them to an intermediate event and then building a relationship makes it more likely they will carry out the ultimate behavior. For example, hospitals hold educational seminars—building relationships between staff and attendees during the events—as a means of stimulating attendees to make the hospital their health-care center.

For most planned public relations programs, a natural triggering event does not occur. The practitioner must be skilled in creatively finding ways to trigger stakeholder behavior again and again, using those small steps along the continuum as research to understand and be able to trigger the ultimate step at some point. Jackson said, "Public Relations is a process by which organizations establish positive relationships which lead to positive behavior." Therefore, *PR* could stand for "positive relationships" as well as "public relations."[3]

The goal or focus of modern public relations practice is positive behavior. This may be a positive behavior that is maintained, that is established for the first time, or that is converted from a negative behavior. Regardless, positive action from the primary publics is the goal.

## A FIVE-STEP PUBLIC RELATIONS STRATEGY FOR THE TWENTY-FIRST CENTURY

A highly effective strategy for **planning and programming** emerges from the Behavioral Public Relations Model. This strategy is demonstrated in numerous cases throughout this book. It integrates the focus on behavior and relationship building with two-way communication methods and credible delivery mechanisms (opinion leaders and the organizational family). With such a wide variety of social media options available, the practitioner does not have to be restricted to the news media as the only way to communicate with the organization's stakeholders. The practitioner is back in control of the message and the relationships with the organization's publics. The key steps are to:

1. *Go direct:*   Go around the critics and gatekeepers to get to the important people whose support is needed for the program's success. The Internet is replacing mass media in effectiveness, while opinion leaders remain the strongest intervening public.
2. *To key stakeholders:*   Those who are interested can give supportive behaviors now or stop needed action through their opposition.
3. *Via opinion leaders:*   Publics do not just spontaneously act; they are stimulated by the movers and shakers called *opinion leaders.*
4. *Using members of the organizational family:*   Involve employees at all levels in customer relations activities, ambassador programs, and community relations outreach teams; put them in charge of building *local* relationships that earn *supportive* behaviors.
5. *On a local basis:*   People operate within their local environments; all issues are local.

## THE CRITICAL IMPORTANCE OF RESEARCH

No public relations program should be undertaken without good research. Research gives the practitioner the in-depth understanding of what a stakeholder group is thinking and feeling and how stakeholders are currently behaving and why. Good research describes the status quo,

---

[3] See "The Behavioral Public Relations Model," *pr reporter*, January 1, 1999.

explains it, and predicts how to improve it, thereby enhancing the practitioner's ability to create positive behavior. When problems do arise, they can usually be sorted into three distinct categories:

1. Ignorance
2. Apathy
3. Hostility

When *ignorance* is the problem, then education is usually the answer. When *apathy* is the problem, then motivation is the answer. These are the easy solutions. But when *hostility* is the problem, persuasion is the answer, and this is not easy to accomplish.

## THE PERSUASION MODEL

Persuading people to change their behavior is difficult for many reasons. Oftentimes, it is not worth the effort it would take to win the enemy over. Unless the success of a planned program of public relations is contingent on total buy-in, a better use of time and resources is to focus on the positive and uncommitted publics and not stir up the opposition (see the Phil Lesly model in Chapter 9).

The **persuasion model** is a successful model for persuading those who are hostile to an idea and who are required for the success of a program. First developed by San Diego practitioner Kerry Tucker, the model involves four steps:

1. Creating "dissatisfaction with the status quo"
2. Offering the program as a viable option to the status quo
3. Presenting the benefits of adopting the new idea and the consequences of rejecting it
4. Modeling the desired behavior[4]

The key, of course, is creating dissatisfaction with the status quo. In effect, the subject has to see and agree that the existing behavior (and the attitudes behind it) is wrong. This is why persuasion is so hard. Something called *self-persuasion* kicks in any time existing beliefs are challenged, and the normal reaction is to fight back to defend one's beliefs and behaviors.

However, if a crack can be made in that wall of self-defense, then the second step is to quickly offer the new idea as a solution to the cognitive dissonance established by that crack. **Cognitive dissonance** was first explored by Leon Festinger in 1956 to understand how and why people resolve conflict in what they know, think, or believe.[5] His conclusion was that people would resolve conflict created by competing or even contradicting information by acquiring or inventing new thoughts or beliefs. Tucker relies on this conclusion in his persuasion theory.

The subject, upon hearing that past or existing behavior could be "wrong," will want to resolve this conflict. Tucker's theory posits that offering the desired behavior as a resolution at this point can lead the subject to adopt the new behavior.

Outlining the benefits of such adoption and the consequences of failing to do so simply reinforces the subject's decision and helps resolve doubts about changing his or her mind. In most cases, the benefits will be obvious and the consequences will be equal to, and opposite of, the benefits.

Finally, modeling the desired behavior presents a picture for the subject of the new world in which the new behavior is the norm. Such "modeling" enables the subject to mentally "fast

---

[4] Tucker, Kerry, *PR Writing: An Issue-Driven Behavioral Approach*, 3rd ed., Prentice Hall (1997).
[5] Festinger, Leon, *Theory of Cognitive Dissonance*, Stanford University Press (1959).

forward" to a point in time when the positive results of this decision are obvious. It is a "better" world, because the subject is benefiting from the new behavior.

The cases in Chapter 9, "Public Issues," demonstrate how difficult it is, however, to move stakeholders from long-held beliefs. Often they move to strike out the conflicting information as "not believable or credible" in an effort to bring order to their own belief system.

## THE ROOTS OF BEHAVIOR

Jackson, Tucker, and others worked long and hard to understand behavior, knowing that one must understand how and why decisions are made before attempts to alter behavior can be successful. What this research revealed may be common sense, but it is important to review it.

Behavior, whether positive or negative, begins with the subject's personal history, which helps to shape the subject's core values. *Core values* are those values that are not subject to much change, regardless of the circumstances. Former U.S. Senator Howard H. Baker, Jr. (R-TN) once defined core values as those values that "wouldn't change even if tempted by money, power, or political advantage." That's a pretty good definition.

A person's **core values drive attitudes that help to form opinions**. These attitudes and opinions are constantly challenged by new circumstances, experiences, and information. The wise person will examine attitudes and opinions regularly to see that they are still congruent with any new personal or societal changes that might have occurred.

Regardless, most people act on what they perceive to be in their best interest. The key word is "perceive," because in some instances people act in ways that are not really best for their long-term survival. (Smoking tobacco comes to mind. Some 20 percent of the American public still smokes, even after 50 years of medical evidence on its adverse impact on a person's health.)

So what drives the positive behavior that is the goal of the public relations process? It might be good to look at what *doesn't* work. What doesn't work is simply providing information. As Tucker says, "No one is sitting out there waiting for your information."[6] Few people get up in the morning and log on or turn on the TV, for example, before getting dressed and going on with their lives. Thus, the one-way, asymmetrical communication models of the past—getting a story in the newspaper, for example—rarely creates any positive behavior.

## THE TWO-WAY SYMMETRICAL COMMUNICATION MODEL

What does work is two-way, symmetrical communication. First introduced by Jim and Larissa Grunig at the University of Maryland, two-way symmetrical communication has its roots in first understanding the wants and needs of the subject and public and then shaping the organization's decisions and actions to meet that need.[7]

The concept is close to what Bernays called the "merging of public and private interest." His idea was to use good research to determine which prosocial actions (as opposed to antisocial actions) would lead to the merger of public and private interests.

The Grunigs' theory has more to do with communication style. They considered and rejected both one-way asymmetrical communication and two-way asymmetrical communication because neither one emphasized the subject. According to the Grunigs, communication must

---

[6] Personal interview with Kerry Tucker, 1992, PRSA Annual Conference.
[7] Grunig, James. F, and Larissa Schneider Grunig, "Toward a Theory of the Public Relations Behavior of Organizations: Review of a Program of Research," *Journal of Public Relations*, Vol. 1, No. 1–4 (1989), pp. 27–63.

start with understanding the wants and needs of the subject public, something that asymmetrical communication fails to do.

## Four Frameworks of Practice

1. *Press agentry:*   Propagandistic, seeks media attention; a one-way asymmetric model.
2. *Public information:*   Disseminates accurate information, but does not volunteer negative information or seek input; a one-way asymmetric model.
3. *Two-way asymmetrical:*   Identifies those messages most likely to gain support of publics without having to change the behavior of the organization; thus, it is manipulative. Change benefits the organization, but not necessarily the publics. The organization knows best and does not need the free marketplace of ideas.
4. *Two-way symmetrical:*   Uses bargaining, negotiation, and conflict-resolution strategies to effect change in the ideas, attitudes, and behaviors of both the organization and its publics for mutual benefit.

## WHEN COMMUNICATION IS NOT ENOUGH

Oftentimes, communication alone does not get an organization where it needs to go. A final theory, **beyond communication**, involves altering the way *society* thinks and acts in order to achieve the level of change needed to satisfy an organization's goals. A case illustrating this model is presented in Chapter 8 (MADD case). This concept involves using good communication strategy and tactics to make major societal changes.

The first step in societal change is to **affect mores**. *Mores* (pronounced "morays") are the informal rules by which we all agree to live. Although they are rarely written or formally adopted, they are very much a part of the way people live and work. Because of their informality, they are subject to change easily, which is a good thing. Flexibility is a desirable element in modern society.

How do mores work to shape behavior? Mores help to determine what society will or will not accept. Certain words are now permissible in public conversation, whereas a generation ago, those same words would have been impolite. What is acceptable in the future will likely be different (for better or worse) from what is considered acceptable today.

Once mores have been in place long enough to become established policy, frequently **laws are enacted** to give them an official status. For example, whereas it was once impolite to smoke in an elevator, it is now against the law in most instances. Changing mores and creating new laws frequently help to move an organization's agenda well past what could be done through communication alone.

A final step in the process is the **engineered solution**. When persuasion, mores, and laws are ineffective, a way to physically prevent the behavior might follow. An example is driving while under the influence of alcohol. There's no doubt that Mothers Against Drunk Driving (MADD) has created a new, positive environment where mores say drunk driving is wrong, and the law agrees. Yet people continue to drive while impaired. An engineered solution might be a device built into a car's ignition system that requires a sobriety test before a car can start. For smokers, such a solution is a ceramic "cigarette" containing a small vial of nicotine. Puffing releases small doses of nicotine for the "smoker," while eliminating any noxious odors or danger from secondhand smoke for those around the smoker.

Driven by new theory, modern public relations practice is prepared to "move beyond communication to behavior," as Pat Jackson preached for over 30 years. This "behavioral PR" puts public relations in a position to compete with other organizational departments in that its results can now be quantified and compared with previously established goals. Only when this happens can public relations hold its own in a corporate or organizational environment.

## 20 Great Truths of Public Relations

1. The long-term security of the organization or product is far more important than short-term expediency.
2. Perception is reality, facts not withstanding.
3. Unfulfilled expectations create most PR problems.
4. Planning and preparation are invaluable. When disaster strikes, it's too late to prepare a crisis plan or build a legacy of trust.
5. The value of research is inestimable:
   a. Every planned PR program should start and end with research.
   b. Every PR plan should evolve from research.
   c. Research should be conducted at every step of the program.
6. PR needs to always play its position and let other departments—legal, operations, marketing, and so on—play theirs.
7. Communication must always follow performance. Act before you talk.
8. PR frequently turns on timing. Knowing when to act is as important as knowing what to do.
9. If your client, product, or organization is challenged:
   a. Don't ignore the challenge.
   b. If the challenge is unfair, fight back as hard as you can.
   c. If the challenge has merit, fight for corrective actions.
10. The media—mass media or social media—are important, but limited, intervening publics. Positive relationships still lead to positive behavior.
11. Ad hoc pressure groups won't give up or go away. You have to deal with them directly or they will consume you in the court of public opinion. (Social media have made this especially true.)
12. PR has to be involved from the beginning to have maximum impact.
13. Full and complete disclosure and communication is the best way to keep from getting greedy when entrusted with the public's money.
14. Doing the right thing is more important than doing the "thing" right. There is no such thing as "corporate" ethics. People are either ethical or they aren't, and these people determine the ethics of an organization.
15. If you have to say something, the truth is always best.
16. Appeals to others' self-interest are seldom unrewarded.
17. Involvement in the planning stages provides "ownership" and support.
18. If top management is not sold, the project will never succeed.
19. Absent trustworthy information, people assume the worst. Rumors thrive in the vacuum of no information.
20. Most negatives can become positives with a little creative effort and a lot of hard work.

*Source:* © Frank R. Stansberry, 1991.

# 3

# Employee Relations

The first public of any organization is its employees—the people who make it what it is. As management guru Peter Drucker reminds us, an organization is "a human community" that needs the contributions of everyone to function and be successful. Many times it appears that management does not recognize this fact. Sometimes managers act as if *they* are the organization and the others just an impediment. An interchange at the annual meeting of an auto company illuminates the truth of the matter. A shareholder asked the CEO why funds were being allocated to improve employee benefits instead of increasing dividends. "Because," he responded, "you and I don't know how to build cars, and they do!"

The situation is complicated by the fact that, in the overwhelming majority of business organizations today, managers and administrators are employees. They do not own the company, but merely manage it for the stockholders. Senior managers may own stock—but so may production workers, secretaries, and janitors. Executives can be hired and fired like everyone else. The true employer is the board of directors elected by the stockholders to oversee the business. In community hospitals, school districts, public interest organizations, government agencies, or membership associations, of course, there is no question of management ownership.

## A DANGEROUS ATTITUDE

It is easy, and perhaps all too common, to view employees as a cost in a line-item budget determining the price of a product or service. This attitude fosters the idea that the less an organization has to pay its employees, the lower the price of the product or service and, therefore, the more competitive the product or service can be in the marketplace.

This one-dimensional view of the labor force provided fertile soil for the tremendous growth of unions, which fought to have labor seen in a multidimensional view. Throughout the decades, unions forced their way into the smallest and largest companies. They won concessions on wages, safety, medical benefits, and vacation and retirement benefits, to mention just a few. Unions became as big as big business. Their influence was reflected in national and state laws as well as in volumes of judicial and regulatory decisions.

The 1980s, however, saw a tapering off of union influence. Union membership dropped; part of this drop is attributed to the significant population move from the unionized Northeast and Midwest to the Sunbelt, which has significantly fewer unions. The impact of foreign competition—foreign cars, for example—as well as the exporting of jobs to countries where labor is cheaper are two other trends that have had an impact on the labor market.

And recently unions have been fighting for their very existence. Right-to-work laws have been passed in 22 states. These give an employee the right not to join a union or pay dues even if the workplace is unionized.

Another major change in the employer–employee relationship is automation. The computer radically changes the role of the individual in many workplaces. The individual now competes with the robot for a place in the assembly line; in most instances the individual will lose the contest. If the computer and the robot take on most of the heavy work in the steel mill, most of the positions on the assembly line, and much of the information gathering and dissemination usually associated with general office work, what is left for the current and future individuals who would fill those jobs?

The trend is to a downsizing of the work force and to a service-oriented economy. This movement creates major reshuffling of jobs and people, with all the emotional stress attendant on such upheaval and readjustment. Layoffs and restructuring of organizations also weaken the loyalty of workers, which can affect morale and productivity. Mergers and acquisitions can have the same effect.

Then there are legislative influences, such as NAFTA, the North American Free Trade Agreement, which allows organizations to move their production facilities around the continent, avoiding regulations and higher employee–benefit costs that impact pricing and profits.

Thomas Friedman, in his book *The World Is Flat: A Brief History of the Twenty-First Century,* writes at length about a variety of ways employees are being squeezed, including the two most prevalent: outsourcing and offshoring. Says Friedman, "No matter what your profession—doctor, lawyer, architect, accountant—if you are an American, you better be good at the touchy-feely service stuff, because anything that can be digitized can be outsourced to either the smartest or the cheapest producer or both."

During this significant time of transition, employer–employee relations change, but they are no less critical than in the past. Indeed, most people would argue that they are now more important than ever.

In a very real sense, frontline workers *are* the organization. They produce the product, provide the service, operate support systems, count the money, deal with customers, work with vendors—in short, they drive the activities that make the organization function.

## BENEFITS OF EMPLOYEE PARTICIPATION

Because they are accountable to the board—the real and legal seat of power in most organizations—executives have responsibility as "the employer." Others, those needed to carry out the operations, become "the employees." Yet, if there is one significant trend in successful organizations worldwide, it is the melding of interests and heightened cooperation between management and employees. Recognition of several benefits from a united effort has brought this "workplace democracy" about:

1. As the founder of Honda puts it, just as cars are gauged by horsepower, so organizations can be gauged by "mindpower." If only the CEO thinks about possible improvements, there is one mindpower. If only management, maybe 100 to 500 mindpower. But

if everyone is encouraged to think about the company and his or her work in it, and then make suggestions, an organization can have 20,000 or more mindpower.

2. In a highly competitive economy, successful organizations are those that deliver customer delight. But customer delight depends on employee satisfaction; that is, dissatisfied employees are unlikely to delight customers, because their own irritations or feelings of abuse will get in the way. (The next time a retail clerk fails to give you delightful service, remember that he or she is probably the lowest paid, least valued, least trained worker in the store—and most likely part-time to boot. Yet the retail industry expects such employees to conduct *the* most important job, serving customers.) Success involves *everyone*—those who make the policies, those who design and produce the product or service, the sales personnel, janitors who keep the premises attractive, secretaries who answer the phone, and so on.

3. To build trusting relationships with customers, shareholders, communities, government, and other stakeholder publics, organizations need to speak with One Clear Voice. Management cannot say one thing in official pronouncements from the ivory tower and then have employees telling another story to the people with whom they interact. Achieving one voice requires shared values, which arise when employees are encouraged to participate in organizational decision making.

The benefits of mutually satisfactory employee–employer relations are significant. There are fewer work stoppages, less absenteeism, higher productivity, and fewer errors. Sometimes the benefits are symbolic, as when the employees of Delta Air Lines gave the airline an airplane during tough economic times. In a similar case, the 480 employees of Piggly Wiggly Carolina, a Charleston, South Carolina, grocery store and distributing business, conceived and organized the $40,000 "Rig for the Pig" campaign. Ninety-eight percent of the employees participated, voluntarily contributing two days' pay. In the end, they raised $7,000 more than was needed to buy the tractor-trailer truck they gave to the company.

## PUBLIC RELATIONS' ROLE

The public relations function, providing the communications channel between employers and employee groups, is important on both sides of the relationship. Practitioners are called on to participate more or less continuously in four phases of an employee's work experience:

- ***The start.***  For example, recruiting programs or help-wanted advertising, orientation sessions, tours, or kits of information.
- ***On-the-job working conditions.***  For example, employee publications, bulletin boards, feedback systems, training meetings, morale boosters, surveys of attitudes, complaint sessions, and teleconferencing.
- ***Rewards and recognition.***  For example, award programs, implementation of employee participation in civic affairs, staging of political science or economic education events, old-timers' parties, open houses, wage increases or bonuses, promotions, annual reports to employees, and so on.
- ***Work stoppage or termination.***  For example, communications during a strike, layoff, or boycott problem, news about benefits for retirees, a retiree publication, projects to help laid-off employees relocate, or exit interviews.

In carrying out duties related to these four phases, the public relations people are usually teamed up with the human resources department in a large organization. In small organizations, all the duties related to employee relations and communication may be vested in one public relations or human resources employee.

No matter who is assigned the duties, the responsibility is as communicator, interpreter, and persuader for the employer. The duties include feedback of employee opinion and ideas as a guide to management. So public relations practices are the fulcrum of a two-way relationship-building and communication system, and therefore must earn the trust of the employees.

## RULES OF EFFECTIVE EMPLOYEE RELATIONS

Although a variety of tools are available to further employee–employer communications, five basic principles prevail as guidelines for the practitioner:

1. ***Employees must be told first.*** Employees should be the first to be told information affecting them and their jobs; the employer should speak directly to them. The relationship is adversely affected when employees learn from outside sources about matters that affect them. If this happens, two-way trust is jeopardized. As a practical matter, external sources cannot do as complete a job of informing employees as the employer can. The grapevine is one of the worst possible sources in the eyes of employees, even though it ranks as high as No. 2 in actuality, according to a recent survey. News media as a source are just as bad.

2. ***Tell the bad news along with the good.*** All too often, organizations exploit internal news channels to report only "good" news, usually complimentary to the employer. That practice wears thin. The tools and the messages lose credibility. Motives become suspect. Employees look to other sources, such as unions and the grapevine, for a more balanced, objective perspective. Revealing good and bad news, openly and candidly, builds trust, common purpose, and productivity.

3. ***Ensure timeliness.*** Information important to employees has the same obsolescence as news of other kinds. Getting it out fast and accurately builds dialogue and trust. Delay opens the door to sources with half-truths, distortions, and bias unfavorable to the employer. Delay is the cause of most rumors, and, once started, rumors are difficult to dislodge. The employer's task is to be the first and most reliable source for employees. To do or be otherwise puts, and keeps, an employer on the defensive with those on whom the organization depends most for its success.

4. ***Employees must be informed on subjects they consider important.*** Years of studying employees' views of communication within their organizations reveals specific items they want to know about—often quite different from what management thinks they want to know about (or *ought* to be told). The list has changed very little during the years such research has been conducted (See Table 3.1).

5. ***Use the media that employees trust.*** Recent studies replicate older ones about which sources of information employees prefer. Even in recent years, with the advent of e-mail and intranets, employees are still keen to get information face-to-face—from immediate supervisors, small group meetings, and top executives. In order, they prefer:

   **a.** Immediate supervisors
   **b.** Small group meetings
   **c.** Top executives
   **d.** Large group meetings

**TABLE 3.1  Subjects of Interest to Employees Change Little**

| Rank | Subject |
|------|---------|
| 1 | Organizational plans for the future |
| 2 | Job advancement opportunities |
| 3 | Job-related "how-to" information |
| 4 | Productivity improvement |
| 5 | Personnel policies and practices |
| 6 | How we're doing vs. the competition |
| 7 | How my job fits into the organization |
| 8 | How external events affect my job |
| 9 | How profits are used |
| 10 | Financial results |
| 11 | Advertising and promotional plans |
| 12 | Operations outside of my department or division |
| 13 | Organizational stand on current issues |
| 14 | Personnel changes and promotions |
| 15 | Organizational community involvement |
| 16 | Human interest stories about other employees |
| 17 | Personal news (birthdays, anniversaries, etc.) |

   **e.** Employee handbook or other booklets
   **f.** Orientation programs
   **g.** Regular local employee publications
   **h.** Bulletin boards
   **i.** Annual reports to employees
   **j.** Regular general employee publications
   **k.** Upward communication programs
   **l.** Audiovisual programs
   **m.** Unions
   **n.** Mass media
   **o.** Grapevine

Employees were asked in the above study which were their *actual* information sources, as opposed to this listing of *preferred* sources. Two were far out of line: *grapevine,* last on the preferred source list, was ranked second as an actual source; *bulletin boards,* number eight in preference, in actuality ranked third.

Participants in a 1999 communications study by IABC and Watson Wyatt cite e-mail as the most frequently used communications tool now (90 percent). But it is not a magic communications pill, according to the study. It received a low (55 percent) effectiveness rating. Clutter is a factor in its ineffectiveness. Employees receive a significant number of e-mails each day, both business and personal. An organization cannot be sure its employees are really taking the time to process and understand their electronic messages.

Using a focused communication strategy that combines a mix of methods and tools brings the most success, finds the study. This mix includes in-person meetings, printed newsletters, intranets, open-door policies, and e-mail.

- Key strategy is face-to-face interchanges, with managers and supervisors seen as communication links first and foremost—not only from the top down and the bottom up, but also laterally (between departments and work groups). Consequently, public relations departments often must coach and train supervisors and managers in interpersonal communication skills.

## FRONTLINE SUPERVISORS AS THE KEY COMMUNICATORS

The source employees most want to receive information from is their immediate or frontline supervisor—the most effective vehicle for communicating with employees, according to the previous list. Frontline supervisors are trusted and therefore more believable.

The communication process that passes information from top management down to employees through their immediate supervisors is sometimes called *cascading meetings*. It involves:

- Providing resources and training for frontline supervisors to relay information to their direct reports;
- Giving supervisors advance notice and in-depth and meaningful information to share with employees; and
- Making subject matter experts available to immediately answer questions.

This process helps relationship building within the management team. Supervisors get information in a timelier manner and feel more plugged into what's going on. And messages are delivered face-to-face to all employees in 24 hours using this process—which beats both the news media and the grapevine.

## TRUST IS ESSENTIAL

Trust directly impacts an organization's success and profits.[1] It contributes to job satisfaction, which leads to effectiveness, financial strength, competitiveness, and productivity. Trust must start with initiatives from the top.

If we look at organizations realistically, it is apparent that the most important people are those at the bottom—the frontliners. They make the product, deliver the service, sell the goods, and provide essential support mechanisms. In short, they more than anyone *are* the organization.

If, as shown in the diagram, you draw a line above the frontline supervisors (whether called team leaders, managers, or whatever), everyone above the line is overhead. The top of the pyramid is cost, not income generating. Those positions exist to support what the frontliners do.

Therefore, if management wants to earn trust, it must acknowledge this, and then formulate policies and processes that prove and continually symbolize it to the frontliners.

There are six components of trust:

1. *Openness.*   Good news and bad must be shared with employees or they may suspect secrecy and conspiracy. Divulge plans in a timely fashion explaining the "whys."

---

[1]According to a study by the International Association of Business Communicators, "Measuring Organizational Trust: A Diagnostic Survey & International Indicator." For more information, call 800-776-4222, or e-mail service_center@iabc.com.

2. ***Shared values.***    Management must share its vision with all employees and encourage employees to offer theirs.
3. ***Consistency of words and actions.***    Consistent treatment of all employees as well as consistency between management's words and actions are needed.
4. ***Appreciation.***    Management must show appreciation for employees' commitment to the organization.
5. ***Feedback.***    Employees' input must be solicited and considered, and they must be allowed to speak out with impunity. Often, trouble stems from executives believing theirs is the only workable way.
6. ***Autonomy.***    Management must give employees respect, allowing them to work independently and monitor their own performance without breathing down their necks.

## COMMUNICATING THROUGH TECHNOLOGY: PROS AND CONS

The convenience and speed of technology make it an alluring communication medium, but it needs to be used wisely. Once awareness has been created—preferably by face-to-face communication where possible—technology (e-mail, the Internet, and intranet sites) is useful for reinforcing the message.

The advantages of technology include a quick way to give and get feedback, which shortens the communication cycle time, convenient information storage and retrieval, reduced communication costs, a flatter corporate hierarchy when an employee with an idea or concern can share it directly with an individual (from a senior manager to an immediate supervisor) without having the message reviewed and filtered by others, and the ability to collaborate with others. It allows people on different floors, different time zones, and different continents to have immediate access to working documents and data.

On the negative side, it's impersonal and increases the risk of dehumanizing relationships; it's generally done quickly, even impulsively, and thus increases the likelihood for misunderstanding; it's a pull medium, which means the receiver must want it and seek it; information security is still a big concern for many; and often the information received is not *information mapped* (a visual layout that makes text easy to read and understand, reduces long paragraphs to bite-sized chunks bulleted for easy scanning, and offers a source for more details).

The main impact of technology, as one PR firm CEO put it, is "speed without analysis, data without wise interpretation."[2]

### Trustworthiness Now Means Holding Back Nothing

Public relations counselor Bruce Harrison advises that in dealing with key publics such as employees, it's not enough to just communicate honestly. Organizations are finding that in order to foster trust, they must be entirely open and show all evidence, a method called "transparent communication." Organizations need to let constituents know:

- Here's how we're making the decision. Here are the facts that led us to make this decision.
- Here are the options. Let's look at them together so you can help us make the decision.
- We believe we're being forthright and candid, but you judge for yourself. Here are the data. What do you think?

---

[2] *pr reporter*'s "30th Annual Survey of the Profession." Vol. 41 No. 38. September 28, 1998.

Intranets are one way to implement this strategy with employees. Minutes of meetings, policies, plans and strategies, financial results, and other data are posted there for any interested employee.

This type of policy is the key for any organization to be considered trustworthy today.

*Source: pr reporter* Vol. 35 No. 36, September 21, 1992, p. 3.

## References and Additional Readings

Bailey, John, and Richard Bevan. "Employee Communication." Chapter 12 in *Lesly's Handbook of Public Relations and Communications*. 5th ed. Chicago, IL: NTC Business Books, 1998.

Barr, Stephen. "Smile! You're on Corporate TV." *Communication World* 8 (September 1991): 28–31.

Beer, Michael, Russell Eisenstat, and Bert Spector. "Why Change Programs Don't Produce Change." *Harvard Business Review* (November/December 1990): 158–166.

Brody, E. W. *Communicating for Survival*. New York: Praeger, 1987.

Casarez, Nicole B. "Electronic Mail and Employee Relations: Why Privacy Must Be Considered." *Public Relations Quarterly* 37 (Summer 1992): 37–40.

Cutlip, Scott, Allen Center, and Glen Broom. "Media for Internal Publics." Chapter 9 in *Effective Public Relations*. 8th ed. Upper Saddle River, NJ: Prentice Hall, 1999.

Davids, Meryl. "Labor Shortage Woes: How Practitioners Are Helping Companies Cope." *Public Relations Journal* 44 (November 1988).

Drucker, Peter. "The Responsible Worker." Chapter 21 in *Management: Tasks, Responsibilities, Practices*. New York: Harper and Row, 1974.

Friedman, Thomas L. *The World Is Flat: A Brief History of the Twenty-First Century*. New York: Farrar, Straus and Giroux, 2006, p. 15.

Herman, Roger, and Joyce Gioia. *How to Become an Employer of Choice*. Winchester, VA: Oakhill Press, 2000.

Holtz, Shel. *Public Relations on the Net*. New York: AMACOM, 1999.

Pfeffer, Jeffrey. *The Human Equation: Building Profits by Putting People First*. Boston. MA: Harvard Business School Press, January 1998.

*pr reporter Special Report: A Probing Look at Employee Relations Today: How to Shape World-Class Internal Relationships and Communications*. Exeter, NH: PR Publishing, 1998.

*pr reporter* Vol. 42 No. 29 (July 26, 1999). "'Are You Being Served?' Study Finds Employee Politeness Is Huge Determinant of Customer Loyalty, as PR Has Insisted."

*pr reporter* Vol. 42 No. 1 (January 4, 1999). "In an Era of Mistrust and Skepticism, Making Your Organization One People Can Trust Is the Ultimate Differentiator."

*pr reporter* Vol. 40 No. 15 (April 14, 1997). "The Psychology of Customer Delight: PR's Vital Role."

*pr reporter* Vol. 39 No. 34 (August 26, 1996). "Some Metrics on How Well Employee Participation Pays Off."

*pr reporter* Vol. 37 No. 21 (May 23, 1994). "Action Research Unites Staff and Management in Satisfying Customers."

*pr reporter* Vol. 36 No. 40 (October 11, 1993). "Communication, PR Ideas Drive Unique Re-Engineering Plan"—An outstanding case study that puts all the organizational trends together.

*pr reporter* Vol. 34 No. 49 (December 16, 1991). "PR's Role in Culture Change."

*pr reporter* Vol. 32 No. 34 (August 28, 1989). "Survey Finds Trust in Management Translates into Quality."

Skutski, Karl. "Conducting a Total Quality Communications Audit." *Public Relations Journal,* April 1992, 20–32.

Smith, Alvie. *Innovative Employee Communication: New Approaches to Improving Trust, Teamwork and Performance*. Upper Saddle River, NJ: Prentice Hall, 1991.

# ⭐ Case 3-1 Communicating through Acquisition: Southwest Airlines Takes on AirTran and Blends Employee Cultures

Often one of the hardest parts of a merger or acquisition is blending the different cultures so that employees are able to do their work to the best of their ability with the least amount of frustration and conflict. Those employees whose organization's name and culture ends up subsumed by the new entity often feel a sense of loss and diminished loyalty. This fact is often overlooked, and a newly created organization can lose precious time and productivity trying to excise the resulting angst and conflict for years.

## How SWA and AirTran Avoided Culture Wars

The Southwest Airlines (SWA) **acquisition** of AirTran became official in early May 2010. However, the SWA communications team began planning far in advance, knowing that a smooth transition to "one-department communications" would not happen overnight.

This was the first merger for SWA, and a lot was at stake. Over the years, it had carved out a unique niche in the airline industry and had managed to hold onto its passenger-friendly, employee-friendly culture, even through leadership transitions.

"We were fortunate that AirTran shares a lot of the same core beliefs in terms of the culture of employees first and treating customers right," says Todd Painter, SWA communications manager.

## Research First

The first step was to meet with AirTran's communications team to figure out how it communicated to employees and compare that to how SWA was doing it. AirTran had a strong communications team, but the department structure did not line up exactly with SWA's structure. At SWA, for example, media relations, employee relations, and social media were all in the same group, which helped them achieve One Clear Voice. They had also established an Internal Communicators Exchange (ICE) which enabled them to communicate with all professional communicators throughout the organization weekly.

Much of SWA's communications program design was based on results from an ongoing, company-wide employee survey program. SWA began these surveys in 2006, and an outside firm still conducts them every two years. "We look at a lot of topics: leadership, direction of the company, morale, etc. Feedback from the survey is reviewed by different cross-sectional committees who then take action on the recommendations. The idea of having an employee blog and the ability to comment on podcasts came from feedback that we needed to increase two-way communication," said Painter. The need for texting and a mobile app also came up in survey feedback.

---

Highlights from SWA Employee Survey and Quarterly Intranet Poll

- 80% say SWA provides up-to-date information on company happenings.
- 97% of SWA employees are willing to go the extra mile for customers.
- On the quarterly SWA Life poll: 90% of employees consistently say they are proud to work for SWA.

*(Continued)*

### Integration Messaging Presented as a United Front

To make the transition, SWA and AirTran decided that all messaging on the integration would be shared and that both companies would continue using their own communication vehicles for at least six months during the transition. Bob Jordan, president of AirTran (and executive vice-president of SWA), established a weekly toll-free message for employees, and Gary Kelly of SWA also delivered a weekly message to SWA employees. The audio messages were then posted as podcasts. SWA continued its daily e-newsletter, "Today at SWA," while AirTran continued publishing its vehicle "Aline" for six months before the two publications were consolidated into one.

"We also had to iron out some systems inconsistencies," said Painter. "For example, all SWA employees had company-issued e-mail accounts but AirTran employees didn't, so we had to get those lined up."

The "publication of record" for SWA is SWALife, the intranet site that is refreshed with three to five stories a day. During the transition period, AirTran employees had access to SWALife, but they also kept their intranet, Sharetran. SWALife has a very interactive blog that gets monitored closely to get a sense of what issues stimulate the most responses and which messages resonate best with employees. "All comments are monitored by the communication team," said Painter. "If we deny a posting, we'll e-mail the employee back and let him know why."

A little over a year after the merger (summer 2011), SWA launched its mobile app and AirTran employees gained access at the same time. Shortly before that, in April, SWA launched "opt-in-texting" for employees. This is reserved for breaking news such as the decision to fly to a new city or quarterly financial results.

In addition, most stations have their own Facebook pages that are fed by local employees, though, again, the communications department oversees them. SWA also developed a Corporate Social Media Handbook for all employees that provides background on SWA's social media philosophy and spells out employee guidelines for social media use; it also includes FAQs on this topic.

SWA has some traditional communication vehicles like the monthly LUVLines newsletter for employees and their families and a special e-newsletter for SWA leaders. "We post our daily newsletter on bulletin boards in the field and have slots for every day of the week in which we can place a one pager—and we do get feedback that crews take the information on flights," said Painter.

### The Mission of Southwest Airlines

The mission of Southwest Airlines is dedication to the highest quality of Customer Service delivered with a sense of warmth, friendliness, individual pride, and Company Spirit (Figure 3.1).

| The Mission of Southwest Airlines | To Our Employees |
|---|---|
| The mission of Southwest Airlines is dedication to the highest quality of Customer Service delivered with a sense of warmth, friendliness, individual pride, and Company Spirit. | We are committed to provide our Employees a stable work environment with equal opportunity for learning and personal growth. Creativity and innovation are encouraged for improving the effectiveness of Southwest Airlines. Above all, Employees will be provided the same concern, respect, and caring attitude within the organization that they are expected to share externally with every Southwest Customer. |

**FIGURE 3.1**

## Culture Consistency

Part of SWA's secret to maintaining its unique culture rests on the fact that leadership has had a consistent commitment to employees. Current CEO Gary Kelly spends a lot of time with employees in the field. He travels to six different locations to deliver his "Message to the Field," an annual state-of-SWA speech, and encourages employees to participate in Q&A sessions. He is not the only visible senior leader. SWA does "organized leader visits," during which three or four leaders go to a particular location and visit with employees. Throughout the year, every SWA city is visited. It helps that founder and Chairman Emeritus Herb Kelleher and President Emeritus Colleen Barrett are still involved. "Colleen was the person behind our customer service culture," said Painter (see the box "Employee Focused Culture Has Deep Roots").

SWA has a Companywide Culture Committee (CCC) made up of employees from all work groups and locations across the organization. Its main goals are to promote and foster a fun and healthy work environment, to help build morale, and to appreciate and recognize the hard work of fellow employees. The CCC includes more than 100 active members and close to 200 alumni members (after three years, a committee member becomes an alumnus). "This is the group that goes out and cooks with our ground operations employees . . . typically on the ramp where the planes are. We grill, play games, play music, and just have fun. We do the same for the mechanics. We also do a hokey day where we surprise flight crews with goody bags and let them have five or 10 minutes of down time," said Painter. *(Interesting observation: More than 30 positions at SWA have the word "culture" in their titles.)*

## Outside Expert Verification

External measures verify that SWA is doing something right when it comes to building and maintaining employee relationships. In 2011, it was ranked 17th by Glassdoor, a jobs and career community in its 4th annual Employee Choice Awards as reported by *Forbes Magazine* in their 100 Best Places to Work list.

## Employee Focused Culture Has Deep Roots

The concept for SWA began in 1966 when Rollin King, a San Antonio entrepreneur who owned a small commuter airline service, and his banker, John Parker, approached Herb Kelleher, then one of their lawyers, with an idea for an airline that would introduce healthy competition to the airlines that serviced Houston, Dallas, and San Antonio. King and Kelleher raised the capital to launch SWA but spent four years and nearly all of the funds fighting restraining orders and lawsuits filed by competitors in order to earn the right to exist.

By the time it was ready to fly, SWA had just four planes and fewer than 70 employees. It was forced to set outrageously low fares to attract customers. The competition, feeling the heat, matched SWA's fares, forcing the new airline to reduce prices even more and putting itself in financial jeopardy. To continue, they needed to decide whether to lay employees off or sell a plane.

Management chose to put employees first. In return for not laying off a single employee, SWA asked employees to master the "10-minute turn" so the airline could keep the same flight schedule it had planned with four airplanes. By doing this, the company could manage more flights per day and ultimately lower operating costs.

From its earliest days, the company has incorporated a focus on fun and LUV (SWA's ticker symbol on the NYSE)—for both passengers and employees—into its unique management style. Employees are comfortably dressed. Flight attendants use humor in their normally mundane announcements; one was even captured on YouTube "rapping" emergency instructions! This relaxed and open working environment has encouraged customer service agents to hold holiest sock contests and to encourage passengers to make faces at ground crews while waiting to board the plane. "We look for a sense of humor, a sense of service," says Colleen. "We don't care if you're the best pilot in the USAF, but if you condescend to a secretary, you won't get hired."

## Why Employee Culture—Not Just Communications—Is a PR Responsibility

Productivity is the lifeblood of an organization and it can be compromised significantly by a culture that blocks communication and cooperation, or one that is closed off or punitive. Whereas employee communications is a core responsibility of PR, employee *relations* has traditionally been the responsibility of human resources. But HR's work has tended to focus on the huge responsibility of personnel management and compliance.

Gradually, public relations practitioners have been taking on more and more responsibility, not only for communicating *to* employees about organizational issues, but also for addressing bottom-up and lateral communications. This brings PR to the very feet of corporate culture. Managing employee relationships to enhance productivity is an integral part of our work since communication is at the very core of a positive relationship, work or otherwise. A practitioner's skill in helping individuals or groups better understand each other can be invaluable. And helping senior management be aware of a problematic culture (that often stems from dysfunction right in the C-suite) can be among the most valuable tasks a practitioner can perform.

# Case 3-2 Buffeted by Management Changes and a Rocky Economy, a Strategic Communication System Keeps Employees Focused

Located in the picturesque town of Bennington, VT, Southwestern Vermont Health Care (SVHC) is a 99-bed hospital system serving an area of about 65,000 people. In late 2007, the Great Recession had yet to occur, but SVHC was feeling the impact of a national health-care funding system that was making it difficult to operate profitably. Complicating matters, this fairly remote and rural part of Vermont has few large employers, which meant that many of the approximately 1,200 SVHC employees had been working in the system for years. Hospital officials began to suspect part of the problem of operational efficiency and profits lay with internal communication.

## Research First

After several employee opinion surveys indicated that morale could be improved, the public relations team commissioned an outside firm to conduct a communications audit that included 15 focus groups (approximately 150 employees) targeting all staffing levels (including day, evening, and night shifts) and satellite locations. To give all employees a voice in the process, a Web survey followed up on the focus groups. The survey was open to all employees, and 310 responded anonymously. The outside firm also conducted face-to-face interviews with senior managers and performed an expert review of all communications materials and the SVHC intranet.

- Findings pointed to a communication system that was both confusing and overwhelming.
- Employees were barraged with e-mail daily, much of it having little to do with them or their jobs.

- Supervisor communication was hit or miss—it depended on the skills of the supervisor and the structure of the department. Staff meetings occurred or didn't; information was conveyed or not.
- The grapevine was actively filling in the gaps, often not accurately. Silos were strong and created roadblocks causing lateral communications to suffer.
- The intranet was accessed primarily for specific data (phone numbers, policies, etc.).
- There were a variety of tools for top-down communication but no formal, recognizable system that employees could count on.
- No formal system for bottom-up communication was in place, so whoever had the time and skill to find and talk with senior managers got their concerns addressed—often resulting in the appearance of haphazard planning.

## A Strategic System Established

Systematizing top-down communications was the first order of business. The public relations team focused on how employees preferred to get their need-to-know information. Supervisors, staff meetings, targeted e-mails (with someone designated to posting them for those without e-mail), Town Hall meetings, and the intranet were channels adopted. Use of "Keep In Touch," the monthly newsletter, was continued but limited to nice-to-know information. A "red-alert" e-mail was established for true emergency communication. The system therefore was self-reinforcing—the important items would end up in multiple venues for emphasis.

*(Continued)*

Systematizing communication was as much about reducing clutter that clogged communication channels as it was about adding new tools. Stopping "all-list" e-mails for non-emergency subjects helped reduce the number of unnecessary e-mails received. And though some senior managers agreed that *others* should stop sending unnecessary e-mails/all-list e-mails, it took some arm twisting to get *them* to see that they were culpable too. Engineered into the system was a rule that "all-list" e-mails had to be approved by the communications department or incident commander (administrator in charge at the time). This was a foot-in-door approach to changing an ingrained behavior.

## Supervisors as Communicators

Supervisors were to be the main information source for employees, but supporting them and holding them accountable was going to be a challenge. A new daily bulletin was created and named "In Touch Today," to link to the monthly newsletter (Figure 3.2). This one-page-only document covered system-wide news of need-to-know importance, left space for departmental leadership to include their need-to-know news, and included a few "passing parade" announcements and a "thought for the day." Including general announcements here made it easier to eliminate overhead announcements throughout the hospital, which had been disturbing patients and interrupting staff.

"In Touch Today" also helped lay out for supervisors the talking points for their now required daily five-minute meetings with staff. Supervisors were tasked with forwarding questions and concerns that needed further action through the appropriate channels.

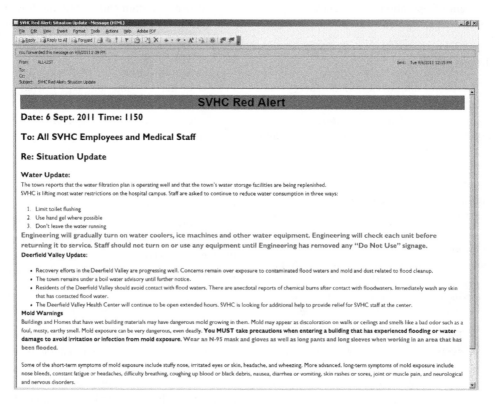

**FIGURE 3.2**   SVHC Red Alert Binder

Southwestern Vermont Health Care's Daily Bulletin

**30 August 2011**

**SVHC News:**

**SVHC Reaches Out to Employees Affected by Irene**

Hurricane Irene has departed the area but her effects are still being felt by many of our employees. Some employees have sustained significant losses including the loss of their homes. To assist our employees who have experienced a significant loss, SVHC will provide an interest-free loan for up to $10,000. If you are one of those employees who have sustained a significant loss and are classified as a regular full-time or part-time employee, please complete the "SVHC Hurricane Irene Emergency Request Form" (attached as a flyer) and return it to Polly Cipperly in Human Resources for processing.

In addition, please remember that all SVHC staff and immediate family members have access to our Employee Assistance Program. This service is free of charge and is entirely confidential. To utilize this service please contact United Counseling Service at (802) 442-5491. For more information about this program, contact Human Resources.

**SVHC Supports Our Communities After Irene**

Hurricane Irene proved to be a tremendous challenge both for the health system and for the communities it serves. SVHC's administration would like to thank all the staff, physicians, volunteers, and caregivers who have worked extra shifts, stayed overnight, braved the elements, and just stepped up to meet the challenge. SVHC not only managed to keep the hospital operating with minimal disruptions, we also have opened up Northshire and Deerfield Valley campuses for urgent care, worked with emergency management teams from across our region to provide medical and nursing expertise, and deployed over 100 cots, pillows, and blankets to the shelter set up for Bennington at Mount Anthony Middle School. Some communities remain affected by the hurricane, including the Deerfield Valley. SVHC's Incident Command Team continues to reach out to these communities to help them care for and comfort people there.

**Departmental Announcements:**

Managers, add your departmental or unit announcements or information here.

**Passing Parade:**

- **Magnet Backpack Donations:** In light of the devastation in the Bennington area, the deadline for backpack donations has been extended until Friday, Sept. 2.
- Managers, please add items as needed relevant to your department.

**Thought for the Day:**

Nature hates calculators.
**Ralph Waldo Emerson** (American Poet, 1803-1882)

**FIGURE 3.3** SVHC Daily Bulletin "In Touch Today"

*(Continued)*

# Monthly Staff Meeting Agenda
## November 2010

**I.  SVHC-Wide Agenda Item: Tobacco-Free SVHC**

a. Entire Health System campus will go tobacco-free effective Jan 1. 2011.
- SVHC is not requiring anyone to quit using tobacco: we are simply asking people not to use tobacco on our campus.
- No tobacco use on campus, including in cars and on UCS property since they are also Tobacco-Free.
- Smoking shelters will be eliminated

b. Tobacco Use Prohibited For Visitors and Patients on campus:
- Patients have access to nicotine replacement therapy through their doctor's orders
- Visitors and others can purchase nicotine replacement from the Gift Shop or the SOS Tech after hours
- Security and the Emergency Dept. will have access to crisis packs containing nicotine replacement therapy

c. Tobacco Use Prohibited for employees on campus or on paid time
- Employees should plan for the transition and provide their own nicotine replacement therapy during work.
- Gwen Hannan, tobacco cessation counselor, is available to help employees pick the right nicotine replacement strategy for work. She also is available to counsel employees who may wish to discuss quitting.
- Leaving Campus: employees are discouraged from leaving campus to use tobacco products. Employees who choose to leave campus for any reason must punch out and respect the property rights of SVHC's neighbors. Time away from campus is considered unpaid time.

d. Policy Enforcement
- Violations by Visitors and Patients:
    1. SVHC's security personnel are primarily responsible for enforcing the policy.
    2. Staff are requested but not required to assist in discussing the policy with violators.
    3. Directors and managers are expected to assist.
    4. Repeated violations will be subject to SVHC's disruptive person policy and may be asked to leave the property.
- Violations by employees
    1. Members of management and SVHC's security personnel are required to speak to employees in violation of the policy and to report violations to the Administrative Director of Human Resources.
    2. Staff are requested but not required to discuss the policy or report violators.
    3. As with all policies, violations may be subject to correction action.

e. Communications: SVHC will be conducting widespread communications with the Bennington community to make community members aware of this change.

f. Opportunity to address questions or comments about other SVHC-wide issues. *(This section is designed to allow staff to raise concerns for management to address)*

g. Follow-up on previous concerns raised in section I.c. *(This is the section where a manager can provide information directly to staff about questions or comments on SVHC-wide issues they have raised.)*

**II.  Department Issues**

(Department managers own the agenda from here on. Insert your own agenda items) a. Department-Specific Financial Report

**FIGURE 3.4**   SVHC Monthly Staff Meeting Agenda

## Lateral Communications

Getting departments to communicate across silos proved to be a harder nut to crack. A variety of ideas were considered, including reviewing standing committees to rotate members and establishing a process for how new task forces and committees would best be formed. Intervening events, however, stopped the train of progress.

## The Economy Goes South and Turmoil Abounds

The Great Recession of 2008 came roaring in and the hospital system, already under duress, suffered significantly. Financial issues, seemingly greater than had been advertised, resulted in a sweeping change of leadership at the top. Many employees who had worked with the long-term CEO and members of his team were devastated and lost trust in management. The communication systems in place were used to keep employees informed as the ground was shifting underneath them. More than 100 positions were eliminated throughout the hospital.

Kevin Robinson, communications director, reflects back: "With major uncertainty among employees, having a single place to go for reliable information became more important than ever. With our communications system, employees could focus on their work instead of spending their time trying to figure out what was going on. It didn't make them feel any less anxious, but it helped quiet the typical chaos and rumor mills that abound in these situations, especially when there is a communications vacuum."

As the hospital system brought on new management, it continued to use the new system for communication to ease the transition. The communications systems allowed for ramped-up coverage without introducing anything new into the mix—something that would have been difficult and costly.

## Evaluations Show System Working Well

Four years later, the system still works well. Regularly, PR staff conduct dipstick studies to see what employees know and to gauge communication effectiveness. In 2010, a formal survey found 82 percent of employees feel informed about what is going on at SVHC. They like "In Touch Today" and are interested in it covering more discussion of ongoing issues and the future of the system. Supervisors still need to develop more skills at running the five-minute meetings, and senior management needs to be more visible. In 2011, SVHC did another check by running focus groups. Earlier findings were reinforced.

As always, however, there is tweaking to be done. Robinson notes, "We continue to struggle with feedback as part of the monthly staff meeting agenda. When it comes in, we respond to it, but it doesn't come in often enough. If we get multiple questions on the same subject, we send a response back to the individual directly who asked and include it in an issue of "In Touch Today." If a handful of people are asking, it's likely there are more wondering about the same thing."

---

Supervisors, a key component of any communication system, constantly need training to be good in this pivotal role. Supervisors are often promoted because they "do their jobs well," not because of their communication skills. PR and HR need to work together to assure that all managers understand their responsibility for good communication and how to glean what needs to be communicated up, down, and laterally.

---

## Never a Dull Moment

With SVHC still dealing with economic issues, but working its way back, August 2011 brought Hurricane Irene through Vermont. Eleven

*(Continued)*

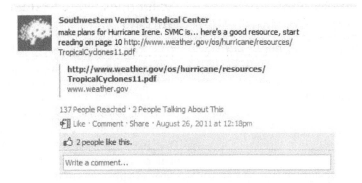

**Southwestern Vermont Medical Center**
make plans for Hurricane Irene. SVMC is... here's a good resource, start
reading on page 10 http://www.weather.gov/os/hurricane/resources/
TropicalCyclones11.pdf

**http://www.weather.gov/os/hurricane/resources/**
**TropicalCyclones11.pdf**
www.weather.gov

137 People Reached · 2 People Talking About This

⏎ Like · Comment · Share · August 26, 2011 at 12:18pm

👍 2 people like this.

Write a comment...

**FIGURE 3.5**   SVHC's Facebook page

inches of rain caused major flash flooding of a magnitude not seen since 1927. It washed out 500 miles of roads and a dozen bridges. Bennington suffered severe flooding, power outages, and destroyed roadways. But the hospital had to remain open. Whereas social media had not been a big part of how the hospital communicated with its staff on a daily basis, it now was the only alternative. "It was critical to helping employees get to work—where we needed them," said Robinson. "Facebook was our best option; otherwise we would have had to call everyone—not something we could do easily (Figure 3.5). We posted all kinds of information on our Facebook page, and that served not only employees who were trying to get to the hospital but community members as well." Red-alert e-mails were also sent to keep staff informed.

"Our intranet is the only unfinished piece of communication we have at this particular time," says Robinson. "It needs a face-lift and a hard

| **Economic Crisis Communication Strategy** | |
|---|---|
| **Low Anxiety, Concerns, Fear** | **High Anxiety, Concerns, Fear** |
| **Strategy:**<br>• Traditional but continuous comm.<br>• Monitor and respond<br>• Isolate and Solve<br>• Supervisor as Communicator<br>• Goal focus | **Strategy:**<br>• High Touch<br>• Secure and Hold<br>• Isolate and Solve<br>• Management as communicator<br>• Objectives Focus |
| **Tactics:**<br>• No new methods but increase frequency<br>• Research — dipstick, opinion leaders<br>• Workshops: financial, stress mgmt,<br>• MBWA senior management<br>• Goals that contribute to bottom line<br>  (energy savings, customer service)<br>• Employee Action/Role (ambassadors) | **Tactics:**<br>• Face-to-Face<br>• One-on-ones<br>• Education: financial, stress mgmt<br>• Cheerleading w/o spin<br>• Small steps on critical goals<br>• Customer Service Strategies<br>• Employee Action/Role (ambassadors) |
| **Message Strategy:**<br>• What makes a difference<br>• Reinforce what is going right<br>• Productivity & performance<br>• Role of employee as ambassador | **Message Strategy:**<br>• Reality w/o fear — calming<br>• Transparency<br>• Education |

**FIGURE 3.6**   Economic Crisis

look at how information is organized. We occasionally get requests to deliver our daily newsletter by e-mail only. We decided against that for now because of the nature of what we do here. Everyone has an e-mail address, but despite the use of computers at the bedside, not all of our staff are able to check e-mail regularly. It is important to understand the behavioral aspects of your employee body and communicate to them in a way that puts their needs first."

## Economic Crisis Communication Strategy

Communicating during a severe economic crisis requires subtle shifts in how and when organizations communicate. Figure 3.6 gives guidelines for communicating during tough economic times.

## References

http://abcnews.go.com/US/hurricanes/hurricane-irene-flooding-cuts-off-towns-vermont-york/story?id=14402696

http://www.nytimes.com/2011/12/06/us/vermont-rebounding-from-hurricane-irene.html?pagewanted=all

# Case 3-3 Establishing the Organization Culture under a New Leader Early: How 100-Day Plans Work

Leaders only get one chance to make a good first impression. It is well documented that new leaders receive a grace period, most often called a honeymoon, during which making the right transitional steps can enhance their general effectiveness and ultimately their ability to effect needed change. Wise leaders make the most of it.

Since President Franklin Roosevelt's plan to pass the majority of his New Deal programs within his first 100 days in office, the 100-day plan has become axiomatic for new leaders in business, government, higher education, and other sectors. This period tends to delineate the new leader's honeymoon with the organization—a time when it might be easier to get things done.

Leadership changes are a time of opportunity, but also a stage when potential missteps could threaten to damage a new leader's prospects before the transition is complete. A well-thought-out and thoroughly coordinated 100-day plan can mitigate the danger and maximize the opportunities for a successful transition and allow the new leader to get off to a great start, and be much more effective over time.

## CNCS's Past Along with the Present-Day Environment in Washington Set the Stage

Recently, the Corporation for National and Community Service (CNCS) faced a vitally important CEO leadership transition. CNCS is a small agency of the federal government with the mission to improve lives, strengthen communities, and foster civic engagement through service and volunteering. It is primarily a grant-making entity that funds AmeriCorps members who serve with well-known grantees such as Teach for America, City Year, Public Allies,

and lesser-known efforts such as the St. Bernard Project, which is constructing houses in areas devastated by Hurricane Katrina and the tornado that hammered Joplin, Missouri, in 2011.

CNCS also funds long-standing programs such as AmeriCorps VISTA and Senior Corps, which includes the Foster Grandparents, Senior Companions, and the Retired Senior Volunteer Program (RSVP). Senior Corps is the largest volunteer program for people over 55.

In total, CNCS engages five million Americans in community service each year, and national service participants serve in 70,000 nonprofits throughout the nation. Its stakeholders are many, are highly diversified, and are found in nearly every community in America.

While CNCS itself has existed for slightly less than 20 years, its antecedents have roots 50 years deep in President Lyndon Johnson's War on Poverty, and before that in President John Kennedy's iconic call to service, "Ask not what your country can do for you. Ask what you can do for your country."

More recently, CNCS's bipartisan supporters have included Presidents George H.W. Bush and Bill Clinton. In 2009, Senators Edward Kennedy and Orrin Hatch teamed to sponsor the Kennedy Serve America Act, which called for a dramatic expansion of national service programs, but narrowed their focus to areas of significant community need, requiring rigorous performance measures to ensure high impact and effectiveness.

Many different circumstances merged to make critical the transition to a new CEO at CNCS. The agency had been without a Senate-confirmed CEO for approximately 18 months out of the previous three years. Beyond this, the bipartisan, presidentially appointed board of directors had dwindled to less than one-third of its full strength due to gridlock on Capitol Hill. More telling, just prior to the new CEO's Senate confirmation, the *"Chronicle of Philanthropy"* published a five-part series on the future of national service that called for strong leadership at CNCS.

These circumstances, coupled with the head winds of federal fiscal austerity—the House of Representatives' second attempt at eliminating the agency and the necessity of the agency showing unambiguous return on investment—only served to intensify the imperative that the new CEO make a strong start from day one.

Every leadership transition is unique, but the process can be researched on the Internet where a range of articles discussing 100-day plans and several transition templates can be found. This is a rich resource from which to draw. A number of these sources are foot-noted, allowing for the development of an in-depth understanding of the process and common mistakes made, as well as for developing alternative approaches.

## Research Helped Lay Out a Strategy

In CNCS's case, research indicated that the new CEO—coming from the national service field as the head of a state governor's volunteer organization primarily responsible for dispensing state AmeriCorps grants—was known to and would be well received by many CNCS employees and stakeholders associated with the AmeriCorps world. However, a number of employees and other stakeholder groups would not know her. Moreover, in Washington, as in any organizational setting, strong relationships with a broad range of stakeholders, peers, customers, regulators, the media, and others are a necessary condition of success.

An approach determined to be the most appropriate would build on the new leader's high-energy and high-touch leadership style. A premium was placed on face-to-face meetings, a strong social media presence, and recalibrating

relationships from her prior roles in the field, thus demonstrating accessibility and instilling confidence. A lot needed to be done in a short period of time.

## The Plan Was Thorough, Straightforward

The plan was organized into actions and activities that had to take place upon Senate confirmation, on the first day; within the first week and month; and within the following 60 days, with easy wins and quick victories foremost.

### Senate Confirmation

- Press release
- Acting leader all-staff message
- Acting leader message to stakeholders
- Acting leader message to board of directors
- Web updates

### First Day-1

- Acting leader thank-you message to staff and workers in the field

### First Day

- Press release
- New-leader call with board chair and message to board of directors
- New-leader Web and social media messages and introductory video
- E-mails to all staff, workers in the field, and stakeholders
- Meeting with direct reports
- Meeting with senior leaders
- Meeting with CEO's office staff
- All-staff meeting with interactive streaming to employees in 50 states
- Meeting with the Inspector General
- Calls to key members of Congress
- Calls to key national service association leaders

*(Continued)*

- Calls to key White House staff
- Walkabout at headquarters to meet employees in their workplaces

### First Week

- Meeting with CNCS political appointees
- Meeting with union leadership
- Walkabouts continue
- Meetings with employee affinity groups
- Meetings with key White House staff
- Meetings and phone calls with key members of Congress and staff
- Thank-you notes to supporters
- Media preparation and review of key messages
- Calls to leaders of partner federal agencies

### First Month

- Begin contacting state governors and key mayors
- National service site visits
- Meetings with national service champions and ambassadors
- First board of directors meeting
- Meetings with members of Congress and key staff continue
- Begin meetings with key stakeholders
- Accept important speaking opportunities in Washington
- Begin deep dives into CNCS operations and cultural assessment
- ID quick wins for the next six months
- Develop supporting communications strategy

### Remaining 60 Days

- Accept important national service speaking opportunities
- Attend National Conference on Volunteering and Service
  - National debut speech in front of the entire national service community

- Featured panelist with the Secretary of Education during an education town hall
- Major speech at closing plenary session
- Networking strategy
- Remarks for at least a dozen stakeholder meetings

## A New Direction Set Early and Successfully

In execution, the plan of action and more was accomplished in terms of the number of intragovernmental and stakeholder contacts and field site visits and of organizational morale building. The new CEO was willing to work diligently to move quickly. Within the first six weeks, the new CEO met and delivered speeches at events with four cabinet officers. The President of the United States himself joined a CEO conference call with members of AmeriCorps.

The new CEO worked to cement key relationships, making contact with 86 members of Congress and key staff members, 12 governors, and the chairman of the United States Conference of Mayors within the first two months, all the while ensuring that other stakeholders and partners had been touched. In addition, she joined with members of Congress to announce AmeriCorps grants awarded to their states. Simultaneously, she launched an aggressive social media strategy including tweeting photos and smartphone video vignettes from important site visits, thus gaining close to 1,000 new followers.

The evaluation of the 100-day program was informal and not tied to any qualitative or quantitative data gathering due to restrictions on government information collection. But in an environment that is not shy on expressing its approval or disapproval, reliable informal feedback channels exist. And all indications from leaders across the national service spectrum were positive. Loud applause and standing ovations at the national conference, plus an avalanche of enthusiastic e-mail and phone calls, were feedback that the new leader had established credibility. Feedback in print media, social media, and verbal feedback from all audience segments was universally warm and enthusiastic, reaffirming the CEO's messaging and direction. The initial signs of buy-in and support from the national service rank and file for the new CEO's leadership were overwhelming.

One of national service's most visible leaders, who leads the field's most prominent advocacy organization, offered this emblematic assessment at the 60-day mark: "[The new CEO] is a great example of having the right leader at the right place at the right time. [Her] combination of management expertise, deep knowledge of the field, and unparalleled ability to communicate the value proposition national service and community volunteering represent has quite literally transformed the agency and its positioning in a very

short period of time. From lifting morale inside the agency and throughout the field to working on a bipartisan basis to educate governors, mayors, and members of Congress, [she] has put to use her talent, her intellect, and her leadership ability at a critical time for the agency and the national service and community volunteer movement."

Left remaining are the staff adjustments, full articulation of adjustments in strategic direction, and adjustments to the communications strategy that are needed to achieve the necessary across-the-board buy-in. However, the stage has been properly set for a successful leadership transition.

This case was written before completion of 100 days.

# ⭐Case 3-4 Producing Good Employee Ambassadors Means Educating Effectively: Kaiser Permanente Makes the Effort

Social scientists explain that "social behavior is the result of an exchange process," typically between two people. They call this "social exchange theory." They think that an individual will weigh the benefits and risks in a relationship, and if there are more rewards than risks, the relationship will thrive. If not, the relationship will end. Public relations practitioners believe this theory can be applied to the relationship between an employee and an organization. When there are "rewards," a positive relationship will result, and that can benefit both the employee and the organization.

Rewarding employees is a tricky business. Monetary rewards, while greatly appreciated at the time, become drawbacks when they are not given again either because the organization has not been as successful or the employee has not been as productive. Frederick Herzberg's Theory of Motivation holds that "hygiene factors" (pay, quality of supervision, job security, working conditions, etc.)[1] can only increase employee satisfaction to a point. Herzberg and his colleagues at Psychological Services of Pittsburgh (1957) found other factors, "motivational factors," that are responsible for increasing satisfaction past a certain level. These include such things as "career advancement, personal growth, recognition, and responsibility," to name a few. So the "reward" in social exchange theory must be carefully considered when building an employee ambassador program.

Kaiser Permanente, one of the largest not-for-profit integrated health-care delivery systems in the United States, is headquartered in Oakland, California. It encompasses both a health plan and a hospital system and includes a 65-year relationship with the Permanente Medical Groups, which include more than 16,500 family practice physicians and specialists who deliver care to more than 9 million Kaiser Permanente members.

Kaiser Permanent's annual employee research confirmed that employees—more than 170,000 staff in nine states and the District of Columbia—were a very strong part of the brand. Internal research showed that employees were very committed to the organization's mission. The majority of staff were not only team members, but Kaiser Permanente members, meaning that they and their families receive their health care from Kaiser Permanente, which may provide additional reason to provide the very best care possible.

Through its Labor Management Partnership, the organization formed unit-based teams (naturally occurring work groups of frontline staff, supervisors and managers, and physicians) to allow for more input into problem solving and process improvement. As a result, employees were more eager than ever to talk about the organization because of their own role in its success. Therefore, Kaiser Permanente believed that using employees as "brand ambassadors" was a logical step in building strong relationships with all stakeholders. The challenge would be to support the work force in speaking with One Clear Voice on behalf of the organization and its members.

- Kaiser Permanente's mission is: To provide high-quality, affordable health-care services and to improve the health of our members and the communities we serve.

---

[1] http://psychology.about.com/od/sindex/g/socialexchange.htm

## What Is a Brand Ambassador?

All employees are "ambassadors." Each time they interact with a customer or tell someone where they work, they convey information about the organization—sometimes good, sometimes bad.

Employees are some of the most credible sources of information and perceptions for external stakeholders. And those who do not sit in traditional seats of power in an organization (secretaries, clerks, receptionists, tellers, technicians, etc.) have some of the highest credibility ratings, which has been demonstrated by a plethora of studies over time.

It behooves an organization to make sure employees are well versed in the vision and language of an organization when they do speak out, and that their satisfaction with the organization as an employer and product or service provider is as good as possible.

## Feeding the System the Right Information

With such a sizable workforce, communicating to all levels *consistently* was critical to Kaiser Permanente's success. It created an internal message architecture (complementary to its external message architecture for public relations work) to ensure that leaders and communicators were speaking with one voice. This included such specifics as providing phrasing for key internal messages that leaders used in correspondence, presentations, and department meetings.

How the messaging would be distributed required engaging frontline employees who did not have access to the Internet or e-mail at work. To find a way to reach them, they were gathered with communicators for ideation sessions. Ideas were generated on how to get to this difficult-to-reach audience. Some were pilot tested to see what might work—ideas such as digital signage boards and comic strips. Kaiser Permanente also did an audit of current systems, to not reinvent the wheel and to use systems that were already successful.

In addition, and probably its most innovative step, Kaiser Permanente engaged in video ethnography, following frontline workers with video cameras to see what a day in their lives really looked like. Using this behavioral method, they were able to analyze the video for any opportunities to connect with employees in their natural flow of work.

## The Architecture Itself

Depending on their job, employee access to, and use of, information systems varied widely. Kaiser Permanente maintains both online and traditional communications systems to make sure everyone has access in a way that is both comfortable and convenient.

Online tools include:

- *A strategy Web site* brings the mission and strategic imperatives to life for employees, so they can understand how their work contributes to the organization's goals and objectives.
- *Self-paced online modules* for managers increase their business literacy and teach them how to communicate about the organization.
- Hundreds of courses help with professional development and support the culture as a continuous learning organization.
- E-mails are sent when information is important and timely.
- The intranet, customized by region, provides online news and information, features, and leadership columns that reinforce mission, brand promise, and the service credo, "We're here to make lives better."
- The external KP News Center Web site is accessible from work or home. Through the site, employees can get up-to-date information, read feature stories and blogs, and watch video blogs at their leisure.

*(Continued)*

Traditional methods of internal communication include:

- *Group huddles*: 15- to 20-minute daily sessions when staff gather at the start of their shifts in their units and talk about what is going on. Managers answer questions, and teams address problems.
- Monthly *town hall meetings* are available across the organization via teleconference and are recorded for future listening. One town hall is hosted by the chairman and CEO, along with The Permanente Federation's executive director, at which they share information and update the priorities of the organization. Often, a guest speaker is featured.
- A print magazine, "Hank" (named for Henry J. Kaiser, the founder of Kaiser Permanente), distributed at facilities and placed in staff mailboxes and on newspaper racks in break rooms and lobbies. It is written in a frontline-friendly way and is filled with stories and examples that team members can easily relate to.
- For bulletin boards, "bulletin board packets" are distributed to facilities each quarter with headline cutouts, fliers, photos, and information that speak to business priorities.

One tool useful for this program is the "CEO celebration letter." Once a week, the CEO personally writes about something that Kaiser Permanente should be celebrating and the people who make it happen. The letter is sent to all employees and physicians via e-mail, and many managers read or discuss it in group huddles. This weekly delivery of good news increases organizational understanding and arms each employee with tangible examples they can share with others in their role as ambassadors for the organization.

## Social Media Is Incorporated into the Mix

Making ready use of a natural communication system that employees are involved in anyway, Kaiser Permanente has its own Facebook business page and is on Twitter and YouTube. The social media outlets are also accessible by other stakeholders, so they are used primarily for messaging that is applicable and interesting to all audiences. Kaiser Permanente's News Center (kp.org/newscenter) serves as an online hub for press releases, positions on hot topics, and more, and it links to other social media and owned media platforms. It is heavily used by community members and employees.

## Accountability

Key to making the system work is for all communicators to use the message architecture every time they are communicating information to the organization.

"Consistency, with customization for regional and local nuances, is key," says Diane Gage Lofgren, SVP and chief communications officer. "Making sure that everyone is talking about our organization and our brand with one voice is of paramount importance for team members to understand our business and deliver on our mission. We work hard to provide clarity and avoid a game of telephone when communicating messages to the next level."

Surveys are conducted after message series are released to make sure they reached all points of the organization. Feedback is provided on how conversations went in huddles. Surveys are completed annually to find out whether employees are having their information needs met and whether they understand how their work supports the goals of the organization. The intranet portal has been redesigned to easily give feedback on any article, ask a question, or request additional information.

## Evaluation Is Ongoing

The communications teams in the various units are constantly checking the ongoing messaging against the architecture to see if they are in agreement and whether the messaging is being used. Teams measure message pull-through on a quarterly basis and track improvements on relevant measures in the annual employee "pulse" survey.

Research on external stakeholders and customers is carried out quarterly and shows a strong uptick in the understanding of the Kaiser Permanente brand, likely as a result of the brand ambassadors themselves—Kaiser Permanente employees.

## Questions for Discussion

1. Do you believe employees should be responsible for being good brand ambassadors for their organization? How do you reconcile this expectation with our individual expectations of freedom of speech?
2. Face-to-face communication, directly from supervisors, has been proven to be one of the most effective communication tools in an organization. But in many organizations, making time for this is next to impossible. How else might you see structuring "face time" between supervisors and employees?
3. How might you recommend Kaiser Permanente use its brand ambassadors beyond what they are doing now?

## PROBLEM 3-A   WHAT PRICE "GOOD" EMPLOYEE RELATIONS?

Safeplay, Inc., has competed in the sports and recreation equipment market for more than 25 years. The market is hotly contested.

One of the programs for employee morale and productivity long used by Safeplay has been the retention of former athletes of national repute on its payroll at each of its five manufacturing plants. Although the athletes are part of the human resources department staff, the public relations department makes them available for news interviews, conducting sports clinics at schools, and sitting on committees for newsworthy civic events.

One of the Safeplay plants is located in the small city of Westward, which has a population of 20,000 and is located on the outskirts of a metropolitan city. This plant, with an average of 900 employees, specializes in leather items such as baseball gloves, golf gloves, basketballs, footballs, soccer balls, and leather carrying bags for sports clothing.

This plant has a former professional baseball notable on the payroll as an assistant HR director. He makes for good copy on occasion, can speak with authority about the products, and directs a recreation program for employees.

## A Tolerant Attitude

At Safeplay plants and in sales offices, there is some pilferage of products by employees. Company policy is that any employee removing company property from the premises without authorization is subject to dismissal. So far, this policy has never been invoked where products are concerned. The unspoken attitude of management is much the same as exists in many consumer-product companies, particularly those that make food, confections, or inexpensive clothing items. It is tolerant, treats pilferage quietly as a minor cost written into the price of products, and looks the other way rather than confront employees, with the risk of possible repercussions if someone is falsely accused. Put another way, management reluctantly concludes that the cost of a baseball mitt taken home in a lunch pail or paper bag to a kid on occasion is not high if employee turnover is low and working enthusiasm is high.

As a means of trying to discourage pilferage, Safeplay offers employees a discount on any products they buy from the store in the personnel office, and on the 10th birthday of any employee's child the employee can select any product priced under $20 and take it home free.

## Tolerance Abused

Recently, however, the "mysterious disappearance" of sports items has gone beyond the boundaries of normal pilferage and management tolerance. Whole containers of items in the stockroom and in the shipping area have disappeared. Inventory records have apparently been doctored.

Obviously distressed, the home office has sent in a private detective agency. The agency's preliminary investigation and analysis are disturbing. It appears that there is an organized thievery ring involving as many as 25 of the Westward plant's employees. It appears, also, that the former athletic star on the payroll is somehow involved, but to what extent is not clear. Someone on the inside, not yet identified, deals with an outside "fence," and someone else on

*(Continued)*

the inside, also not yet identified, handles the pay-off to all the cooperating employees. Some of the involved employees are members of the union, and some are in the office "white-collar" jobs.

## The Decision Process

At an executive decision-making meeting, you, as director of public relations, have been called in, along with the director of personnel and a company lawyer from the home office. The three of you have been asked to assess the repercussions if the town's police are called in and legal action is taken. You are asked to offer any other resolution that would "better serve the interests of all involved."

The lawyer says that as soon as an airtight case can be constructed, which would include photographs and eyewitness accounts of products being removed and being transported to a "fence" and an actual money transaction completed, she favors appropriate law enforcement action and legal redress against those involved.

The personnel manager says he prefers to bring charges only against the leader or leaders inside and all those involved on the outside. He prefers to handle the cooperating employees individually, possibly allowing some sort of plea bargaining to keep the employees the company considers of real value on the payroll. He feels this approach will adequately frighten all employees, halt the activity, and avoid having to replace some trained and competent employees.

It is your turn to speak, using whatever notes you have taken while the others stated their positions. What is your view, taking into account the impact not only on internal relations, but on other publics directly or indirectly involved—including families of employees involved, neighbors, local law enforcement, news media in the trade, the Westward community, and shareholders of Safeplay? Are there others?

What actions, and in what sequence, would you propose and why?

How would you deal with the recommendations of the lawyer and the human resources manager without setting up an adversarial situation?

## PROBLEM 3-B    KEEPING MERGER HAVOC AT BAY

You are the vice president of public relations for a computer manufacturing company. The CEO called you and the vice president of human resources in for a meeting. Your company is planning to merge with another computer manufacturer.

You are aware of the havoc mergers inflict on employees. You also know that unhappy, disgruntled employees don't perform their tasks as well, can damage customer relationships, and can ultimately wreak havoc on a company's profits. You are worried about how to present this merger to the employees.

Communication with employees currently is done through an intranet site called "What's Happening." It's read by most employees, but not regularly, as not all have access to a computer. A newsletter goes out periodically—at least quarterly, but more often if needed. The CEO meets with upper management weekly to be informed of goals and how well they're being met. He is a friendly, people kind of person, not afraid to speak before large groups, and thinks well on his feet. He enjoys the weekly meetings with upper management. He has from time to time thought about being more available to all employees but until now he hasn't had the time or motivation to accomplish that.

The CEO has said he does not want anyone to lose his or her job. Some may need to be retrained but no one will be let go. The merger will take place in two weeks, but the timeline for blending the organizations will be over several months.

He is asking that you and human resources work out the employee communication details and report back to him in two days.

Put together the key messages you want delivered to employees, and who will deliver them and how. Also, plan the timing of the messages in conjunction with when the merger will actually take place. If you plan to use two-way communication, through what vehicles will employees communicate and with whom? Who will respond to their comments and questions? Is there a way to measure effectiveness? What programs will you recommend be put in place to blend the cultures of the two organizations?

# 4

# Community Relations

A community is a social organism made up of all the interactions among the residents and the organizations with which they identify. As a social organism, a community can take pride in its scenery or in its high school basketball team; it can be factionalized on the basis of who lives on which side of the railroad tracks, or who is well-off or poor; it can be a heterogeneous collection of suburban residents drawn together only by a common desire to escape living within a metropolitan area.

It is necessary for organizations to live by the community's ordinances and social mores. Permits must be sought to expand facilities, dig up utilities, change traffic flow, or even to operate at all.

A neighborhood, town, city, or state is obviously a human community. Like organizations, they require positive interrelationships among all members to function smoothly and efficiently. Because a company, hospital, school, or other organization would have difficulty operating effectively in a community that is disrupted or inefficient, it is necessary for it to accept the responsibility of corporate citizenship.

Therefore, mutual trust engendered by positive public relationships is essential for both the community and organizations located within it to function in a reasonable manner. A community is not merely a collection of people who share a locality and its facilities.

## THE OLD-FASHIONED VIEW OF COMMUNITY RELATIONS

Traditionally, employers have tended to regard their relationships with home communities as being extensions of their employee relations. The idea was that employees who were treated decently would go into the home communities singing the praises of their employer. In this traditional viewpoint, employers felt that their dollar payroll, their local tax payments, the occasional loan of a facility for a meeting, and the annual contribution to the United Way discharged their community obligations.

Their attitude seemed to say, "Look what we are giving: jobs, taxes, meeting facilities, and charitable donations." Employers who held this view tended to assume that with little more than a snap of their fingers they would be provided the practical necessities for efficient operations: streets, sewers, water lines, power and telephone, police and fire services, recreational areas, health-care centers, schools, shopping centers, residential areas, cultural and religious facilities, and all the rest. The viewpoint tended to say, "These are what we are entitled to in return for what we give. The community owes us these."

This attitude has changed. Employers now know that they must have more than a general concern for the efficiency and adequacy of community services for themselves and for their employees. They have learned that they must become involved in specific community decisions and actions concerning fiscal policies; honesty in public offices; attracting new businesses and holding older ones; planning for the future; and generating the enthusiasm of volunteers in charitable, cultural, fellowship, educational, recreational, business, and patriotic endeavors. In general, they must apply the collective talents of the organization to the community in which it operates. The combination of these concerns involves having representatives in the policy-making structure of the community, sometimes directly and openly, sometimes behind the scenes.

- Community relations, as a public relations function, is an institution's planned, active, and continuing participation within a community to maintain and enhance its environment to the benefit of both the institution and the community.[1]

## COMMUNITY ISSUES

**Community relations (CR)** work is a dynamic aspect of public relations. If there were no other reason, the changing physical and social makeup of communities would make it so, but there are many other contributing factors. Among them: Few people stay in the communities where they are born. Families move not once, but several times. Community communications programs must deal with this constant turnover of residents. Also, employers move. Sometimes they move from a congested central city area to a suburb. When they move, both areas are disrupted. A manufacturer may move a headquarters or a manufacturing facility from one city to another, mortally wounding the economy of one and perhaps starting a boom in the other. Branches of businesses and institutions are opened in areas of growing population and closed in areas that are shrinking or that are poorly managed. A new interstate highway bypasses a community formerly dependent on travelers for its trade. Undesirable elements get control of government. A community also undergoes change when there is a movement for reform or rehabilitation.

Almost all the needs of a community as a desirable place to live and work can be placed into 10 categories:

1. Work for everyone who desires it
2. The prospect of growth and new opportunities
3. Adequate competitive commercial enterprises
4. Competent municipal government with modern police, fire, highway, and other services
5. Educational, cultural, religious, and recreational pursuits
6. Appropriate housing and public services
7. Provision for helping those least able to help themselves
8. Availability of legal, medical, and other professional services
9. Pride and loyalty
10. A good reputation in the area and beyond

---

[1]Wilbur J. Peak, "Community Relations," in *Lesly's Handbook of Public Relations and Communications* (Chicago: NTC/Contemporary Publishing, 1998) 114.

### A New Type of Community

Today we are in the advent of a new type of community, one that is not defined by streets or buildings but by the Internet. Virtual communities are springing up by the minute, on subjects close to people's hearts—animals, illness, romance, motherhood, divorce, etc. And though these communities do not interact at the grocery store or the little league field, they operate in many ways similarly to the ones of old. There are opinion leaders whom others tend to follow and find credible; there are those who are more involved—interested members—and the casual observers. But they have all chosen to be a part of this community, opting into a group and showing an affinity for the subject. Whether they ever act on it beyond the click of a "join" or "like" may be up to us.

## THE ROLE OF PUBLIC RELATIONS

Public relations work of a basic nature is involved in at least nine areas of an organization's community relationships:

1. Issuing news of interest to the community and providing top officials of the organizations with information on the status of community relations
2. Representing the organization in all sorts of volunteer activities, including fund drives— and getting employees to do likewise
3. Managing the contributions function—giving donations if a corporation, raising funds if a nonprofit organization
4. Counseling management on contributions of employees as volunteer workers or board members; arranging for use of facilities and equipment by community groups
5. Functioning as the organization's intermediary with local governmental, civic, educational, and ad hoc groups concerned with reform, social problems, and celebrations
6. Planning and helping to implement special events such as ground breaking or dedication of new facilities, change in location, anniversaries, reunions, conventions, or exhibitions
7. Preparing advertising or position papers aimed at residents or local government as needed or desirable
8. Preparing publications for distribution to resident groups
9. Planning and conducting open houses or tours as needed or desirable

With the dynamics of change mentioned earlier, public relations work is becoming less concerned with the "routine" and more with the unusual: controversies between factions in the community; activism on social issues; and dealing with calamity, crisis, and governmental regulations as they affect the local community or as they are echoed in local ordinances affecting an organization.[2]

## CAN COMMUNITY RELATIONS BE THE CORE OF PR PROGRAMMING?

Yes, community relations can be the core of public relations programming because it sets the tone of what an organizations stands for—not in words (rhetoric) but in actions (behavior). Today, how organizations conduct themselves in the communities where they do business is driven by two factors that make it more than just "getting the house in order":

---

[2] For an example of a sudden and drastic change in local relationships, see news accounts of the oil spill of the *Exxon Valdez* in Alaska in March 1989.

1. Instant communication, encompassing burgeoning information networks that go far beyond news media data gathering. It has the capacity to capture and transmit home behavior far and wide.
2. Global competition and the "global village" have created interest in such information, at least by competitors, activists, government agencies, and others who have reason to broadcast it.

Three strategic levels need to be planned:

1. *Defensive:*  guarding against negative acts, or acts of omission
2. *Proactive:*  being a leader in positive acts that appeal to key publics
3. *Maintenance:*  finding ways to retain relationships with publics not currently key, but still able to influence a company's reputation by forthright expression of their perceptions of it

This approach is far different from "doing nice things for the community." Assigning community relations to indifferent or inexperienced staffers because it's "easy" no longer suffices—and of course misses the centrality of community relations today.

## TWO TYPES OR LEVELS OF PROGRAMMING EMERGE

Standard community relations involves basic, arm's-length, "good corporate citizen" activities that reach out, invite in, create awareness, and let facilities be used. For example:

1. **Membership networking,** assigning "official" representatives to all important community groups
2. **Speakers bureau,** placing talks to key groups on topics vital to the organization
3. **Make facilities available**
4. **Open houses,** visits, tours
5. **Programs around holidays**
6. **Service on boards** of directors
7. **Take part in public events** and back "must-support" causes

The second level of community relations involves becoming part of the fabric of the community by placing people throughout its planning and decision-making networks:

1. **Ambassador or constituency relations** programs
2. Hold regular **opinion leader briefings** or idea exchanges
3. Set up local **community relations advisory boards**
4. **Employee volunteer programs**
5. **Community research,** jointly with a college perhaps
6. **Social projects** that tackle the real community needs as seen by your key publics
7. **Make expertise available**

Neither list is exhaustive, but the two suggest the differences in the two levels of activity. In most cases, some of both levels are useful.

### Other Considerations

Employee volunteerism has so many serendipitous benefits that it raises the issue of **spouse, family, and retiree** participation. Those organizations that involve these individuals and groups generally report expanded impact and a widening network.

**Feedback data banks** may provide the biggest opportunity, capturing what is heard and observed from opinion leaders and community members in a formal way. Use of data banks is *really* listening to the community for invaluable information, which is instantly actionable through community relations programs.

## SUCCESSFUL COMMUNITY RELATIONS ARE PLANNED, ORGANIZED, AND SYSTEMATIZED

In community programs, five considerations should come into play:

1. *Targeting*
   - Which *groups* in the community must be targeted?
   - What *behaviors* need to be motivated?
   - What specific *activities* will lead to this motivation?
   - What *information* must be gathered and assessed before starting?
2. *Participate or own*
   If your reputation needs improving, working on projects with accepted partners who can use their reputation to pull yours up; if yours is good, projects you can own offer more benefits and visibility without any dilution.
3. *Here versus there*
   Should a program be based within the organization, or should it be an outside program? Should it take place on-site or off-site?
4. *"Official" versus employee volunteer activities*
   If the latter, how will the organization get credit? Should employees be able to do some volunteer work "on the clock"?
5. *Reaching opinion leaders*
   What design will assure that this critical goal is met?

## TURNING WORKERS INTO GOODWILL AMBASSADORS

People trust people, so turning employees into ambassadors within the community is an effective way to be known, spread goodwill, and develop relationships. Employee ambassadors can be used to build solid community relations programs in four ways:

1. Using speakers bureaus to get information out to local opinion leaders
2. Employee participation in volunteer or outreach programs
3. Direct opinion leader contacts, sharing news and gathering insight and feedback
4. Sponsored memberships (where employees are designated to belong to and attend a specific group's activities on behalf of the organization)

### Public Relations Role in Online Communities

The role of the practitioner in online communities related to our organization is twofold: (1) as a listening source to keep track of what is going on, what is being said, difficulties, frustrations, and potential latent crises, and (2) as a helpful, responsive purveyor of information and enlightenment. Because individuals typically feel a sense of ownership of their online community, too much input from the organization can feel overbearing and controlling. We must avoid our organization's voice becoming the obnoxious acquaintance that dominates conversation and err on the side of the friendly, helpful, and objective touch.

## References and Additional Readings

Arnstein, Caren. "How Companies Can Rebuild Credibility and Trust." *Public Relations Journal* 50 (April 1994): 28–29.

Bagin, Don, and Donald Gallagher. *The School and Community Relations,* 7th ed. Needham Heights, MA: Allyn & Bacon, 2000.

Brion, Denis. *Essential Industry and the NIMBY Phenomenon.* Westport, CT: Quorum, 1991.

Burke, Edmund. *Corporate Community Relations: The Principle of the Neighbor of Choice.* Westport, CT: Praeger, 1999.

Chynoweth, Emma, et al. "Responsible Care: Listening to Communities: What Do They Want to Know?" *Chemical Week* 153 (December 8, 1993): 68–69.

*Corporate Community Relations Letter* published by The Center for Corporate Community Relations at Boston College, www.bc.edu/cccr.

Cutlip, Scott, Allen Center, and Glen Broom. "Corporate Philanthropy." Chapter 14 in *Effective Public Relations,* 8th ed. Upper Saddle River, NJ: Prentice Hall, 1999.

Frank, Helmut, and John Schanz. *The Economics of the Energy Problem.* Joint Council on Economic Education, 1212 Avenue of the Americas, New York, NY 10022. Pamphlet, 1975.

Hunter, Floyd. *Community Power Structures.* Chapel Hill, NC: University of North Carolina Press, 1953. A community relations classic.

Hussey, John. "Community Relations," in *Experts in Action Inside Public Relations,* 2nd ed., eds. Bill Cantor and Chester Burger. White Plains, NY: Longman, Inc., 1989: 115–125.

Kruckeberg, Dean, and Kenneth Starck. *Public Relations and Community: A Reconstructed Theory.* Westport, CT: Greenwood, 1988.

Lerbinger, Otto, and Nathaniel Sperber. "Community Relations." Chapter 6 in *Manager's Public Relations Handbook.* Reading, MA: Addison-Wesley, 1982.

Lundborg, Lolls. *Public Relations in the Local Community.* New York: Harper and Row, 1950.

Continues to be definitive. By the public relations staffer who advanced to CEO of Bank of America.

*Making Community Relations Pay Off: Tools & Strategies.* Washington, DC: Public Affairs Council, 1988. Tells how companies are meeting the test of effective community relations.

McDermitt, David. "The 10 Commandments of Community Relations." *World Wastes* 36 (September 1993): 48–51.

O'Brien, Paul. "Changing Expectations of Community Relations." *Executive Speeches* 8 (October/November 1993): 33–36.

*pr reporter* Vol. 41 No. 49 (December 14, 1998). "Hyundai's 'Blind Date' with Community Improves (Part 2)": 2.

*pr reporter* Vol. 41 No. 48 (December 7, 1998). " 'Blind Dates' with Communities Don't Work; Steady Courtships Do": 2–3.

*pr reporter* Vol. 41 No. 35 (September 7, 1998). "Even Superior Community Relations Not Beyond Reach of Entrepreneurial Trial Lawyers—But It Can Defeat Them": 1–2.

*pr reporter* Vol. 36 No. 28 (July 19, 1993). "Can Community Relations Be the Core of Public Relations?": 1–2.

*pr reporter* Vol. 36 No. 4 (January 25, 1993). "Model for Employee Participation and Outreach Programs": 1–2.

*pr reporter* Vol. 35 No. 15 (April 13, 1992). "Inviting the Public Inside Is Effective and Unexpected Way to Deal with Community Issues": 3.

*The Public Relations Body of Knowledge.* New York: PRSA. See abstracts dealing with "Community Relations."

Rich, Dorothy. "Business Partnerships with Families." *Business Horizons* 36 (September/October 1993): 24–28.

Skolnik, Rayna. "Rebuilding Trust." *Public Relations Journal* 49 (September 1993): 29–32.

# ⭐ Case 4-1 A Classic: Chemical Industry Takes Responsibility for Community Concerns

## Trade Association Takes the Initiative

The American Chemistry Council (ACC) is the trade group for the chemical industry. Its members represent 90 percent of the productive capacity of industrial chemicals in the United States. Dues are based on a percentage of a company's chemical sales.

Chemical companies must be constantly innovative to remain competitive in today's global marketplace. Like most trade associations, ACC helps members stay abreast of issues and techniques. It provides assistance in complying with laws and regulations. ACC also offers **leadership training** and **task force groups** to develop skills and knowledge in the managerial, legislative, technical, and communications areas.

> "Many of the challenges that our industry will face in the coming years can best be addressed through the strong performance platforms that have been laid through Responsible Care®."
>
> B. CHUCK ANDERSON, PRESIDENT, OCCIDENTAL CHEMICAL CORPORATION

As public awareness of environmental health and safety issues has increased over the past few decades, the chemical industry has been scrutinized by activists, regulators, and consumers more closely than ever before. As environmentalists make louder protests, legislators respond with more stringent regulations.

Since 1990, the Superfund Amendments and Reauthorization Act (SARA), also known as the Emergency Planning and Community Right-to-Know Act, requires chemical manufacturers and other organizations to inform employees and the community about the nature and hazards of the materials with which they work.[3]

As pressures from legislation mounted and NIMBYists[4] began paying closer attention to environmental issues in their communities, the chemical industry realized that it needed to reach beyond one-way communication of its side of the story. It needed to do three things:

1. *Listen to and recognize the perceptions and fears* of the public, especially neighbors of chemical plants
2. *Own up to any performance problems*
3. *Take action* to correct problems and address perceptions

## Proactive Response to Public Concerns: Responsible Care®

For almost 25 years, since 1988, the Responsible Care® program has helped ACC member companies significantly enhance their performance, discover new business opportunities, and improve employee safety, the health of the communities in which they operate, and the environment as a whole. Responsible Care® is a global initiative that began in Canada in 1984 and is practiced today by 55 national and regional associations in 60 countries around the world. Although not established as a public relations program, Responsible Care® does offer the chemical industry the opportunity to highlight its performance-improvement successes. A pillar of the Responsible Care® program is environmental, health, safety, and security (EHS&S) performance monitoring and reporting, both for individual companies and the chemical industry overall. All ACC member companies

[3] Bernard J. Nebel, *Environmental Science.* (Upper Saddle River, NJ: Prentice Hall, 1990) p. 290.

[4] *"Not In My BackYard."* An update is NOPE (*Not On Planet Earth*).

*(Continued)*

**FIGURE 4.1** Symbol of Responsible Care®
*Source:* (Courtesy of ACC)

are required to publicly report, through Responsible Care®, specific performance measurements in the following areas:

- **Environmental metrics,** including hazardous air pollutants released, $SO_x$ and $NO_x$ emissions, and net water consumption
- **Energy metrics,** including greenhouse gas emissions and energy efficiency
- **Safety metrics,** including number of process safety incidents, DOT-reportable distribution incidents, OSHA-recordable lost workday incidence, and fatalities
- **Accountability metrics,** including community outreach and emergency response initiatives

Some of these metrics are reported on a company-by-company basis, while others are reported as aggregated industry statistics. This *public reporting* is meant to enhance transparency and accountability and drive performance of ACC member companies. ACC uses these reported metrics to openly demonstrate the commitment of ACC members and their partners along the supply chain to continuous improvements in the EHS&S performance of their operations and businesses.

Responsible Care® is *proactive public relations*. Rather than waiting for an accident to occur, or the public to become fearful or upset, it actively *invites* people to learn which chemicals are produced at a plant, how the plant is operated, and what protective measures are in place should an accident occur.

Studies have shown that *fear* of an unknown event is more powerful than an actual *bad occurrence*. In a study of a group known to have

1. **Community Awareness and Emergency Response Code (CAER)**

    to reduce potential harm to the employees and the public in an emergency as well as bring the chemical industry and communities together

2. **Pollution Prevention Code**

    to improve the industry's ability to protect people and the environment by generating less waste and minimizing emissions

3. **Process Safety Code**

    to prevent fire, explosions, and accidental chemical releases

4. **Distribution Code**

    to reduce employee and public risks from the shipment of chemicals

5. **Employee Health and Safety Code**

    to maximize worker protection and accident prevention, through training and communications

6. **Product Stewardship Code**

    to ensure that the design, development, manufacture, transport, use, and disposal of chemical products is done safely and without environmental damage

**FIGURE 4.2**    The six Codes of Management Practices turn guiding principles to practical application.

*Source:* (Courtesy of ACC)

latent tendencies for developing Huntington's disease, the majority of those whose genetic tests showed they would most likely develop this incurable malady felt that knowing was beneficial. "Better to know than be always wondering." Those who knew they were likely to get the disease reported their quality of life and psychological health was better than those for whom testing was inconclusive.

This holds true for knowing and communicating about chemical risks as well. Most people can handle truth better than being left in doubt. Open communication shows respect for people by treating them like responsible adults. However, the Huntington's study also indicates that all people do not react the same when learning of risks. About 10 percent had trouble adjusting to the news, even when it was good (i.e., they would probably not develop the disease). Apparently, for some, just handling the change or believing the test was accurate was of greater impact than the relief. As always, no rule fits everyone.[5]

Responsible Care® is composed of 10 elements:

1. Guiding Principles: followed by every member and partner company

2. Codes of Management Practices: environmental, health, and safety guidelines
3. Dialogue with the Public: to identify and address public concerns
4. Self-Evaluation (figure 4.2): annual reporting on a company's implementation of the Codes
5. Measures of Performance: to view progress of Responsible Care®
6. Performance Goals: company-specific goals reported on annually
7. Management Systems Verification: independent review of companies' implementation of Responsible Care®
8. Mutual Assistance: company-to-company dialogue
9. Partnership Program: helping companies along the value chain participate in Responsible Care®
10. Obligation of Membership: to participate in Responsible Care® and follow these elements

ACC member companies adhere to 12 Guiding Principles addressing product and process safety, sound environmental practices, and informative public communications. Figure 4.3 illustrates these principles.

[5] *pr reporter* 36, May 3, 1993, pp. 2–3.

(*Continued*)

- To lead our companies in ethical ways that increasingly benefit society, the economy and the environment.
- To design and develop products that can be manufactured, transported, used and disposed of or recycled safely.
- To work with customers, carriers, suppliers, distributors and contractors to foster the safe and secure use, transport and disposal of chemicals and provide hazard and risk information that can be accessed and applied in their operations and products.
- To design and operate our facilities in a safe, secure and environmentally sound manner.
- To instill a culture throughout all levels of our organizations to continually identify, reduce and manage process safety risks.
- To promote pollution prevention, minimization of waste and conservation of energy and other critical resources at every stage of the life cycle of our products.
- To cooperate with governments at all levels and organizations in the development of effective and efficient safety, health, environmental and security laws, regulations and standards.
- To support education and research on the health, safety, environmental effects and security of our products and processes.
- To communicate product, service and process risks to our stakeholders and listen to and consider their perspectives.
- To make continual progress towards our goal of no accidents, injuries or harm to human health and the environment from our products and operations and openly report our health, safety, environmental and security performance.
- To seek continual improvement in our integrated Responsible Care® Management System to address environmental, health, safety and security performance.
- To promote Responsible Care® by encouraging and assisting others to adhere to these Guiding Principles.

**FIGURE 4.3**   ACC member companies adhere to a list of 10 guiding principles about safe plant operations and proper public communications.

## Responsible Care®'s Target Audiences

The goal of Responsible Care® is to continuously advance the level of chemical industry performance, demonstrating commitment to a better, safer world. This message is targeted to:

- The chemical industry
- Teachers and students
- Employees
- Federal, state, and local officials
- The media
- The general public
- Plant neighbors
- Local and national interest groups
- Supply chain customers

## Building Public Relationships

### Activities to Reach External Audiences

ACC member and partner companies use a combination of one-way and two-way communication activities to invite external publics to communicate with their local plants. One-way (or information-transfer) efforts include:

- **Brochures** featuring shelter-in-place messages and explanations of Responsible Care®
- **Annual Responsible Care® reports** that target the business community, as well as community stakeholders, and report on the company's environmental, health, and safety performance
- **The ACC Website,** www.americanchemistry.com/rc, highlights ACC member company performance in meeting specific metrics
- **Advertisements** at the local level
- **Community newsletters** sent to plant neighbors to keep them informed about the company and its activities

Two-way (or relationship-building) efforts include:

- **Community advisory panels** (CAPs), groups of citizens with diverse backgrounds and feelings toward the chemical industry. CAPs are sponsored by local chemical plants and encouraged to voice community concerns with industry representatives. Well-run CAPs provide dialogue between a plant and the community. ACC members and partners have sponsored nearly 300 CAPs across the country with great success. One example is the Le Moyne (Alabama) Community Advisory Panel, which works to improve emergency response service to the local community and sponsors an annual "Responsible Care® Night" at member company plants to help residents understand the initiative.

> "If a company is a member of Responsible Care®, it lets me know that they are committed to communicating with neighbors more frequently, more sincerely and with more depth."
> DIANE B. SHERIDAN, COMMUNITY ADVISORY PANEL FACILITATOR

- **Hazardous material drills** involving plants and local emergency responder groups. These exercises help improve knowledge and response time in the event of an incident. For more information, visit www.transcaer.org.
- **Responsible Care® fairs/days/open houses** are sponsored by the plants or CAP groups. These events are opportunities for the community to tour a plant and learn about its operations.
- **Inviting state legislators and local and national activist leaders to speak at association meetings** and sending ACC delegates or scientists to meetings of environmental, regulatory, and community groups.

## Activities to Change Behavior of ACC Members

To maintain ACC membership, companies are required to implement the Responsible Care® Guiding Principles and Codes of Management Practice. ACC sponsors regional workshops and an annual conference to educate company executives and managers about implementing Responsible Care®. In addition, many have found creative ways to reach their new objectives. For example, some have tied managerial bonuses to achieved objectives. Others use peer pressure or recognition to motivate and support the Responsible Care® initiative.

As codes are implemented, ACC requires every company to report its progress along the way. All of the more than 220 companies taking part in Responsible Care® in the United States undergo headquarters and facility audits to ensure that they have a structure and system in place to measure, manage, and verify performance.

## Evaluation: External Publics

The National Association of Public Environmental Communicators commended Responsible Care® for its one-way and two-way communication vehicles.

## Evaluation: Internal Publics

### Reductions in Chemical Emissions

ACC members reported that Responsible Care® companies reduced hazardous emissions released to the air, land, and water by 75 percent from 1988 to 2010. Responsible Care® companies have improved energy efficiency by more than 10 percent and reduced greenhouse gases by more than 16 percent from 1992 to 2010.

## Self-Evaluation

The ACC Responsible Care® initiative includes a self-evaluation process. Member companies are required to furnish ACC with an annual report of their progress in implementing the Codes of Management Practices. They have shown significant gains in Process Safety, Distribution, Community Awareness, and Emergency Response.

(*Continued*)

Although these results show improvements, ACC recognizes that company self-evaluations are subject to challenges of credibility. ACC is now identifying additional code measurement systems that continue to meet objective public scrutiny.

## Performance Measures

Performance measures exist to demonstrate the progress being made through Responsible Care® and are used to help drive performance improvement throughout the membership. The performance measures include Community Awareness and Emergency Response, Pollution Prevention, Process Safety, Distribution, Employee Health and Safety, and Product Stewardship.

## Performance Goals

Member and partner companies are asked to:

- Establish at least one goal for a Responsible Care® performance result
- Make steady performance improvement toward that goal
- Publicly communicate the goal or goals and progress toward meeting them
- Annually report to the Council the established goals, progress, and public reporting mechanism

This case demonstrates the trend of public relations programs to *begin with responsible action* by organizations, with public relations practitioners playing a key role in *design and strategy*. The *communications and relationship-building activities* then follow, to gain recognition for the responsible action.

**Questions for Discussion**

1. To what extent can a voluntary performance improvement initiative by private industry forestall government legislation and regulation on environmental matters? Explain your position.
2. What else could ACC do to attain higher credibility for Responsible Care® with:
   - The public
   - Its own members
   - Associated industries
   - Legislators and regulators
   - Activist groups
3. How could it measure an increase or decrease in credibility?
4. List other industries whose products or operations engender fear. What steps are you aware of that each is taking to allay public apprehensions? How does Responsible Care® compare with what these industries are doing?
5. Imagine yourself living across the street from a chemical plant. List all the feelings you can think of that you might have about the plant – positive, negative, or neutral. What specific actions would representatives from the plant need to take to address your feelings?
6. Draft a letter from a chemical plant manager to those living near the plant announcing introduction of the Responsible Care® initiative.

# Case 4-2 Community Relationships Maintained During Hospital Closing[*]

Throughout the 1980s and early 1990s, business and the government began trying to trim whatever fat there was from the health-care system. In 1997, Congress passed the Balanced Budget Act in an attempt to reform Medicare and trim waste from the system. But cuts went billions of dollars beyond expectation. The health-care system was in a financial crisis. Health premiums weren't paying for the cost of services. Hospitals were being squeezed by managed care companies having their own financial troubles. One consequence was the closing of hospitals.

## Mercy Hospital–Detroit's Struggle

The east side of Detroit is among the most troubled urban areas in the United States, struggling with a multitude of social and economic challenges. Mercy Hospital–Detroit was an important anchor in this neighborhood, not only providing access to health care, but also security, employment, leadership, and a place for social interaction. It relied heavily on Medicare, Medicaid, and other government sources for its business—nearly 80 percent of its total admissions.

In the early to mid-1990s, Mercy Hospital–Detroit found it increasingly difficult to maintain its fiscal health; operating losses were supplemented by the hospital's parent company, Mercy Health Services (MHS).[6] Then, in 1997, the Balanced Budget Reconciliation Act severely reduced Medicare and Medicaid reimbursements. The already struggling hospital was devastated by the cuts. Losses of $1.5 million per month began to mount. The federal and state funding cuts similarly affected operating margins at Mercy's other hospitals. The MHS board was faced with systemwide financial constraints that put the system's bond rating at risk. Operating losses at Mercy Hospital–Detroit totaled nearly $100 million from 1990 through 2000.

In the hope of finding a buyer, a series of discussions with major Detroit health systems ensued in 1999, but all were facing the same circumstances: increasingly ill patients with no health insurance and decreasing reimbursements from the government. The decision was made to close the hospital in December 1999. Mercy Hospital–Detroit quickly became a national example of the evolving health-care crisis in the United States.

## Several Public Relations Issues Emerged

- How can the hospital close without giving the impression of abandoning the city and its poorest residents?
- Is it possible to close the hospital while still maintaining the excellent reputation of MHS and its sponsor, the Sisters of Mercy?
- How can Mercy coincidentally acquire a similar-sized hospital in a predominantly white suburban community without attracting major criticism and, worse yet, accusations of "racism"?

## Research

Preparations began when Mercy Hospital–Detroit commissioned a research study to obtain community opinion and attitudes. The study

---

[*] Thank you to Stephen Shivinsky, APR, vice president of corporate communications and public relations at Trinity Health for this case study.

[6] Renamed Trinity Health after a May 2000 merger.

(Continued)

showed that the parent company, MHS, was held in high esteem and that the local community not only counted on Mercy Hospital–Detroit but saw it as an entitlement for the community.

Meanwhile, the commitment to the community from the Sisters of Mercy and the MHS board led MHS management to conclude that it should donate the 10-year-old building to the community. Instead of simply selling the hospital campus to a developer for commercial use, MHS decided the hospital should be converted to a long-term community asset to enhance neighborhood revitalization, and the new owner or owners and users should share the mission and values of the hospital's parent, MHS. Additionally, MHS decided to keep a presence on the hospital campus by earmarking $2 million for a primary care clinic for the uninsured. In doing so, Mercy supported its mission of "care for the poor and underserved" while seeking a new owner for the larger block of property and buildings.

The next step was a major study in early 2000—just after the announcement of closure—consisting of personal interviews with 198 Detroit community and opinion leaders, including elected officials, clergy, and major business and social service agency representatives, to obtain ideas about how to "do the right thing" and "give back" to the community, rather than simply closing the hospital and moving on. The personal interviews provided valuable input on specific community needs, possible organizations that met the criteria for a new owner, and communication tactics for most effectively reaching the important audiences of key community leaders and area residents, many of whom were without transportation or telephones. The interviews also helped crystallize other audiences to target:

- Mercy Hospital–Detroit employees, medical staff, board members, and volunteers
- Mercy's leadership group (40 top management personnel nationwide) and other corporate office employees

- Community religious leaders
- Local physician leaders
- Regional and national partners
- Major insurers
- The Archdiocese of Detroit and bishops in all MHS markets
- Michigan's governor and staff
- Detroit's mayor and key aides
- The Wayne County executive and key aides
- The Detroit City Council
- Trade and health-care consortia
- 99,000 residents in the primary service area

## The Public Relations Plan

A public relations plan was developed to reach these audiences using a variety of tactics—not relying on advertising—including specific ways to obtain their input and feedback. Tactics in the plan included using e-mail; a telephone hotline; staff and community town hall meetings; targeted letters to volunteers, community leaders, and others; the hospital newsletter; editorial board meetings with Detroit's two daily newspapers, weekly business newsmagazine, and an African-American weekly; formal closure notices in community newspapers; direct-mail letters; and news releases, fact sheets, and backgrounders.

The **key messages** to communicate were: "Mercy can no longer tolerate this level of losses or be supported by others within the Mercy system," "Mercy is 'doing the right thing' by donating the property to help meet community needs," and "Mercy continues its ministry for the poor with a new primary care center for the uninsured—investing $2 million per year to make that happen."

## Plans Were Executed with Precision

Plans began with a carefully implemented effort to obtain balanced stories—as early as September 1999—about the difficult financial situation and the possibility that Mercy Hospital–Detroit may close. This was followed by a series of editorial board meetings with Detroit's two dailies, the weekly business newsmagazine, and an African-American weekly. Similar meetings were later held with community leaders and the Detroit City Council. The generally fair and favorable editorials and news coverage resulting from the meetings helped educate Mercy's key audiences and would later help them understand the reasons for closing.

Media coverage reached a crescendo in January 2000 and continued through March 2001, including *NBC Nightly News* and several national trades. A total of 10,000 letters were mailed to residents' homes within three eastside ZIP codes. All audiences received the news of Mercy Hospital–Detroit's closing and, although disappointed that Detroit's east side would lose an acute care hospital, they were generally understanding of the situation.

Except for a "public notice" advertisement placed in local newspapers, a regulatory requirement, no other form of advertising was used to reach the audiences.

## Evaluation

In late 2000, the Mercy Hospital–Detroit building was donated to a multiservice community organization (SER Metro) and a Catholic organization serving youths and families (Boysville). Other new tenants on the former hospital campus include Mercy Primary Care Center, to serve the uninsured, the National Council of Alcoholism and Drug Dependence, Head Start, Child Care Coordinating Center, the Detroit Fire Department, and McAuley Commons' independent housing. The revamped campus promises to continue providing a positive, major impact on the community. Balanced media coverage told the story fairly. Personal interviews with a sample of 20 (from the list of those previously interviewed) were extremely positive. Internal meetings were equally positive. Employees from Mercy Hospital–Detroit, many of whom

would be without jobs, gave Mercy–Detroit's CEO a standing ovation after he explained the closing and transfer of the hospital.

The final test came when MHS announced the purchase of St. Mary's Hospital, a 300-bed hospital in the Detroit suburb of Livonia, only four months after closing the inner-city Detroit hospital. Without the effective public relations program on the closing of Mercy Hospital– Detroit, the announcement to acquire a new hospital in a predominantly white suburb could have caused significant editorial scrutiny and community backlash that would surely damage MHS's reputation (just one month after its merger with another major national health system to create Trinity Health) and hamper its future growth. With minor exceptions, all internal and external audiences met the announcement of the St. Mary's Hospital acquisition with support and encouragement.

Today, Mercy Primary Care Center continues to operate in one of the most impoverished areas of Detroit. It provides a range of primary care services, regardless of ability to pay. In 2011, it served almost 6,000 patients, providing medication, lab tests, limited radiological studies, physicals, preventive care and health education, management of acute and chronic diseases, pelvic exams and pap tests, enrollment into medical plans, social services, and limited specialty care to uninsured, low-income patients. Mercy Primary Care Center also has a specialized personal assistance program that provides clothing, showers, and laundry services for homeless persons. It provided almost 77 showers a week in 2011.

### Questions for Discussion

1. You are the public relations director of the closing hospital. Your public relations plan calls for a community town hall meeting. Some people in the community don't have phones or computers. How will you alert everyone about this meeting? When will you hold it?

(*Continued*)

How many times? Who will attend from the hospital? What is your goal for the meeting and how will you achieve that? Put together a plan addressing these issues.

2. Many depend on the hospital for their own and their children's health needs. The plan calls for input and feedback from the community. What will you do with the feedback? What if your CEO is unwilling to listen?

3. Take as an example the hospital closest to where you live. Who do you think are the opinion leaders for that hospital? Make a list and identify them by their position in the hospital, how they would be contacted, and what their message strategy would be.

4. Ten years later, social media is potentially a useful tool. Analyze the pros and cons of using it with these stakeholder audiences and discuss how the approach might have been different today. Consider what protest groups might have arisen as a result and incorporate your insights into your plan.

# ⭐Case 4-3 The Struggle for Nuclear Power

After a 30-year decline in the support for nuclear power, a combination of triggering events started to dramatically shift public opinion (soaring gas prices, Iraq and Afghanistan wars, the rise of China's consumption of oil). Americans had become fearful that energy—a critical component of our own economic engine—would not be available or affordable in the 21st century.

Energy companies, seeing a softening of resistance, started once again floating the idea of building nuclear power plants. They felt that they could sell them now as a safe and reasonable alternative to oil from the Middle East.

And then, in the blink of an eye, the naturally occurring triggering event of an earthquake and tsunami in Japan stopped the growing public acceptance in its track. Nuclear power was once again persona non grata, the gradual shift in latent readiness erased in a flash as the world watched the Fukushima nuclear plant on the northeast coast of Japan become inundated with water and three reactors melt down over the course of days. Large groups of people, where possible, were evacuated. Food sources, fish, and land were contaminated for the foreseeable future. The impact on humans is still yet to be determined, and only decades will tell what the full effects will be. The *New York Times* reported that the plant's owners and regulators were accused by insiders of ignoring "years of warnings that a larger-than-expected tsunami could take place." These industry insiders attributed this behavior to "a culture of collusion in which powerful regulators and compliant academic experts looked the other way while the industry put a higher priority on promoting nuclear energy than protecting public safety."[*]

This major disaster in Japan put an immediate stop to the revival of plans for nuclear power in the United States and refueled the concerns that drove the antinuclear movement at the beginning.

## How the Antinuke Movement Began

The environmental movement had its beginnings in the 1960s and 1970s, originally in protest of the nuclear power industry. Since that time, the movement has broadened its concerns, becoming involved in efforts to curb air, water, and ground pollution; global warming; overpopulation; and more. Many of the tactics used today by the environmental movement are the same as those it used in the 1970s.

The building and expansion of nuclear power plants over the last 30 years had pretty much dried up for numerous reasons. Activist actions and demands had driven up the costs of nuclear power projects. According to the Office of Nuclear Energy, Science and Technology, barriers to the deployment of new nuclear power plants included significant cost and schedule uncertainties associated with the new untested licensing processes for siting, licensing, and operating new nuclear power plants and the high capital cost of existing certified design. No new nuclear plants have been ordered in the United States for more than 30 years, but the strategies and tactics of the activists who protested these plants live on in most activist movements today.

## Seabrook Station

Seabrook Station became a national symbol of the nuclear power debate in the 1970s and 1980s. Located in Seabrook, New Hampshire, 40 miles north of Boston, it was built on New Hampshire's 17-mile North Atlantic coastline in an extensive salt marsh area. During the

---

[*] http://www.nytimes.com/2012/03/10/world/asia/critics-say-japan-ignored-warnings-of-nuclear-disaster.html?pagewanted=all

*(Continued)*

prolonged construction and licensing process, Public Service Company of New Hampshire (PSNH)—the original owner—encountered persistent opposition from various sources.

- Initially, opposition came from environmentalists who were concerned about the potential impact a "once-through" water cooling system would have on ocean temperature. Among other issues, they were worried about possible irreparable damage that warming ocean waters would have on the biological populations in and under those waters.
- As plant construction progressed, a broader section of the community became increasingly concerned about the safety of the reactor and the proposed evacuation plans.
- The cost of the plant and its possible effect on the region's electricity rates sparked additional opposition. Increased power costs were perceived as an obstacle blocking industrial development and the prosperity of northern New England.

---

Perhaps the first sign of problems for Seabrook Station occurred when the proposal to build came before various official boards. The builders showed an illustrated model with the containment unit at a proposed height of 250 feet, mostly hidden from view by trees. But redwoods don't grow in New England!

---

- Some citizens protested the plant because they doubted New Hampshire's need for a new power source.

Seabrook Station encountered delays as activists started demonstrating. The opposition intervened in the Nuclear Regulatory Commission's (NRC's) adjudicatory review boards. The legal case was led by the Seacoast Anti-Pollution League (SAPL), while other grassroots activists spearheaded by the Clamshell Alliance led

protests. Its activities ranged from peaceful demonstrations to forceful attempts at site occupation with mass arrests.

After nearly 18 years of licensing, construction, and regulatory review, Seabrook Station began regular full-power operation on August 19, 1990. Through the years, Seabrook Station has become more sensitive to the needs and concerns of its publics. Seabrook was focused on the sorts of things that don't make electricity, such as community relations, public education, and environmental information.

## The Opposition

After the Three Mile Island and Chernobyl accidents, safety became the main concern of opponents. Seabrook opponents did include many gate-bashers, the form of opposition that comes to mind where nuclear power is concerned. But many other activists sought a different route to get their message heard. The issues of the opposition ranged from complete rejection of nuclear power to concerns about the location of Seabrook Station.

To this day, some dedicate their lives to opposing nuclear power. SAPL still monitors Seabrook and other nuclear power plants in New England.

Construction ceased temporarily in 1984. Then New Hampshire Yankee (NHY), a division of PSNH, took over the project and with the Seabrook Joint Owners[7] (other power companies with an interest in the plant) reaffirmed its determination to complete Seabrook. People from PSNH were moved into top position at NHY.

## Developing Strategies

NHY's community relations team focused on Seabrook's publics in the seacoast area (see box *Identifying the Seabrook Publics*). The public relations team initially used reactive programming to address and resolve the opposition's

---

[7] Originally, Seabrook Station was jointly owned by a large number of companies, with PSNH holding the largest percentage of ownership. In 2002, Seabrook was sold to FP&L Energy.

---

### Identifying the Seabrook Publics

The Seabrook communications staff identified important publics for Seabrook.

#### Internal Publics

- All Seabrook Station employees who live in communities around the plant site
- Employees who do not live in the area

#### External Publics

- Massachusetts and New Hampshire residents living both inside and outside the emergency planning zone
- Local and national news media
- The financial community

Seabrook community relations staff targeted—in 23 New Hampshire and Massachusetts towns—public and private schools, day-care facilities, police and fire departments, local officials and opinion leaders, local media, advocacy groups, large (over 50 employees) and small businesses, chambers of commerce, network organizations such as the Lions and Rotary clubs and the local United Way, and citizens living within a 22-mile radius.

---

concerns and to resolve cognitive dissonance.[8] They then used one-way and two-way communication techniques to address these goals.

## One-Way Techniques

1. Created a series of hard-hitting ads featuring Seabrook employees offering words of reassurance.
2. Distributed a "safety kit" consisting of information on Seabrook, waste management, radiation, and safety systems.
3. Circulated "Energy," a community-targeted newsletter, between 1988 and 1989 to all publics in the emergency area. The articles focused on issues related to energy.

## Two-Way Techniques

1. In 1986, NHY formally invited the surrounding community to tour the nuclear plant. More than 7,000 people from the surrounding New Hampshire and Massachusetts communities attended this event.
2. Seabrook Station's Science and Nature Center allows viewers to explore nature and science simultaneously. The Center displays information about electrical generation and contains an ocean aquarium 260 feet below sea level. A total of 30,000 people visit the Center annually.
3. According to NRC regulations, the state must inform the public in the 23 affected towns about emergency and safety procedures. NHY took this one-way task and made it into a two-way strategy. Public relations staff created a calendar decorated with photographs of the seacoast and mailed copies to all homes in the area. The calendars included public notification information, including which radio stations broadcast emergency bulletins and instructions. Employees hand-delivered calendars to approximately

---

[8] The theory of cognitive dissonance, first put forth by Leon Festinger in 1947, suggests a human desire for consistency between what people know and what they do. Any conflict creates a disturbance. See Glen Broom, Allen Center, and Scott Cutlip, *Effective Public Relations*, 8th ed., Toronto, Ontario: Prentice Hall Canada, 1999.

(*Continued*)

4,000 of the 7,000 small businesses in the area. Only 2 percent of those businesses rejected the information.

Seabrook did encounter some heated public opposition to the evacuation plan, and that attracted a lot of media attention. Some schools were unhappy with the proposed evacuation plans because teachers would be required to stay with their classes even though their instinct would be to rush to their own families. These perceptions of the proposed evacuation plan's shortcomings forced many towns to reject the emergency procedures.

4. Communicators representing Seabrook met with school superintendents and business executives to educate them about emergency planning. They also developed relationships with Massachusetts emergency medical squads and fire departments.
5. NHY communications employees approached the media proactively. If a siren that had nothing to do with Seabrook sounded off in a surrounding town or if a rumor about Seabrook was circulated, NHY called the media before the media called them.

These efforts helped Seabrook Station achieve online status. NHY won its contested case before the NRC's adjudicating boards.

## The Need for Proactive Measures

Seabrook public relations teams did not stop once the plant was on line. "We did the things we needed to do to get our license according to the rules and regulations. And then we went a step farther to be proactive and adopt a policy of 'management of expectations' for our community relations efforts," wrote Richard Winn, director of communications for NextEra Energy Seabrook.

Seabrook utilized a strategy to build one-on-one relationships. Now that the plant was up and running, those relationships needed to be maintained. According to Seabrook research at that time, the greatest percentage of people was not definitively for or against nuclear power. Therefore, public relations staff believed it was vital that the public feel comfortable about contacting Seabrook whenever there was a concern.

## Reinforcing Relationships

NHY took measures to reinforce the relationships it had established:

1. NHY continued to send out an emergency plan information calendar to all of its external publics. The calendar consists of 33 pages of emergency planning and safety information.
2. The Science and Nature Center was made accessible for school- and community-based field trips. The Center provides hands-on exhibits featuring energy and environment and the Owascoag nature trail—approximately 1 mile of preserved woods and marshlands with a variety of plants and animals.
3. NHY established a local hotline for citizens in surrounding communities to call and inquire about specific problems and concerns.

## Focusing on the Community

Seabrook Station employees and volunteers participated in several community-oriented events and activities. Each quarter, the community relations department initiated at least one new program encouraging community involvement.

1. Employees participated in Lions Camp Pride, a summer camp facility offering educational and recreational overnight programs to children with special needs. Volunteers installed docks, stained and painted buildings, and cleaned and set up bunkhouses.
2. Employees participated in the seacoast's Seafood Festival. They raised money

at the event by selling popcorn, and donated all proceeds to My Greatest Dream, an organization that benefits terminally ill children.

3. Volunteers participated in Coastweeks, a nationwide celebration of the nation's coastal areas. NHY cleaned up Hampton Beach, a New Hampshire state park about 2 miles from the Seabrook plant.

4. Time and building materials were donated to Action Cove Playground, an innovative playground in West Newbury, Massachusetts. The children's area was designed for explorative and imaginative play.

5. NHY founded a local Project Homefront, an effort to assist families whose relatives were called to serve in the Persian Gulf War. A total of 163 volunteers offered services and assistance in transportation; auto, electrical, and plumbing repair; carpentry; and babysitting. Employees also donated $1,135 to this project.

Other community endeavors aided organizations such as Wish Upon a Star, which provides anonymous Christmas gifts to needy children, and the Girl Scouts of America. According to Martha Netsch, Director of Communications for the Swift Water Girl Scout Council, the Girl Scouts frequently visit Seabrook Station's Science and Nature Center, work with staff on scout education programs about solutions to today's energy problems, and recognize the Science and Nature Center as support for young women interested in mathematics, science, and technology.

Seabrook encouraged employees to become involved in local civic organizations and in local government. Many are on town and city boards; on volunteer emergency medical squads and fire departments; in Rotary, Lions, and Kiwanis clubs; or are active in school organizations. Every year employees serve as judges at local science fairs.

## Through the 1990s, into the 21st Century

In 1992, the control of Seabrook was bought by Connecticut-based Northeast Utilities, which earlier took over bankrupt PSNH. Legislation was passed in 2000 that deregulated the energy industry. It required those who distributed energy to divest themselves of energy sources that produce power. Thus, Seabrook was sold again in 2002 to FP&L Energy, a Florida energy provider that set up a separate energy-producing company from its delivery side. It promptly dismantled the second cooling tower on site. Although management has changed, very little else has. FP&L Energy was renamed NextEra Energy Resources in 2008.

Some activist groups continue to exist, though most are now peaceful in their approach. According to SAPL's Joan and Charles Pratt, their mission is to make sure Seabrook complies with NRC regulations. The Citizens' Radiological Monitoring Network acts as a support group that focuses on how to live with potential hazards. Its goals are to monitor every air and water emission from Seabrook, to hold Seabrook socially accountable for every emission, and to expect a responsible attitude from the station itself. All these awareness groups keep a close eye on Seabrook.

Despite the controversial issues, Seabrook employees, for the most part, maintain professional relationships with activist groups. A small number of people opposing the plant remain very reserved and refuse to speak to anyone who works at Seabrook Station. The plant's community relations department believes it is in its best interest to deal cooperatively with these groups.

The Seabrook Station communications team noted at the time, "A subtle community relations shift occurred at Seabrook Station as the plant became more accepted and proved itself to be a good neighbor. Initially, the value of a solid community outreach program in large part was to help support the plant's efforts to

*(Continued)*

get licensed and begin generating power. Now that Seabrook has done that, our community outreach is just as important now as it ever was. In many ways, our community relations activities have become more of an extension of our own employees' personal lives and commitments to their neighborhoods."

The Seabrook Station Science and Nature Center, its "most valuable PR outreach vehicle," continues its efforts to educate people about nuclear energy. The Center also informs visitors about the many initiatives taken by the Station that helped transform a town dump into a thriving ecosystem.

## Evaluation

Has Seabrook Station prevailed in the court of public opinion? In one sense it has, in that it is now an accepted part of the community.

Seabrook Station continues its two-way communication efforts by upholding its good neighbor policy and offering ongoing educational information to the public, and through the involvement of its employees—becoming Seabrook Station's ambassadors—in their neighborhoods and community organizations. However, according to the Office of Nuclear Energy, Science and Technology, "Until nuclear power becomes an energy solution once again, we won't know for sure if Seabrook and its string of owners have done enough with stakeholder education and relationship building to be successful in building new plants."

**Questions for Discussion**

1. What responsibilities, if any, does a business have to the community?
2. Should a business that produces a controversial product or service have obligations that surpass legal and regulatory mandates? Why or why not? Does your answer depend on whether the product (or production of the product) is potentially hazardous or lethal to the environment or humans?
3. Develop some proactive and reactive strategies that Seabrook will need when decommissioning the plant, disposing of the spent fuel rods, and if the radiological emission risk correlations show that the plant has become dangerous.
4. After the problems in Japan, what messages or activities can the nuclear power industry use to revive what was the growing interest in returning to nuclear power in the United States?

# Case 4-4 Driving Community Behavior to Save Energy and the Environment

By 2011, the general public had descended into two prominent camps—those who firmly believed global warming was a fact and those who did not. Little was being done about global warming itself because political forces couldn't agree whether scarce money should be spent solving something that may or may not be happening. And even those who did believe couldn't agree on what to do about it.

But a small town in New Hampshire, urged on by a swath of environmental programs around the state, had quietly started making changes. And this is the story of how their grassroots public relations efforts moved this community from its sleepy rural nature to something else.

In 2007, the town of Temple, New Hampshire, had little going on in terms of energy- and carbon-reduction efforts. Although it had a conservation commission that focused on preserving open spaces, preserving land, making woodland trails, and so on, the town never recycled at its Harvest Festival or other events, and people weren't talking about energy savings, climate change, or lowering the town's carbon footprint. An environmental scan at the time would have shown a small town (1,500 people) that leaned slightly more Democratic in the 2008 election. The median age was 37, and though most had a high school education, only a third had graduated from college. (See more Temple statistics at http://www.city-data.com/city/Temple-New-Hampshire.html.)

It was in the year 2007 that a grassroots movement took hold across the state of New Hampshire. Its purpose was to have communities sign a New Hampshire climate change resolution prior to the 2008 presidential election. One hundred and sixty-four New Hampshire communities, including Temple, passed the resolution at their annual town meetings. This vote led to the appointment of a Temple town energy committee tasked with making recommendations to reduce emissions and save energy at the local level. The committee used the resolution's passage as a triggering event to kick-start environmental-conservation and energy-saving programs within the town.

## New Hampshire Climate Change Resolution

To see if the town will go on record in support of effective actions by the President and Congress to address the issue of climate change which is increasingly harmful to the environment and economy of New Hampshire and to the future well being of the people of _____.
These actions include:

1. Establishment of a national program requiring reductions of U.S. greenhouse gas emissions while protecting the U.S. economy.
2. Creation of a major national research initiative to foster rapid development of sustainable energy technologies, thereby stimulating new jobs and investment.
   In addition, the town of _____ encourages New Hampshire citizens to work for emission reductions within their communities, and we ask our selectmen to consider the appointment of a voluntary energy committee to recommend local steps to save energy and reduce emissions.

The record of the vote on this article shall be transmitted to the New Hampshire Congressional delegation, to the President of the United States, and to declared candidates for those offices.

*(Continued)*

The energy committee sought to build on their success, but with the 2007 through 2008 deep recession in play, getting the community to spend money to "save the environment" was a difficult sell. Committee members decided to work through a relationship strategy that built trust, gathered resources, and made connections. They connected with a myriad of other resources available outside of the town. And within the town they sought to teach through modeling behaviors and offering information—but not through preaching or pushing. The methods used included:

- Providing recycling at town events (role-modeling and foot-in-door)
- Free weatherization for low-income residents—relationship building and problem personalization
- Befriending naysayers—defusing the opposition
- Creating community celebrations—cheerleading successes
- Serving great food at all events—foot-in-door

A second major triggering event occurred in 2007—a hole and major leak developed in the Fire Department's roof. When volunteer fire department personnel volunteered to fix the hole and replace the roof for free if the town supplied the materials, the town was ecstatic. Money was tight and the town couldn't afford anything fancy. So, when the energy committee threw a wrench into the plans by advocating for energy efficiency being built into the structure, and that stopped the ongoing plan, feelings ran high. But relationships had been built and education done. The town's residents were able to pause and consider without descending into chaos. The hole in the roof was fixed, but a new roof was put on hold. Early in 2008, the energy committee conducted an exhaustive energy inventory for the town's municipal buildings, uncovering the bad news that there were three very energy "leaky" buildings. The committee recommended professional energy audits for those buildings to determine what could best

be done to "tighten them up" and save the town money. When the audits were completed, the committee invited the board of selectmen and the planning board to attend presentations of the findings from the inventory and energy audits. The boards became convinced that energy retrofitting and upgrades were in order, to stop wasteful fuel expenditures. But financing was not in the cards during the recession.

A third major naturally occurring triggering event occurred that winter, the ice storm of 2008, which wiped out power to the town for 14 days just before the December holidays. The need for change felt critical. Suddenly, residents were looking for alternative power sources—renewables. One trigger led to the next. The planning board was now willing to consider the energy committee's offer to write an energy chapter to add to the town's master plan. After a year of arduous work with the board and many drafts, an energy chapter was added to the master plan. It included a land-use plan plus recommendations for zoning ordinance upgrades and policies that guide the town toward lowering its energy usage, reducing emissions, and supporting the installation of renewables across all sectors. It has become the town's road map going forward.

Once public opinion and the energy committee's actions moved in the direction of energy efficiency and environmental care, the gates swung open. Again, one trigger led to another. In this case, all the previous triggers, one way or another, led to a most pivotal event—the Regional Greenhouse Gas Initiative (RGGI) awarded Temple a $332,000 RGGI grant in 2009, to conduct a deep energy-efficiency retrofit for the three audit-identified "leaky" municipal buildings and for the expansion of the energy committee's educational program. The stunningly successful retrofit greatly reduced the town library's energy usage and improved its comfort level. It also resulted in an 81 percent reduction in the town's municipal building and fire department's heating fuel usage and $CO_2$ emissions—lowering taxes for years to come.

The energy committee expanded their educational Web site, initiated a recycling and environmental program with the kids in Temple's elementary school, expanded their free weatherization program for low-income residents, held several free weatherization workshops for residents, and inspired their community to win a four-town carbon footprint competition.

Compared to the other towns competing, Temple had the highest percentage of households to take new steps to lower their energy usage. Fifteen percent of its residents stepped up to the challenge, saved $35,484, and reduced emissions by over 255,092 pounds. Their victory was rewarded with an ice cream social, catered by nearby environmental steward Stonyfield Farm, which jumped at the opportunity to honor the town of Temple in its success.

The relationships that grew out of the friendly competition among the leaders of the four towns triggered an important next step for all of them. They joined with other environmental leaders in the region to form a nonprofit grassroots organization, the Monadnock

Energy Resources Initiative. Its aim is to bring low-cost home weatherizations and solar hot water installations to the region, using the community-building models of neighbors helping neighbors and barn raisings. Weatherization trainings and solar installations are in the works.

Meanwhile, Temple's Energy Committee continues to focus on helping their town become as adaptive and resilient as possible in the face of rising fuel prices and the approaching collision with peak oil.

**Questions for Discussion**

1. While Temple, New Hampshire, has been successful in its efforts, other communities still struggle to get environmental programs off the ground. A particularly difficult group to reach is wealthy homeowners. Many are not motivated by saving money. What strategies, tactics, or messages might you recommend for a wealthier town?
2. What other methods could you devise to reach out to community members

Installation of insulated R40 cool-vent roofing
http://www.teec.info/Photo-Montage.html

*(Continued)*

to get them to come and participate in town functions—particularly when it is freezing outside?

3. Discuss how these changes might have been achieved even if the ice storm had never happened or the RGGI grant had not been awarded.

## PROBLEM 4-A   HELPING ISN'T ALWAYS EASY

You are a member of a civic organization that has 300 members locally and is the local chapter of a national organization. Most of the membership is well educated and falls into the middle- and upper-income brackets. The local organization has a reputation for civic involvement—working for better schools, increased voter registration, and equal rights for minorities and women.

About 18 months ago, the executive committee made a presentation to the organization on illiteracy in your city. Studies show that 25 percent of the adult population is "functionally illiterate." By the year 2020, the number of functional illiterates is projected to reach more than one-third of the population. Although the problem is spread throughout the population, the percentage of minorities in this group is high.

Soon after the executive committee's presentation, the organization voted to establish a literacy council for adults in the city. The primary function of the council is to solicit and train volunteers to act as tutors and match these persons with individuals wanting to learn to read and write. The organization is able to generate heavy news coverage of the council and public-service announcements about the need for tutors and students. Despite the coverage, very few persons have volunteered to tutor; even fewer persons have requested the service.

Because of your expertise as a communicator, the organization has asked you to become involved in this program. Your review of the program indicates there is general agreement among individuals that something has to be done, but no one is quite sure what. Your organization sets an objective of obtaining and training 50 volunteer tutors and matching these with 50 students in the next six months.

As a well-trained public relations professional, you recognize that your organization has fallen into the trap of believing that widespread and positive publicity will influence behavior. You agree to help

the cause but stipulate that research is essential to discover why the program hasn't taken off.

Describe how you will design and budget (in time and money) a research program to give you the information necessary to implement a successful recruiting program for students and tutors.

## PROBLEM 4-B   ADJUSTING TO A CHANGE IN COMMAND

For 10 years, George Loyal has been a one-person public relations department at Siwash, a college of 3,500 students in Ohio. They have been 10 good years in terms of George's working conditions. There has been plenty of publicity material to pump out, and there has been cooperation on the part of news media.

Of great assistance to George has been the attitude of the Siwash College president. He takes an open stance publicly. He is articulate, handsome, and personable. He has been effective in attracting quality faculty, activating alumni support, and adding notable trustees who have been important in raising funds and making sure that Siwash is favorably regarded by legislators in the state capital.

But all these good things seem to have come to an end. The president was struck down by a massive heart attack and suddenly passed away. The trustees moved quickly to name a successor, who turned out to be a senior member of the Siwash faculty. He is a professor of anthropology, a scholar who is well published, quiet, and nonpublic.

The new president, in the month since his selection, has informed George that he is not going to be active in alumni affairs, visible at sports events, or available to talk with news media whenever they want him to. He spends most of his time closeted with a few of the older faculty members. His secretary seems to feel that her job is to protect him from intrusions or outside visitors. He has not sent for George or sent him a memo about any specific job to do or any change in his responsibilities.

George's work has almost come to a standstill except for routine news releases. He frankly is not sure where he stands. The cooperative relationship he has had with news media seems to be threatened. The director of alumni relations is as baffled as he is. Two trustees have quietly indicated that they are stepping aside rather than stand for reelection when the time comes. The local sports editor has tipped George off that the newspaper's managing editor plans to ask for a meeting with the new president soon if he doesn't "come out of his shell."

The question before George is, What options does he have in trying to preserve the gains in public relations attained during the past 10 years?

1. What would be the most effective way of establishing a proactive relationship with the new president?
2. What would be your overall strategy for maintaining the college's relationships with its important stakeholders?
3. Given the personality of the new president, what role would you allot to him in maintaining the college's reputation?
4. How would you gain support for this strategy?

## PROBLEM 4-C  BRINGING THE COMMUNITY TO CONSENSUS

You are an employee of a public relations firm that focuses on raising money for the fine arts. A large client of the firm wants to find funding to relocate the city's largest Center for the Arts within a yet-to-be-built state-of-the-art facility. You meet with your peers and discuss taking on this large assignment.

Several key factors must be considered; most important is how the community will react to such a change. The Center's current home is legendary, dating back to when the city was first built. It has held many memorable performances. Parents love to bring their children to the plays and musicals that are performed there; many enjoy its opera and classical music performances. Film festivals and dance performances have also been presented there.

However, the Center is old and in need of repair. Estimates for the repairs and for long-term upkeep are high. This client feels it would be more financially sound to build a new facility than to pour more money into the old building. The advantages for building a new Center—state-of-the-art acoustics, up-to-date technology, expanded and more comfortable seating, etc.—weigh greatly against the community's desire to keep the old building and find funding to repair it in future years. There is also the matter of convincing the board of directors. Some of the members are in favor of keeping the old building and feel that it is too valuable, historically, to abandon.

Knowing that you need to sway opinion within the community as well as the board of directors, how would you begin? What information do you need and how would you get it? What specific audiences would you target? Which audience must you reach first? How do you propose to reach all the various audiences? How would you use two-way communication in your plan? Would opinion leaders work here? If so, how would you find them? Consider also the future use of the current building. How can that become part of your plan?

# 5

# Investor Relations

Financial investment is no longer the purview of the wealthy alone. With the advent of the IRA, 401(k), ESOP (Employee Stock Ownership Program), and online trading, the body of investors has swollen with middle-class wage earners looking to a more secure future. These people follow the market with the same fervor as traditional institutional investors and probably suffer more over the ups and downs of the market than any high rollers.

One aspect of financial affairs that increasingly affects the national mood is U.S. investors' evaluations of the corporations in which they have invested. The major measurements are dollar sales volume, profit, the increase or decrease in interest or dividends paid, and whether the price of the stock or bond has increased or decreased from the original purchase price. Other factors include the rank of the company among competitors in its field and what percentage of dividends is paid in comparison with the purchase price.

Experts in the financial world who make a living, and sometimes a fortune, by analyzing and trading equities for themselves and for customers have to be aware of changing conditions in the money supply, raw material prices, international monetary affairs, national economies around the world, and much more. They use sophisticated measurement tools such as stock market trend lines, a company's management capabilities, debt to asset ratio, and several others.

In addition, there is the element of government finance—borrowings by the Treasury Department, municipalities, or state agencies in the form of bonds or debentures. Government spending, too, is a major factor in the financial fortunes of the nation.

Today, with stock market news and international monetary or economic status constantly reported and talked about, public relations practitioners also must keep abreast of these topics. A small percentage of practitioners will specialize in investor or financial relations. However, *all* practitioners need to be familiar with the economic climate and its impact on the organizations they represent—corporate, governmental, or nonprofit.

## THE PUBLICLY OWNED CORPORATION CONCEPTUALIZED

In the U.S. business system, as an ideal, the publicly owned corporation's mission, performance, and behavior represent the consent granted, and the consensus of views held, by all those who have a stake in its financial success. This concept embraces shareholders, employees and their pension funds, community neighbors, suppliers, and certainly customers. On the sidelines, appropriately, are those associations and governmental agencies designated to encourage, over-see, referee, or discipline in the name of all taxpayers, or the voters. In this idealization, publicly owned corporations might be seen as instruments of a people's capitalism. In actuality, such a concept is simplistic and does not exist, for these companies quickly take on the personalities of those who manage them—competitive, greedy, self-serving, or just the opposite.

A publicly owned business is created and managed to be profitable and to be competi-tive with others that sell the same product or service. In order to get started at all, there must be capital or credit and a product or service for which a market is perceived or waiting to be created. Prudent use of capital and skill in producing and marketing the product or service become the province of a small group that manages the enterprise day by day. Survival comes first. Beyond that, growth, diversification, and expansion make up goals that fuel ambition and drive all participants on the payroll. Profit, what's left over after all expenses are paid, makes everything else possible.

Given these realities, it is simply not practical for all those who have a stake in the out-come of an enterprise to take an active part in a forum for major decisions or as links in the decision process. Apart from being largely inaccessible, the stakeholders of a publicly owned corporation are too diverse in their self-interests and in their views of what a business should do, except in the case of a few public issues such as quality of the environment, to rally and force action. Given the realities, it should not be surprising that profit, and the power it brings, frequently leads to excesses, abuses, and corruption. These bring investigation, prosecution where indicated, and regulatory measures to preclude recurrence, in the name of the ultimate public interest.

## REALITY HAS A LONG HISTORY

Corporations are not ordained by Mother Nature but are a creation of the state. Until the early 1800s, someone starting a business had no "corporate shield," but put all his or her assets at risk. If the business failed, the owner was personally responsible for all debts to the point of per-sonal bankruptcy. Because this situation discouraged the formation of new business, laws were enacted allowing for the formation of **corporations**—business entities in which shareholders risk only the amount of their investment.

What the state creates it can regulate. Regulatory measures started a long time ago, such as those governing interstate commerce mandated by the U.S. Constitution. However, the federal government began to institute more stringent controls over business. In 1890, the Sherman Antitrust Act, aimed at regulating concentration or monopoly within several indus-tries, was passed. This act was supplemented by the Clayton Act in 1914, and in the same year the Federal Trade Commission Act set up a mechanism to keep channels of interstate trade open to competition. The 1929 stock market crash and the Great Depression of the 1930s stimulated legislative and regulatory actions in the investment area. First was the Securities Act of 1933, which required a corporation to publish a prospectus (a preliminary printed state-ment that describes an enterprise and is distributed to prospective investors) when it prepares to sell securities to the public. Then came the Securities Exchange Act of 1934, creating the Securities and Exchange Commission (SEC) and dealing with the conflict of interest involved when a corporate official reaps personal financial gain on information not known to the public. Rule 10b-5 in 1942 tightened the act, prohibiting fraudulent and deceptive practices in the purchase or sale of securities.

## THE MATURING OF FINANCIAL PUBLIC RELATIONS

In spite of the Teapot Dome scandal and other problems stemming from overcontrol of many economic areas by the so-called robber barons, financial public relations didn't spring up in the 1920s, but publicity specialists such as Ivy Lee and Ed Bernays were called in at that time for their expertise.

Financial relations in the 1930s was recognized by employers as a useful communications element, but was considered secondary to the publicity and special events that supported marketing efforts as the economy struggled out of the Depression. It didn't rise in the pecking order and earned no particular voice in the decision process during World War II. Then the corporate focus was on boosting employee morale and thus increasing productivity, which was necessary to arm the Allies. The focus was also on increasing the sale of war bonds to finance arms production. After the war, with so much pent-up consumer demand to be satisfied, it was hard not to be successful and keep stockholders satisfied, so financial relations specialists were not needed.

A financial relations breakthrough came in the 1960s, in a classic situation of insider trading, in which a single news release was deemed by a court to be the critical factor in whether the investing public had been misled (see Case 5-4). Out of the case came the understanding—as determined by the SEC, the New York Stock Exchange, and corporate officials—that financial communications were important and could create or obviate legal liabilities for the corporation. Shingles labeled "Financial Public Relations" appeared by the thousands. Qualified practitioners began to sit in on the financial decision-making process of their corporations.

## AT THIS JUNCTURE

Corporate growth has become almost a religion in U.S. industry. The means of getting to heaven have involved huge investment in research and technology, diversification of products and services, acquisitions, mergers, conglomeration, and multinationalization. From these actions has come an increasing concentration of corporate ownership among a few thousand very wealthy individuals, investment funds, and banking and insurance interests, both U.S. and foreign. Boards of directors of huge corporations have been woven in a crisscross pattern of a few thousand individuals whose views of the system are similar and whose posture is dependably reactive when the system comes under criticism of any kind.

In the 1970s and into the 1980s, conditions were not reassuring for the small investor or average wage earner. Inflation helped wages but hurt buying power. Interest rates for money borrowed for a car or home were high, mortgaging the future. Available jobs for traditional functions shrank as corporations went abroad for cheap labor and automation displaced people. Savings decreased or disappeared for a great many.

In the latter 1980s, conditions were ripe for the rich to get richer and for the high-rolling risk takers and arbitrageurs to find market manipulation and insider trading irresistible. The mood seemed to be that "anything goes if you don't get caught." Each new rumor of a corporate raid takeover, issuance of junk bonds, or bit of privileged information spurred speculation.[1]

---

[1] Elliot D. Lee. "Takeover Predators Now Share the Prey," *The Wall Street Journal,* April 29, 1988. The article lists takeover activity at the time, including Campeau Corp. buying Federated Stores for $6.6 billion and GE acquiring Roper Corp. from Whirlpool. William Celis. "Low Stock Prices Spur Takeover Flurry," *The Wall Street Journal,* March 1, 1988, revealed six takeover transactions in a single day, totaling $5.4 billion in assets. Among those involved were Homestake Mining, Media General Inc., and USG Corp. A chart showed the total value of transactions increasing from $10 billion the first two months of 1987 to $28 billion in the same period of 1988.

Black Monday came in October of 1987. It was a rude awakening as the market's Dow Jones average plummeted some 500 points, taking with it some of Wall Street's big dealers. In the wake, a Tender Offer Reform Act was proposed as an amendment to the Securities Exchange Act of 1934. Too little, too late.[2]

Things quieted down, but not completely or permanently. In 1988, another case made financial headlines when a young trainee in Morgan Stanley's mergers and acquisitions department was alleged to have fed material information to a wealthy Hong Kong customer, who then traded on that information, garnering $19 million in gains. Then, for the next several months, it seemed each week brought a new Wall Street scandal, making the names of such men as Michael Milken and Ivan Boesky infamous.

The 1990s saw the government, through the SEC, get tough on insider trading issues. With an outpouring of public comment—nearly 6,000 comment letters, the vast majority from individual investors in favor of adopting Regulation Fair Disclosure (Reg FD)—the SEC adopted the ruling. Reg FD's intent was to end the special relationship that existed between public companies and analysts and brokers—to level the playing field for *all* investors. Prior to Reg FD, analysts and brokers often received information from companies that was material to investment decisions but was not shared with the general public. As one comment letter noted, "The explosion of the Internet provides ways for information to reach all investors. Analysts are one way, and in the past they were the principal conduit. But now that's changing."

On October 23, 2000, the new ruling took effect with cries from the analyst community that it would chill communications from companies. In fact, it has both promoted and inhibited corporate communications. A survey by the National Investor Relations Institute (NIRI) of its membership found that 28 percent are providing more information to investors than before the new rule, 48 percent are issuing about the same amount, and 24 percent are providing less information. NIRI is concerned about that 24 percent. Further study is needed to determine the reasons and what can be done about the situation.

By the beginning of the 21st century—in light of all preceding activities—one would have expected to find investors more careful, regulators more attentive, and managers more ethical. Yet, some of the biggest corporate failures due to poor management practices, corrupt ethics, and questionable financial methodologies have led to financial ruin for many investors. The excesses of such organizations as Enron, WorldCom, and Tyco have led to further regulation. The Sarbanes–Oxley Act sought to solve some of the problems. Some feel it hasn't done enough—others feel it went too far. The SEC continues to seek out and prosecute senior managers when they step over the line and play havoc with investors' nest eggs. In 2006, Ken Lay and Jeffrey Skilling of Enron fame were both found guilty and sentenced to years in prison. (Lay died suddenly in July 2006, thus vacating his guilty verdict and throwing civil suits against him into disarray.) Bernard Ebbers of WorldCom was already serving his time while Dennis Kozlowski of Tyco was busy fighting on appeal. Martha Stewart had also served her time and was back on network television as if nothing had happened.

The financial "bubble" that burst in 2007 threw the market into a panic, causing stock prices to fall, banks to fail, insurance companies and real estate subsidiaries to look for bailouts, and common investors to watch their portfolios decrease by 50 percent.

---

[2] George Getschow and Bryan Burrough. "Pickens, Acting Bitter, Finds Takeover Game Isn't Much Fun Now," *The Wall Street Journal,* April 5, 1988. Detailed profile of Texas oil man T. Boone Pickens, who said in 1983 he wanted to take over Gulf Oil Corp, later decided not to go ahead, but made a $518 million pretax profit when speculators bid up the price of Gulf stock on the basis of his intent. In 1988, he was weary and bitter, lashing out at investment bankers, advisers, local and national news media, and many others.

From that experience, of course, came new legislation, this time in the form of the Dodd–Frank bill, which brought the most significant changes to financial regulation in the United States since the regulatory reform that followed the Great Depression. These changes in the American financial regulatory environment affect all federal financial regulatory agencies and almost every aspect of the nation's financial services industry.

The bill even went into executive compensation, requiring reporting by all public companies on CEO to median employee pay ratios and other compensation data, enforces equitable access to credit for consumers, and provides incentives to promote banking among low- and medium-income residents. (Wikipedia)

## THE ROLE OF PUBLIC RELATIONS

Now the question is, and it will always remain, what is the role of the public relations practitioner in the organization and in relation to the stockholders when shady dealings are at work?

NIRI's survey also found that, prior to the new ruling, 60 percent of its member companies were providing full public access to their conference calls to discuss quarterly earnings results and guidance. After Reg FD, 89 percent are doing so, mostly through Webcasts. Eighty-four percent of companies are notifying investors and the media of their upcoming conference calls in a news release, 75 percent post a notice on their company's Web site, and 55 percent are using "push technology"—directly notifying interested investors who want an e-mail alert.

The one-on-ones between companies and analysts and investors are continuing, according to NIRI's survey, contrary to the fear that these might be severely cut back for fear of violating Reg FD. However, there is important information, much of which is nonfinancial, that companies can and should discuss with analysts and investors. This nonfinancial information offers important measurements of a company's well-being, which can directly affect the bottom line. Analysts may have to do more work now with Reg FD. No longer can they be guided in their analysis by the companies. Information will be distributed equally. Knowledge and the ability to analyze data are key.

## AN ENVIRONMENT OF STRONG VIEWS

Financial relations present a worthy challenge to the practitioner. As prime audiences, you have millions of small investors fighting to be on an equal footing with those who "control" the market (such as managers of pension funds and mutual funds, and other money managers) and leaders of publicly owned corporations who can make decisions that are helpful or harmful, choosing short-term expedients or long-haul public interest. Then there are the regulators—and the ever-inquiring media, economists, and legislators—who can make and change the rules.

The positive views small investors have of the corporate world stem in part from good news such as dividends or appreciation in the value of their investments, bullish forecasts by corporate and investment spokespersons, and profiles of company leaders portraying them as intelligent, honest, and planning for future success.

Their negative views are formed in part by information in proxy statements about lavish executive salaries, bonuses, and stock options not based on the health or performance of the corporation. Investors read news items about costly indulgences such as private aircraft, executive dining rooms, limousines, club memberships, and junkets, all in the name of incentives or customer relations that are recovered in higher prices for the products or services. And they are not reassured when such free-spending corporations, unable to compete with foreign products, run to the government for protection.

## A Language of its Own

A generation ago, practitioners had to learn new financial semantics. Terms such as *privileged information, conflict of interest, insider trading, timely and adequate disclosure, due diligence,* and *a material fact* became part of communications as well as legal language.

An infusion of words appeared during the late 1980s and early 1990s. Practitioners needed to understand *arbitrage* and *arbs, junk bonds, payment in kind (PIK), green mail, raiders, programmed trading,* and *hostile takeover.*

Today, new lingo continues to emerge on the Street, for example, Regulation Fair Disclosure (see page 99).

Large investors—directors chosen to guide the corporations and the people hired to manage the businesses—constitute a relatively small audience with some deeply ingrained convictions in common. They claim that the system works well. Criticism or threats of regulation tend to harden their positions and to render spokespersons less flexible rather than more open and accessible. When challenged, this posture provides an example of the *artificial censorship principle.* At times, unwelcome criticism or questions concerning economic matters are labeled as expressing an unacceptable political viewpoint—thus the strategy or tactic of *changing the issue.*

- The role of the corporate financial relations specialist or consultant tends to be that of *interpreter and mediator* between the prime audiences. He or she usually comes on as a moderate or neutral in economic and political philosophy. The position requires skill and objectivity in representing the average investor, the middle-class unsophisticated citizen, while representing private enterprise and conservative views publicly.

Among the interveners financial relations must take into account are the financial news media, those who run and support nonprofit institutions such as education, and those charged with making and enforcing the securities laws.

## THE SPECIFICS OF THE FUNCTION

The financial public relations role can be summarized as:

- Communications strategy appropriate to management goals in investor relations
- Preparing public literature, including reports required by law, and establishing press contacts
- Managing relationships with the financial community, including analyst meetings, tours or visits, and so on

Among the specific situations requiring communication are:

1. A company goes public, splits its stock, or arranges added financing.
2. A corporation wishes to make a tender offer to acquire another corporation, to merge with another corporation, or to head off or oppose an unwanted offer. An acquisition or merger may result in a change of identity such as name, logo, headquarters location, or ownership.
3. A timely announcement is needed for significant new products, services, expansion, or acquisition, which might affect the price of the company's stock.
4. Periodic reports of financial results, including an annual report, need to be issued.

5. Arrangements are required for meetings with investors and for public reports of proceedings, including the annual meeting—and, in some enlightened corporations, an employee annual meeting.

6. Special literature is required, dealing with a corporation's philosophy, policies, and objectives; its history or anniversary; and its scope, "identity," or "culture." Any of these may also be the subject of advertising.

## References and Additional Readings

Berkeley, Alan. "Stand by for Change: The Future of Investor Relations." Address at the University of Texas, April 30, 1987. Synopsis in *pr reporter* 30 (August 17, 1987).

Berle, A. A., Jr. *Power Without Property.* New York: Harcourt, Brace and World, 1959. A classic book.

Cheney, Richard. "What Should We Do About Takeovers?" *tips & tactics, pr reporter* 25 (supplement, April 6, 1987).

Cutlip, Scott, Allen Center, and Glen Broom. "The Practice: Business and Industry." Chapter 14 in *Effective Public Relations.* 8th ed. Upper Saddle River, NJ: Prentice Hall, 1999.

Dobrzynski, Judith. "The Lessons of the RJR Free-for-All." *BusinessWeek* (December 19, 1988). Raises and answers questions about the battle for RJR Nabisco.

"Four Barometers Analysts Apply in Measuring Management Performance." *Investor Relations Update* (October–November 1992): 15. Summary in purview, supplement to *pr reporter* (February 15, 1993).

Holliday, Karen Kahler. "Understanding Investor Relations." *Bank Marketing* 24 (August 1992): 22–25.

Leeds, Mark, and Bruce Fraser. "Why Wall Street Matters." *Management Review* 82 (September 1993): 23–26.

Lees, David. "A Strategy That Pays Dividends." *Management Today* (March 1994): 5.

Lerbinger, Otto, and Nathaniel Sperber. "Financial Relations." Chapter 7 in *Manager's Public Relations Handbook.* Reading, MA: Addison-Wesley, 1982.

Metz, Tim. *Black Monday: The Catastrophe of October 19, 1987 . . . and Beyond.* New York: William Morrow, 1988. A chronology of the stock market drop of 500 points and the theory concerning the mystery of it.

Miller, Eugene. "Investor Relations." Chapter 11 in *Lesly's Handbook of Public Relations and Communications.* 5th ed. Chicago, IL: NTC Business Books, 1998.

Moore, Philip. "Ciba Takes Investors into Account." *Euromoney* (September 1993): 37–38.

National Investor Relations Institute offers a wealth of information, including *IR Update,* a monthly newsletter. National Investors Relations Institute, 8045 Leesburg Pike, Suite 600, Vienna, VA 22182; 703/506-3570; www.niri.org.

The *Public Relations Body of Knowledge.* New York: PRSA. See abstracts dealing with "Financial and Investor Relations."

Seely, Michael. "Hit the Financial Bull's Eye with Well-Aimed IR Programs." *Corporate Cash Flow* 14 (July 1993): 26–30.

# Case 5-1 Bankruptcy: Communicating for Future Success[*]

Nothing strikes fear into investors like the possibility of bankruptcy in a publicly held company. Under bankruptcy law, investors are the last consideration in the distribution of assets of the bankrupt entity. In the Enron collapse, for example, some $80 billion in shareholder value was lost, including more than $2 billion held by Enron employees and retirees. That value will never return.

But not all bankruptcies involve liquidation. Many struggling companies find relief in bankruptcy, taking advantage of the shelter of Chapter 11 to reorganize, absent the pressure of creditors or—commonly—legal verdicts that would otherwise prevent a company from continuing daily operations. This case addresses the reality of bankruptcy and the need for effective communication throughout the process.

When a company files for bankruptcy, it is using an important management tool for effectively operating an enterprise. Executives have the expectation that the bankruptcy "remedy" will help protect their business at a time when they've exhausted other options and are operating beyond their current financial capabilities.

Companies and people who file for bankruptcy protection are not "bad," but they might be looked at negatively if they fail to meet the public's demand for effective and timely communication. Everyone who is affected by the bankruptcy filing, including employees, customers, shareholders, and suppliers, wants to know how they will be impacted. They want straight answers. They shun rhetoric, complicated phrases, and smoke screens.

Customers want their deliveries; employees want their jobs and paychecks; shareholders want a return on their investment; and suppliers want to be paid. And the media want to report the facts. It's really quite simple.

Bankruptcy communication, like all crisis communication, requires credibility. Although there is nothing wrong with saying, "I don't know," it's important to add the phrase, "but I'll get back to you as quickly as I can with the answer." Then, live up to your word. Don't guess and don't go beyond the information currently available.

Some issues in a filing cannot be answered or resolved immediately. Telling a "white lie" that will satisfy the questioner in the short term (e.g., "The check will be sent next week") will probably result in a long-term loss. The cardinal rule of crisis communications—and a bankruptcy is generally considered a crisis—is always tell the truth. There are no exceptions.

Many companies today have a crisis communications plan that details actions to be taken when something goes wrong. Typically, the plan addresses manufacturing or packaging errors, a regulatory investigation, a lawsuit, an accident, or a boycott. No one anticipates bankruptcy, however, and it often isn't included in preplanning efforts despite the keen public interest and media attention filings receive. Although every crisis situation is different, each demands the same basic response—proactive contact with all concerned constituencies on a continuing basis.

When a filing is imminent, public relations professionals must think about the key messages that need to be conveyed and anticipate

*(Continued)*

[*]Appreciation to James R. Frankowiak, APR, president, Public Communications Inc., Tampa, Florida, for their assistance in preparing this case.

what questions are likely to arise. Before the various constituencies are notified, answers should already be in place. The most credible spokesperson for each public should be designated and thoroughly briefed. Other company executives must know who the appropriate spokespersons are and refer inquiries to them. It's important to be rumor sensitive so that misinformation is quickly corrected. Keep an ear to the street—especially Wall Street.

Conditions that change during court protection proceedings will have an impact on the communication plan. Public relations professionals need to be proactive so that new information, whether good or bad, is communicated before important audiences read it in the newspaper.

Examining recent bankruptcy communications programs can provide valuable insights.

## Harvard Industries

Harvard Industries, a large, publicly held original equipment manufacturer of automobile components, sought protective action because of serious losses at its Doehler-Jarvis subsidiary, which manufactures manifolds, transmission housings, and other castings. Strategically, the subsidiary offered good long-term potential, but continuing losses made it impractical to realize that potential in the short run.

The company's public relations counsel, PCI, developed a comprehensive communications plan in the event Harvard's board of directors determined a Chapter 11 filing was necessary. This was done in advance of the board's ultimate decision to seek Chapter 11 protection. The key message was that Harvard Industries planned to submit a reorganization plan quickly and that operations would continue uninterrupted. A commitment for $175 million in debtor-in-possession financing would help assure continued operations while the company was under court protection.

A planned rehearsal was scheduled for constituent leaders, plant managers, controllers,

and human resource representatives just before the court filing. Once court action was taken, the company disclosed the action to the SEC, as required under the SEC's "full and complete disclosure" tenets.

Tailored versions of letters signed by the CEO were faxed to all key audiences, including customers, investors, employees, and suppliers. A news release and a question and answer document were enclosed. Hard copies were mailed as a follow-up. Selected customers were visited personally, and a series of toll-free telephone lines were established for individual stakeholder groups.

A strong emphasis was placed on monitoring constituent questions and concerns so that responses could follow quickly. Daily call logs that included the nature of the call and the call-back telephone numbers were shared with senior management. Media calls and article clippings were monitored by the public relations firm with response suggestions made to the CEO. Follow-up communications with suppliers also used a telephone hotline.

Employee meetings were held to address concerns. Employees were offered the opportunity to submit anonymous questions to management. Reorganization updates were posted throughout the court protection period.

The company is working aggressively with creditors to develop a feasible plan of reorganization. Stakeholders are updated periodically. When Harvard is ready to reestablish its leadership role as a leading industrial manufacturer, all stakeholders will know it.

## Celotex Corporation

Celotex Corporation, a major building materials manufacturer for domestic and international markets, filed for bankruptcy protection in 1990 due to the threat of asbestos litigation. Its public relations council, PCI, was asked to assist senior management with the development and implementation of a comprehensive communication plan to support the company's filing. At the time of the filing, Celotex consisted of two divisions: an affiliated research and development division and an international sales and marketing affiliate.

Celotex had 26 manufacturing facilities across the United States, plus regional sales offices, all networked via e-mail communications. The company employed nearly 3,000. In many of the company's plant locations, Celotex was a dominant employer and purchaser of local goods and services.

The communication plan, which was constructed with the participation of senior management representing finance, purchasing, human resources, sales and marketing, and corporate communication, identified and considered the special communication needs of every Celotex stakeholder. The plan set the stage for proactive communication initiatives throughout the nearly seven-year period of protection and beyond.

Key milestones during the company's period of protection were communicated in advance to all stakeholders. Toll-free numbers were established, and calls were returned within 24 hours. Special editions of the company's publication, "IMAGE," were produced and distributed to support the communication program, and comprehensive rumor-monitoring systems were established for internal and external stakeholders. Misinformation was corrected as quickly as possible.

When appropriate and necessary, senior management supported communication activities by telephone and in person. The company worked diligently to ensure that all stakeholders were updated on any steps related to the bankruptcy. Having a stakeholder read about an important process milestone in the newspaper or seeing it on television was simply not acceptable.

Senior executives visited all company locations each year and held candid conversations with employees. Those staff members wishing to submit questions and concerns anonymously were encouraged to do so by calls to the toll-free lines. When it became apparent that many stakeholders had similar questions or concerns, the company produced materials to address those issues. The period of

protection was marked by a series of business ebbs and flows related to the future of Celotex.

The outcome of similar bankruptcy cases in the recent past had been less than favorable. Through hard work and good fortune, Celotex achieved consistent, record-setting sales and revenues in the final years of its protection period. Management began to plan for the company's future.

Although Celotex had done well operating under protection, it became apparent that the new Celotex would have to better position itself to effectively compete in the marketplace. In late 1996, less than six months before emerging from protection, Celotex consolidated its divisional structure into a single operating unit to enhance customer service and staff productivity. The company's R&D and international divisions and its former corporate parent all became part of the new Celotex.

The Celotex response relied on the same basic strategies that helped other companies in similar situations: Recognize the information needs of all audiences, be the sole source of related information, provide a solid way to express concerns and questions, and respond immediately. Rumors and incorrect information were not tolerated. Proactive communication with all stakeholders on a continuing basis became the rule for Celotex.

*(Editor's note: When Celotex emerged from bankruptcy, ownership was vested with a trust that was to manage the company's assets in such a fashion that future asbestos claimants would have access to funds to pay individual claims. The trustees determined the best course of action would be to sell the assets of the company to the highest bidder, and that was done.)*

Bankruptcy communication parallels communications in other corporate crisis situations in that it demands proactive, continuing contacts with different groups. Yet, bankruptcy is almost always unanticipated and therefore a response to it is not included in many crisis plans. Paying close heed to corporate bankruptcy success stories offers valuable lessons in today's complex business climate.

## Questions for Discussion

1. Why would a company that is not totally failing want to declare bankruptcy?
2. Does the stigma of bankruptcy damage a company's reputation and business?
3. How does bankruptcy affect a publicly held company's relationship with the SEC?
4. How can a reputable company "take bankruptcy" and avoid its legitimate debts and obligations? Is this good public relations?
5. How does communication at a company in bankruptcy differ from that at a healthy company?

# Case 5-2 Aflac Gives Shareholders a Say on Pay

## Deriving Reputational Gain from a Corporate Governance First

By 2008, the American business community had spent 20 years lurching from one crisis of confidence to another. The 1990s were tainted by the insider trading revelations of Ivan Boesky and Michael Milken. The early 2000s saw the scandalous implosion of Enron as well as the convictions of CEOs at WorldCom and Tyco. And the global credit meltdown of 2008 was blamed by many on the questionable behavior of business interests including banks and traders.

Against this dark backdrop, Aflac (NYSE: AFL)—the number-one provider in the United States of guaranteed-renewable supplemental insurance—was among the few companies to recognize the real and actionable advantage of a reputation for transparency in corporate governance. Indeed, among shareholder activists, "transparency" became a drumbeat of demanded reform and was the basis for the regulatory innovations of Reg FD, Sarbanes–Oxley, and, more recently, Dodd–Frank. Moreover, Aflac recognized that investors were increasingly willing to place a premium on the stock of companies perceived to be ethical. *The Economist*'s 2007 global business barometer reported that 85 percent of investors believed corporate responsibility was a "central" or "important" consideration in investment decisions. That figure was almost double the 44 percent who responded to a similar survey five years before.

**FIGURE 5.1**  Aflac logo

Aflac's corporate communications team constantly is monitoring issues pertinent to the company, the industry, and American business. By 2006, executive compensation had risen to the top of the list of investor concerns. The 2007 Corporate Board Effectiveness Study[1] reported that about one in three directors of U.S.-based public companies said CEO pay is "too high in most cases." Also, the Chartered Financial Analysts (CFA) Institute responded to member demand by issuing a manual for frustrated shareholders on analyzing the fairness, transparency, and long-term effectiveness of executive compensation agreements.[2]

---

The following was contributed by Paul Dusseault, a 25-year veteran of Fleishman-Hillard, one of the world's leading communications firms.

[1] "10th Annual Corporate Board Effectiveness Study," by Heidrick & Struggles and the University of Southern California Marshall School of Business, 2006–2007.

[2] "Compensation of Senior Executives at Listed Companies: A Manual for Investors," CFA Institute Center for Financial Market Integrity, December 2007.

Aflac investor relations, along with corporate communications, developed an initiative centered on the issue of executive compensation. While most American companies resisted the growing movement for greater shareholder voice in matters of executive compensation, Aflac decided to embrace it. Aflac saw an opportunity to reinforce its credentials as ethical and progressive in matters of corporate governance and, in 2008, became the first large, American, publicly traded corporation to invite a shareholder vote on executive compensation.

**Planning**

Third-party endorsement was crucial to the communications strategy. While it is fairly typical for large, brand-name companies to receive letters from shareholder rights advocacy organizations asking for various corporate governance reforms, Boston Common Asset Management was the first to send such a letter to Aflac. Aflac began a dialogue about shareholders' right to have a say in the process of executive compensation. The investor relations group secured agreement from Boston Common to participate in communications activities surrounding the Aflac vote. "While Aflac viewed the shareholder vote as the right thing to do, we also were eager to *not* be perceived as lecturing other corporations about what they should do," said Laura Kane, Aflac's vice-president for corporate communications. "Having Boston Common as a willing communications partner helped reinforce that Aflac was responding to shareholder concerns rather than initiating reforms unilaterally, thereby anticipating and deflecting some possible criticism."

The investor relations/corporate communications team prepared a variety of materials to be shared with Aflac shareholders and business media including:

- The 2008 proxy and other correspondence issued to shareholders
- Background on the Say-on-Pay issue
- Stock performance tracked to the CEO's tenure
- Comparisons of Aflac CEO compensation policies with those of other companies with CEOs as long serving and successful[3]

The investor relations team commenced a year-long schedule of direct communications with shareholders; the Aflac corporate communications team was charged with reinforcing (via business media coverage) the company's rationale for setting compensation for the CEO and other senior executives, the commitment by Aflac to pay-for-performance, and its loyalty to shareholders. The team determined that only Daniel P. Amos, chairman and CEO, could be the company spokesperson on such a high-level, transcendent issue. Among the talking points used by Amos in numerous media interviews:

- Aflac's compensation policy is pay-for-performance, not just for our senior executives but for all our employees. During my tenure as CEO, the company's market value has grown from $1.2 billion to $30.5 billion.
- Aflac's board of directors listens to company shareholders, as well as groups that advocate transparent corporate governance, such as Boston Common Asset Management.
- Our shareholder vote on executive compensation is just the latest episode in a long track record of progressive corporate governance policies at Aflac.
- Though the shareholder vote is officially nonbinding, a significant negative percentage would result in immediate changes in Aflac executive compensation policies.

---

[3] From August 1990, when Amos was appointed Aflac's CEO, through 2007, the company's total return to shareholders, including reinvested cash dividends, exceeded 3,800 percent, compared to a 660 percent increase for the Dow Jones Industrial Average during the same time period.

## The Program

Aflac's corporate communications team:

- Negotiated exclusive national release of news of the history-making announcement of Say on Pay in February 2007 to help improve the placement and prominence of the news articles (*USA Today*, Feb. 14, 2007).
- Referred reporters to pertinent shareholder activists (typically critics of corporate large corporations) to add a counterintuitive aspect to the story (*Newsweek*, June 4, 2007).
- Arranged prominent thought-leadership coverage just prior to the historic shareholder vote (CEO interview, *The Wall Street Journal*, March 7, 2008).
- Negotiated unprecedented access to the CEO for select national media (e.g. *CBS Evening News*, April 29, 2007; *The Today Show with Matt Lauer*, March 28, 2008.).

- Made the CEO available for nationally broadcast interviews (*Fox News, Nightly Business Report*, CNBC, etc.).
- Issued multiple corporate press releases leading up to the vote, to create a crescendo of attention:
  - "Aflac Adopts Non-Binding 'Say On Pay' Shareholder Vote," (Feb. 14, 2007).
  - "Aflac Moves Up 'Say on Pay' Shareholder Vote to 2008," (Nov. 14, 2007).
  - "First 'Say on Pay' Vote Goes to Aflac Shareholders," (March 25, 2008).
  - "Aflac Shareholders Have Their 'Say on Pay'" (May 6, 2008).
- Leveraged overlapping news trends and events to tell Aflac's Say-on-Pay story well after the historic first vote (e.g. "The Pay Debate," *The Boston Globe*, June 24, 2009).

Whether or not Mr. Amos' salary was too high, too low, or just right was not the province of the public relations staff. But how that conversation was to be managed was definitely their responsibility. By limiting shareholder input or just ramming through board decisions, fallout issues could have been immeasurably damaging to the organization's reputation and trust levels, and could have taken immeasurable time and attention from other important tasks. Taking the high road and giving people a voice in decisions is the role of the practitioner in this situation.

## Evaluation

- In 2008, 93 percent of shareholder votes were cast in favor of Aflac's executive compensation policies and procedures; in 2009, the favorable vote was 97 percent.[4]
- Aflac leapt from number seven in 2008 to number one on *Fortune*'s 2009 list of the World's Most Admired Companies in the Health and Life Insurance category.

- Since 2007, Aflac has been named one of the World's Most Ethical Companies by *Ethisphere* magazine four times, and was named by Reputation Institute in 2008 as the Most Respected Company in the Global Insurance Industry.
- In 2009, *Corporate Responsibility Magazine* added Aflac to its list of 100 Best Corporate Citizens, based on the company's high level of public disclosure and transparency.

[4] In 2008, Daniel P. Amos earned as chairman and CEO of Aflac, Inc., a total compensation of $10.8 million, which included a base salary of $1.3 million, stock and options grants of $9.2 million, and other compensation of just under $200,000. In 2009, Amos earned total compensation of $13.1 million, which included a base salary of $1.3 million, a cash bonus of $4.1 million, stock and options grants of $7.45 million, and other compensation of just over $200,000.

## DISCUSSION QUESTIONS

1. Large, public, American companies now routinely host nonbinding shareholder votes on executive compensation; indeed, such votes are called for under the Dodd–Frank Act of 2010. How did being the first to invite a shareholder vote have an impact on media interest in Aflac?

2. In terms of media strategy, what role did third parties play in the Aflac Say-on-Pay episode?

3. How did Aflac's corporate communications team extend favorable national business media coverage over a period of nearly two years based on a single corporate announcement?

4. Regarding corporate reputation, what are the lasting effects of such a flurry of positive business media coverage?

5. Why did the corporate communications team insist that the CEO be the lead spokesperson on this initiative? Why not the CFO? Or the COO?

# Case 5-3 Money Smart Week®:
# Getting America to Spend Wisely

**FIGURE 5.2**   Contributed by Alejo Torres, Senior Outreach Manager, Chicago Federal Reserve Bank. This illustration was a signature piece of the 2012 MoneySmart Week campaign.

*(Continued)*

Contributed by Dr. Barb DeSanto, APR, Fellow PRSA, professor, A.Q. Miller School of Journalism and Mass Communications at Kansas State University & Alejo Torres, Senior Outreach Manager, Chicago Federal Reserve Bank, Chicago, Illinois.

September 2008 was a month that really brought together the state of the U.S. economy and personal finances. Americans all felt the aftershocks in the form of lost jobs, mortgage foreclosures, retirement and pension growth losses, and the realization that retirement plans and dreams had changed forever. They heard the nation's huge investment banks and some corporations admit they were in dire straits and needed millions of federal bailout dollars. The words "recession" and "depression" were daily media fare.

A crisis of confidence developed that continued to plague national recovery efforts. Job creation, rebuilding the housing market, and stabilizing America's credit rating dominated a world in financial disarray. For individuals, money, retirement planning, job security, savings, managing credit, and paying off debt were everyday worrisome conversation topics. A 2012 Gallup Poll[1] found that the number-one worry of 55 percent of Americans with incomes below $75,000 was jobs and unemployment. The second most reported worry was the continued decline and instability of the U.S. economy (Gallup, January 2012)

## How Americans Behaved Differently

Americans' financial behavior following the 2008 meltdown shows some interesting effects. For example, America's primary financial philosophy is grounded in capitalism, which includes private ownership of business, making money, and a competitive market place as unfettered as possible by regulations. Individuals' personal finance is also a feature of capitalistic economies; This means that markets grow when people buy products and services. Therefore, Americans' rates of saving, debt reduction, and spending are constant

topics in the media as well as in personal conversations.

One of the nation's leading financial news services, Bloomberg.com,[2] reported that Americans doubled their savings rate to an average of 4.8 percent in the two years after 2008. However, consumers then began to expand their spending, which pushed the savings rate down. Several factors contributed to this decrease in personal saving: (1) Unemployed people had to dip into their savings to survive, and (2) the Federal Reserve's policy of keeping interest rates at historic lows helped consumers decide to spend rather than save to accounts that yielded almost no interest.

The bottom line, and a potential silver lining, in this scenario is that Americans are generally very conservative and cautious about spending money; are wary, unsure, and confused about how to wisely save money and plan for retirement; and are educating themselves in many different ways about money.

## The Role of Federal Reserve Banks

Throughout American history, bank panics and financial crises have been common, with the panics that led to bank failures and bankrupt business hitting an all-time high in the late 1800s and early 1900s. In 1913, Congress passed the Federal Reserve Act that established 12 Federal Reserve banks and 25 branches responsible for ". . . supervising and regulating certain financial institutions and activities, for providing banking services to depository institutions and the federal government, and for ensuring that consumers receive adequate information and fair treatment in their business with the banking system" (Federal Reserve Web site).[3]

Historically, the 12 Federal Reserve districts operate as independent entities, because a large part of their charge is to address the

---

[1] Jeffrey M. Jones, "U.S. Financial Worries Rival Those of 1992 Worry about Job Loss Up to 34%," January 25, 2012. Retrieved from http://www.gallup.com/poll/152180/financial-worries-rival-1992.aspx.

[2] Timothy R. Homan, "Slump Taught Profligate Americans Value of Saving: Economy," April 20, 2012. Retrieved from http://www.bloomberg.com/news/2012-04-20/recession-taught-americans-value-of-saving-economy-correct-.html

[3] Federal Reserve Board of Governors. Retrieved from http://www.federalreserve.gov/

regional and local economic and financial needs of the areas they serve. The 12 districts meet at regular intervals in Washington, D.C., to share information and inform each other about specific issues that impact their districts, such as weather calamities, business development, and unemployment numbers. Similarly, each district develops its own community education and outreach programs, and like most entities in a capitalist society, is protective of information, ideas, and reputation.

The Chicago Federal Reserve Bank was the first to recognize the need for community financial education well before the 2008 financial crisis when it created and carried out its first Money Smart Week® in 2002. Little did the Chicago Fed (as it's routinely referred to) realize how important this week would grow to be.

## The Chicago Fed's Money Smart Week® Development

In July 2001, members of the Chicago Fed's Money Smart Advisory Council, a diverse group of more than 40 Chicago-area organizations working together to promote personal financial literacy, agreed to share resources and ideas to achieve greater public awareness of financial programs and services available in Chicago. The event created was Money Smart Week®, six days of focused presentations by community groups, financial institutions, government agencies, educational organizations, and financial experts, all designed with the goal of helping consumers learn to manage their personal finances better. The event's objectives included helping consumers become aware of financial information sources, bringing different organizations together, and mentoring these organizations to work together to help share their financial expertise—without spending a lot of money themselves.

## The First Money Smart Week®

April is financial literacy month, and the advisory council saw that month as a natural link to creating a week of financial education

events in its home area of Chicago and through its branch Federal Reserve Bank in Detroit. The first year, the Chicago Fed had to solicit partners to create and deliver pilot events and seminars. Schools and libraries were sought as partners, because they had the physical space to accommodate people. One of the challenges for the Chicago Fed was financing the week's event. (Because Federal Reserve banks are quasi-governmental agencies, they cannot ask for money, seek sponsorships, or raise funds. They can, however, accept in-kind donations and ad hoc sponsorship monies for dedicated events.) So, finding community partners with available space to host the events was essential, as were the partnerships the Chicago Fed has developed with Allstate Insurance and the *Chicago Sun-Times* to be included in the *Sun-Time*'s annual financial education for kids newspaper insert. Likewise, finding qualified community presenters required the Chicago Fed to persuade individuals that this was a corporate social responsibility opportunity. The cardinal rule for all presenters since the first Money Smart Week® is NO selling, just education and information.

Money Smart Week® grew slowly from 2002 through 2007. The program did not need a physical city or Federal Reserve branch bank to be successful. Events could be held in any type of community that had a Money Smart Week® planning team. In Wisconsin, by 2012, one Money Smart Week® planning team had grown to 50 teams. In 2007, Iowa, Indiana, and downstate Illinois all piloted statewide programs.

## A Triggering Event

The financial meltdown of 2008 was most certainly an event that public relations pioneer practitioner and educator Pat Jackson would identify as one of his iconic "triggering events," a set of circumstances and events that immediately grabs people's attention and affects their behaviors. The Chicago Fed Money Smart Week® program would agree. It received an avalanche of calls asking, "How can we get

*(Continued)*

onboard with Money Smart Week®?" Personal finance awareness had arrived.

The intense interest in the Chicago Fed's Money Smart Week® model was both a blessing and a curse. The Chicago Fed was able to bring new states and communities under its Money Smart Week® umbrella as partners. However, many other states and cities, primarily in other Federal Reserve districts, tried to copy the Money Smart Week® on their own terms, creating their own logos, Web sites, and program offerings ranging from the established week to month-long programs, which created confusion about what the original Money Smart Week® program was and, more importantly, could have had a negative impact on the quality of the Chicago Fed's groundbreaking program. The Chicago Fed's strategic thinking and planning resulted in three activities that helped it solidify its leadership position in community financial education:

1. First Money Smart Week® leadership conference
2. National partnership with the American Library Association (ALA)
3. National partnership with the Visa credit card company.

To preserve the integrity of its program, the Chicago Fed, in October 2011, hosted the first Money Smart Week® leadership conference for 13 states (Colorado, Illinois, Indiana, Iowa, Michigan, Missouri, Nebraska, New Jersey, Oregon, Texas, Washington, West Virginia, and Wisconsin) involved in Money Smart Week® programs.

The conference had two goals: (1) to help states understand and value their relationship in the multistate financial education campaign developed by the Chicago Fed and (2) to share the best practices different locations had and combine them into a best practices resource document for others participating in the leadership conference. The Chicago Fed saw the conference as a ". . . step in the right direction toward interstate communication between partners at all levels" (TORRES LETTER).[4] To facilitate that, a national steering committee of representatives from all 13 states was developed in 2012.

## Partnerships in Sync

The educational mission of the ALA fit well with the educational mission of the Chicago Fed, and the partnership with the ALA helped recognize and reinforce the Chicago Fed as the "owner" of Money Smart Week® as a national brand. The Chicago Fed found three reasons to partner with the ALA: (1) Libraries are great promoters in their communities and have great community ties; (2) libraries are in the business of educating, not selling; and (3) libraries measure things, which provides built-in measurement. "Libraries help create an ecosystem with state and regional coalitions to help form the web of communication and partnership essential to Money Smart Week®," said ALA Director of International and Chapter Relations Michael Dowling.[5]

Visa also brought its National Football League's (NFL's) Financial Football program to Money Smart Week®. Financial Football uses major league athletes in public service announcements to create awareness of financial literacy and Money Smart Week®; and other major league sports figures have joined the financial literacy effort.

## Money Smart Week® Programming and Logistics

Planning for each annual Money Smart Week® begins in May following the April national week of events. To continue to develop Money

---

[4] Alejo Torres personal correspondence.

[5] "ALA's Michael Dowling discusses first ever Money Smart Week @ your library April 2–9 EIN" Presswire. Retrieved from http://www.einpresswire.com/article/365100-ala-s-michael-dowling-discusses-first-ever-money-smart-week-your-library-april-2-9

# MONEY SMART WEEK

APRIL 21-28, 2012 | MONEYSMARTWEEK.ORG

## Money Smart Week® Logic Model

Situation: Everyone needs to know how to spend, save, and borrow money wisely to achieve their financial goals. Financial institutions, not-for-profits, schools, libraries and other community partners can join together to support financial education during Money Smart Week.

| INPUTS | OUTPUTS | | OUTCOMES – IMPACT | | |
|---|---|---|---|---|---|
| | Activities | Participation | Short term | Medium term | Longer term |
| What we invest | What we do | Who we reach | | | |
| **People**<br>Federal Reserve Staff<br><br>**Partners**<br>Money Smart Advisory Council & partners– refer to website for list of current organizational members<br><br>**Materials**<br>calendar of events, posters, inserts, bookmarks, shreds, comics, other Fed promotional materials | **Planning processes**<br>Regular meetings via telephone or in-person<br><br>**Kick-off the week** with statewide press conferences and local launches<br><br>**Capture the attention of consumers and organizations** with media stories, promotions, and advertising<br><br>**Select winners** of state and local contests<br><br>**Offer personal money management workshops, seminars, and activities** that are mostly free and open to the public. | **Residents** in the Seventh Federal Reserve District, from young people to seniors. Courses in other languages are offered in certain locations<br><br><br>**Community Partners** involved in money management education | **Participants** will:<br><br>Increase knowledge of effective money management practices and be inspired to be more engaged in their own finances<br><br>**Partners** will: Increase their knowledge & awareness of the MSW effort; improve relationships with other organizations; be aware of resources & curriculum available for teaching consumers | **Participants** will:<br><br>Adopt best practices to manage money more effectively<br><br><br><br><br><br><br>**Partners** will: Strengthen local collaborative efforts through the networking Money Smart Week affords participants. | **Participants** will:<br><br>Build long-term financial security and wealth<br><br><br><br><br><br><br>**Partners** will: Create a sustainable environment for personal financial literacy efforts in their communities |

**FIGURE 5.3**    Money Smart Week* Logic Model

Smart Week®, Senior Outreach Manager Alejo Torres created a partner kit to help regional event leaders create and implement their own events. Partners are expected to provide leadership, communicate internally and externally, possess or acquire general financial literacy knowledge, and be committed to the Chicago Fed's Money Smart Week® program. Partners include businesses, financial institutions, schools, libraries, not-for-profit organizations, government agencies, and the media. Partners register online with the Chicago Fed, thereby agreeing to the Fed's guidelines, and receive materials, updates, a copy of Money Smart Week®'s best practices, and assistance in planning their events. From October to March, Torres conducts monthly conference calls with regions, cities, counties, and communities to

*(Continued)*

help each one develop and carry out its program. Each location has a chairperson who recruits his or her own committee chairs, who handle the individual week's elements, from the essay contest to speakers and presentations. Torres also created a partner media toolkit containing general and customizable news releases, fact sheets and talking points, media coverage tips, and public service announcements. A PowerPoint presentation summarizing the previous year's activities and successes is distributed to partners to help them recruit future presenters.

The 2012 Money Smart Week® began with a series of kick-off events in different locations, followed by a week of activities, seminars, and events. More than 500 free events were offered in Chicago for all ages, ranging from sessions on unemployment and job transitioning, money management for women, and savvy shopping and bargain hunting, to healthy habits that save. Creativity is a key point in getting people interested in personal finance; this year's sessions included advanced funeral planning on-site at a funeral home; smart food shopping on-site at a supermarket that featured how to use the store's couponing system; how to survive the financial part of a divorce; and how to deal with gambling addictions.

To get children and schools involved, the Chicago Fed and its partner organizations, including Visa, sponsor a Money Smart Kid essay contest to students in grades five through eight. Students write a 300-word essay answering the year's question to win a scholarship. Essay finalists are selected to attend the Money Smart Week® kick-off at the Chicago Fed. To see the current essay question go to http://www.chicagofed.org/webpages/education/msw/index.cfm.

The Chicago Fed relies on print media for the majority of its promotions, as the serious nature of financial literacy works well with traditional media. Thirty percent of all event attendees report they learn about Money Smart Week® from printed materials. The Chicago Fed also uses street and guerilla marketing

such as Ben Franklin giving out flyers, a dollar bill character walking the streets distributing materials, and students in Money Smart Week® t-shirts. The Franklin character has generated his own following and appeared on or in various media interviews, including ones on radio.

Social media is a new venture for the Chicago Fed. Because of the conservative nature of Federal Reserve banks and each Federal Reserve district's specialized regional and local information, sharing in the open forum of social media has been slow to develop. The Chicago Fed's Facebook page is just two years old, and the entire organization has one social media person. It has no Twitter account. Building relationships with partners, however, has grown, as partner organizations have their own Facebook pages and link to the Chicago Fed's, thus creating a network. In addition to information, this network provides online analytics to keep track of current financial concerns and activities among Money Smart Week® partners and consumers.

## Proving Success: Evaluation

Just how much impact has Money Smart Week® had on financial literacy? In 2012, the Chicago Fed had more than 500 free events during Money Smart Week®, and it hoped to surpass the more than 32,000 people in the Chicago area who attended events in 2011. Torres developed a session rating sheet that presenters have attendees complete. In addition, media coverage is tracked by a national media tracking firm.

The Chicago Fed has had two measurable goals it wants to achieve: (1) to turn its regional and local coverage into more national coverage, and (2) to develop its social media plan.

## A Step Toward Enhancing Reputation

The Money Smart Week® story combines financial education and community outreach and adds a different face to a government organization that suffers from the public's lack of knowledge about what it does, as well as a somewhat negative reputation because of Americans' distrust of almost anyone involved in their finances. Working toward understanding average Americans' financial situations in all different stages of life shows that building relationships can literally pay off.

## Questions for Discussion

1. The program is evaluated by session attendees and by the extent of media coverage it receives. What would you suggest it adopts as a more behavioral evaluation?

2. Do you believe this program alone can impact the Fed's reputation or the reputation of the financial industry in general? How?

3. What social media sources would you recommend it adopt and how would you suggest they be used?

4. Does having Visa (credit card company) as a partner diminish the objectivity of Money Smart?

# Case 5-4 When Actions of a Few Can Lead to Organizational Failure; What Is PR to Do?

The advent of the 21st century brought stark changes to the world of financial trading. Technology took away much of the human control of the past and threw financial markets into turmoil again and again, due often to something often described as a "computer glitch." In addition to the ever present "glitches," however, there have been and continue to be individuals whose ethics (or lack thereof) have propelled them into behaviors that also damage the system and the companies for whom they work—with insider trading. Names such as Raj Rajaratnam, Rajat Gupta, Martha Stewart, Mark Cuban (owner of the Dallas Mavericks), Jeff Skilling (Enron), George Soros (billionaire investor) recall just a few of the scandals of the recent past. And their actions have damaged their organizations if not destroyed them entirely. It is a PR responsibility to handle these scandals. How they are dealt with often will determine whether the organization lives to fight another day.

## A Classic Case Teaches Valuable Lessons

For nearly 30 years after the enactment of the Securities Exchange Act in 1934, which prohibited manipulation and deception in the financial world, the role of public relations in stock transactions was not taken seriously by corporate management and the relevant sectors of the SEC. As a result of a landmark court case involving Texas Gulf Sulphur Company (TGS), the role of public relations changed drastically.[1] This case is definitive in understanding some of the problems and requisites in the performance of financial relations.

- At the heart of the case was a single news release drafted by a public relations consultant and the vice-president of Texas Gulf. The manner in which the news was released to the media raised questions of whether the content was deceptive.

## Precedents

Until 1942, insider trading, or using private information, had not been outlawed. Questions of integrity or ethics went largely unasked publicly until the Sherman Antitrust Act was passed in 1890. Even after the Securities Exchange Act was passed in 1934 and Rule 10b-5 was made public, the laws were not enforced and went untested for two decades.

Since the depths of the Great Depression, the SEC has tried to prevent insider trading. Insiders—anyone with facts or news not yet released to the general investing public—have a distinct advantage until that knowledge is available to the public. Thus, insiders are in a position to "cash in" on that information to the detriment of the investor who might buy or sell shares absent the information known only to insiders. The Securities Exchange Act of 1934 was written to forbid insiders from benefiting from information unique to them.

## The TGS Case

The TGS scenario started with some late 1950s activities related to mineral exploration in

---

[1] The name was subsequently changed to Texasgulf. In 1981, the company was acquired by the French corporation Elf Aquitaine, Inc., for $5 billion and then purchased by Potash Corporation of Saskatchewan in 1995 for more than $800 million.

Section 10 of the 1934 Securities Exchange Act, and Rule 10b-5, promulgated by the SEC in 1942, state that persons may not "make any untrue statement of material fact or...omit to state a material fact" that would have the effect of misleading the public in connection with the purchase or sale of any security.

*A precondition would be that a person did, in fact, possess information whose disclosure or nondisclosure could have an effect on the value of a security. Thus, "insider" information, the disclosure of such information, and the purchase or sale of securities are mutually involved. Private gain is implicit.*

eastern Canada.[2] Aerial geophysical surveys over a large expanse of land were made until potential drill sites were selected. The people who participated in the surveys included:

- **Richard D. Mollison,** a mining engineer and later a vice-president of TGS
- **Walter Holyk,** a TGS geologist
- **Richard H. Clayton,** an electrical engineer and geophysicist
- **Kenneth H. Darke,** a geologist

They selected a segment of marshland near Timmins, Ontario, that was promising enough to trigger a survey on the ground. This land was not owned by TGS. One of the first problems was getting title or drilling rights via an option from the owners. Contact with the owner of part of the desired area was first made in 1961.

Eventually, in mid-1963, some land was acquired and drilling began in November. On visual inspection, the sample—obtained by diamond-core drilling—seemed to contain sulfides of copper and zinc.

On Sunday, November 12, 1963, Darke telephoned his boss, Walter Holyk, at his home in Connecticut with an optimistic report. Holyk called his boss, Richard D. Mollison, nearby in Old Greenwich, and later that evening called Dr. Charles F. Fogarty, TGS executive vice-president, also nearby in Rye, New York. Holyk, Mollison, and Fogarty subsequently went to the site—called the Kidd 55 tract—to see for themselves. The group concluded that the core was indeed promising and should be shipped to Utah for chemical assay.

## A Lid on the Information

Pending the results, they wanted the acquisition program for other desired land in the area to proceed as quickly as possible. They knew obtaining rights might be difficult. To facilitate matters, TGS president Claude O. Stephens instructed the group to keep the unconfirmed results a secret . . . even to other officers, directors, and employees of the company. Following traditional prospecting and camouflage customs, the first hole was marked

*(Continued)*

---

[2] The narrative and facts that follow were gleaned from some of the same sources that formed public opinion during the period when the events in this case took place. Among the sources are a complete text of the court's opinion in *SEC v. TGS,* 446 F2d 1301 (2nd Cir. 1966); an article by John Brooks. "Annals of Finance: A Reasonable Amount of Time," in *New Yorker* magazine, November 9, 1968 (and from a critique of the John Brooks piece provided by TGS public relations consultant William H. Dinsmore); *The Wall Street Journal* articles, "Big Boards Expands, Tightens Standards on Timely Disclosure of Corporate News." July 18, 1968; "Texas Gulf Ruled to Lack Due Diligence in Minerals Case," February 9, 1970; "Rise Detected in Use of Inside Information to Make Stock Profits," October 31, 1972; "Most Executives Say They Won't Give Insider Data to Analysts," August 16, 1968; "New Structure Prompt Firms to Revise Policies on Disclosure of News." October 9, 1968; and "Rules on Disclosure Don't Bar Exclusive Interview, Cohen Says," October 9, 1968; and "No Comment—A Victim of Disclosure," *New York Times,* August 25, 1968. Also helpful was an analysis provided to officers of Motorola, Inc., by its legal counsel, entitled "Corporate Information Releases." We also drew on several references in issues of the *Public Relations Journal, PR News, pr reporter,* and other business and professional publications. An appeals brief for the defendants was requested of attorneys but was not received.

and concealed, and another one, *barren*, was drilled and left in sight.

## Calendar of Events: 1963–1964

- November. Seven TGS employees were the "keepers" of significant information. In the same month drilling began, Fogarty, Clayton, Mollison, and Mrs. Holyk bought TGS stock totaling 2,050 shares at $17 to $18 a share.
- One of the most famous instances of insider trading was Charles F. Fogarty's purchase of TGS shares during 1963–64. Fogarty, knew that the company had discovered a rich mineral lode in Ontario that it couldn't publicize before concluding leases for mineral rights. In the meantime, Fogarty purchased 3,100 shares.[3] His "investment" yielded about $300,000 profit in 2006 dollars.
- December. The chemical assays of the test core came back, largely confirming the TGS estimate of copper and zinc content, as well as discovering a silver content. TGS scheduled the resumption of drilling in March.
- January–February. Inside informers and those they gave "tips" to owned 8,235 shares. At this point there were also 12,300 calls (options to buy a specified amount of stock at a fixed price) to buy TGS stock.
- February. The company issued stock options to 26 of its officers and other employees, five of whom were the insiders on Kidd 55. The option committee and the company's board of directors had not been made aware of the find.
- March 31. The company resumed drilling.

After further drilling of three more holes by April 10, there was evidence of a body of commercially minable ore. (The accuracy of the estimate later came into contention between SEC experts and TGS officials.)

## Leaks and Rumors

By this time, there had been enough activity at the Kidd site that rumors of a possible major ore strike were circulating in Canada. A press item on February 27, in the *Northern Miner,* reported rumors of TGS "obtaining some fat ore indications" from its work north of Timmins. On March 31, TGS invited a representative of the publication to visit and see the exposed, barren site for himself, and a date was set for April 20. Then, on April 9, the *Toronto Daily Star* and the *Globe and Mail* carried stories. The *Globe and Mail* headline read, "Wild Speculation Spree on TGS: Gigantic Copper Strike Rumored." The phone lines and the conference rooms at TGS headquarters, 200 Park Avenue, New York, were busy on April 10. According to John Brooks, writing later in the *New Yorker* magazine:

> President Stephens was sufficiently concerned about the rumors to seek advice from one of his most trusted associates, Thomas S. Lamont, senior member of the Texas Gulf board . . . and bearer of a name long venerated on Wall Street. Stephens asked what Lamont thought ought to be done about the "exaggerated" reports.
>
> "As long as they stay in the Canadian press," Lamont replied, "I think you might be able to live with them." However, he added, if they should reach the papers in the United States, it might be well to give the press an announcement that would set the record straight and avoid undue gyrations in the stock market.[4]

[3] David D. Haddock, "Insider Trading: The Concise Encyclopedia of Insider Trading," in *The Concise Encyclopedia of Economics.*

[4] J. Brooks, *Business Adventures,* New York: Weybright and Talley Division, David McKay. Originally published in "Annals of Finance," *New Yorker* magazine, November 9, 1968.

## Public Relations Called In

The stories in Canada were picked up and printed on Saturday, April 11, by such U.S. media as *The New York Times* and *The New York Herald Tribune,* with the rumor of a major copper strike. Robert Carroll, a Doremus & Co. public relations consultant, helped Dr. Fogarty, the executive vice-president, draft a news release over the weekend, and it was released at 3:00 P.M. on Sunday, April 12, to appear in Monday morning's papers.

## News Media and Stock Market React

The Monday *New York Herald Tribune,* an important financial medium, headlining its story, "Copper Rumor Deflated," quoted passages from the TGS press release and hedged on the optimism in its earlier story out of Canada.

On the New York Stock Exchange, TGS stock price on April 13 ranged between $30^7/_8$ and 32, closing at $30^7/_8$. When compared with an $18 high in November, the $30 price represented a 65 percent rise in five months. Meanwhile, the internal, nonpublic reports from Timmins became so rosy that an official announcement confirming a major ore strike was readied for April 16.

There was a problem in the synchronization of communications. A reporter for the *Northern Miner,* a Canadian trade journal, had interviewed Mollison, Holyk, and Darke and had prepared an article confirming a 10-million-ton strike for publication in his April 16 issue. The story, submitted to Mollison, was returned to the reporter, unamended, on April 15. Separately, a statement drafted substantially by Mollison was given to the Ontario minister of mines for release on the air in Canada at 11:00 P.M. on the 15th, but was not released until 9:40 A.M. on the 16th. Also, separately, in the United States an official statement announcing a strike of at least 25 million tons ($2^1/_2$ times the Canadian trade-journal story) was read to the financial press in New York from 10:00 to 10:15 A.M. on April 16, following a 9:00 A.M. directors' meeting. The news showed up on the Dow Jones tape at 10:54 and on Merrill Lynch's private wire 25 minutes earlier at 10:29, another peculiar circumstance. *(Possibly, the "news" was not as obvious to Dow Jones as it was to Merrill Lynch. Possibly the "news" was given to Merrill Lynch earlier.)*

## The Trial and Appeals

An SEC complaint indicated that company executives had used privileged information to trade in the company's stock before the information had been disclosed publicly. In May, the complaint was argued before Judge Dudley B. Bonsal of the Southern District Court at Foley Square, New York. He ruled in favor of all the defendants except David M. Crawford and Richard H. Clayton, who had engaged in TGS stock purchase after the first press release on April 12 and before the second one, on April 16, was public knowledge.

The lower-court judge dismissed the case against the defendants who had purchased stock prior to the evening of April 9, on the grounds that information they possessed was not "material," that their purchases or tips to others were educated guesses or hunches, and that executives should be encouraged to own shares in their own company. As for trading by insiders following the April 16 directors' meeting, and whether they had waited a "reasonable time" for the disclosure to become public knowledge, the judge decided the controlling factor was the time at which the release was handed to the press, not when it appeared on the Dow Jones stock market tape.

## Public Relations Involvement

The trial court judge gave a big lift to the public relations profession because a public relations consultant had been involved. The judge decided that because corporate executives had sought the advice of public relations counsel, they had exercised reasonable business judgment.

*(Continued)*

## The Press Release: April 12, 1964

New York—The following statement was made today by Dr. Charles F. Fogarty, executive vice-president of TGS, in regard to the company's drilling operations near Timmins, Ontario, Canada. Dr. Fogarty said:

> During the past few days, the exploration activities of Texas Gulf Sulphur in the area of Timmins, Ontario, have been widely reported in the press, coupled with rumors of a substantial copper discovery there. These reports exaggerate the scale of operations, and mention plans and statistics of size and grade of ore that are without factual basis and have evidently originated by speculation of people not connected with TGS.
>
> The facts are as follows. TGS has been exploring in the Timmins area for six years as part of its overall search in Canada and elsewhere for various minerals—lead, copper, zinc, etc. During the course of this work, in Timmins as well as in eastern Canada, TGS has conducted exploration entirely on its own, without the participation by others. Numerous prospects have been investigated by geophysical means and a large number of selected ones have been core-drilled. These cores are sent to the United States for assay and detailed examination as a matter of routine and on advice of expert Canadian legal counsel. No inferences as to grade can be drawn from this procedure.
>
> Most of the areas drilled in Eastern Canada have revealed either barren pyrite or graphite without value; a few have resulted in discoveries of small or marginal sulfide ore bodies.
>
> Recent drilling on one property near Timmins has led to preliminary indications that more drilling would be required for proper evaluation of this prospect. The drilling done to date has not been conclusive, but the statements made by many outside quarters are unreliable and include information and figures that are not available to TGS.
>
> The work done to date has not been sufficient to reach definite conclusions and any statement as to size and grade of ore would be premature and possibly misleading. When we have progressed to the point where reasonable and logical conclusions can be made, TGS will issue a definite statement to its stockholders and the public in order to clarify the Timmins project.[5]

As for the news release itself, a major point of contention in the hearings was whether it was encouraging or discouraging to investors. A Canadian mining security specialist said that he had had a Dow Jones (broad tape) report that TGS "didn't have anything basically." A Midwest Stock Exchange specialist in TGS was "concerned about his long position in the stock" after reading the release. TGS defense attorneys contended that the financial media had been at fault in not publishing the full text of the controversial release. The trial court stated only, "While in retrospect, the press release may appear gloomy or incomplete, that does not make it misleading or deceptive on the basis of the facts then known."

## The Complaint Moved Up the Court Ladder

The SEC appealed all dismissals, and the case was argued in the court of appeals. In essence, the appellate decision reversed the lower court's findings on the important issues,

---

[5] From the appeals court opinion, *SEC v. TGS*, 446 F.2d, 1301 (2nd Cir. 1966).

except for the convictions of Crawford and Clayton, which were affirmed.

The case was remanded to Judge Bonsal of the lower court for the "appropriate remedies." He:

- Ruled that TGS and its executives failed to exercise "due diligence" in the April 12 news release.
- Ordered certain defendants to turn over to TGS profits made by trading on inside information.
- Issued injunctions against Crawford and Clayton, barring them from further purchases or sales based on "undisclosed" information.
- Denied a request by the SEC that TGS, as a corporation, be enjoined from issuing false, misleading, or inadequate information, pointing out that there was no "reasonable likelihood of further violations."
- Because there was no "reasonable likelihood," did not issue injunctions against Darke, who had left the company; Holyk, chief geologist; Huntington, a TGS attorney; Fogarty, then president of TGS; and Mollison, a vice-president.
- Noted that Coates, a director, had paid $26,250 in an approved settlement, including $9,675 said to be profits to several "tippees," and that Crawford returned "at his cost" the stock he purchased.
- Assessed paybacks of $41,795 from Darke personally and $48,404 for his "tippees," $35,663 from Holyk, $20,010 from Clayton, and $2,300 from Huntington.[6]

### Some of the Echoes

In the immediate wake of the TGS settlement, several predictable measures were taken to avoid a repetition of what had occurred. Publicly owned corporations reexamined their practices of disclosing financial information to be sure they were in compliance. The New York Stock Exchange expanded its policies regarding timely disclosure and issued new pages for its company manual.

Financial news media, somewhat defensively, placed responsibility for the published information on the corporate sources of such information without permitting those sources to control what was published. While insisting on the media's right to edit financial releases according to the news values perceived in them, some comments by financial editors suggested that corporate practitioners constituted obstacles rather than facilitators in getting out all the relevant facts.

Corporate financial relations people, for their part, undertook with notable success to exercise a more important and outspoken role in corporate decisions regarding the "what, when, and how" of significant information to be released publicly via press or controlled media. This meant a seat in management councils for financial relations people when decisions were made regarding whether a particular item of information was newsworthy and whether it was capable of influencing the value of the corporation's shares in the stock market. This also meant attending meetings with groups of analysts where material information might inadvertently be introduced, and calling for immediate broad disclosure.

The trade literature abounded with analyses of the risks and requirements implied by the TGS case. Financial public relations was coming of age.

### Relevance to Public Relations Practice

With the dollar stakes involved in the stock market so large today as to seem almost

(*Continued*)

---

[6] Extracted from the opinion rendered in 65 Civ. 1182 by Judge Dudley J. Bonsal, United States District Court, Southern District of New York, February 6, 1970.

fictional, the day-by-day practice of public relations may seem remote or unrelated. It is neither.

Every large corporation, bank, brokerage firm, charitable foundation, and other financial institution has public relations counsel or staff. The professionals providing counsel and implementing the communications involved in financial affairs can qualify legally as "insiders." They can be found guilty, as individuals, of knowingly releasing financial information that is false, deceptive, or misleading or of trading on privileged information. In court cases, it has been evident that financial relations practitioners are not in the clear by pleading "I only did (or said) what the client told me to." Practitioners must make reasonable efforts to verify facts disseminated. "Hold harmless" clauses no longer constitute a shield.

Although TGS didn't create the financial relations industry, its aftershocks certainly drew clear guidelines for practitioners. A law that had been on the books since 1934 now had some teeth, and those who understood the new circumstances were sure to be more valuable to their employers than ever before.

Perhaps more important, however, were the precedents established by the TGS rulings. From that day forward, every publicly held company knew (or should have known) that the SEC requires:

- Full and complete disclosure of every material fact in a timely manner
- A complete ban on insider trading
- Corporate and personal responsibility of public relations counsel

These tenets would be the backbone of what is now the highest-paying segment of the public relations profession—investor relations.

### Questions for Discussion

1. What if the TGS case happened today? How might things have been handled differently with today's technology? Do all the recent "insider training" scandals make this case seem less or more problematic?
2. Think about a different situation. Suppose that a weekly financial e-mail newsletter "Tips and Rumors" regularly got into some people's hands a day before each issue of the magazine came out, and some of the stocks mentioned were suddenly traded heavily and run up in price. Suppose, also, it turned out that a clerical person in the magazine's public relations department privately had been sending an advance rough draft of the column as a favor to a friend at a brokerage firm. Neither that clerk nor the friend at a brokerage firm traded or made any profit. As you understand SEC's Rule 10b, who is legally liable? Put another way, where does common sense tell you the responsibility for the privacy of material facts belongs?
3. Objectively, was the initial TGS news release about the ore strike at Timmins misleading on the basis of what was known *at the time the news was released?* Or did it go only as far as a cautious, prudent management was willing to go for fear of overstating and getting in trouble for that? Or, what else does your objective evaluation say might have been the determining consideration?

## PROBLEM 5-A   CAN AN ANNUAL REPORT PLEASE EVERYONE?

Preparation of the annual report for a publicly owned corporation is probably the most frustrating, if not the most difficult, communications task generally assigned to the corporate communications staff. This statement is true whether the job is handled internally or with the aid of outside counsel.

As the management "report card" aimed at those who own the company as shareholders and for those in the financial community who can influence others for or against owning shares, it is an ultrasensitive and personal document. In many cases it is an ego trip for the head of the firm, for the top financial officer, or for officers hoping one day to become CEO.

The top official, when the company has had a good year, both competitively and in operating results, may want a lavish four-color booklet. The senior financial officer may prefer one or two colors (the second being silver or gold), demonstrating prudence as well as success. The heads of operating divisions, wanting to broaden the circulation to customers and prospects, may want lavish product or service pictures, particularly of the products or services of their particular division or subsidiary. The director of personnel will probably want pictures showing how happy the employees are at their jobs. Systems analysts will want their latest cost-reducing equipment shown. If the corporation is international in scope, the export department will want to emphasize "hands across the seas."

Shareholders who may receive dividends of $1 per share of stock may receive an annual report that costs $1 to $2 per copy to produce, not counting the time to put into it by executives and members of the communications staff. In many corporations, thinking about the next year's report starts as soon as one year's annual report has come out and been distributed, feedback has been received, and the annual meeting of shareholders has taken place. Given the high vanity quotient involved; the diversity of views within a corporation; the inherent "competition" for attention, recognition, and prominence among corporate divisions; and possibly financial results that are not the best, public relations has its work cut out for it.

Persuasion, compromise, and reconciliation are needed. See how you would go about this task: Select a corporation and acquire an annual report. Assume that you have to plan for the next year's report.

1. What questions will you ask and what research will you do before you start your basic strategic plan for the report?
2. Your research indicates the desirability of some major changes in the content and design of the report. Draw up a formal outline of your approach, including:
   • Overall theme in words and graphics (with your rationale)
   • Table of contents indicating obligatory information
   • Preliminary concepts for cover and layout
   • Photography needs or other visual techniques with costs
   • Printing costs, including number of copies
   • A timetable with deadlines

3. How will you suggest reducing the cycle time required to produce the annual report?
4. What would be the pros and cons of an electronic option? With or without a print version?

## PROBLEM 5-B  HERE COMES THAT MAN NADER, AGAIN

The article "Ralph Nader's group nominates 10 companies for Hall of Shame" appeared in the national newspaper *USA Today*. Companies earned a place on the list based on their "unethical conduct, narrowness of vision, lack of foresight, and unwaveringly steady focus on the short-term bottom line."

You are newly hired, a business school graduate with an emphasis on public relations, in the shareholder relations section of a department in one of the 10 companies named in the news story.

After the story appeared, there were a few well-chosen expletives expressed in your company regarding Nader and his associates, but there was no request from senior financial officers or top management that any responsive or reciprocal action be taken. Your immediate boss asked nothing of you, and the vice-president for public relations made no request of him. The position of your employer, apparently, is much the same as the "cool-it" posture of GM when Nader's Campaign GM was on. There is a new development, however.

A letter has come in, addressed to Director of Shareholder Relations. The letter includes these passages:

My husband was a successful businessman. His success is the reason I am able to live comfortably on my investments, one of which is ownership of 100,000 shares of your stock. I might say that I own more of your stock than some of the people on your board of directors.

Having more of my money invested in your stock than some of your directors who get paid fees concerns me somewhat. But my major concern is that you do things that invite attention and distrust because they appear unethical, illegal, short-sighted, or just plain greedy, and contrary to what investors and consumers are entitled to expect. Isn't this a legitimate reason to question the justification for the huge salaries, bonuses, and stock options you give yourselves?

*(Continued)*

I know I have the alternative of removing my funds from the company and investing them elsewhere. The news article, however, suggests that the standards you set for your conduct, and your performance, are typical of all big business. That leaves me no place to go except to foreign businesses, or to government with demands that they regulate you more strictly, or take over your industry and run it for the benefit of everyone. Frankly, your speeches complaining about regulation leave me a bit cold.

Isn't it high time that those in business take the lead in self-discipline so that government and everybody else will have real leadership to follow?

This letter has been passed down the line, and it stops with you. The note of instruction on it reads: "We may get a bundle of letters pretty much like this one. Upstairs [the president's office] they want a reply, to be signed by the president. Let's see what you can come up with."

1. What will you do before you fire up your computer to write the letter?
2. Write a draft of the letter with a cover sheet explaining to the president the rationale for your approach.

## PROBLEM 5-C   PLANNING THE ANNUAL MEETING WITH A TWIST

You work for the corporate communications department of a major corporation in California. Your duties vary on what projects come up, but your focus as of late has been internal. As a function of your job, your department is responsible for arranging the annual meeting of shareholders. Your corporation has decided to merge with another leader in the industry, and the company has decided to release this information at the annual shareholder meeting.

Planning the annual meeting is a large task to take on, but with the added information that will need to be communicated you realize that you have a huge job on your hands. This merger will have a significant effect on many aspects of the corporation. First, it will be a larger operation. As you are already a leader in the industry, this merger will put your company at the top and possibly put it in the *Fortune* 500. Second, the company will expand its services and products and will have to make changes internally to support the new business that it will be taking on. Job descriptions will need to be changed as well as departments consolidated so that they may become more cohesive and focus on their new tasks. Third, many jobs will be eliminated from both companies to complete the final merger. Some of the company's shareholders are employees; some of them might lose their jobs in this process.

Knowing all of this, how will you communicate this information to shareholders at the annual meeting? Would you make a presentation to employees separate from shareholders and allow them to voice their concerns? What media would you use to relay this information to the public outside of the company? In what sequence would you release this information?

Public relations practitioners often play the role of interpreter or mediator in situations like these. What recommendations will you make to the CEO that might help her present this news in a positive light?

# 6

# Consumer Relations

"Who are the three most important publics?" asks an old trick question. The answer is "customers, customers, and customers." If you don't succeed in attracting them and then building continuing relationships with them, you'll be out of business and nothing else will matter.

During the rise of marketing as a cure-all in the mid-1980s, this view frequently prevailed in corporations. Hospitals, universities, public agencies, and even churches adopted marketing as a response to the increasing competition for people's interest and dollars. On balance, the marketing revolution was helpful to many organizations—particularly large or very successful companies, which had often forgotten that it is the customer who pays the bill, and to nonprofit entities, which often treated users of services as a nuisance to their routine, rather than the reason for their existence.

Ironically, while this trend reestablished a key point of public relations philosophy, it sometimes pushed public relations departments into a role secondary to marketing. A much-debated point was whether public relations is a part of marketing or vice versa or whether they are both essential strategic services and thus equal in importance.

The question was prominent because marketing became a part of organizations that traditionally did not use marketing concepts. Hospitals in particular began marketing their "products" in an effort to gain their share of the health-care market. Their patients began making it clear they did not want to be sold health care, and hospitals retreated—putting the function back into perspective.

Marketing and public relations share some fundamental concepts. These include analyzing market opportunities (research), selecting target markets (publics), developing a marketing mix (communication and action plan), and managing the marketing effort (evaluation).

The sharing of these concepts illustrates the close working relationship of the two fields. Despite these similarities, keep in mind that marketing is ultimately product-specific or service-specific. Public relations is a much broader discipline. *pr reporter* illustrated the differences, stating that public relations as a strategy does four things marketing cannot do:

- Public relations is concerned about internal relations and publics.
- Public relations cares about noncustomer external publics and the environment in which the organization operates.

- Public relations operates on the policies of human nature (what makes the individual tick), whereas marketing focuses on consumer behavior (purchasing and economics, often expressed in number-crunching research).
- Public relations may work to stabilize or change public opinion in areas other than products.[1]

In the 1990s and into the 21st century, the functions have come close together, as demonstrated by the dominant customer relations strategy: relationship marketing. As the name suggests, this approach adopts public relations principles such as personalized, one-on-one dialogue regarding marketing of products and services.

The buyer–seller relationship concerns every public relations department and every public relations counselor. Ideally, the role of the public relations counselor is to help create conditions of understanding so that the objectives of sellers can be attained by satisfying needs of consumers. As a landmark conference between public relations and marketing leaders concluded,[2] public relations must both (1) help motivate purchases and (2) create a hospitable environment for the organization to sell product and services.

## HISTORICAL BACKGROUND

Starting in the late 1940s, following an almost universal base of hardship during the Great Depression, consumer "wants" were for material possessions, labor-saving devices, convenience, ease, and luxury. To producers and sellers, these were seen as consumer "needs." In the succeeding decades of increasing prosperity and affluence, it followed that if a product or service could be sold, it "deserved" to be sold. If a desire for it could be induced, it was what the people "wanted." Wants translated with adept interpretation into needs. A hula-hoop, a Frisbee, a pair of jogging shoes became "needs" for wholesome recreation or health.

For product and service sellers, the 1950s were happy times, as they were for marketing, promotion, advertising, and publicity personnel. The economy was based and dependent on increasing consumption. Trading in one's car annually, building a summer home, discarding clothes for each fashion change, engaging in fads, buying on time with credit cards, maintaining a big mortgage, stocking a basement with appliances, using hair tonics and electric shavers—these were "marks of distinction." Buying was promoted as though it were patriotic. Communications served these times well, especially when television came on the scene to give printed and audio media tough competition.

With this set of conditions, it was inevitable that sellers would stretch the boundaries of quality, service, and safety in products and services. They would exceed the limits of truth and accuracy in their claims and would abuse the privilege of using the public media. On occasion, through inadequate concern for quality, they would kill and injure some people and alienate many others.[3]

The first significant government restraint in the 1960s came in the Kefauver–Harris Drug Amendments in 1962. Through the decade, other federal laws were passed, involving abuses in packaging, labeling, product safety, drugs, and truth in lending. Regulatory agencies became

---

[1] *pr reporter,* Vol. 27, January 2, 1984, p. 3.

[2] "A Challenge to the Calling: Public Relations Colloquium 1989" held at San Diego State University on January 24, 1989, sponsored by Nuffer Smith & Tucker.

[3] For further insight, see Earl W. Kintner, *A Primer on the Law of Deceptive Practices,* New York: Macmillan, 1971.

more active and aggressive.[4] A presidential assistant was appointed to represent and help protect the consumer. A tough adversarial relationship with business was established.

Meanwhile, business approaches to the consumer were shifting. "Share of mind" superseded "share of market" for many national product advertisers. Programs spoke more about "benefits" and "value." Publicists were engaged more in concepts to sell "an idea," "industrial statesmanship," "a good company to do business with," or the "philosophy" or "personality" rather than the sheer pleasure of owning the product or enjoying the service.

In public relations programming, public service was increasingly hitched to marketing. Recipes were provided for home economists; commemorative events were tied to products; dinosaur models went on exhibit; cars were tested by the loan of one to each family in a small town; a blimp roamed over public events, aiding national telecasts. The introduction of a new line of sports equipment endorsed by a celebrated athlete might be accompanied by a personal appearance. On tour, the athlete might sign autographs in stores, be interviewed by local writers on controversial sports subjects, be photographed at bedside in children's hospitals or wards, and conduct free clinics on sportsmanship at a local school.

- Today, this approach has become the rule: People want to be *served,* not sold.

Further business response to growing consumer protectionism and advocacy came in the activation of ombudspersons, 800 numbers, understandable warranty statements, devices for improved listenership and response, calls to customers to check satisfaction after a purchase, quick settlement of injury claims, and product recalls. This attitude elevated the importance of public relations and its implementation, but it did not stop all the abuses.

Television commercials were louder by several decibels than entertainment broadcasts. Among the largest advertisers were makers of products that were the most profitable but among the least necessary to human survival or uplift—cosmetics, liquor, and tobacco, to name a few. Going into the 1970s, consumer disenchantment with sellers, their wares, and their words expressed itself as more awareness of alternatives and here and there a boycott.

## THE LINK BETWEEN REPUTATION AND MARKETING

In the 1980s, a new rash of crises shared the front page; they involved violence, drugs, greed, pollution, and lack of integrity. Business has adjusted to this situation. Advertising and publicity talk about reforestation, human dignity, education, rehabilitation, and "caring." Projects and speeches focus on safety, health, and the minority, neglected, and disabled groups in society.

There are other problems. Conglomeration and divestiture tarnish traditional identities. What happens when Armour, not only a prestigious name on a pound of bacon but a landmark at the Chicago stockyards and a family intertwined for generations in the culture and society of the city, is swallowed into a bus company, also with a well-known name, Greyhound? Or when Twinkies becomes a product of International Telephone and Telegraph?

Multinationalism is another matter. Does anything significant happen in consumer relationships when a company that has proclaimed its "loyal American heritage" goes abroad to manufacture because wages are lower?

Savvy consumers make buying decisions based on how companies run their businesses, according to a 1995 survey by public relations firm Porter Novelli.[5] Five major influences on

---

[4] Early cases of FTC intervention and decisions include Carter's Little Liver Pills in the 1950s and Geritol in the 1960s. There are many more recent cases.

[5] *pr reporter,* October 2, 1995, pp. 3–4.

buying habits were (1) product quality, (2) the company's method of handling consumer complaints, (3) the way a company handles a crisis in which it *is* at fault, (4) challenges by a government agency about product safety, and (5) accusation of illegal or unethical trading practices. Communication with consumers began moving from a product or service focus to information about how the organization operates and what values guide its decisions.

The first decade of the 21st century saw reputation become an even stronger element in the marketing mix. A sophisticated new generation of consumers, subjected to a constant barrage of marketing since their youth, now look intently for real distinctions between competing products.

### Role of Social Media in Consumerism

This has exploded recently as social media has taken hold. Now the consuming public no longer has to wait for a mass media outlet to inform consumers about potentially dangerous or risky products. Anyone with an interest and passion can establish his or her own soapbox to bring change to a product or service (see Case 7-2, Change.org). Web sites are devoted to evaluating products, and Facebook groups are dedicated to bringing the "truth" to consumers along with random e-mails. And then there are sites established simply to debunk urban legends (www. snopes.org).

## THE ROLE OF PUBLIC RELATIONS

Technically, both marketing and public relations support the sales function. "Nothing happens until a sale is made," says an old bromide. The difference is that marketing is totally engrossed in selling, whereas public relations is more holistic. It supports sales to customers, but also is concerned with relationships with all other stakeholders of the organization.

Originally, public relations supported sales almost exclusively through media publicity, promotional events, and consumer information programs. The objective was to make people:

1. Aware of the product or service in the first place
2. Knowledgeable about the benefits and advantages of the particular product or service
3. Constantly reminded of their favorable feelings toward the product or service

Such activity ties in with advertising and authenticates product claims. Media used include newspapers, magazines, radio, television, features, photos, planned events, sponsorship of sports or musical activities, and many other venues for promotion. These are one-way communication vehicles touting the name and claims of the product or service.

Although the emphasis on marketing pushed some public relations departments back to this role, the changing conditions of the marketplace also brought forth several new activities, such as:

1. Forming user groups (as computer makers did) or customer service departments (as some automakers and utilities did) to personally build customer loyalty
2. Adopting customer satisfaction programs in which the entire organization is focused on delivering not just a product or service but also the quality and personal interactions consumers expect when making a purchase (as retailers, utilities, and brand manufacturers did)
3. Concentrating the publicity and promotion activities on taking customers away from competitors (which the beer and cigarette makers state as their primary reason for publicity and advertising)

**4.** Protecting the reputation of the product or service, and of the organization, in a period of consumer activism, government regulation, competitive predation, global marketing, and similar conditions that bring a continual bevy of public issues to bear on every organization and industry

## CUSTOMER DELIGHT REPLACES CUSTOMER SERVICE

Yet even as organizations trimmed and shaped themselves to meet their customers' needs and values, two related challenges surfaced: (1) how to discipline and motivate the organization (and its employees) so it (2) delights customers who then become regular, repeat, and loyal.

The importance of customer service is shown in recent research of a major national company. It found that 64 percent of surveyed customers were perfectly satisfied with the product or service, but changed because of the way they were treated. Seventy percent chose a particular organization, not because of its product or service (which they knew they could also get elsewhere), but because of how they were treated.

Organizations that compete for customers know that the goal has shifted to *delighting customers*—which offers the ultimate competitive edge. Even if competitors satisfy customers, your organization can prevail by delighting them. Elements of a customer-delight program include:

1. *The promise:* A plainly stated vision of benefits for customers. Take care that these benefits are not undermined by employee actions or by ad copy that promises the moon.
2. *Customer expectations:* These arise chiefly from (a) your actual promise, (b) competitors' delivery of delight, and (c) customers' perceptions of service quality in general.
3. *Delivery:* The gap between promise and delivery is frequently huge. Management must recognize that frontliners—those who actually serve the customers—are not the bottom rung of the organization, but its most important resource. Keeping those frontliners motivated means using teamwork, continuous training, employee evaluation and reward systems, and a method for measuring customer delight.
4. *Aftermath or maintenance:* This is where reputations are solidified as shown by the classic study[6] in which satisfied customers tell four or five others about their experience, while dissatisfied customers whose cases are not resolved speak to 10 others.

## References and Additional Readings

Aaker, David. *Managing Brand Equity.* New York: Free Press, 1991.

Broom, Glen, and Kerry Tucker. "Marketing Public Relations: An Essential Double Helix." *Public Relations Journal* 45 (November 1993): 39–40.

Crispell, Diane. "What's in a Brand?" *American Demographics* 15 (May 1993): 26–32.

Cutlip, Scott, Allen Center, and Glen Broom. "Consumer Affairs and the 'Marketing Mix.'" Chapter 14 in *Effective Public Relations.* 8th ed. Upper Saddle River, NJ: Prentice Hall, 1999.

Davidson, Kenneth. "How to Improve Business Relationships." *Journal of Business Strategy* 14 (May/June 1993): 13–15.

Degen, Clara, ed. *Communicators' Guide to Marketing.* New York: Longman, 1990.

Feeman, Laurie. "Direct Contact Key to Building Brands." *Advertising Age* 64 (October 25, 1993): S2.

Felton, John. "Consumer Affairs and Consumerism." Chapter 16 in *Lesly's Handbook*

[6] *pr reporter,* November 9, 1981.

*of Public Relations and Communications,* 5th ed. Chicago, IL: NTC Business Books, 1998.

Hardesty, Monica. "Information Tactics and the Maintenance of Asymmetry in Physician–Patient Relationships." In D. R. Maines and C. J. Couch. eds., *Communication and Social Structure.* Springfield, IL: Charles C. Thomas, 1988: 39–58.

Harns, Thomas. *The Marketer's Guide to Public Relations.* New York: John Wiley & Sons, Inc., 1993.

International Customer Service Association (ICSA) has a variety of materials related to the total quality service process and encourages professional dialogue to achieve customer satisfaction. For more information, contact ICSA, 401 N. Michigan Ave., Chicago, IL 60611–4267; www.icsa.com.

Kotler, Philip. *Principles of Marketing.* 9th ed. Upper Saddle River, NJ: Prentice Hall, 2000.

Lerbinger, Otto, and Nathaniel Sperber. "Consumer Affairs." Chapter 4 in *Manager's Public Relations Handbook.* Reading, MA: Addison-Wesley, 1982.

Mazur, Laura. "A Consuming Ambition." *Marketing* (January 13, 1994): 23–24.

McManus, John. "Disaster Lessons Learned: Customer's Lifetime Value." *Brandweek* 35 (January 24, 1994): 16.

Murphy, John. *Brand Strategy.* Upper Saddle River, NJ: Prentice Hall, 1990.

Ott, Rick. *Creating Demand.* Richmond, VA: Symmetric Systems, Inc., 1999.

*pr reporter* Vol. 43 No. 46 (November 20, 2000). "Relationship Marketing: What Precisely Is PR's Role? Creating the Environment, Counseling, Running the Show?"

*pr reporter* Vol. 37 No. 12 (March 21, 1994). "Elements on Making Your Organization Customer-Friendly."

*The Public Relations Body of Knowledge.* New York: PRSA. See abstracts dealing with "Marketing, Marketing Support, and Consumer Relations."

Rich, Judith. "Public Relations and Marketing." Chapter 14 in *Lesly's Handbook of Public Relations and Communications.* 5th ed. Chicago, IL: NTC Business Books, 1998.

Sanford, David, and Ralph Nader, et al. *Hot War on the Consumer.* New York: Pitman, 1969.

Wilcox, Dennis, et al. *Public Relations: Strategy and Tactics.* 6th ed. New York: Longman, 2000.

Zandl, Irma, and Richard Leonard. *Targeting the Trend-Setting Consumer.* Homewood, IL: Business One Irwin, 1991.

# Case 6-1 Chevrolet Ditches the Traditional for Unprecedented Campaign to Attract New, Millennial Buyers

It's not all the time that a company gets the chance to break down its traditional methods and challenge itself to think outside of its comfort zone. But with the Chevrolet Sonic, the company's new subcompact, Chevrolet knew it had to deconstruct its systems and try something that would potentially reinvent the way automakers spoke to Generation Y, also called Millennials.

Sonic was due to arrive in dealerships fall 2011. The company was fighting a crowded, competitive market and had a run-of-the-mill reputation in the subcompact market. Recognizing the need for change, Chevrolet pulled together a new system to align its marketing and communication efforts that would, in the end, transform the way the company launched vehicles.

To flip this process on its head, Chevrolet implemented a new system in which the company's agencies would be intimately involved with each other, working together for many months prior to the dealerships receiving the vehicles. This new process allowed the various agencies—from advertising to media buying to diversity outreach to social media to public relations—to pitch creative platforms and executions to Chevrolet as one integrated launch plan. This, in itself, was a new way of working.

Chevrolet was determined to get this right, which meant it needed a more strategic approach, ultimately linking the multiple agencies together as early as possible in the process. Previously, the public relations agencies would support the marketing plans after the decisions were made. In the new model, the public relations agency would be completely involved in the strategy and tactical decisions, which led to a more cohesive and well-thought-out launch activity. A new paradigm was created that rallied the supporting teams around one strategy.

With this news system, Chevrolet would attempt to stand out from the crowd and make a robust statement about its newest subcompact in a marketing effort called "Let's Do This!"

## Situation Analysis: It's Going to Be a Tough Sell

From the beginning, Chevrolet faced some tough facts. Unfortunately, it wasn't replacing a dominant Chevrolet entry in the small car market. Its previous small car, Aveo, was "midpack" at best in terms of sales and appeal.

In addition, the brand wasn't very relevant to the buyers it needed to reach the most as new vehicles began rolling out of the company—cars such as the Cruze and the Spark—later in 2012. The company had to find a way to balance relevance and ability to relate in a way that would not seem overbearing or forced. It would have to fit with their customers' digital, social, and fast-paced lifestyles.

Chevrolet had to overcome:

- A lack of awareness of the Chevrolet Sonic nameplate,
- Current segment avoidance of the brand, and
- Increased competition in the subcompact market.

*(Continued)*

**FIGURE 6.1** © 2012 Chevrolet Motors, LLC

And it had to exploit:

- Favorable market conditions, including subcompact segment growth and rising gas prices, and
- A legitimate product that challenged segment sales-and-image leaders.

Chevy wanted to achieve the following objectives:

- Make Chevy relevant to small car buyers,
- Leverage Sonic to increase Chevy consideration,
- Earn consideration of 15 percent of potential buyers by August 2012 (one year after the start of production), and
- Support Sonic sales objectives.

To do all this, the company made the decision to aggressively go after the future of the brand—the youngest buyer group, Millennials. They are the men and women between the ages of 18 and 34 years in 2012.

## Target Audience: The Elusive Millennial

Beyond studying the demographic data of Gen Y, Chevrolet also studied their media consumption patterns and lifestyle habits to understand not only who they are, but what they do and where they receive their information.

This targeted group's biggest differentiator was how they consume media. Millennials live online. They watch less TV than their parents and read fewer magazines. Instead, they talk and text their friends; they swap videos with each other; they are constantly gaming; and they love connecting with their "faves." So Chevrolet built a plan around their specific media habits and decided that the digital space was going to be where the brand connected with its new audience.

Using a psychographic analysis of its target, Chevrolet identified launch strategies that formed the basis for the integrated marketing and communications plan. Moreover, each tactic had to support one of the objectives below:

- Focus the work on the needs and habits of the customer
- Singularly focus on Chevrolet's primary target
- Create a strong persona that complements positioning

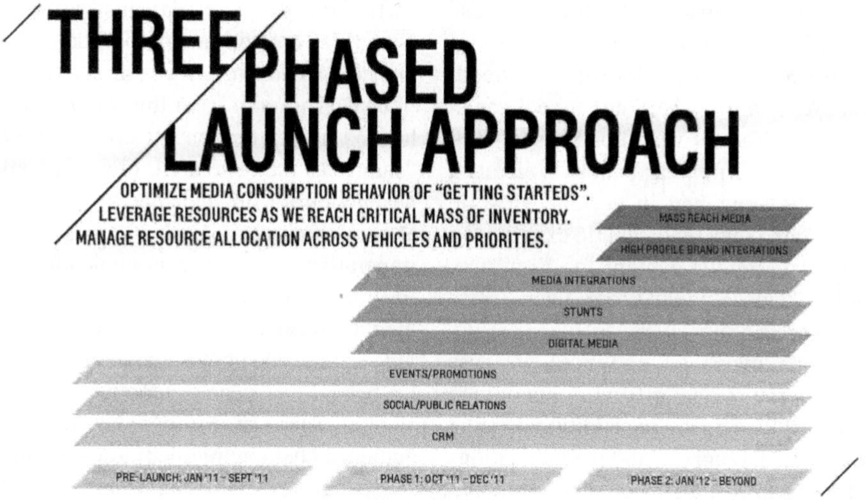

# THREE PHASED LAUNCH APPROACH

OPTIMIZE MEDIA CONSUMPTION BEHAVIOR OF "GETTING STARTEDS".
LEVERAGE RESOURCES AS WE REACH CRITICAL MASS OF INVENTORY.
MANAGE RESOURCE ALLOCATION ACROSS VEHICLES AND PRIORITIES.

MASS REACH MEDIA
HIGH PROFILE BRAND INTEGRATIONS
MEDIA INTEGRATIONS
STUNTS
DIGITAL MEDIA
EVENTS/PROMOTIONS
SOCIAL/PUBLIC RELATIONS
CRM

PRE-LAUNCH: JAN '11 – SEPT '11    PHASE 1: OCT '11 – DEC '11    PHASE 2: JAN '12 – BEYOND

**FIGURE 6.2**    © 2012 Chevrolet Motors LLC

- Tap into the experiential nature of the target
- Engage in out-of-the-box thinking

This led to the term "Getting Starteds" and the following definition:

"Getting Starteds" are excited and optimistic to launch into the next phase of their lives, thriving on adventure and new experiences. They not only want to find the next big thing, they want to be the first to share it with all of their friends. They are experiencing many firsts in their lives—getting their first real job, moving out and getting their first home or apartment, traveling through Europe with a group of friends, or even doing something as simple as trying a new cuisine at a local restaurant.

The bottom line was that Chevrolet wanted to capture the target audience's optimism, spirit of adventure, and fun that the potential buyers exhibited in their everyday lives. The campaign was built around connecting to the emotion of experiencing something for the first time.

## Strategy: The Risks That Are Worth Taking

Chevrolet had to seed a new name in a very crowded segment in a highly memorable way. With insights about the target audience, about how they consumed media and what they valued, Chevrolet launched Sonic's "Let's Do This!" campaign in September 2011 with public relations activities beginning a few months prior with exclusive media drives. The "Let's Do This!" campaign would demonstrate how Sonic best fit the Millennial lifestyle by showing how it's a "car for firsts," and the "firsts" would be larger-than-life "stunts" that the car would perform.

It wasn't easy to convince all of Chevrolet that a digital launch was going to more effective than a traditional advertising campaign with the "heavy-up" broadcast media they were accustomed to seeing. It would take time and some risk, but building a new image and reputation for Sonic wasn't going to be easy. By creating several highly visible, first-time stunts, Sonic content would have strong potential to go viral and gain the attention of the target audience

Sonic was then personified and began performing its own impressive "firsts" to prove it
*(Continued)*

was up for anything that the "Getting Starteds" were. The approach was direct. It would not feature Sonic with celebrities. Instead, Chevrolet wanted to make Sonic a cool car to own and drive. The car would be the star. But, by partnering with popular bands, Web sites, and celebrities engaged in certain lifestyle activities, Chevrolet would tap into existing fan bases to create unique content for YouTube, Facebook, Chevy.com, and more. Each "first" targeted a specific subculture, such as gaming, extreme sports, music, art, and more, and was paired with promotional efforts to encourage deeper engagement, including additional media buys, social media support, and media relations outreach, for a truly integrated launch activity.

For the media relations activities, the public relations team, supported by Boston-based Mullen, related the "firsts" theme to vehicle attributes that were a first for the subcompact segment, such as it being

- The first and only small car to have 10 standard airbags
- The first small car to have standard alloy wheels and standard OnStar navigation
- The only small car made in America
- The first vehicle in the United States to use a unique water-based "three-wet" paint process
- The first and only small car to offer a turbocharged engine and the most available torque in its class
- A segment leader in interior roominess and versatility

## Tactics: Putting "Firsts" into Context

Chevrolet decided that for the first four to five months of vehicles arriving in dealerships it would begin with a strictly digital launch campaign with the traditional heavy advertising launch following. This digital campaign would rely on an integrated approach that would tap all communication functions to help extend the message further in the digital realm.

Before any activations or outreach, Chevrolet created an online "home" for the launch—a dedicated Web site for Sonic called "LetsDoThis.com." On this site, the company housed all of the content created around the "stunts" as they occurred, giving a convenient destination for the audience to watch or relive Sonic's activities. With every stunt, it was imperative that each communication effort—from a tweet to a Facebook status update to a media advisory—drive the audience to watch videos, view the photos, get more details, or see the behind-the-scene materials on this Web site.

Chevrolet also ran contests for the target audience challenging them to create their own "firsts," record them, and post them on the site. Participants would then be eligible to win a Sonic of their own during the first few months. Once the Twitter, Facebook and LetsDoThis.com sites were live and had an active community, Chevrolet began executing stunts.

The first stunt was a bungee jump off a 100-foot structure in Long Beach, California, where visitors were encouraged to visit LetsDoThis.com and click on a special arrow. With every click, the Sonic moved closer to the edge. Finally, after nine hours and more than 2.5 million clicks, the Sonic took a dive into a pool of water at the bottom. This dive signified the launch of Sonics in dealerships and began the digital engagement with the target audience.

For the second stunt, Chevrolet performed a takeover of the YouTube home page by placing an obvious red button with the words "Do Not Press" on screen. Anyone seeing a button and those words would want to click on it. Once they clicked, they would activate a video of the second Sonic stunt—a sky dive.

The Sonic and a team of the world's best skydivers went up 14,000 feet over the Arizona desert and let the Sonic drop from the plane's cargo area. Dozens of cameras recorded the event, and the video received nearly 500,000 views on YouTube.

Next, Chevrolet teamed with 20-year skateboarding veteran, television star, and entrepreneur Rob Dyrdek, who performed an incredible skateboarding move, called a kickflip, with an actual Sonic. Rob featured the kickflip in March on his *Fantasy Factory* MTV show, and the stunt generated nearly one million views on YouTube.

On the same weekend, Chevrolet created and projected a 3-D interactive claw game on the Roosevelt Hotel on Hollywood Boulevard in downtown Los Angeles. Observers and passers-by were allowed to play and, using a gigantic shift lever, pull prizes from the 3-D digital machine image, until one lucky winner found and extracted a new 2012 Sonic.

After the first three stunts, Sonic rose to number two in sales in the small car segment without running a single broadcast or print advertisement. The public relations team supported the stunts via media invitations and storytelling.

Possibly the biggest stunt of the campaign was Sonic performing the first-ever music video by a car with the "viral" group OK Go. It included nearly 2,000 instruments laid out over a gigantic musical road course. The band activated instruments by extending their arms from the car. And the band's official online video of "Needing/Getting" received five million views and was the number one YouTube video on day one. Within the first 10 days online, the video hit a high of 15 million views. As of June 2012, the video has had more than 20 million views on YouTube.

About this stunt, *AdAge* asked the question: "Is OK Go's Chevy-sponsored music video one of the best product placements ever?" Music Editor Simon Dumenco said, "The reception has been wildly positive, with even the blatant product placement being warmly received."

One of the most up-voted comments on the Reddit site said, "I think this is a great use of corporate funds/product placement. The band gets an amazing music video that would be prohibitively expensive without Chevy's money, and Chevy reaches their 18–34 demographic with a spot that has the car as a central figure."

It was clear Chevrolet was beginning to get some buzz online for Sonic because the Millennial target was talking—both digitally and IRL (in real life)—about the launch. But the company needed to use the Sonic and the new campaign to help change the perception of the brand with a broader audience. So it expanded its launch into traditional media, as planned, by putting together highlights of all the stunts into one 60-second commercial "Anthem," which debuted on the world's largest broadcast platform, the Super Bowl. As of June 2012, this ad has had more than three million views on YouTube.

"Anthem" was one of the highest rated Super Bowl commercials. One reason was the music track, the song "We Are Young" by the group Fun. The song was originally covered on an episode of a major prime-time television show, and Chevrolet leveraged it for the first commercial spot for Sonic. The combination was powerful: The song rose from number 38 on the Billboard charts to number one within four days of the ad airing during the Super Bowl. The song stayed number one for seven weeks.

The next stunt tapped into a specific lifestyle interest toward which the Millennial audience has begun to gravitate. Sonic created its own street art scene—the first ever painted by a car. Teaming with urban street artist Jeff Soto, Sonic painted a mural on a wall in Northern California using an iPad controlled by Jeff and robotic arms with custom controls. This stunt was documented and added to LetsDoThis.com and promoted on YouTube.

Sonic had an additional television spot, "Night Swim," that began running during the 2012 Billboard Music Awards. It tells the story of five college-aged kids who push the envelope a bit and go for a nighttime dip in their skivvies at a lake. They realize the keys were locked in the car and use the myChevrolet app to "remotely" unlock the car. Directed by Jason Reitman, a Hollywood high-flyer whose film credits include "Juno" and "Up in the Air," the commercial was received with great reviews.

*(Continued)*

## Results: How'd They Do?

The campaign proved successful, especially when comparing sales of Sonic to Aveo. The difference was dramatic. Compared to Aveo, Sonic had a 33 percent higher transaction price and 90 percent less incentive spend, and Chevrolet's conquest rate (buyers from outside the GM family) was near 50 percent. In addition, nearly one-third of the buyers were under age 35, which was 50 percent more buyers under 35 than Aveo had.

By June 2012, Sonic was firmly established in the segment as the second-best-selling car with hopes of becoming the best-selling. Sonic also became the most popular small car on Facebook as of June 2012, with nearly 440,000 fans, which were nearly 180,000 more than any other small car. The sales of the car were matching expectations, and the Sonic community was engaged.

## Summary: The New Public Relations

The role of the public relations practitioner changes every day as technology continues to change the way messages are delivered. The lines are blurring between advertising, marketing, and communications, and the modern practitioner needs to remain malleable and strategic. In the case of the Chevrolet Sonic launch, media relations efforts supplemented the program through automotive media drives, target lifestyle outreach aligned with each stunt, and custom stories related to the product and company.

The public relations practitioner was also relied on by the larger integrated group as a trusted advisor in the planning stages. Because public relations professionals can foresee how the target audience will perceive a brand, they are often the most valuable people at the table, helping to shape the messages and programs.

### Questions for Discussion

1. What would you recommend Chevy do to tweak this campaign for your generation rather than the Millennials?
2. What might be some fallout issues from this campaign? How might GM and Chevy prepare for them?

# Case 6-2 Firestone: A Recall Revisited*

*"Those that fail to understand history are doomed to repeat it."*
—Jean Jacques Rousseau

Large production companies are in business to make a profit. However, when products fail and lives are lost much more than profit must be considered. In August 2000, Ford Motor Company took on the largest recall in history because of Firestone tires failing on the road. Many deaths and injuries were caused by the bad tires, and many lawsuits were filed against Ford and Firestone, but the greatest impact of the fiasco was on the public reputations of the companies involved. The media coverage was sensational, and everyone who owned a Ford Explorer was taking a close look at the tires. The situation was in need of a strong public relations response, but there was none to be found.

## A Little History

In the early 1970s more than 20 million Firestone 500 radials were sold to customers who then experienced problems and failures with the tires. They registered their complaints with Firestone.

Two years later, Firestone's director of development reported to top management that the design of the radial 500 was of "inferior quality." In 1975, Firestone did some "severe torture" tests in its R&D division and found that half of the tires did not pass the test. No report was filed or made public, because the government did not require one. Firestone kept the information to itself and sold millions more 500s.

In 1976, numerous consumer complaints about tread separation were sent to the Center for Auto Safety. The complaints were then sent to the National Highway Traffic Safety Administration (NHTSA). Finally, in 1977 Firestone recalled only the 500s from the years 1973 and 1974. It stated that one of nine plants was having problems on the production line and that this was the cause of these failures. Firestone said that the 500s were a good tire and that only the ones from the specific plant were faulty. Company officials also said that any other problems with the 500s were due to improper inflation or abuse by customers.

The NHTSA decided to do some tests of its own. Random tire brands were tested for blowouts, tread separation, and distortions. The results showed that 46.4 percent of problem tires were the Firestone brand. The NHTSA planned to release the information to the public, but Firestone obtained a restraining order to prevent the release of the news. This caught the attention of the national media. Everyone wanted to know what Firestone was hiding.

Test results from the NHTSA were leaked to the Center for Auto Safety, and in March 1978 the Center released the information to the media. It became a media frenzy, with nearly every paper covering the story on the front page. In August 1978, Firestone was forced by the government to recall all the 500s. In the end, the 500s caused 29 deaths and 50 injuries.[7]

## History Repeats Itself

Beginning in the 1990s, many tire failures and fatal SUV rollover cases were reported, causing the NHTSA to investigate. In midsummer of 2000, Ford acknowledged the problem, igniting continuing legal battles concerning what Ford knew and when it knew it.

*(Continued)*

---

* This case was researched and written by Jason Rock, a public relations major at the University of Central Florida.
[7] "Firestone's Reluctant Recall." *PR Practices, Fourth Edition.* p. 276, Case 8-1.

Ford and Firestone had a large crisis on their hands, much like the one Firestone had before. In August 2000, Bridgestone/Firestone announced a voluntary recall of 6.5 million tires, the largest recall to date. The information about the recall along with all other communication was put on the Firestone Web site.

The NHTSA was closely watching Ford and Firestone during the recall. After doing its own testing, the NHTSA supplied the media with an extensive list of tires that needed to be recalled. Included were Firestone's 15-inch and 16-inch tires used on Explorers.

It was not long before information was leaked that pinpointed the reason the tires were failing and the SUVs were rolling over. A missing layer of nylon in the tires was to blame for the rollovers and the many accidents. Jacques Nasser, CEO of Ford, said that Ford would do what needed to be done. However, Ford began to blame Firestone for the problem, and then Firestone blamed its employees at a plant in Illinois.

In September 2000, Firestone's public relations firm Fleishman-Hillard walked out saying, ". . . it became evident that we could no longer be of service to Bridgestone/Firestone."[8] Firestone named Ketchum as its new public relations firm after Fleishman-Hillard walked out.

John Lampe, CEO of Bridgestone/Firestone, said that all tires on the NHTSA's list needed to be tested, but for now the company was recalling only the 15-inch tires. He offered free inspections to any who were unsure of their own tires. Throughout the next year, Ford and Bridgestone/Firestone communicated internally and searched for who to blame. The majority of external communication to the public was through company Web sites and a handful of press conferences. Research on Ford SUVs and Bridgestone/Firestone tires continues, but there have been

more than 200 deaths—not to mention thousands of injuries.[9]

## The Facts

In the 1990s, consumers experienced failures with their tires and after investigation and research the largest recall ever was conducted. By November 2001, more than 200 lives had been lost in Ford Explorer rollovers. Ford used its Web site to facilitate the recall and display written communications, because it was an inexpensive medium. However, Ford's Web site for the recall could not handle the flow of traffic the day the recall was announced. Within the first eight days, the site received some 5.1 million hits. The majority of people trying to get to the Web site were unable to because it was down for 11 hours due to the overload.

Ford, which is a U.S. company, was the first to jump on the consumer's side, with Nasser saying Ford would "stand behind and replace the tires." Bridgestone, a large Japanese company, owns Firestone. Japanese senior executives perhaps did not understand the difference between Japanese and U.S. cultures in a time of crisis. Tradition in Japan is that an issue will fade out of the news as soon as a public apology is given.[10] Therefore, Bridgestone/Firestone did its part and apologized to its public in Japan. However, the United States has a different tradition when it comes to crisis—the public demands more than an apology. Firestone's sales dropped 50 percent after the recall, causing profits to drop by 80 percent.

Ford and Firestone have a long history together. Traditionally, new Ford vehicles have come with Firestone tires. But Ford can choose another name brand of tires if it decides to. As a result, Firestone had the most to lose. It made much of its money selling tires to Ford. Thus, the crisis impacted Firestone's future more than Ford's.

---

[8] "Is Firestone's Clock Ticking?" CNNfn, New York. September 8, 2000.

[9] "Ford Is in the Driver's Seat." *The Orlando Sentinel.* October 31, 2001. C1 and C7.

[10] "The Ford-Firestone." FindArticles.com. October 2000. Maryann Keller.

The CEO of Bridgestone/Firestone, realizing that the company was losing in the court of public opinion, finally acknowledged, "We know that we have been slow in responding to public concerns, that we underestimated the intensity of the situation, and that we have been too focused on internal details." This was as much of an apology as Bridgestone/Firestone would make.

Firestone maintained that the Explorer was the problem, and ties between the companies were severed. Meanwhile, the case continued in the courts of law and of public opinion. Ford won a few lawsuits against Firestone and is using that money to do more research on why the tires failed more on the Explorers and not as much on other SUVs. Consumer legal actions were expensive for both companies.

This public relations issue is still playing out for both companies. They became victims of their own actions.

## The Perceptions

The media was the public's eye in this situation. Before the recall took place, frequent images of SUV rollovers appeared on the nightly news, creating national awareness of the problem with the Firestone tires. Consumers saw the damage first hand because of videotapes and still images of the horrific rollovers. Death tolls and injury numbers were growing as the recall became public. Lawsuits were filed and investigations began.

Owners, aware of the many accidents and lawsuits pending against Ford and Firestone, were checking their own Fords to make sure the tires were not part of the recall. As consumers were rapidly shaping their opinion about Ford and Firestone, little was being done to address consumers' concerns.

The media were unsure of who to blame. The NHTSA's test results were published, and consumers were pointing fingers at everyone. The media kept the public up to date on the recall and the court decisions. Rollovers and injuries continued to happen, and each one made the news. Ford and Firestone could be found on news and investigative shows on a regular basis.

Other tire companies capitalized on the information vacuum. Goodyear offered information about Firestone's recall on its Web site. In addition, competing local tire businesses offered consumers free tire inspections.

Ford had actually communicated well internally and had made some good decisions. Initially, the public viewed Firestone as the culprit, but with more research needed, Ford might have been to blame also. As a whole, the public was confused, but consumers knew to stay away from Ford and Firestone. The public was also entangled in the blame game, hopng for someone to blame who could then fix the problem. That hope began to wane, however, as the former partners parted and pointed fingers at each other.

## Public Relations Impact

Public relations is supposed to play a major role in a crisis such as a recall, but Ford and Firestone didn't appear to be up to speed with the sensitive consumers of the new millennium. Firestone could have learned its lesson from the first recall. Learning to deal with the media, not blaming consumers, and working with the NHTSA were problems not addressed at that time—nor in the later crisis. News coverage in the papers during the first recall read, "The success of a corporation nowadays depends not only on how it makes and markets its products, but also how it is perceived by the public." Society has progressed since the 1970s, and more important now than the court of law is the court of public opinion. This concept seemed lost on Firestone.

It is understandable that the Japanese company, Bridgestone, did not understand American public relations. However, because it is a company that conducts much of its business in the United States, it should have been able to handle communication in the U.S. market.

Ford didn't communicate much more effectively. Much of the news from Ford was released to the media and also posted on the Web site. However, information was not

*(Continued)*

released in a timely manner. Because of this, many of the public's opinions were shaped and finalized before the recall could take full effect. Ford was too late and therefore unable to control the agenda and set expectations. Competitors were only too eager to offer information on the situation as well.

A decade after the dust had settled, some things are still murky. As the American Automobile Association commented:

> Ten years later, it's still not clear where the bulk of the blame lies. The original Explorer had a relatively narrow track and a high center of gravity, which made the SUV more prone to rollover than a contemporary sedan or station wagon. The Firestone tires in question did suffer from a higher incidence of delamination, especially when underinflated. Rather than point fingers and place blame, it's important to look at how vehicles have improved in the years since. Beginning with the 2007 model year, manufacturers began incorporating tire pressure monitoring systems (TPMS) into new vehicles. These TPMS readouts give warning when tire pressures drop below an acceptable threshold, advising drivers of a potentially dangerous situation almost as soon as it occurs. Modern vehicles have improved standards for both rollover protection and occupant safety, and today's Ford Explorer is lower and wider than earlier counterparts, making it less prone to rollover even in extreme situations. Electronic aids, such as vehicle stability control, also help to ensure that drivers don't get in over their heads in a sudden avoidance maneuver or tire blowout.[5]

## Lessons Learned

Ford and Firestone could have done many things differently before, during, and after the tires became an issue of public concern. In a consumer-based society, just getting bad tires off the road is not enough. The lost relationships between customers and the two companies are going to be difficult to rebuild.

Neither company seemed to have a plan in place for dealing with such a crisis. The scenario of a possible recall should have been addressed before it happened. No one was "expecting the unexpected." Deciding who to blame should take a back seat to fixing the problem.

Both companies should have focused their efforts on (1) fixing the problem; (2) focusing the agenda on this solution; and (3) providing consumers with a realistic timetable for the solution to be in place and working.

Absent this, the companies are left with an agenda set by the media and the government—something that no company wants to endure—and the unrealistic expectation that the problem should have been resolved yesterday.

### Questions for Discussion

1. Compare and contrast the situation Firestone faced in 2000 with the similar situation of 1975.
2. How does Ford's involvement in 2000 change the scenario?
3. Discuss Firestone's decision to recall only the 15-inch tires. Was that a good "PR" move?
4. Recalls occur daily in the automotive industry. Why do you think a total recall was such a sticking point with Ford and Firestone?
5. Discuss the role the Internet played in Ford and Firestone's communication strategy. How would the situation been affected by today's Twitter-happy society?
6. How did Japanese ownership affect this case?
7. Why do you think the PR agency for Firestone quit in the middle of the crisis?

---

[5] AAA via thecarconnection.com

# Case 6-3 Johnson & Johnson Then and Now: How Handling a Crisis Can Make or Break a Reputation

In 1982 and 1986, Johnson & Johnson's (J & J's) timely and comprehensive responses to the Tylenol crises were recounted in various media outlets and incorporated into the best practices of management, marketing, public relations, and the interface among all three.[11] It was accepted that J & J had established a "gold standard" for managing crises, using effective public relations.

## Tragedy and the Response—the Gold Standard

In 1982, an unknown culprit or culprits tampered with packages of Tylenol, planting cyanide-laced capsules within them. These were sold in Chicago-area stores and killed seven people. J & J, the parent company of McNeil Consumer Products Division, Tylenol's manufacturer, pulled the drug from all shelves and issued a recall, at a cost of over $50 million. Following an investigation, the product was reissued in tamper-resistant containers. Consumers were offered a sealed package of capsules to replace potentially lethal ones. J & J pioneered tamper-resistant consumer product packaging, gained credibility, public trust, and esteem, and exceeded the market share it held before the crises. Packaging regulations were tightened by the Food and Drug Administration (FDA, under the Department of Health and Human Services [HHS]).

## Practical Realities

Information available at that time suggested that J & J's triumph was because:

1. The company had a history of success and service as a producer of health-care products.
2. The company took pride in its public visibility and its reputation for integrity.
3. The company benefited from its founder's focus on social responsibility ". . . that went far beyond the usual sales and profit motives"[12] and a legacy of high ethical standards.
4. The J & J credo was supported and interpreted by succeeding generations of executives during challenging times and was reinforced during the Tylenol crises.
5. In their relations with employees, neighbors, investors, customers, and government agencies, J & J's spokespeople—including the CEO—showed leadership and authority.
6. J & J recognized the public interest and its legitimate representation by the news media. It did not hesitate to disclose news, whether good or bad, in a timely way.

*(Continued)*

---

Contributed by Rachel Kovacs, Professor of Communications, City College of New York

[11] For accounts that address these issues further, see *pr reporter,* February 13, 1983; *Public Relations Journal,* March 1983; *Public Relations Review,* Fall 1983; "The Tylenol Comeback," Johnson & Johnson, undated booklet; "Tylenol's Rebound," *Los Angeles Times,* September 25, 1983; "Tylenol Deaths Still a Mystery," Associated Press, September 26, 1983; and "Tylenol's Miracle Comeback," *Time,* October 17, 1983.

[12] Lee W. Baker. *The Credibility Factor.* Homewood, IL: Business One Irwin, 1993, p. 54.

7. The corporate public relations function was part of management, participating in the decision process and in implementing the decision when communication was involved.
8. Mechanisms for feedback from publics were available and public input was highly valued.
9. The company worked collaboratively with the FDA's press office. FDA updates about the initial recall of 93,000 bottles of Tylenol, a subsequent national recall, and its new, uniform standards for manufacturing tamper-resistant, nonprescription drug packages quelled panic.

## A Copycat Crime and Its Aftermath

In February 1986, a New York resident died after ingesting cyanide-laced Tylenol capsules purchased at an area A & P. J & J immediately ceased Tylenol capsule production and again offered refunds or exchanges for tablets or caplets. Additional tainted capsules were later found at Woolworth's, nearby. The cost for the 1986 recall was $180 million, which included "*communication expenses* to reassure consumers of the safety of non-capsule Tylenol." This action, consistent with J & J's public image, received positive news coverage.

In the late 1980s, in the competitive market for pain-relief medications, advertisers made claims and counterclaims to net companies a bigger cut of the profits. A poll taken close to the time of the copycat incident showed that despite the crises, J & J's name did not have negative associations for consumers. Of those polled, 76 percent thought the company's efforts to avoid tampering had sufficed. Most

people saw that isolated acts of violence and terrorism were unavoidable.

## The Public Mattered

J & J's commitment to corporate responsibility, as it was understood at that time, enabled it to contain the Tylenol tragedy without sacrificing its credibility. It had no crisis plan prior to the Tylenol incidents, yet "Johnson & Johnson developed and geared activities to protect and communicate with its customers, to react to their fears, and provide what consumers needed."[13] It recognized its responsibility to the public and the necessity for positive public relationships. This demonstrated that companies enhance their profitability when they give special attention to the public and its needs.[14]

At the time, James Burke, J & J's CEO, stated, "I think the lesson in the Tylenol experience . . . is that we . . . have extraordinary leverage with our most important asset . . . the goodwill of the public. *If* we make sure our enterprises are managed in terms of *their obligations to society,* that is also the best way to defend this democratic capitalistic system . . . ."[15] In 1986, the Council on Economic Priorities gave the company its American Corporate Conscience Award. A *Company That Cares,* a centenary history of J & J, was written by Lawrence Foster, its then-head of public relations, and the company received many more industry honors.

## Different Decade, Different Response

Since the time of the crises, J & J successfully launched additional Tylenol-based remedies and has prospered. At the end of fiscal year 2011, J & J reported that ". . . full-year sales

---

[13] Eileen Murray and Saundra Shohen. "Lessons from the Tylenol Tragedy on Surviving a Corporate Crisis." *Medical Marketing and Media,* February 1992.

[14] *pr reporter.* Vol. 27, February 6, 1984, p. 3.

[15] Ibid.

of $65.0 billion increased 5.6%."[16] Yet J & J's reputation today has suffered from recent recalls and allegations, and its response—or lack of it—is in stark contrast to the company's actions and reputation in the 1980s.

## Revisiting the J & J Credo

Beginning in at least 2009, journalists, regulators, industry observers, consumers, health-care professionals and other publics began to question whether indeed J & J had prioritized the interests of its customer base and health-care professionals over those of its investors and other stakeholders. J & J's decisions recently have raised concerns about the company's commitment to its publics, given allegations of J & J misconduct, misrepresentation, ethical lapses, and dubious communication practices.

## A Trusted Name in Baby Care, Spread Thin, Experiences Quality Control Problems

Although J & J and its subsidiaries have generally been identified with a range of recognized brands, its reputation is most closely associated with its baby care line. J & J, as the parent company, has striven, above all, to maintain the integrity and promote the purity of its baby products. Nevertheless, since 1932, when it became decentralized, with various companies at home and abroad, J & J has considered itself a global family of companies (more than 250), and those executives in charge of the various subsidiaries have had substantial autonomy.

## J & J from 2008 to the Present: More Crises, Differing Responses

From 2008 through 2011, J & J faced allegations of recalls, "phantom" recalls, faulty medical devices, an attempted cover-up of manufacturing and safety problems, and kickbacks to a pharmaceutical sales company. In this period, many of the recalls included over-the-counter children's and adults' medication manufactured by McNeil Consumer Healthcare (the manufacturer of Tylenol). There were more than 50 voluntary recalls by the company in the period between early 2010 and March 2011.[17] One plant was closed in Ft. Washington, Pennsylvania, for problems that J & J identified as faults with cleaning procedures and documentation of the procedures,[18] and McNeil agreed to comply with "comprehensive inspections" of two other plants, one in Las Piedras, Puerto Rico, and another in Lancaster, Pennsylvania.[19]

The January 2011 recall occurred just after the State of Oregon sued J & J. The state alleged that the company knowingly sold defective Motrin tablets nationwide and hired a contractor in 2009 to quietly remove the tablets from store shelves—that is, they

*(Continued)*

[16] Johnson & Johnson. "Johnson & Johnson Reports 2011 Fourth-Quarter and Full-Year Results." Published Janaury 24, 2012. http://www.jnj.com/connect/news/all/johnson-and-johnson-reports-2011-fourth-quarter-and-full-year-results (accessed on February 28, 2012).

[17] Voreacos, David, Alex Nussbaum, and Greg Farrell. "Johnson & Johnson's Quality Catastrophe." *Bloomberg Businessweek*. (March 31, 2012). http://www.businessweek.com/stories/2011-03-30/johnson-and-johnsons-quality-catastrophe (accessed on July 6, 2012).

[18] Loftus, Peter. "J & J Issues Another Round Of Drug Recalls." *Wall Street Journal* (March 30, 2011). http://online.wsj.com/article/SB10001424052748704471904576231042179455516.html (accessed on July 5, 2012). (See also Johnson & Johnson. "Johnson & Johnson Provides Update on McNeil Consumer Healthcare Remediation; Announces Completion of Internal Assessment Phase Of Comprehensive Action Plan." *All News.* http://www.jnj.com/connect/news/all/johnson-and-johnson-provides-update-on-mcneil-consumer-healthcare-remediation (accessed on July 4, 2012).

[19] Diamond, Michael L. "Secret Recall, Plant Shutdown Congress Calls Hearings on J & J $100 Million on Upgrades. FDA Raised Concerns Over J & J Medicines." *Asbury Park Press* (November 20, 2011). http://www.app.com/article/20111121/JNJ/101050009/Secret-recall-plant-shutdown-Congress-calls-hearings-J-J-100-million-upgrades (accessed July 5, 2012).

planned a "phantom" recall (this lawsuit was nearly concurrent with multistate suits against J & J).[20]

An alleged phantom recall by J & J would have prevented public knowledge of any product flaws and formal action by the FDA. The latter would have deprived consumers and health-care professionals of information about any dangers of the drug. Without this knowledge, consumers and health-care providers would not have known to stop using it.

In May 2010, J & J announced the recall of numerous products, including children's Tylenol, Zyrtec, Benadryl, and Motrin. It was reported that McNeil had begun the recall voluntarily, based on allegations of "manufacturing deficiencies."[21] The author of that story also cited allegations of a higher dosage of active ingredients in certain infants' and children's brands than the labels indicated. McNeil acknowledged the potential of the medication to be immediately toxic.[22]

The same month, the House Committee on Oversight and Government reform investigated allegations against J & J. Representative Edolphus Towns, committee chairman, said its behavior depicted a company "willing to put the health of children at risk."[23] Although the FDA's Dr. Joshua Scharfstein criticized J & J

for its quality control and on other counts, the agency itself was rebuked for taking so long to recall the drugs.[24] William Weldon, J & J's then-CEO, also testified: ". . . we let the public down . . . . We did not maintain our high quality standards . . . ."[25] Although Weldon said he ". . . most regrets that 'there are children who need' Motrin and other recalled McNeil products," *he added,* "There has never been a serious injury resulting from everything that happened here . . . ."[26]

J & J reached a settlement regarding another of its products, the Ortho Evra birth control patch. Use of the patch increased the risk of blood clots, which led, in some cases, to stroke or heart attack.[27]

To top the allegations plaguing McNeil, the J & J subsidiary DePuy manufactured artificial hip implants that allegedly leached toxic cobalt and chromium, sickened patients, and caused deterioration of surrounding soft tissue. Patients worldwide faced additional surgeries to remove and replace the implants.[28] More than 500 New Zealand patients with the implants were affected; they could not sue but those affected elsewhere could.[29]

In addition, J & J allegedly paid kickbacks to Omnicare, a major nursing home supplier. According to a lawsuit filed in Boston, this

[20] Riley, Charles. "Johnson and Johnson Recalls 45 Million More Products." *CNN Money* (Janaury 17, 2011). http://money.cnn.com/2011/01/14/news/companies/johnson_johnson_recall/index.htm (accessed August 3, 2011).

[21] Singer, Natasha. "Children's Tylenol and Other Drugs Recalled." *The New York Times* (May 1, 2012). http://www.nytimes.com/2010/05/02/business/02drug.html (accessed August 3, 2011).

[22] Ibid.

[23] Abelson, Reed. 2010. "Lawmakers Grill J & J and FDA Officials." *The New York Times* (July 30, 2010). http://prescriptions.blogs.nytimes.com/2010/09/30/lawmakers-grill-jj-f-d-a-officials/ (accessed August 5, 2011).

[24] Ibid.

[25] 111th Congress. "Johnson & Johnson's Recall of Children's Tylenol and Other Children's Medicines and the Phantom Recall of Motrin (Part 2)." Hearing before the Committee on Oversight and Government Reform, House of Representatives, One Hundred and Eleventh Congress, Second Session (September 30, 2010). http://www.gpo.gov/fdsys/pkg/CHRG-111hhrg63148/html/CHRG-111hhrg63148.htm (accessed July 5, 2012).

[26] David Voreacos, Alex Nussbaum, & Greg Farrell, G. Op. Cit.

[27] Pringle, Evelyn. "J & J Concealed Dangers of Ortho Evra Birth Control Patch." *Lawyers and Settlements.com.* April 16, 2007. http://www.lawyersandsettlements.com/articles/drugs-medical/ortho-evra-harm-00761.html (accessed June 25, 2011).

[28] Taylor, Phil. "Kiwis Can't Claim for Faulty Hip Joint." *New Zealand Herald.* (July 11, 2011). http://www.nzherald.co.nz/nz/news/article.cfm?c_id=1&objectid=10735888 (accessed August 4, 2012).

[29] Lakhani, Nina. "Thousands of Patients Left in Agony by Faulty Hip Replacements." *The Independent.* September 12, 2010. http://www.independent.co.uk/life-style/health-and-families/health-news/thousands-of-patients-left-in-agony-by-faulty-hip-replacements-2077180.html (accessed on August 4, 2011).

was to promote sales of its drugs, including Risperdal, to nursing homes.[30] In April 2012, an Arkansas jury ruled that Janssen, the J & J subsidiary that manufactured Risperdal, downplayed and hid the drug's risks.[31] J & J has continued to recall products from various subsidiaries, and the FDA now has oversight of more than one J & J facility.[32]

## How J & J Communicated with its Priority Publics—One Telling Outlet

One important measure of how a company relates to its publics is the way that it presents itself on its Web site. Given the number of recalls and concerns about J & J products, presenting timely and accurate information to those publics would be important. Press releases go back two years, but those addressing the recalls are limited. A March 2012 review of *All News (a section of the J&J website)* revealed that between the end of December 2010 and mid-February 2012 a total of six press releases relating to the recalls were published.[33] During this 14-month period, the Web site listed or provided links for numerous support services and other resources for consumers.

A second review, in June 2012, showed only four press releases related to any recall,

In order to know that one of the releases was a recall of the HIV/AIDS drug Prezista, manufactured abroad and distributed in Canada, readers had to scroll down the page.[34] Two weeks later, a press release issued in the United States about Prezista made no mention of the recall.[35] Omitting this information is problematic because some Americans buy their drugs in Canada. How would patients know about the problems with Prezista, distributed in Canada, unless the Web site would tell them? What health consequences might consumers face without this information?

J & J's clear focus on its Web site is the purity of its baby-care image (although advocacy groups recently disclosed the presence of possible carcinogens in J & J's No More Tears baby shampoo,[36] and J & J recalled one lot of Aveeno baby lotion because of possible contamination[37]) and on celebrities who have agreed to endorse its products. What do these communication choices mean for J & J and its public relations and what questions do they raise?

J & J, by engaging in nontransparent behaviors, has opened itself up to public scrutiny about its actions and intentions. The style of communication on J & J's Web site alone might make people question whether it has set the public's interest above its own.

*(Continued)*

---

[30] Johnson, Linda. A. "U.S. Attorney: Johnson and Johnson Paid Millions in Kickbacks to Boost Sales of Schizophrenia Drug in Nursing Homes." *The Huffington Post.* (January 15, 2010). http://www.huffingtonpost.com/2010/01/15/johnson-johnson-kickback_n_424604.html (accessed August 2, 2011).

[31] Bartels, Chuck. "Johnson & Johnson Subsidiary Hid Risks Associated with Risperdal, Drug that Made Company Billions." *The Huffington Post.* (April 10, 2012). http://www.huffingtonpost.com/2012/04/11/johnson-johnson-risperdal-risks_n_1417999.html#es_share_ended (accessed July 1, 2012).

[32] Feeley, Jeff, and Eric Francis. "J & J Hid Risperdal's Risks from Arkansas Doctors, Lawyer Says." (April 12, 2010). http://www.bloomberg.com/news/2012-04-10/j-j-hid-risperdal-s-risks-from-arkansas-doctors-lawyer-says-1-.html (accessed July 5, 2012).

[33] Johnson & Johnson. *All News.* http://www.jnj.com/connect/news/all. (May 11, 2012). *All News.* http://www.jnj.com/connect/news/all (accessed on March 7, 2012).

[34] Johnson & Johnson. *All News.* http://www.jnj.com/connect/news/all. (May 11, 2012). *All News.* http://www.jnj.com/connect/news/all (accessed on May 11, 2012)

[35] Johnson & Johnson. "FDA Issues Complete Response Letter for 800 mg PREZISTA® (darunavir) Tablet." *All News.* (May 29, 2012). http://www.jnj.com/connect/news/all (accessed on June 2, 2012).

[36] Epstein, Samuel S. "Multiple Carcinogens in Johnson & Johnson's Baby Shampoo." *The Huffington Post.* (December 28, 2012). http://www.huffingtonpost.com/samuel-s-epstein/johnson-baby-shampoo_b_1151807.html (accessed on July 6, 2012)

[37] FDA. "Firm Press Release Recall: Aveeno Baby Calming Comfort Lotion." *FDA* (January 27, 2012). http://www.fda.gov/Safety/Recalls/ucm289619.htm (accessed on July 6, 2012).

## Questions for Discussion

1. Tylenol is a product of the McNeil Consumer Products wing of J & J. When the original deaths occurred, the parent organization moved in and took over both responsibility and spokesmanship. What are the pros and cons of that strategy for the CEO and the communications people in McNeil? What about the news media?

2. Why do you believe J & J has acted so differently between the first series of problems in the 1980s and the recent problems? What internal communication problems do you surmise might have impeded a more successful handling of the issues? What would you counsel the company to do going forward?

3. One of the Great Truths of PR is that there is no such thing as corporate ethics. How can an organization install and enforce an ethics policy that works? How might it keep it intact even through leadership changes?

4. In the 1980s, J & J acted according to its credo and recovered from two separate, fatal tampering problems. Might the credo have provided some guidance in the more recent situations?

# Case 6-4 Marriott On the Move Cultivates Customer Relationships

During a flight home from Europe in 2007, Bill Marriott sat next to his new executive vice-president and chief global communications and public affairs officer, Kathleen Matthews. She explained to him that the company needed to find a powerful way to communicate with customers in today's message-saturated environment.

Her solution: Create a CEO blog that would be a personal way for Marriott to engage customers who sought a deep connection with the company and wanted to join the company in conversations.

---

A CEO or corporate blog is just one tool in a toolbox filled with ways to reach stakeholder audiences. Selecting the right tool to reach an audience means evaluating the way the audience naturally receives information now. If it is a very connected audience, used to accessing and reading online content, then a blog is likely a good choice. Initial research helps determine current behaviors around medium use. Finding a natural fit for each audience is imperative as is not expecting people to change their behavior to fit your preferred communication style. Like a stream in the woods, follow the natural bank and do not force nature to bend to your will.

---

## Deciding Whether to Dive into the Blogosphere

"The first consideration is to have something to say that will interest people," explained Jay Hamilton, who directs digital corporate relations for Marriott. If the CEO has an abundance of engaging content to share, a communications team can then consider the benefits and drawbacks of creating a blog.

Some of the potential benefits of having a CEO blog for customers include:

- Humanizing the company by helping customers to get to know the CEO
- Building the company's brand by educating customers about the company's history and culture
- Providing key updates about the organization's activities and plans
- Serving as a direct channel for conversations between the CEO and customers

These benefits can enhance customer loyalty. Potential drawbacks, however, include:

- Amplifying critical comments by hosting them on an official blog that high-value customers would read
- Monopolizing significant CEO time over a sustained period
- Needing to supply fresh content over a sustained period that would engage readers
- Taking the risk of possibly making a misstatement that could result in negative reactions

"The CEO has to want to blog," explained John Wolf, vice-president of global brand public relations for Marriott. "In this world of transparency, you need to be ready to talk about things. Spin doesn't work. It's about authenticity and transparency. You need to have a CEO who understands what he or she is getting into, wants to do it, and understands that it won't be all positive."

*(Continued)*

---

Contributed by Tiffany Derville Gallicano, Ph.D., University of Maryland

Wolf also explained that with the myriad ways that people can express their views online, it is at a company's own peril to not be a part of that conversation. By having a blog, a CEO can host the discussion, listen to blog readers, and share his or her views in a venue that is more extensive than microblogs or social networking sites, which can be used to engage in short conversations and encourage people to read the blog.

## Earning Buy-In from HR, Legal Counselors, and Executives

Human resources and legal counselors expressed concern about employees posting comments that could cause problems. They also discussed potential problems that could arise from the mention of employees' names in comments. The communications team alleviated these concerns by explaining that:

- All comments would be moderated
- A terms-of-use policy would be created to describe the kinds of comments that the blog editor would approve and the kinds of comments that would not be accepted
- As described in the terms-of-use policy, the blog would be positioned as a communication tool for external audiences only; employees would be directed to report concerns to their managers, human resources, or the Marriott business integrity line (five years later, Marriott launched an internal blog through the company's intranet)
- The last names of Marriott employees would be deleted from comments to protect employees' privacy

Both positive and negative comments would be welcome; however, the terms of use would explain that feedback about a hotel stay should be reported to the Marriott customer care group (and a link to a form was given) rather than posted on the blog. Comments would need to be relevant to the conversation.

The communications team earned executive support by forming a blog advisory board of senior-level executives, to make them part of the process. As the communications team developed components of the blog, such as the editorial policy and terms of use, it shared regular reports with the advisory board. Setting a launch date was important. The internal deadline helped the team propel the project forward in a timely fashion, which can be a challenge in a global corporation.

## Orienting the CEO to the Blogosphere

The communications team talked with executives from other organizations, such as Boeing and IBM, who had blogs, to find out what they thought made a successful blog. The team presented what they learned to Marriott and showed him the blog of Randy Tinseth, the vice-president for marketing for Boeing in Seattle, and the blog of the first CEO blogger, Jonathan Schwartz of Sun Microsystems.

The communications team also needed to overcome the barrier to technology. The CEO, who was 75, did not use computers. Marriott and his team wanted the blog to be truly authored by Marriott, rather than having someone ghostwrite his blog posts. "That's not the way it works," explained Hamilton. "You can't fudge these things; you can't pretend you're Bill Marriott."

Marriott decided he would dictate his posts to an audio recorder or a member of the communications team who would then transcribe what he said. An audio recording would be published with each blog post. All comments would be printed and delivered to Marriott for his review. He would decide which comments to respond to and would dictate his responses. To be transparent about the process, Marriott presented these details in a section of the blog titled About Marriott Blog.

To handle the challenge of generating a steady stream of varied content, the communications team decided to meet each month to discuss ideas and establish a month-long editorial calendar. The team considers Marriott's travel calendar and encourages him to write blog posts about the places he visits. They also encourage Marriott to tell stories each month about the company's culture. For example, the company's philosophy is to take care of employees, they'll take care of the guests, and the guests will keep coming back. Highlighting an event designed to honor top employees is one vehicle for discussing the company's philosophy.

The team also encourages Marriott to discuss the company's recent innovations and global growth. For example, a recent blog post describes Marriott's partnership with Conservation International and a local provincial Chinese government to support a producer of honey that follows sustainable practices. The blog announced that with Marriott's addition of its 100th hotel in China, it has worked out an agreement with its juice vendor to bottle the honey, serve it in Chinese Marriott hotels, and donate a portion of the profits to the sustainability program.

In addition, Marriott has various topics he wants to address each month. The monthly editorial calendar helps the team ensure that there is a robust pipeline of stories to share on the blog.

When considering story ideas, Hamilton advises, "The best blogs aren't promotional, they're individual, and they're from the heart. You don't sell products—people don't want to see that."

Marriott introduced his blog on January 15, 2007, by discussing why he decided to start a blog, how he felt about entering the blogosphere, and the kinds of topics he planned to cover.

## Profiting from the Results

The communications team hoped to get 5,000 visits in the first two weeks; however, the blog received 20,000 visits and numerous comments. The launch received coverage in online media, as well as *The Washington Post* and *USA Today*. The blog has a steady readership of travel journalists and bloggers who go to the blog for story ideas.

Today, the blog receives approximately 30,000 visits a month, and during a big news month, the number of visits tends to escalate to about 60,000 a month. The year 2012 is its fifth anniversary. Because Marriott is one of the few octogenarian bloggers and one of the few top executives to blog, *The Huffington*

*(Continued)*

*Post* announced that Marriott is now a *Huffington Post* contributing blogger.

## Research About Ghost Blogging

Ghost blogging occurs when a public relations practitioner without disclosure writes a blog post on behalf of the stated author of the blog; this practice is controversial.

A recent survey of public relations practitioners by Gallicano, Brett, and Hopp (2012) found that most respondents thought it was permissible to engage in ghost blogging, provided that the stated author provided the ideas for the content and gave final content approval. The results also showed that approximately 41 percent of the respondents had at least one executive blog, and slightly more than half of these respondents acknowledged that their executive blogs were ghostwritten.

This study generated wide discussion and disagreement at the International Public Relations Research Conference. Among those disagreeing was social media measurement specialist and thought leader Katie Paine, who termed the study "Most Disturbing to Bloggers" in her summary of the conference.

Although most respondents in the survey approved of ghost blogging, opinions might shift as people learn the results of a subsequent survey of 507 readers of corporate blogs, 510 readers of politicians' blogs, and 501 readers of nonprofit blogs, which was conducted by Gallicano, Cho, and Bivins (2012). Regardless of the work setting, readers did not widely approve of the practice of having a communications person draft a blog post for the stated author, even if the blog post ideas came from the stated author and the stated author gave final content approval.

### Questions for Discussion

1. Visit www.blogs.marriott.com/marriott-on-the-move and read at least five blog posts. What do you think about the blog?
2. Explain the distinctive benefits and drawbacks of a blog, as compared with other social media channels, such as microblogs and social networking sites.
3. If your CEO expressed an interest in starting a blog, what would you need to discuss before deciding to move forward?
4. Marriott rejected ghost blogging. Explain and justify your position about whether a blog's stated author should delegate the writing of the blog posts to a public relations practitioner.

## Sources

Gallicano, Tiffany. D., Brett, Kevin., and Hopp, Toby. "Is Ghost Blogging Like Speechwriting? A Survey of Practitioners About the Ethics of Ghost Blogging." Paper presented at the meeting of the International Public Relations Research Conference, Miami, FL (March 2012).

Gallicano, Tiffany D., Cho, Yoon. Y., and Bivins, Thomas. H. "What Do Blog Readers Think? A survey to Assess Ghost Blogging and Ghost Commenting." Paper presented at the meeting of the Association for Education in Journalism and Mass Communication, Chicago, IL (August 2012).

# Case 6-5 Toyota: Growing Too Fast, Responding Too Slowly

On a Thursday morning in February 2010, readers of the national newspaper, *USA Today,* opened the business section to see two full-page ads. One from Toyota outlined "Our Commitment to Customers," a pledge to "make things right for our customers today and in the future."

The second, from General Motors, proclaimed "A Statement About Us. Not From Us." It seems that one of GM's vehicles had been named a "best buy" by some consumer magazine.

That the two ads appeared four pages apart on the same day might (or might not) have been a coincidence, but the attitudes expressed certainly were not. Toyota, once the world leader in consumer vehicles, was trying to win back drivers and buyers after a horrific stretch of accidents, incidents, and recalls. GM, emerging from bankruptcy and a government bailout, was crowing that one of its vehicles had won an award. The silent comparison was deafeningly loud.[1]

How Toyota, long a leader in safety and quality, found itself on the defensive is a lesson in corporate communication.

## The Situation

The situation literally exploded on the national scene in August 2009 when a Lexus being driven on the San Diego, California, freeway accelerated out of control and crashed, killing four passengers. The accident was "caught on tape" as one of the passengers called 911 to report the car's acceleration, and that tape was replayed over the mass media and social media thousands of times.[2]

But trouble may have been brewing for Toyota for years. As far back as 2002, according to a report by a consumer advocacy group,

Safety Research and Strategies, reports of unintended acceleration among Toyota models spiked.[3]

The National Highway Traffic Safety Administration (NHTSA) conducted an inquiry in 2003, and two minor recalls were issued in 2005 and 2007. But it was the highly visible crash in San Diego that brought the issue to the front burner (and front pages) for American drivers. Over the next two years, Toyota would recall some 10 million vehicles, see its market share drop, post its first operating loss in 50 years, and see its precious consumer franchise crumble beneath the weight of accusations that the company put profits before safety.[4]

Toyota's automotive problems were two-fold: The first was the sudden, unexpected acceleration of its cars, which ultimately was traced to sticky gas pedals, faulty floor mats, and improper installation of aftermarket mats. The second came a year later when some Prius and Lexus hybrids were recalled to address brake problems.[5]

Exacerbating the safety issues was the economic downturn worldwide, which hammered sales and profits across the industry. Those conditions led Toyota to idle two factories in the United States, keeping the workers on the payroll in keeping with the Toyota business model.[6]

## Facts versus Perceptions

With the benefit of hindsight, the facts are pretty clear.

1. Some Toyota vehicles were accelerating out of control.
2. Drivers were concerned over brake times and distances.
3. Accidents and deaths were occurring.

*(Continued)*

**4.** Toyota sales and profits were down.
**5.** Toyota's stock price was falling, an indication of loss of faith by the public.

The acceleration problems stemmed from friction (stickiness) related to wear in the gas-pedal assembly and from floor mats catching (and holding down) the gas pedal. Braking problems required a software adjustment. The corrections were relatively simple. The question was: Why didn't Toyota just acknowledge the problem and fix it?[7] The answer to that question is much harder. Some of it is a matter of perception—engineers versus consumers.

One of the Great Truths of PR (see p. 20) says, "Perception is reality; facts notwithstanding." Dr. Jeffrey K. Liker, in his book, *Toyota Under Fire,* notes that the cultural differences between Japan and the United States played a part.

"This started in the United States," writes Liker, "and at first Toyota viewed it as a regional perception problem that could be handled by management in the United States, but in the Internet age, nothing stays local for very long, and it soon became a global crisis."[8]

Also, the Toyota culture was to study a problem thoroughly before taking any action. That might have slowed responses.

"The Toyota Way demands that any problem be thoroughly investigated before any conclusions are reached. It demands that problem solvers 'go and see' the problem firsthand and not rely on abstract, third-hand reports. It demands thoughtful and critical reflection to find root causes and develop effective solutions . . . ."[9]

The perception issue came into play in the way Japanese engineers saw the problem. As Liker explains, "If the sticky pedals kept drivers from stopping, or materially increased the time required to bring the car to a halt, then the sticky pedals were clearly a safety defect and required immediate corrective action. If, on the other hand, braking performance was unaffected by the sticky pedals, then, engineers felt,

the pedals were not a safety defect but a customer-satisfaction and component-reliability issue."[10]

Because a Camry with a wide-open throttle could be brought under control more quickly than a competitor's car with a similar problem, the Japanese engineers concluded "that the sticky pedals were not a safety issue, and that there was no reason to issue a recall."[11]

Interestingly, the sticky pedal issue was growing in Europe prior to its eruption in the United States. Toyota had issued technical bulletins asking distributors in Europe to keep an eye out for the problem. But as it was thought to be a problem only in Europe, similar notices were not sent to the United States. The NHTSA was as surprised as anyone, fining Toyota $16 million for not reporting in the United States a safety problem well known in Europe. It is the maximum fine for such offenses, and the largest ever levied on an automobile company.[12]

Unfortunately for American consumers, "major decisions on engineering, safety, and recalls were still being made almost exclusively in Japan, not in the affected region. Just as important, recall decisions, separated as they were from the region, were based primarily on the input of engineers who did not have direct access to customer feedback. Toyota's culture of fact-based decision making, which has served it so well, essentially excluded from consideration customer complaints or customer sentiment, relying almost entirely on engineering judgments."[13]

Meanwhile, American managers for Toyota were stuck. Their consumer feedback was telling: Toyota cars are not safe. Japan engineers were saying there is no need for a recall. One American manager, Irv Miller, wrote in an e-mail five days prior to the massive Toyota recall, "We need to come clean" about the acceleration problems. "The time to hide this one is over."[14]

The sticky pedal recall covered 2.3 million vehicles in the United States, in addition to the 3.8 million cars recalled for floor-mat problems. (These numbers may include some overlap.)

As Liker explains:

The gap in perception between the United States and Japan was large. In Japan, the perception was that the sticky pedal recall was an example of Toyota putting customers first by issuing a recall for a very rare situation that had not caused any accidents and wasn't perceived as a true safety defect. In the United States, however, this latest recall was completely undermining Toyota's reputation for quality and safety, and the trust that so many Americans had put in it.[15]

Faulty breaks on the Prius and Lexus further added to the cultural and perception crises. In 2010, Toyota received more than 100 complaints about brake performance on the Prius. People said the brakes seem to be unresponsive on bumpy, slick surfaces. As Liker explains,[16] the operative word was "seems" because the issue was not that the brakes didn't slow the car, but that the response "seemed" to be slower than drivers expected. The actual time lag was about 3/100 of a second, during which the brake pedal seemed to be "softer" than drivers expected. "There was no effect on the braking ability or distance," Liker says, "just on the feel of the pedal."

Because braking efficiency wasn't affected, Toyota didn't at first issue a recall, much as it had decided that the sticky accelerator didn't warrant a recall, even though the company had changed the production software on cars still in assembly. The media had fun piling on, and Toyota recalled nearly 500,000 cars to alter the software.

The recall continued Toyota's woes, and added to the growing sentiment that Toyota had suddenly lost the ability to make a safe car.

Consumer perceptions of Toyota's problems were driven largely by media coverage. *The Los Angeles Times* devoted major amounts of space to the ongoing problems Toyota was suffering, offering more than 100 stories during the crisis.[17]

Transportation Secretary Ray LaHood said Toyota was "safety dead" and needed a trip from federal safety officials to Japan to "wake them up."[18] *USA Today,* in an editorial following Toyota's Congressional testimony, said, "Toyota recalls reflect a company that lost its way."[19]

Congress, of course, used the opportunity to posture for American voters, calling Toyota president Akio Toyoda to Washington to apologize for his company and its products.[19]

A so-called "blue ribbon" panel formed after the initial recall, criticized Toyota for being "too centralized," "dismissive of outsiders," and too "quick to equate safety with quality."[20]

The San Francisco public relations firm Fineman PR, in its annual "Top Ten PR Blunders," cited Toyota in 2010, saying "Toyota poorly communicated, provided inconsistent solutions, blamed parts suppliers, and targeted drivers themselves . . ." in addressing the problems related to its vehicles.[21]

Of interest, however, is the reaction of those who currently owned Toyota vehicles versus those who drove competitors' cars and trucks. "Toyota's history insulated it from a great deal of the potential damage from the crisis," Liker says. "Drivers of Toyota vehicles, although they were the ones who were directly affected by the recalls, felt much more positive about the company than those who were not customers."[24] A survey of car owners showed that at the height of the crisis, Toyota owners were twice as likely to buy a Toyota than those who owned competitors' cars."

In February 2010, calls from car owners "were heavy" at dealers around the country, *USA Today* reported.[25] "Most of the people just wanted information," said a service manager in California. "Most of them have been very calm."

## The Problem

Toyota, Liker says, "bears some culpability for what happened . . . . The primary problems

*(Continued)*

were not technical. They were, first and foremost, in how Toyota communicated, both internally and with customers, the public in general, the media, and NHTSA. The root cause of these errors, Toyota later concluded, was the way it historically handled safety and quality concerns, which was overly centralized in a quality department in Japan and focused on an engineering perspective, while the company had lost direct touch with customer perspectives and concerns."[22]

Mr. Toyoda said in his remarks to Congress, "Toyota has, for the past few years, been expanding its business quite rapidly. Quite frankly, I fear the pace at which we have grown may have been too quick. I would like to point out here that Toyota's priority has traditionally been the following: First, safety; second, quality; and third, volume. These priorities became confused, and we were not able to stop, think, and make improvements as much as we were able to before . . . .We pursued growth over the speed at which we were able to develop our people and our organization."[23]

Had Toyota's rapid growth caused it to lose sight of what made it the largest car manufacturer in the world?

"Here's one good reason Toyota became the world's largest automaker," *USA Today* said in an editorial. "In 1989, when the company discovered that the Lexus LS400, its new flagship luxury car, had three flaws, it sped into crisis mode. Within weeks, Toyota came up with three fixes. It produced a video to train dealers, and it recalled 8,000 cars. It even sent mechanics to buyers' homes to repair the Lexus in their driveways.

"Here's one good reason the auto giant has sunk to its current lows: In 2006, when Lexus owner Rhonda Smith reported that her car suddenly accelerated, sped out of control to 100 miles an hour and wouldn't stop even as she stood on the brakes and pulled the emergency brake, Toyota all but called her a liar. In a letter, the company insisted the brakes will always override the accelerator."[26] (The lady later traded her Lexus for a Toyota Tundra.)

## The Public Relations Impact

Another Great Truth of PR (see page 20) says that if your company is challenged, perform research to see if the challenge has merit. If it does, then remedial action is needed to correct the problem, and corrective actions are then the basis of subsequent communication. Communication always follows performance.

For Toyota, coming to the realization that the crisis was real was the first step in coming to grips with the solutions. As Toyota president Akio Toyoda said, "There was a gap between the time that our U. S. colleagues realized that this was an urgent situation and the time that we realized here in Japan that there was an urgent situation going on in the U. S. It took three months for us to recognize that this had turned into a crisis. In Japan, unfortunately, until the middle of January, we did not think this was really a crisis."[27]

The strategy, from the beginning, was to:

1. Accept responsibility
2. Don't blame the customer, dealer or supplier
3. Put customers first

Included in this was the determination to change the culture from "study the problem" to "solve the problem."[32]

Toyota began by making sure the corrective actions were in place. Then it was able to start addressing consumer perceptions. Its 1,223 dealers took a lead position in rebuilding trust, sending tow trucks to those who were reluctant to drive suspect cars to the dealership. This was a service Toyota offered to any customer who wanted it.[28] Toyota even bought back cars from those afraid to continue to drive them. To be sure the dealers could meet customer expectations, Toyota committed a $30 million pool to be divided equally among the dealers.[29]

Toyota's call center (in California, not offshore) was getting some 96,000 calls a day (up from 3,000). Its call center manager called in everyone who had any experience to handle the increased volume.[30] These workers were empowered to authorize expenses (like towing) or service appointments, loaner cars, and extended warranties.

As Jim Lentz, president of Toyota's U.S. operations said, "Obviously, we're tracking spending. But we're doing whatever is necessary to fix any shortcomings that we had in our current process, make sure that we have the right process, and make sure we're taking care of our customers . . . ."[31]

The new policies were put to the test almost immediately. Soon after the 2010 Lexus GX 460 was introduced, *Consumer Reports* wrote that the car failed a rigorous stability test and that it was giving the new Lexus a "do not buy" recommendation.

"In the past, the *Consumer Reports* test would probably have led to weeks, if not months, of internal debate and testing at Toyota," says Liker.[33] "That was no longer Toyota's approach, and a decision to take action was made first, even before a detailed investigation." Toyota stopped sales and issued a voluntary recall to update software that would solve the problem.

To help restore sales, Toyota introduced generous sales incentives that helped bring people back to the dealerships. Toyota also began striking back at critics, pointing out that much of the criticism had come from those with a financial interest in Toyota's plight—plaintiff lawyers and their clients. Negative articles dropped from 235 in February 2010 to seven in August. Toyota paid the fines levied by NHTSA, even without agreeing they were justified.[34]

Today, it's business as usual at most Toyota dealerships. Toyota's safety ratings at the end of 2010 were back to normal for the most part, with 17 models rated "most reliable" by *Consumer Reports*—the most of any manufacturer. *Forbes* rated five Toyota models as most likely to go past 200,000 miles, and Kiplinger put three models on its list of 10 best cars of the past decade.[35]

All the news wasn't good, however. J. D. Power's ratings showed Toyota had slipped behind Ford and Honda in customer loyalty, and 19 percent of new-car buyers were avoiding Toyota because of its "bad reputation."

One blogger, Edward Niedermeyer of the Truth About Cars Web site, said, "Toyota was operating with a halo. And, that halo is gone. It opened the market for a lot more competition. In a numerical sense, Toyota sales haven't gone down as much as they might, but in a strategic sense, it's a much tougher fight saleswise than it might have been . . . ."[36]

## Lessons Learned

Toyota quickly learned that it had not listened carefully to its customers. It didn't know what consumers thought and worried about or even how they used their vehicles.[37] Further, the company's attempts at maintaining close control and efficiency had the "unintended consequence" of causing too many delays in responding to customers and other stakeholders.

Back at corporate headquarters in Japan, Toyota had deliberately kept sales and marketing apart from engineering and design. That way, it could keep design considerations away from cost and price pressures. The thinking was "the quality department could put safety and quality ahead of business concerns and not be unduly influenced by sales or regional units which were concerned with revenue and profitability . . . . But, in trying to protect quality and safety from sales, the company inadvertently choked off a lot of customer feedback . . . ."[38]

In the communication realm, Toyota found that the traditional method of thorough study of an issue resulted in decisions being made in Japan by people who were relatively uninformed about "street conditions" in the States. This had to change.

"We should not just be talking to the customer from a purely engineering viewpoint," said Shinichi Sasaki, executive vice president of global quality. "We have to care more about the customer's feelings."[39]

Toyota is serious about reconnecting with its customers. In June and July of 2010,

(*Continued*)

"Customer First" training centers were opened in Japan, North America, Europe, Southeast Asia, and China "to provide team members with additional training on how to integrate customer needs and feedback into their problem solving and design processes more effectively," Liker says.[40]

In these centers, full-time quality professionals will complete a three-year program, and some 300,000 regular employees will receive between eight and 16 hours of training in the Toyota culture, quality processes, and more.

To further strengthen the bonds with the customers, Toyota extended the two-year free scheduled maintenance program that was originally meant to be a sales incentive. Under this program, the dealer's service crew will see a customer eight times during the first two years of ownership, giving customers face time with the dealer, and the dealer an opportunity to help the owner get the most from his or her car.[41]

What might Toyota have done differently, from a communications perspective?

James Wiseman, who in the midst of the crisis was named group vice-president for communication in North America, believes Toyota could have been more aggressive from the beginning. "Toyota was too risk averse in the early stages of the crisis and should have done more to clearly explain technical issues, speak directly to customers, and explain Toyota's efforts to resolve problems and improve, taking some personal responsibility for this. Generally, I wish we had been more proactive, especially on TV, to speak for our company and all our employees and partners in America. We should have been more visible, including me."[42]

So, in essence, it comes back to Lanny Davis's old saw about putting an end to any crisis: Tell it all. Tell it yourself. Tell it first.

Had Toyota done those things, the crisis might not have been so long, painful, and expensive.

## Questions for Discussion

1. Discuss the pros and cons of Toyota's policy of thorough study of a problem versus a quick response.
2. Why was the American public willing to so readily believe Toyota cars were unsafe?
3. What role did culture play in this situation? Can you think of other situations in which culture might have played a role?
4. How important was it that Toyota had a strong balance sheet and ample reserves during the crisis?
5. Might the definition of safety be different from continent to continent?
6. How might Toyota have (1) predicted or (2) prevented the situation it found itself in?
7. Would you consider buying a Toyota? Why? Why not?

## Citations

1. *USA Today,* February 18, 2010, p 5A
2. Liker, Jeffery K. *Toyota Under Fire,* p. xi
3. *Time,* February 22, 2010, p. 26
4. Liker, p. xii
5. *Time,* February 22, 2010, p. 29
6. *Time,* February 22, 2010, p. 29
7. *Time,* February 22, 2010, p. 30
8. Liker, p. xii
9. Liker, p. xv
10. Liker, p. 96
11. Liker, p. 97
12. Liker, pp. 98–109
13. Liker, p. 101
14. *Orlando Sentinel*, April 8, 2010, p. B6
15. Liker, p. 106
16. Liker, p. 113
17. Liker, p. 123
18. *USA Today,* February 3, 2010, p. 3B
19. *USA Today* , February 25, 2010, p. 10A
20. *USA Today,* May 24, 2011, p. 3B
21. *PR Tactics,* January 2011, p. 4
22. Liker, p. 94
23. *USA Today,* February 25, 2010, p. 10A
24. Liker, pp. 190–191

25. *USA Today,* February 1, 2010, p. 3B
26. *USA Today,* February 25, 2010, p. 10A
27. Liker, p. 128
28. Liker, p. 130
29. Liker, p. 132
30. Liker, pp. 133–134
31. Liker, p. 137
32. Liker, p. 138
33. Liker, p. 141
34. Liker, p. 150–151
35. Liker, p. 195–197
36. Liker, p. 198
37. Liker, p. 163
38. Liker, p. 167
39. Liker, p. 173
40. Liker, p. 178
41. Liker, pp. 179–180
42. Liker, p. 217

## PROBLEM 6-A   A WINE BAR NEEDS POSITIONING

"Berry's" is a wine bar in a southwestern U.S. city with a population of 400,000. In fact, it is the only full-fledged wine bar in the city. While many other bars serve wine, none specialize in fine wines of the United States and Europe as Berry's does. The fact that it is the only wine bar in the city is its problem. Although the city has ample well-educated middle-income people, wine has not developed a following as it has in some larger cities. Because no other wine bars are available, wine drinkers have become used to ordering wine at regular bars rather than at "specialty-shop" wine bars.

Berry's location is good—downtown near some fine hotels and in an area that is being revitalized, further emphasizing its upscale image. The interior is pleasant and has wine vaults for people who want to store their wine there and have it available whenever they come into the bar. All of these vaults have been rented.

The wine bar has been open for only six months. It has a good lunch business, but needs a better evening business (especially during the week).

The total budget for creating the new business is only $11,000. Mr. Berry comes to you because he knows you have just opened your own communications firm. He says, "I know it's not a lot of money, but it's a lot for my business. I can't afford to just buy ads—what do you suggest?"

Consider what type of research you would use to determine how to manage customer satisfaction—how to attract new customers and how to retain the loyalty of existing ones.

On the basis of your research, prepare a one-year strategic marketing plan that prioritizes your publics and uses a mix of one-way and two-way communication activities with evaluation methods built in. Provide a budget that allocates the $11,000 between research and customer relation activities.

Finally, what issues should Berry's be speaking out on, considering the enormity of alcoholism and driving-while-intoxicated problems, so much in the news today? Think about how to position Berry's as a socially responsible drinking establishment.

## PROBLEM 6-B   GOOD INTENTIONS, BAD RESULTS

Earlier this year, when you graduated from college, you were fortunate. You had a job waiting for you at Bart's Cartmart Inc., the largest distributor of motorized vehicles and accessories in Amarillo. The firm's slogan is, "Speed Up with Us!" Bart (Cartwright), the owner, happens to be your father. That saves having to work your way up. Besides, you've already helped out summers, when you weren't using one of the products playing golf, cruising off-road, or mowing the lawn.

This job has great promise. You're an only child, and your dad has long had in mind that you would be taking over the business some day. In preparation, you majored in marketing, minored in public relations, and took several elective courses including one in business law.

To start you out full-time, your dad put you in charge of customer relations. It has been fun and challenging. This first year, you devised a follow-up program in which you or an assistant called on each customer a week or so before the warranty period for the product purchased expired. You asked whether the customer needed anything that you could supply within warranty. Customers praised and liked that attention. And you've had Bart's Cartmart sponsor the winners' awards in one of the major competitive events at the annual Stock Breeders' Exhibition (motor vehicles as well as plaques and ribbons, of course).

This week, the Annual Harvest Festival is on, and acting on a request from the committee running it, you have loaned six used golf carts for the festival events.

*(Continued)*

Your father has been most tolerant of your activities. He obviously wants you to enjoy your job and to relish growing with the company. At the same time, Bart is no softie. He came off a farm and rose in business the hard way. He knows what he wants and is determined to get it. At times he can be tough, if he feels he has to, and even dictatorial.

When you got to work recently, you were handed a morning newspaper by the receptionist. In it there was a story about a 12-year-old boy, the son of a local farmer and Harvest Festival official, who was driving one of your carts around late yesterday afternoon for fun. Something happened, and the cart tipped over on his leg, mangling it, with possible permanent damage. The kid, in the hospital, told his parents, and they told the newspaper reporter, that he "didn't know what happened." He was "just going along fine," when he felt a bump and he couldn't turn the steering wheel. Next thing he knew, the cart was headed for a big harvest machine. He tried to turn the wheel, but it wouldn't work and he became jammed between the cart and the machine. The newspaper carried a head shot of the boy. He was cute. The story indicated that the cart had been borrowed from Bart's Cartmart.

You sought out your father immediately. He said he'd gotten a call from the newspaper late in the evening, but there was no reason to disturb you. He had called the boy's father and mother, with whom he was acquainted, to express concern and sympathy. They were very upset. When he'd mentioned to them that these heavy carts weren't really made for handling by little kids, the father had made some critical remarks about lending out used carts that might have something wrong with them.

"I don't like it," your father said to you. "People don't react reasonably when their own flesh and blood is involved. I doubt we've heard the last of it." You asked him what you could do. Should you send someone in the shop with a trailer to bring the cart back and have it inspected, send the boy a book to read, arrange to retrieve all the loaned carts, or what? "We shouldn't touch that cart," your father said, "not until I can talk to our lawyer. Just sit tight for a few hours, and we'll know where this thing is going."

Within the hour, a lawyer representing the injured boy and his family called the company to say he had requested that local authorities "impound" the cart, and indicated he would want to talk with Bart soon. Also within the hour, your father had talked with the company's lawyer, the agent of the

firm handling the company's insurance, and with a person at the police department who said he would hold the cart. Your father's lawyer, he said, would be talking with the legal department of Rundo, the manufacturer of the carts.

Before the day was over, you and your father talked again in some detail. "This is the kind of thing you dread in a business like this," he told you. "And with so damn many ambulance-chasing lawyers around, good intentions and fair dealing don't always come out the way you had in mind. With the reporters looking for things to blow up into headlines, I can see this thing heating up into a court case and a local issue where people who should be minding their own business stick their noses into ours and choose up sides."

You assure your father that the good intentions in loaning the carts will pay off in the end and that if you're open with the newspeople they'll be fair in whatever they write or say. He says, "We'll see. If you have any ideas as this thing goes along, come tell me. I'll welcome them. But don't go off half-cocked talking with others at the newspaper, with the people on the Festival Committee, or with the next-door neighbors. Come see me first."

Obviously, you are anxious to help, to apply what you learned over four years, and to retain the conviction that if you treat others fairly, you'll be treated fairly in return.

Given the four-step planning process, and the aforementioned events, what might you set as your objective, your strategy, and your main tactics in helping resolve the problem before it boils over into the community and into a courtroom? What might you recommend to your father about the dos and don'ts of customer and community relations in the future, and communications about those relations?

## PROBLEM 6-C  TURNING CUSTOMER COMPLAINTS TO CUSTOMER DELIGHT

Eagle's Wings Airlines is a young company that flies no-frills flights within the United States. You work for its public relations department. Winter holiday time is approaching and flights are booked, but customer complaints are increasing. For now, the cheaper ticket prices are keeping reservations high, but if the level of complaints continues, customers will be lost. In fact, you have just been informed that Eagle's Wings has been named the worst airline in customer service. The number of customer complaints has been piling up on your desk. Flights continually arrive and depart late due to inefficient airport crew members, and the on-flight crew has received poor ratings because of rudeness.

To add to this pressure, flight attendants and pilots are complaining about being overscheduled. They want time off to enjoy the holidays at home with their families, not in some remote location as they wait for a flight back—a result of poor scheduling, which has been happening more frequently.

The number of customer complaints is growing as are employee complaints. You do not have responsibility for human relations but you can see that it impacts customer relations. The head of human relations is very busy and understaffed, but she has agreed to meet with you tomorrow. In the meantime, you need to get a plan formulated because you can't afford to further antagonize customers. In fact, you want to delight customers. How will you do that knowing what you know about this situation? What is your immediate plan of action?

Put together a one-year strategic plan to build consumer relationships, and outline possible problems and solutions. Put into action an evaluation process that will help you gauge the minds of your consumers as well as your employees. This will make it easier for both sides to communicate what they like, don't like, and would like to see improved. You hope this will bring about improvements and repeat customers, which will help business in the long run.

# 7

# Media Relations

The biggest misunderstanding in public relations over the years has concerned the *mass media*: what its role and power really are in modern society and how important media relations are in building effective public relationships.

Many practitioners still go to the extreme of *equating* public relations with publicity. So, unfortunately, do some managers. Others find contemporary journalism so unbalanced in its emphases and objectiveness and its audiences so fractionated that, except in unusual circumstances, they prefer to avoid mass media altogether.

Fortunately, many scholarly studies have given us an objective look from which to devise workable strategies. They find that:

1. ***Mass media influence is cumulative and long-term.*** A single news report, even if covered by media across the country, or an item in a single medium, even if it's the evening news, usually causes little if any behavior or attitude change. But when many media cover a subject over the years, perhaps expressing a viewpoint on the topic, whole generations can be influenced. For example, most of us have no personal experience whatsoever with communism, yet we strongly oppose it—because all our lives it has been a subject portrayed in a negative way in our media. "Going viral" via the Internet will probably speed up the cumulative effects of major incidents.

2. ***The main power of mass media is to make us aware***—of products, services, companies, and ideas—and to provide information about them. By itself, awareness rarely moves us to action or even shapes an opinion. But as a first step in the decision-making process, it is vital. If we don't know something exists, we can't do anything about it. Scholars call this the *agenda-setting role of the media* (see Figure 7.1).

3. ***Mass media concentrate on reporting bad news***—the errors, accidents, and scandals of human society. As an early American political figure said, "In a republic based upon public opinion, it is necessary to excite a spirit of inquiry—to furnish public men with information of their errors."[1] Today, this statement is true not only of elected officials but of all

---

[1] William Plummer, U.S. senator, several times governor of New Hampshire, and historian, in an article titled "To the People," published widely, May 23, 1820.

**FIGURE 7.1** Members of the media, such as the creator of this popular cartoon, recognize the changes that have occurred in news gathering and dissemination. (Reprinted with permission from Universal Press Syndicate. All rights reserved. Calvin and Hobbes copyright 1994 Watterson.)

executives and all organizations as well. As educator Scott Cutlip said, "There are no private organizations today, even if they are totally owned by one or a few persons, because all must abide by the rule of public consent." But research shows we prefer to hear about bad news, rather than good news, by a factor of seven to one. In their own marketing interest, then, it follows that the media would feature bad news. It's what their customers demand.

Clearly the challenge is to create relationships with journalist figures—as with *all* publics—that will permit them to rely on our organizations when we are the focus of interest.

## THE RISE OF SOCIAL MEDIA

Over the past five years, *social* media have come to the forefront of communication—and by default—to public relations. As soon as Facebook, Twitter, and others became the new norm for casual communication, savvy practitioners realized that those media would soon be the media of choice for professional communicators, too.

These new media have some pronounced advantages over the mass media that formed the backbone of traditional public relations communication for a century. The most dramatic improvement brought about by social media is the ability to "go direct" and bypass the gatekeeper and agenda-setting roles of mass media.

Equally important is the immediacy and flexibility of social media. Today's practitioner doesn't have to wait for the six-o'clock news or the home edition to disseminate his or her message. The Internet works 24/7. While most recipients are not sitting by their computers awaiting another message, when they do log on, the message is sitting in their inbox, awaiting an interested set of eyes (and ears) to open it.

Which brings up a third advantage of social media. Sight, sound, color, and motion used to be the purview of only television among the mass media. Now, those attributes can be added to any message via streaming, links to YouTube, or other video.

But the rise of social media has not signaled the end of mass media. Television still remains the number-one choice of American consumers for news and information, according to Pew Research Center (Pewresearch.org). But the public is trending strongly away from mass media. In the past five years:

- TV news as a source of information has fallen from 82 to 66 percent.
- Newspapers' importance dropped from 50 to 31 percent.
- Radio fell from 24 to 16 percent.
- The Internet rose from 13 to 41 percent.

The differences are even greater in so-called "high value" demographics:

- Men 18–49 prefer the Internet over TV by 56 to 55 percent.
- Women 18–49 still choose TV over the Internet 62 to 52 percent.
- Adults under 30 prefer the Internet over TV 65 to 52 percent.
- But the 30–49 crowd still picks TV 63 to 48 percent.

One thing is evident at this point: Our audience's habits are on the move and we must be vigilant in determining what sources are useful for reaching which stakeholders. We must remember that the media—social or mass—are still just a tool in a practitioner's arsenal. They are useful in creating awareness. They are helpful in reaching opinion leaders. Social media can help maintain a relationship that is already established.

Journalists of all hues will continue to report on our organizations, and they have to be dealt with when they do. Practitioners will still have to build positive relationships with journalists if they are to succeed.

Though the generalized relationship between journalists and practitioners may forever be characterized as adversarial, we must remember that the two professions share one basic tenet—the First Amendment—and in pursuit of protecting free speech, we are united.

## WORKING WITH THE MEDIA

An important part of the practitioner's job has been working with the media. This relationship depended on practitioners providing information that news people considered to be of public interest—that is, newsworthy. That relationship is evolving. Newspapers are slowing disappearing, and the journalists left standing have limited time to spend understanding our story, our issues.

As the mass media seek their new position in the Internet age, how they report and present the news is changing. Once that question is settled, if it is ever settled, public relations communicators can determine how best to serve the old and new media alike.

## THE FUNDAMENTALS

For now, practitioners will still have to prepare themselves to serve the old media in traditional ways, even while "going direct" at every possible opportunity. Knowing how traditional media work is important.

Stripped down to basics, the mission of the news media is to inform audiences quickly, accurately, and fully on matters in which audiences express an interest and on matters that affect them significantly, whether or not the audiences have expressed interest, or are even aware of the issues.

In simple terms, the mission of the public relations function is to build working relationships with all of an organization's publics. When appropriate, doing so may require making use of news media when viewpoints or activities are newsworthy.

Along with the opportunity and ability that journalists and public relations practitioners have to shape public opinion go the obligations of truth and accuracy, as specified by the law. A high degree of ethical responsibility involving moral standards and integrity is implicit in serving the best interests of the public.

The freedom of the news media to inform the public and to interpret information without bias is assured by the First Amendment to the Constitution. Abuse of that freedom could lead to loss of credibility with the audience, loss of revenue from advertisers, and public censure. Thus, while news prerogatives are jealously guarded, journalistic education and practices emphasize self-discipline. News media, owned privately and operating competitively for profit, are admittedly careful. When they interject their own views, they are expected to label them as "editorial," "opinion," "analysis," "commentary," and so on.

The public relations function comes under the freedom of speech provision in the First Amendment. Practitioners have the choice of telling their story in paid space or time or offering it as news, subject to editing or rejection by the media. The penalties for abuse of free speech rights by a private organization can be the loss of supportive constituents such as shareholders, employees, neighbors, customers, members, or donors, as the case might be. Then, too, there is monitoring by the FCC, FTC, and other federal agencies, as well as professional and trade societies. Within the professional practice of public relations, the penalties can be sanctions from professional groups such as the Public Relations Society of America (see Chapter 10) or exposure by the news media. The penalties to the individual practitioner for being "clever" in manipulating facts, being "devious" in dealings with journalists, being "unavailable" when sought by the media, or being "unauthorized as the spokesperson" for an employer can be reaped in loss of credibility and integrity in the eyes of the media and consequently loss of some functional value to the employer. The sword has an edge on both sides of the blade.

## A DIFFICULT, DELICATE TASK

The practitioner serves two masters. One is the employer. The other is the public interest. Traditionally, the news media stood between the two. The practitioner travels a precarious and rather thin line. The employer wants his or her best foot put forward in public. There are bound to be times when public exposure can be damaging to a campaign, a product, or a reputation. At these times, employers would prefer no publicity. Then there are times when the truthful and accurate response to a press inquiry is simply not known (the facts have not been ascertained). There are times when an organization's policies, or legal or competitive considerations, give precedence to its "privacy" over the "public's right to know." At such times, the forbearance of the media is desired—but rarely forthcoming.

If a practitioner is not able to handle the flow of information so that favorable news is covered and adverse news is at least treated fairly, the practical value of the practitioner to the employer is somewhat limited. However, practitioners must make it clear to employers and clients that they cannot control the media.

## GUIDELINES THAT HAVE SURVIVED

Although, as noted earlier, it is risky to draw generalizations about relations with mass media, a number of guidelines are widely followed:

1. Start with a sound working knowledge of the methods and the technology involved in gathering potential news, evaluating it, processing it editorially, and putting it into the best format and mode for newsprint, magazine, broadcast, and electronic media. Be able to fit into the process.
2. Be sure that the employer has a designated spokesperson available on short notice. It may be you.
3. Have spokespeople be as candid as possible in response to inquiries—within the limits of obvious competitive and national security and of compassionate consideration for those hurt by the news.
4. Play the percentages, as in a long successful partnership, taking the instances of bad news in stride alongside a record of good news coverage achieved.
5. Continuously educate and train employers and spokespeople on how to handle themselves when in contact with news media.
6. Generate good news situations as a track record to offset instances of undesired news. Do not simply wait defensively for bad news.
7. Advocate an employer's views on public issues among the organization's natural constituencies and in the news media receptive to them.
8. Expect the unexpected and be prepared for it. In particular, have a crisis or disaster plan for every foreseeable circumstance.

## STRATEGY FOR THE NEW CENTURY

In today's environment, people want to be served, not sold; involved, not told. Where do the media fit in when reaching out to and involving these stakeholders? Here's a five-point strategy:

1. *Build relationships face-to-face.* Earning trust through relationships motivates behavior. Once a relationship is formed, people will accept and pay some heed to your communications.

2. *Make internal publics top priority*—inreach before outreach. Only satisfied employees can deliver customer delight.

3. *Consider "going direct" to bypass media.* As journalists become entertainment-oriented voyeurs and media credibility and reach continue to decline, rarely can the media help, even if disposed to do so. Instead, go direct to key publics, and don't make yourself overly visible since that may attract media snooping.

4. *Use accountable, focused, measurable programs.* Once called "soft," these public relations programs incorporate value-adding efforts. Strategic philanthropy, value-added and cause-related marketing, and loyalty programs are prominent examples. The former "we're just nice people" approach never jibed with other organizational behaviors and was not trusted.

5. *Expand research*—far beyond statistical surveys. Research has gone beyond lip-service to be the backbone of programming and strategy setting. Top research techniques are participative: focus groups, panels, Delphi studies, and gap research.

Public relations practitioners know now that one-way information transfer is insufficient. We must pursue the ideal of two-way dialogue. Involving stakeholders and offering them service, information, or events are the keys.

# ✗ Case 7-1 The Role of the Media and Public Relations in Negotiating Public Policy—Real Salt Lake City Builds Stadium in Utah

Spending public money is a contentious issue no matter what level of our government—local, state, or federal. Everyone has an opinion, and so they should, since it is their money being spent. In January of 2005, Salt Lake City decided to build a soccer stadium for the soccer club Real Salt Lake (RSL) after Major League soccer announced plans to bring a team to Salt Lake City. Although the legislature passed a bill by March 2006 to fund the stadium, the process ground to a halt as questions and concerns mounted, partially because the news media ran the public discussion.

## The Media and Conflict Resolution

The media's role in public policy has been to be a *watchdog* of government or an independent third party similar to a mediator. "Mediators and facilitators know that news coverage can benefit a consensus-building process immeasurably" (p. 436), according to Kunde (1999). The news media that provide responsible and balanced coverage that informs the public can legitimize or hinder an ongoing public negotiation, but they help to ensure that the players involved are held accountable in serving the publics' interests. "Indeed, sometimes mediators and participants need press coverage to generate support for a process, and actively seek it out" (p. 436). The reconciliation of a conflict occurs when all parties in the conflict are mostly satisfied with the outcome. As media resources shrink and media technologies expand, so does the ability of other stakeholders—such as RSL, the fans and voters, and state and local governments—to influence the media's role in building consensus in a dispute.

---

### Conflict Resolution and Public Relations

Managing public relations strategically involves a long-term perspective. In conflict-resolution terms, a win/win situation for all parties involved in an issue is better predicted if the parties or stakeholders have a long-term relationship. Stakeholders are more likely to support a win/win in any given short-term involvement if they know they are going to have to deal with one another again and again in the future.

Abdicating responsibility for stakeholder communications to media—be it traditional or social—is a recipe for problems in these situations. Practitioners who rely strictly on the media to communicate information miss the opportunity to (1) communicate information unfiltered, (2) listen for feedback in order to refine messages going forward, and (3) build trust through face-to-face connections. Playing everything out on the front pages not only inflames but infects those who may not have previously heard, considered, or concluded anything about your subject.

---

Contributed by Ken Plowman, associate professor public relations, Brigham Young University

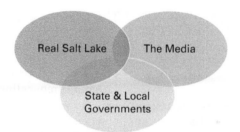

**FIGURE 7.2**    Key Publics or Stakeholders—
A Contentious or Cooperative
Effort

## Timeline of Events

- July 2004—Major League soccer announces plans to bring a team to Salt Lake City.
- January 2005—Salt Lake City leaders announce willingness to buy land for a downtown stadium and consider use of redevelopment agency funds—public funds—for the construction of that stadium.
- May 2005—Sandy, a suburb of Salt Lake, bids on the stadium.
- March 2006—The Utah legislature passes a bill allowing public funds to be used for the project.
- May 2006 through January 2007—A number of funding plans are proposed and rejected for a variety of reasons, including questions about financial viability, the gap between funds offered and actual projected costs, etc.
- January 26, 2007—The Salt Lake County debt review committee votes 4–0 against the stadium proposal.
- January 29, 2007—Salt Lake County mayor Pete Corroon supports the debt review committee decision, and the deal is officially declared dead. The RSL team then announces it is "weighing options," including selling the team.
- February 2007—A new stadium proposal is put forward, and the state senate eventually passes the deal. With the intervention of Governor Jon Huntsman, construction of the stadium finally becomes a reality.

- Oct 2008—The Rio Tinto Stadium opens.

## Events Unfold

"They [Sandy City officials] weren't always happy to see us [Sandy City was the final location for the stadium]," said a journalist who had covered the process. "The media's influence made the discussion heated; every move they made, we (the media) were watching and reporting."

Negotiation was portrayed in the media as a contentious process. The reaction, therefore, was that the media itself was stirring controversy since they were reporting on the problems in negotiations. "The media were reporting on a contentious process, so it became contentious in the media."

Though the media viewed themselves as striving to be objective on this issue, in hindsight they acknowledged that they had been influential. Said one journalist, "Politicians were reading [what we wrote] and making decisions."

The media tried to act as a neutral third-party mediator. They affected the public negotiation. They provided the public with information, thereby fulfilling an agenda-setting role. And the media extended the conflict by framing and amplifying the issue, thus extending the life cycle of the conflict until ultimate resolution. In some cases, the media believed that their presence at meetings about building the stadium introduced more circumspection into deliberations and that in

*(Continued)*

such cases participants were very aware of the media's presence and took that presence into account.

## RSL Struggles

RSL saw the media as trying to promote a contentious negotiation process. "They wanted contention. They wanted to rabble-rouse. They wanted a debate," commented a consultant who worked with RSL.

One newspaper in particular "wanted some agitation," said an RSL representative. [The paper] wanted [Mayor] Peter Corroon to look like he was taking on [RSL owner] Dave Checketts. They framed stories that way . . . . They're selling papers and they need that . . . ." Furthermore, the media not only promoted the idea of a contentious negotiation process, but RSL felt that they were successful in selling their idea of a contentious negotiation process. "Of course they are influential," said an RSL representative, "and they stir up the public."

Media and government representatives felt that this issue—especially when it came to the complicated funding proposals being discussed—was too complex for most of the public to comprehend. "It's a complicated issue that most people don't understand," was the statement made by one RSL representative. "Most people, as much as we tried, didn't understand" that the deal RSL was looking for was not any different than deals that had been given to others who had previously built successful sports and entertainment venues in the state.

As the other players in the negotiations did, RSL recognized that the complicated funding issue was the main sticking point for all sides. Should public money be used to help finance private ventures, and if so, how much money is too much to give? RSL found the state government, and then-governor Jon Huntsman, exceptionally cooperative. Said one RSL representative, "We had support from Greg Curtis (the then-speaker of the House, who helped propose initial funding); we had support from the legislature . . . ."

## The County Weighs In

Salt Lake County, on the other hand, was a different story. In spite of RSL owner Dave Checketts's efforts to reach out to the media, including frequenting editorial board meetings, he was perceived, in the words of one observer, as ". . . the red-headed stepchild that the media loved to kick around, and for two reasons: One, he was out of town and he was viewed as this rich New York millionaire coming in . . . and trying to rape the public, and it was easy to play that stereotype; and two, he was in a very public battle with [another prominent Utah sports franchise owner]."

RSL officials had difficulty understanding why they were being met with such tremendous opposition in the press and, subsequently, from the public who were influenced by the media. The hostile media environment RSL found itself in began to cool, however, once much of the news begins to slip off the front page and onto the sports page. Said an RSL representative, "I'll tell you what: the media ultimately started helping. The sports reporters got interested in the sport. The team became successful and the team became beloved." The negotiation process changed once the public was able to look beyond dollar signs and see a new, exciting sports franchise to cheer for.

One important opinion leader for the public was one of Governor Huntsman's children. "[The stadium negotiations] were the first time in [Huntsman's] gubernatorial career that he stuck his neck out," said one observer, "and he did it because his 16-year-old daughter—or son—I'm not sure which, said, 'Dad, soccer's cool! What are you going to do? Let this get away? You're going to let this get away?' . . . And Jon [Governor Huntsman] made it happen."

Governor Huntsman's efforts came in the nick of time, as RSL had threatened to move to St. Louis if a funding deal was not reached by a certain date. This very real threat (Checketts had a buyer ready to sign a check to buy a portion of RSL and seal the deal for the team's move) proved to be effective in getting a deal done.

When asked if time constraints, and specifically the deadline for moving the team, played a role in moving the negotiations along, an RSL representative replied in the affirmative, stating that, "If there's no line in the sand, it would just get pushed off." Checketts was within hours of finalizing the team's move to St. Louis when Governor Huntsman "stepped in and said, 'We're going to make this happen.'"

## Reframing Clears the Path

While some felt the media was portraying the negotiations as filled with contention, the reframing of the stadium as a sports story helped build public support for the team and for the stadium, despite the fact that many of the main sticking points in the negotiations, specifically the tax issues, were never fully understood by the public.

The newfound public support, along with RSL's self-imposed deadline to move the team to St. Louis if no funding deal was reached, helped persuade the governor to step in and act to create the tax mechanism that would keep RSL in Utah.

## Media in Control

Overall, the presence of the media at committee meetings and other "unaccustomed" places introduced more circumspection and hesitancy into deliberations. They were not neutral in their stance on the issue. And they framed the issue for discussion in the public arena—not with RSL or the cities involved. They actually amplified and extended the life cycle of the dispute before it was finally resolved to the mutual satisfaction of the city of Sandy, Salt Lake County, the state of Utah, and RSL. But the media did play a valuable role, not in mediation, but in education and focus on the issue.

## What This Means for Public Relations Strategies and Tactics

Communicating with key publics does not always mean using the media in a positive way. Some city council members ". . . would turn to the audience and say, don't believe them [the media]—they've got it all wrong." The bulk of the public discourse around the construction of the RSL stadium was concluded nearly five years ago. But changes in the media industry—and in the technology of media delivery over those five years beg the question: How might these negotiations look different if they were being conducted today?

In Utah, significantly fewer reporters cover local governments today than five years ago. A swarm of journalists like the one reporting on the RSL stadium negotiations at that time might be difficult to find today—a reality echoed by one negotiator, who lamented that he had not seen a reporter in his office in two and a half years. And if, in fact, there are no journalists to facilitate a negotiator's ability to "play to publics" what is the cost to the public good?

## The Role of Social Media

At the time, social media platforms like Twitter were not as prevalent as they are today. Today, citizens attending city council meetings can instantaneously tweet the results. The fluidity of the news and the unbroken 24/7 news cycle would have changed the landscape of 2005 to 2007, when the publication of news about the negotiations occurred at regular *stagegates*. This intermittent—rather than continuous—release of news allowed all the negotiating parties "troughs" in between major public developments, enabling them to react, regroup, and reposition themselves before the curtain rose on the next act of this long-running drama.

The "layer of interpretation" provided by the media, who viewed one of their main roles as educating the public about this very intricate issue, would also have been very different. Today's journalists operate in an era of social media sound bites, frequently issued by citizen journalists who may not have the background knowledge to educate the public—and who indeed may not even view it as their job to do so. The RSL stadium issue was complicated

*(Continued)*

enough when it was explained by a seasoned corps of journalists who had spent months or years following and studying it and writing literally dozens of stories about it. How effectively could such a complex topic be communicated in 140 characters or fewer?

"Reporting is becoming more participatory and collaborative," says Alan Rusbridger, editor of Britain's newspaper *The Guardian*, in an article in the *Columbia Journalism Review*. "The ranks of news gatherers now include not only newsroom staffers, but freelancers, university faculty members, students, and citizens . . . . There is increased competition among the different kinds of news gatherers, but there also is more cooperation, a willingness to share resources and reporting with former competitors. That increases the value and impact of the news they produce, and creates new identities for reporting while keeping old, familiar ones alive."

### Questions for Discussion

1. How much did the presence of the media influence the stakeholders in this case? And did it ensure greater responsiveness or responsibility on the part of the negotiating parties? Or did the media merely inform the public and make it aware of the issues involved in the public dispute?

2. Do traditional media still matter when it comes to serving the public interest and

in policy making, especially with the rise of social media, for example, blogs and Twitter, which are becoming more credible in the eyes of the public?

3. Is this process of public policy making and negotiating in the public arena simple or messy and complicated, and is it worth our time in pursuing? What is the responsibility of public relations practitioners in this process? Where do the media stand in the process—what stakeholders do they represent? And, does this process serve the public interest effectively? Or, is it self-serving to the media?

## References

*Deseret News* (2008). http://www.deseretnews.com/article/655192500/Timeline-Real-Salt-Lake-soccer-stadium.html.

Kunde, J.E. (1999). Dealing with the press. In L. Susskind, S. McKearnan, & J. Thomas-Larmer (Eds.). *The consensus building handbook* (pp. 435-62). Thousand Oaks, CA: Sage.

Plowman, K.D. (2006). "Public Relations, Conflict Resolution, and Mediation." In E.L. Toth, ed. *The Future of Excellence in Public Relations and Communication Management: Challenges to the Next Generation."* July, pp. 85–102.

Rusbrider, A. (2009). *The Guardian* editor, http://www.editorsweblog.org/newspaper/2009/10/rusbridgers_mutualized_news.php.

Tofel. R.K. (May 24, 2010). "Why Corruption Grows in Our States." *The Daily Beast.*

# ★Case 7-2 Social Media and Activism: Anyone Can Now Easily Play

The history of social activism has long been rooted in individual commitment and mass media. Organized labor, civil rights, the women's movement, and war protests all counted on making a statement that could be picked up and projected to the masses via the magic of the printing press, radio wave, or television tube.

Protestors still march and sit in. Consider the several Middle Eastern governments toppled with the help of Facebook-driven communication that created something akin to a "flash mob" atmosphere across the Arab world.

To bring attention to what it considered abuses in Washington and Wall Street, the "Occupy" movement "occupied" public spaces from Florida to Washington State. The "99 percent" didn't like being pushed around by the "one percent," so public parks and sidewalks were clogged with people exercising their First Amendment rights.

But, slowly, almost quietly, another option is growing: the online petition.

"Before," said Hayagreeva Rao, a Stanford University professor of communication studies and human resources, "to be an activist, you had to go on a march. Now, all you have to do is log on."[1]

In 2011, a 22-year-old college graduate, Molly Katchpole, was incensed that Bank of America was going to charge its customers $5 a month to use the bank's debit card. She initiated an online petition against the bank using Change.org, a Web site launched in 2007 to do just what Ms. Katchpole was doing—create a groundswell of opinion without leaving the house.[2]

Her petition attracted more than 300,000 supporters in a month, giving the bank sufficient cause to revoke the offending fee. Emboldened by her success, Ms. Katchpole then went after a similar situation

at Verizon, which was charging a $2 fee for some of its online payment options. One day—and 130,000 signatures—later Verizon reconsidered.[3]

Change.org is the brainchild of Ben Rattray, a Stanford graduate who saw the power of the petition joining the ubiquity of the Internet. The result is a Web site that just about anyone can join and use to gain support from people around the globe. In mid-2012, Change.org had 10 million members, 100 employees, and 500 new petitions a day.[4]

Change.org is currently available in four countries, and Rattray hopes to see his baby grow to 20 countries in the near future, comprising 25 million members.[5]

Joining Change.org is free, and there is no charge for posting a petition. Subject matter is not restricted, unless it promotes hate or violence. "We don't tell people what issues they should care about. We let them decide and give them the tools to do something about it," Rattray said.[6]

On its Web site, the company describes itself. "Change.org is a social action platform that empowers anyone, anywhere to start, join, and win campaigns to change the world. We're proud to be a certified B Corp, using the power of business for social good."

A visit to Change.org reveals a long line of "victories" as well as tips on how to start a petition, a list of featured petitions and top causes, and press coverage generated by the site and its petitions. Streaming across the top of the page are "victories" ranging from Katchpole's Bank of America bringdown to that of a fourth-grade class petition to Universal Studios to present its *Lorax* film in an ecofriendly context.[8]

Of particular interest is the amount of press coverage the site has generated. *The New York*

*(Continued)*

## The Agenda Setting Function of the Social Media?

The new media take an approach that is radically different from that of the traditional media, whose approach had been to serve as what Marshall McLuhan called the "agenda setter." Newspapers used to say, "We don't tell people what to think, we tell them what to think about." Included in that mentality was the "gatekeeper" role, personified by the tag line of the *The New York Times*: "All the news that's fit to print." Of course, it was the Times' news personnel who determined if something was "fit to print."

Today, with the shrinking size and budgets of traditional media, they look to the social media forums and bloggers to set the agenda for what they will then print or air. Traditional media provides more information about issues, concerns, and events that the social media world is addressing in real time.

For public relations practitioners, the new, electronic petition is one more way to hear from stakeholders, whether they want to or not, whether traditional media has covered it or not. As *Time Magazine* said:

*"Rattray's site has quietly enabled tens of thousands of people, many with little exposure to social activism, to launch homegrown crusades on issues ranging from corporate malpractice to immigration reform without ever gathering in a park or square. . . . Change.org is putting companies and governments under tremendous pressure to change their policies, sometimes in a matter of a few weeks or less . . . ."[7]*

*Times,* for example, covered the *Lorax* petition, calling Change.org "the go-to site for Web uprisings." A *Washington Post* story cited Change.org and its role in "populist" causes.

What this coverage proves is the power of social media to move ahead of traditional media. Never was this more obvious than in the shooting of 17-year-old Trayvon Martin in Sanford, Florida. The hoodie-wearing teen was shot in the parking lot of a gated community by a neighborhood watch volunteer, George Zimmerman. At first, the police ruled it a justified shooting, and declined to arrest Zimmerman.

Then, 11 days later, a Howard University student originated a petition on Change.org to force Sanford police to charge someone with the killing. A Change.org staffer noticed the petition and thought it would resonate with more people if it came from Martin's parents. Renamed "Prosecute the killer of our son, 17-year-old Trayvon Martin," the petition resulted in 300 signatures a minute at its peak, and more than two million in a week.[9] Zimmerman

was arrested and charged and awaits trial as of this writing.

Once the petitions started hitting the news, the mass media couldn't get enough of the story. Fanning the flames were Al Sharpton and Jesse Jackson, and even President Obama chimed in saying, "If I had a son, he would look like Trayvon."

Every major network, most dailies, and countless reporters descended on Sanford for nearly two weeks until Zimmerman was arrested. Clearly, the mass media would rather follow a story than lead it. Change.org has no problem leading one.

Not every petition gets the extra boost that the Martin drive received. Most of the featured petitions are on the liberal side of the agenda, and conservative causes seldom generate much interest, inside or outside Change.org. As *Time Magazine* pointed out:

*. . . Change.org's membership, judging by its petitions on social and political issues, plainly leans left . . . . (Rattray) allows that a petition with a pronounced*

*conservative objective—say, the closure of an abortion clinic—is unlikely to get singled out for the kind of special assistance made available to Trayvon Martin's parents.*

The success of Change.org is one more step toward individual action and away from persuasion of the masses via mass media. Research by the Pew Research Center reveals more and more Americans are turning from traditional media and toward the Internet for news and information. Television is still the number one source for news, but the Internet is close behind. That is especially true for younger audiences.[10]

In the past 10 years:

- TV news as a source of information has fallen from 82 to 66 percent.
- Newspapers' importance dropped from 50 to 31 percent.
- Radio fell from 24 to 16 percent.
- The Internet rose from 13 to 41 percent.

For those who practice public relations, positive relationships are going to be increasingly important in the future. The ability to bypass mass media and the agenda-setting and gatekeeping roles is certainly a welcome change. But the sword has a second side, and it's sharp.

Just as the PR community can go direct, so can activists.

**Questions for Discussion:**

1. Is the emergence of Change.com a good thing or a bad thing for the future of public relations? How? Why?
2. Is the decline of mass media a positive or negative for PR practitioners? Why?
3. Why does Change.org seem to favor "populist" causes?
4. How would the liberal bent shape your opinion of the service?
5. What steps should businesses and corporations take to maximize the value of a site such as Change.org (or minimize the damage)?

## References

1. *Time Magazine,* April 9, 2012, p. 42
2. Change.org Web site
3. *Time,* p. 42
4. Wikipedia "Change.org"
5. *Time,* p. 42
6. *Time,* pp. 42–43
7. *Time,* pp. 41–42
8. Change.org Web site
9. *Time,* pp. 41–42
10. Pew Research Center (Media Trends, 2011)

# ⭐Case 7-3 There's a Syringe in My Pepsi Can!

Large corporations are always potential targets for those who seek fame or fortune at the expense of those companies. In the summer of 1993, PepsiCo, makers of Pepsi-Cola and Diet Pepsi, among other beverages, found itself an unwilling subject in one of the most widespread news stories of the day, a story in which the PepsiCo was implicated in multiple claims of foreign objects being found in unopened cans of Diet Pepsi.[2]

This confidence crisis put the international soft-drink company before the public in a way no company wants to be viewed. But the ensuing activities of the Pepsi response team and the U.S. Food and Drug Administration (FDA) calmed the crisis and won for the company the coveted "Best of Silver Anvils" award in the 1994 Public Relations Society of America competition.

## The Situation

On June 9, 1993, Tacoma, Washington, residents Earl (Tex) and Mary Triplett reported finding a used syringe in a half-empty Diet Pepsi can. They turned the can over to their lawyer who contacted the county health department.

The next day, local television station KIRO aired a report of this incident, citing a Sudafed tampering just two years previously, and the fact that needles aroused concerns about AIDS. No other news medium covered the story that day.

The following day, June 11, a second needle claim was made in Washington, and *The Seattle Times* and other local media picked up the story, adding that in neither case had there been reports of injury resulting from the incidents.

On June 12, the FDA did not recommend a recall, but did issue a five-state consumer alert, asking consumers to pour soft drinks, particularly Diet Pepsi, into a glass or cup before drinking them. The next day, a New Orleans man claimed to have found a syringe in a can of Diet Pepsi, and by June 14, 10 more claims were reported.

Wire services and national broadcast media picked up the story as more reports came in. The coverage was second only to the Supreme Court nomination of Ruth Bader Ginsburg, as people reported finding syringes, sewing needles, pins, screws, a crack cocaine vial, and even a bullet in Diet Pepsi cans.

By June 16, claims had been reported in 24 states, including one from a reporter for *The Milwaukee Journal* who said she had no plans to sue Pepsi after finding a needle in a can of Diet Pepsi. Meanwhile, *The Los Angeles Times* and CBS reported the needle found by the Tripletts may have belonged to a diabetic relative. In one week's time, more than 50 incidents had been reported to the police, the FDA, or the media. None, however, reported any illness or injury associated with the incidents.

## The Facts

Throughout this seven-day nightmare, neither Pepsi nor the FDA could see any rational reason for the alleged incidents being reported. Soft-drink filling lines are high-speed, high-tech production lines in which empty, open aluminum cans are fed (upside down) down a conveyer at high speeds (1,200 a minute) to be filled. During this roller-coaster ride, the cans are cleaned with heat, water, and air before

[2] This case was prepared by University of Central Florida students under the supervision of instructor Frank R. Stansberry, APR, Fellow PRSA, now retired.

being inverted, passing through a closed filling filter or screen, and emerging filled and capped at the end. At no time is there an opportunity for foreign objects to find their way into the container, except during the brief time in the filling chamber. Further, the objects being reported are not those commonly found in a soft-drink plant or any other workplace.

The geographic spread of the reports was also difficult to understand. Canning plants are regional operations. The plant in Washington serves only five western states. Yet contaminants were being reported all across the county. These products were being produced by numerous canning operations, so there was no direct link among them except for the brand of the product being produced, and the production process. Unless there was a concerted effort to tamper with Diet Pepsi, there was no reason to link the widespread reports to a single production problem. The FDA said continually it could find no connection from a production standpoint among the growing number of complaints.

Pepsi-Cola Company, convinced its production operations were not at fault, decided against any recall of the products involved. Pepsi-Cola Company President Craig Weatherup, taking the "point guard" position on the response team, said repeatedly in interviews that "there is no health issue" related to the reports, citing the lack of any illness or injuries associated with the reports.

In a *Wall Street Journal* interview, Weatherup said, "We've gone through every can line, every plant, numerous records. All the evidence points to syringes going into the cans after they were opened."

## The Perceptions

"All the evidence" was lost on the news media and the consuming public, however. "When the national media juggernaut gets hold of something, and you're it," Pepsi-Cola Company Vice-President of Public Affairs Becky Madeira told a PRSA workshop a year

later, "it's a public trial, and it's not much fun. This was a crisis without precedent."

Fueling the controversy were the continued reports of new contaminants found in Diet Pepsi. In city after city, residents came forth to press their claims of having found foreign objects in their cans of Diet Pepsi. Time after time, the familiar Diet Pepsi logo (being advertised at the time with the popular Ray Charles jingle punctuated by "Uh Huh") was being seen in the media with either an alleged contaminant object or a facsimile.

Weatherup continued the counterattack, saying he was "99.99 percent sure" the incidents were not related to anything under Pepsi's control. But sales slipped. Weatherup, in a follow-up report after the crisis had been put to rest, said, "The week of the hoax, sales dipped only three to four percent . . . ," but three percent of Diet Pepsi's sales still represents millions of dollars. The perception crisis was real, indeed.

Adding to the difficulty in containing the spreading number of incidents was a 10-year pattern of substantiated and unsubstantiated product tamperings—some with fatal consequences. In 1982 (and later in 1986) deaths were reported from Tylenol capsules laced with poison (see Case 6-3). In 1986, rat poison was found in Contac (and other) products; glass fragments were discovered in Gerber baby food; and two people died in Washington after taking cyanide-laced Extra-Strength Excedrin. And there were the deaths of two people in Washington from ingesting Sudafed. The consuming public had reason to be concerned, as did Pepsi. With the number of soft-drink alternatives available, some consumers were opting for the competition.

## The Problem

The problem for Pepsi was how to stem the reports, show the safety of its products, and win back the customer loyalty, which had made Diet Pepsi the number two diet drink in the country.

*(Continued)*

Timing was important because the reports were mounting before the wildfire of news reports. "Speed is essential," said Madeira, "but so is accuracy. It is very dangerous to attempt to explain the cause of the crisis without facts that are corroborated from outside experts. In our case, the expert was the FDA."

The most important question was "Is there a health risk?" The FDA took the lead in answering this question, and almost immediately determined that, in the two Seattle-area reports, there was no health hazard or risk.

A second question involved the presence of syringes and needles in or around the filling chamber. Again, the FDA became the intervening public and determined, after an exhaustive examination of Pepsi's procedures and facilities, that the high speed and integrity of the filling lines made it impossible for any such object to find its way into the canning process. There was no internal tampering. Whatever was turning up in the cans had been placed there after the cans were opened. FDA Commissioner David Kessler agreed that there was no health risk from the tamperings and, most probably, no relationship between the alleged tampering reports popping up coast to coast.

The facts obviously weighed heavily in Pepsi's favor—the randomness of the reports, the security of the filling line process, the dubious nature of all the claims, the variety of objects being reported, and the fact that needles and syringes were never found in production-line situations under normal conditions. No one said there were any health issues resulting from the tamperings. There was no reason to think any of the reports had merit.

Perceptions, fueled by media reports, however, were just the opposite. Consumers in nearly two dozen states were lining up to claim contaminants were found in Diet Pepsi cans. Diet Pepsi cans were on television as much as Jay Leno—nightly. In fact, Leno and his peers were having a field day with the issue, poking fun at the difficult situation in nightly monologues. Editorial cartoonists also joined the spoofing by suggesting that everything from a power drill to the famous "missing sock" was turning up in Diet Pepsi cans. For a seemingly endless 96 hours, the Diet Pepsi scare was the nation's top news story. Something had to be done, and the Pepsi team mobilized and swung to the offensive.

## The Public Relations Impact

When the story first broke on June 9, Pepsi let the local bottler, Alpac Corporation, handle the media inquiry. Operating under the premise that the plant was secure, Alpac also had to investigate any possible way an object *could* have been introduced during the filling process. Working with local health officials and the FDA, Alpac assisted in the investigation and found nothing that would implicate the filling line.

The plant was opened to the media, and the plant owner, manager, and quality assurance manager were made available to the press. All they were able to say at the time, however, was that the situation was unusual and that they would do everything they could to cooperate with local authorities to find the cause of the crisis.

But even these findings did not stem the tide of complaints filtering in or the growing media interest in the problem. Pepsi was going to have to get involved at the national level; the problem was more than Alpac's to solve.

Crisis coordinator Madeira identified four primary publics to be addressed:

- The news media
- Customers (those who purchased the product for retail sale)
- Consumers
- Employees and local Pepsi-Cola bottlers

The **public affairs department,** which Madeira directed, had a team of six media relations specialists prepared to respond to media inquiries and to provide regular updates of facts and developments. "One Clear Voice" was the key approach. A second team wrote and produced video news releases, audiotapes, press releases, charts, and diagrams of the production process and photos for external and internal distribution.

**Consumer relations** had 24 people manning the 24-hour toll-free hotlines, taking calls from consumers, hearing reports and comments, and monitoring public opinion as it developed.

**Scientific and regulatory affairs** assigned technical and quality assurance specialists to work with the FDA and local health departments to evaluate and track each complaint.

**Sales and marketing** personnel were responsible for maintaining relationships with its customers—supermarkets, restaurants, convenience stores, and others who sold Pepsi products to the consumer.

**Manufacturing** experts assisted the FDA and developed simple, easy-to-understand explanations of the filling line process for the news media and the public.

The **legal department** was involved at all stages of the reporting and communication process.

The entire effort was kept in-house as opposed to the company bringing in an outside crisis communication consultant.

Pepsi's response centered on four principles:

- **Put public safety first.** Look at the problem through the perspective of the public and address their concerns.

- **Find the problem and fix it.** Pepsi was convinced the problem was not within its production facilities, so it worked with the regulatory authorities to demonstrate the security of its plants, and to investigate and respond to all complaints.

- **Communicate frequently, quickly, and regularly.** Use both broadcast and print communication tools. Be honest, available, and informed about what the media need and be prepared to meet those needs.

- **Take full responsibility for resolving the crisis.** Pepsi realized quickly that this was a problem that the public expected it to help resolve. Pointing fingers at consumers or ducking responsibility was never an option even though most on the crisis-response team felt the reports of foreign objects were hoaxes.

The chief weapon in the defusing of the crisis would be a compelling video news release showing exactly what happens on a can filling line and how difficult it would be to introduce any foreign element into a can during this process.

Television had brought the crisis into 100 million American homes, and television would be Pepsi's best opportunity to expose the folly of the reports. On June 15, six days after the Tripletts said they found the syringe, Pepsi presented a dramatic look at an ordinary can filling line. The same consumers who had seen the Diet Pepsi cans with syringes now saw millions of the blue and red cans whirring by at the rate of 1,200 per minute. Image confronted image—and news programs picked up the video news release (VNR) in such numbers that soon nearly 300 million viewers had seen the footage.

That initial VNR and three subsequent ones presented the company's position that its production lines were safe and secure. Diet Pepsi was safe when it left the plant. Weatherup, continuing his role of spokesperson, appeared on a dozen major TV shows, and the Pepsi public affairs team had conducted nearly 2,000 interviews within the week.

"Our strategy was to reassure the public that this was not a manufacturing crisis," said Madeira. "What was happening was not occurring inside our plants."

The strategy worked, assisted by some excellent support from the FDA and some good luck. A third Pepsi-Cola VNR contained images from an in-store surveillance camera that showed a woman trying to stick a syringe into a Diet Pepsi can while the cashier was not looking. Tampering with the food supply is a

*(Continued)*

felony, and the woman was arrested. When the arrest was made, the VNR was released and the hoax began to crumble.

Many who had made claims against Pepsi began to recant their stories for fear of prosecution. In states across the country, arrest after arrest was made and reported by the media. Those who tried to profit at the expense of "big business" were located and apprehended. The media had gotten the message and were eager to highlight the consequences faced by the perpetrators. Weatherup continued his offensive and, as the number of arrests increased, claimed vindication for the Pepsi products.

By June 21, Pepsi was being defended and applauded in editorials and columns around the country and the FDA announced happily that "the hoax is over." A year later, 54 people had been prosecuted by the states in which they resided for their roles in the hoax, and all had been convicted. *The Milwaukee Journal* reporter had also recanted her claim but lost her job.

In newspapers across the country, Pepsi ran a clever ad stating "Pepsi is pleased to announce . . . nothing." The crisis was over.

## Second Guesses

Monday morning quarterbacks had a field day with the hoax and its many elements. Most of the second-guessing involved the timing of Pepsi's rebuttal. "I don't understand why Pepsi didn't explain everything on the first day," said Don Smith, the city editor of the *Seattle Post Intelligencer*, who was skeptical about the reports from the beginning. In spite of his misgivings on timing, Smith's evaluation of the Pepsi response was that "they did fine."

Steven Fink, a Los Angeles-based crisis communication consultant, told *The Toronto Globe and Mail* that Pepsi had two crises—one of reality and one of perception. "The crisis of perception is that the company is not protecting the safety of their consumers. . . . If the public has the perception that the company was playing fast and loose with their safety, this will hurt the company in the long run."

The lack of a recall spurred some critics, too. Tylenol's swift (and expensive) recall of its products in 1982 left the impression that a recall was the linchpin of any product safety issue. Pepsi, however, saw no health or safety concerns resulting from its problems and opted against a product recall.

"The cost of a recall is a valid corporate concern," said Mayer Nudell, a crisis management consultant, "but they [Pepsi] have to weigh the short-term implications for the bottom line against the long-term corporate image and therefore market share and public receptivity and everything else. Very often, it's that long-term image that corporations sometimes lose sight of."

While Pepsi eschewed the recall, several retailers grew uneasy with the escalating furor and pulled the product from their shelves. Sheetz, a convenience store company with 250 stores in four mid-Atlantic states, pulled 16-ounce bottles of Diet Pepsi off its shelves after a West Virginia man reported finding a syringe. Other grocers and convenience stores from Iowa to Oklahoma followed suit. Kroger, the nation's largest food chain, offered customers a full refund on Pepsi products if they were uneasy after hearing the news reports.

Madeira concedes things might have been handled better, but points out "time was the enemy. It took us time to conduct the investigation in the plants, await FDA conclusions, and then get the information together to answer all the questions. The dynamics changed every hour. There is no standard crisis communication formula where you pull out your crisis readiness plan and implement it. You have to adapt your plan and process to the circumstances. In this case, this wasn't a product or public health crisis, it was a media problem. The more you saw that visual of the can and the syringe, the greater the concern became."

Looking back, she admits Pepsi did not expect that this would be a national story. "We have things that happen locally, and you do your job locally, and it's over and done with," said Madeira.

While that wasn't the case, few will argue with the success of the response. Sales dipped but soon recovered. Pepsi's positive relationships within the FDA paid huge dividends. In addition to using the FDA experts as counselors during the crisis, Pepsi was able to benefit from those same experts, powerful opinion leaders, who spoke as third-party endorsers of the company's lack of culpability.

Pepsi's strong understanding of the news media and the experience built up over the years also contributed to the success. Even though Pepsi was the victim of a week-long media feeding frenzy at its expense, Madeira and her staff worked with reporters in getting the situation turned around. "Your only defense when your company is on trial in the media," she said, "is to be a participant in that trial."

## Questions for Discussion

1. Discuss the implications of Pepsi's strategy, specifically
   a. Putting public safety first
   b. Taking full responsibility for solving the problem
   c. Using the media to present its case
2. Differentiate between "solving the problem" and "solving the situation."
3. Evaluate Pepsi's decision not to order a product recall. What are the plusses and minuses of such a decision?
4. What options did Pepsi have on June 10, 1993? Did the company select the correct course of action? Why or why not? What other choices could the company officials have made?
5. Discuss the role of the FDA in addressing and solving the situation. Was Pepsi's use of the FDA beneficial? Why? How?
6. Could this "crisis" have been avoided? How? Shortened? How?
7. Did the news media behave responsibly in reporting this story? Cite examples to support your answer.
8. Discuss the communication tools employed by Pepsi in solving the problem. Specifically evaluate the role of VNRs.
9. What was the "turning point" in Pepsi's resolution of this problem? Cite examples to support your answer.
10. When "perception is reality, facts notwithstanding," how can a company such as PepsiCo create new perceptions? Did the company succeed? Cite examples from the case to support your answer.

# ✳ Case 7-4 Universal Studios Florida: Riding "Rat Lady" to Halloween Success*

## The Situation Background

Universal Studios Florida (USF) opened its gates in Orlando in June of 1990 as a major player in the theme park industry (after USF grew and added a second theme park, "Islands of Adventure," and a shopping/dining entertainment complex, "CityWalk," it changed its name to Universal Orlando). In early 1991, USF had already set its sights on capitalizing on the resident market and building turnstile admissions during the traditional off-peak tourist periods.

The awareness-building plan was simple: USF would create an event for Halloween that would be so extraordinarily compelling that it would not only increase park visits during the soft tourist October time period, but it would command a separate evening admission fee. During the daylight hours the theme park functioned as usual, but as darkness fell, the park would be transformed into a morbid collection of haunted soundstages, "spooktacular" shows, and countless surprise guest encounters with the most realistic horror monsters Universal Studios makeup artists could conceive. Halloween Fright Nights (HFN) (later changed to Halloween Horror Nights) was born in concept, and the inaugural event was held for a four-day period immediately prior to and including Halloween day. It was wildly successful and demonstrated that USF could "own" the Halloween celebration scene in Orlando as it had planned.

Building on great first-year attendance and guest enthusiasm, in 1992, HFN was expanded to begin much earlier in the month and include the two weekends (Friday through Sunday) prior to Halloween, plus the days immediately before Halloween and the holiday itself. The need for long-lead publicity to build public awareness of this expanded schedule presented an immediate problem. USF's public relations counsel, tasked with developing a publicity plan, immediately conducted a poll of newspaper reporters and TV news directors to determine where Halloween ranked in news story coverage. The result was unanimous—Halloween was considered a secondary holiday and as such would not become a newsworthy subject until the days immediately prior to Halloween (today, due to events like Universal Orlando's Halloween Horror Nights, Halloween has become one of the top-celebrated holidays in the United States). Reporters and news directors alike said only "extraordinary circumstances" would warrant Halloween news coverage so early October, the period for which USF now needed news placement.

## The Publicity Challenge

The publicity task was clear—create an extraordinary event to *compel* news media to cover the Halloween activities. However, the solution was not as immediately clear. A meeting was set with the USF entertainment and promotions department and public relations counsel to explore all the new scare elements for HFN and determine what might be suitable as a showcase piece for publicity purposes. One element stood out: Guests enter a darkened room, feeling their way around by hand-to-wall contact, and then suddenly the floor lights up to reveal they are standing on a clear Plexiglas floor. They are shocked to see, just inches below their feet, a screaming woman

*Appreciation to Joe Curley, APR, cofounder of Curley & Pynn Public Relations Management, Inc. (Orlando, Florida) for his assistance in preparing this case.

in a coffin flailing her arms and covered with 100 live crawling rats! Rick Hensler of USF promotions immediately dubbed her "The Rat Lady," and the group agreed this scare element had terrific potential. Counsel wondered who was actually going to be the Rat Lady. She hadn't been selected yet, but it would be someone from the USF staff.

## The Strategy Develops

The challenge was to package the Rat Lady to create news, lots of it and early in the month, too. It was determined that a traditional news release—no matter how strong or cleverly written—just *wouldn't* meet the challenge. A totally different approach was necessary. It was decided to hire an "outside" Rat Lady to provide a "third-party" interview opportunity. To find the right candidate, the plan was to place a newspaper help-wanted ad to hire the yet-undetermined Rat Lady. The strategy was to treat the ad's wording as though it was a routine, everyday hiring situation, but with a full tongue-in-cheek approach. The USF human resources department agreed to provide an open Rat Lady staff position to which the public could apply.

The Rat Lady publicity strategy began to unfold. A special post office box was established for the applications, to streamline the process and maintain timeliness. The help-wanted ad was placed in the highest-circulation daily newspaper in each of the major Florida cities and ran Friday through Sunday. The ad read:

**HELP WANTED:** Person to share small dark coffin with 100 live rats. Evening hours. No experience necessary, but must not have irrational fears of being buried alive, confinement, or all over body contact with crawling rodents. High-pitch scream desirable. Mail reply to: Universal Studios Florida, PO Box xxxxxx, Orlando, FL 32853. An equal opportunity employer.

The ad was originally going to read "Woman to share small dark coffin," but

newspapers would not run the ad if it was gender specific, because the work could be done by either a woman or a man.

## The Action Phase

The weekend ad timing was critical to the strategy of not having any USF comment (human resources offices closed over the weekend), thereby letting the Rat Lady ad create some buzz on its own. By early morning on Saturday, radio stations were getting called by listeners who pointed out the Rat Lady ad, which fostered on-the-air patter and generated calls to USF to learn more—but USF offices were closed until Monday. The Rat Lady buzz continued to build, and by Monday morning the post office box was full of applications and the phones were ringing nonstop from news media asking questions on how many applied, who would dare apply, where these people were from, how much the job paid, were the rats real, and so on.

Media members frequently asked for a Rat Lady press kit and were coyly told this was a human relations interview process and there was no press kit (a strategy to reinforce the publicity plan tactics). This response resulted in media taking "ownership" of "finding the story" and actually demanding that they be allowed to interview Rat Lady job applicants.

The huge and growing response (from both applicants and the media) immediately put a strain on USF staffing and necessitated an increase in personnel dedicated to the project. This included additional public relations and entertainment department staff to organize and conduct a Rat Lady "casting call," to provide media the information they were requesting.

The casting-call format was chosen to avoid any confidentiality issues related to publicly disclosing employment applicant information. After USF created a list of first-cut applicants, those agreeing to participate in the casting call were given new public information application forms that focused on basic data such as the applicant's name, city, and why the applicant thought she were qualified to be chosen Rat

*(Continued)*

Lady. Each Rat Lady applicant was required to do a "scream test," handle the rats, and then finally lie in the coffin and allow the rats to crawl all over her body. Media were allowed to tape the session, and they packed the casting-call soundstage and interviewed many applicants (some very strange and bizarre individuals), resulting in extensive story placement.

USF taped the casting-call events and up-linked a national VNR to build even more awareness. Media calls were made to outer markets that had hometown ties to applicants to provide a local angle and motivate pickup.

Follow-up stories continued on the "working" Rat Lady during the regular HFN nights (media taping was allowed prior to and immediately after HFN public operational hours). Sidebar stories were created focused on "behind-the-scenes" of raising the rats:

- The rat litters were hand-raised by USF employees to be human friendly.
- Peanut butter was smeared under the face makeup of Rat Lady to have the rats appear to be chewing on her face.
- The rats changed shifts many times a night to protect the rats and keep them active.
- Special costume alterations were developed that included Velcro ties at the Rat Lady's wrists, ankles, neck, and so on, to keep the rats from entering her garments.
- "I saw the Rat Lady" buttons were sold at HFN vendor booths to provide hype and create more awareness of the stunt (these sold out in the first few nights of HFN).
- Employees adopted the rats as pets following the HFN event, and demand for the rats exceeded the supply.

## Overwhelming Media Results

The media coverage was worldwide: The story was picked up and fed by virtually all major TV, radio, and print news networks and syndicates. The Associated Press pickup resulted in placements in a majority of daily newspapers in the United States; radio pickup covered virtually all news services, including Paul Harvey doing two special reports. The Rat Lady story received widespread international coverage and was translated for the media in Japan. Other media outlets included *Entertainment Tonight,* CNN, CNBC, *CBS This Morning,* the *Arsenio Hall* show, the Sci-Fi Channel, the *New York Times* syndicate, the Associated Press, the Knight-Ridder News Service, *Good Day New York* (FOX), and many other major shows and syndicates.

Rat Lady returned the next year, in 1993, with a friend—Roach Man—who was covered with Madagascar hissing roaches, some that were three inches long!

The solid and continuing Florida media coverage resulted in a record sell-out crowd for the Second Annual Halloween Fright Nights and set the stage for the event to grow to the largest Halloween scare celebration in the world.

## PROBLEM 7-A   EMPLOYER INTERESTS AND MEDIA INTERESTS IN CONFLICT

Ted Square takes pride in his professional integrity. He has never deceived a news reporter, never offered a "pay off" for publicity, and never risked his own integrity for personal or employer gain.

Ted's boss is the owner of a multimillion dollar auto parts manufacturing firm whose foremost customer is a major auto maker. Ted's boss is a man of character. He has never pressed Ted for more publicity or more favorable press at whatever cost. He is a realist, taking and relishing whatever favorable publicity is generated by events, but not worrying about the quantity, accuracy, or completeness of it. With his business strong and growing, the owner exhibits an attitude that is fully supportive of Ted.

One day, the owner is shocked when his vice-president of operations confronts him and says it is time to make him a full partner. He claims that his efforts have made the business grow and prosper. The owner is in a quandary. He has been quietly preparing his son to run the business, figuring he could take over in about five years. Meantime, there is no denying that this vice-president, acquired a few years ago from one of the Big Three automakers, is of huge importance to the parts firm.

The owner refuses to be pressured by the vice-president. He does assure him that in time to come he will earn more and more income, and ultimately, he says, a limited partnership might be available.

The vice-president at this point reveals that he has received an offer from a prime auto parts competitor—to be made a partner and president of the competing firm. He presents his resignation to the owner on the spot.

In the hour following this shocking meeting, several events with public relations overtones take place:

1. The managers of the product design, engineering, manufacturing, and marketing departments turn in their resignations. They are moving to the competing company with the vice-president of operations.
2. All these executives have been promised a "much better deal" by the vice-president of operations.
3. Gossip is going around the office and shop that the business may have to be closed down and all employees terminated or furloughed without pay.

The owner is busy on the telephone, lining up successors for all the "defectors" and trying to reach the buyer at a large auto company, a current customer, to make sure its contract is intact and unaffected. His financial vice-president is busy calling other customers, brokers, and others to reassure them that the business is not threatened. In the meantime, Ted's department is working on statements the owner wants to make to employees, automotive trade press editors, the local media, and wire service stringers.

Midway into these efforts, word is passed to Ted Square by his secretary that the local bureau chief of a financial newspaper, a long-time friend, is on the telephone. Ted has to take the call, and he hopes that it concerns some other subject. But it does not. The conversation goes this way.

"Ted, this is George. I'm up against our deadline in 15 minutes, but we have a rumor down here that your vice-president of operations has resigned."

"Yeah, George. I've been working on a release about it. Do you want the name of the man who will succeed him?"

"Sure."

"It's Lem Jones. He has been the vice-president's right-hand man for several years. So the business will go right along."

"Thanks, I'll get this into the works. Let me have more details as fast as you know them."

That was it. George, despite being a trained newsman, failed to ask Ted where the vice-president

was going or the full circumstances of his resignation. Ted, for his part, was aware of more than he told. He simply answered specific questions and minimized the importance of the events, even though he knew the story would get financial front-page coverage if he added more details.

As it developed later on that day, the financial newspaper was scooped by a local newspaper whose reporter had called the vice-president of operations personally, had gotten the name of the company he was joining, had called them, and had obtained quotable details. The local bureau chief, Ted's friend, was embarrassed. His boss in New York had chewed him out. He blamed Ted for holding back information that was newsworthy, and said, "I'll never be able to trust you again."

"I'm sorry you feel that way," Ted told him. "I had no information from the operations vice-president, or the other guys who were resigning, and no one gave me authority to speculate, or to speak for them. What I had officially from the president, I gave you. You didn't ask for anything else. If you had, I could have referred you to the operations vice-president."

"OK," the bureau chief said, "that's what you say now. But every time you call me, remember, I've got a long memory."

Obviously, this was something for Ted to think about. He reasoned that his obligation was first and last to his employer. He had to release information of news value for which he was the authoritative source. But he did not have to go beyond that, and particularly not if it might be harmful to his employer. The damaged relationship with the major financial newspaper was seriously worrisome.

Who was right: Ted? The bureau chief? Both? Neither? If you had been Ted, how would you have handled the situation so that your employer's interests and your good media relationship with George were both protected? What would you have done differently?

If your company was publicly owned, would you have acted differently when George called?

## PROBLEM 7-B  DEALING WITH THE MEDIA IN A STICKY SITUATION

You are the public relations director of Alger Tiberius (AT) Software Inc., an up-and-coming software development company. Things have been exciting in the last few days since the introduction of a new software program, Manufacturing Efficiency

*(Continued)*

Revolution (MER). When integrated into the computer controls of manufacturing equipment, it will increase the efficiency of that equipment and cut production time in half. This program will revolutionize the manufacturing industry. Magazine previews of the product have been complimentary, and it looks as if the company has an instant best seller on its hands.

But bad news hits one day when your morning coffee is accompanied by a newspaper clipping from *The Local Yokel Times,* quoting Don T. Figgle, your president and CEO, who is particularly proud of the new product and has taken every opportunity to brag about its merits in the press. In an offhand comment he makes to a reporter at a local restaurant, Figgle is quoted as saying that "this product will virtually replace about 15 percent of the American manufacturing work force. It cuts out about half of the unnecessary actions done in factory production."

Figgle's quote is followed by the reaction of the AFL–CIO in response to this new information about the product. Ned T. Green, official spokesman of the organization, is quoted as saying, "This new product was not presented with this information to the labor and computer industries. Efficiency gains in manufacturing were discussed but not the elimination of a sector of our workforce. AT Software in effect lied to the public about the impact this software program will have on the American work force."

Needless to say, this turn in media coverage is unexpected and unwanted. Figgle was correct in saying that the software would revolutionize the computer and manufacturing industries, but his statistics were incorrect. The product would eliminate 10 percent of jobs for the manufacturing work force but would create jobs in a different area for other workers. Those who would lose their jobs could be retrained for other areas. You arrange another press conference for Figgle to disseminate the correct statistics available to the press, but whether the jobs are cut by 15 percent or 10 percent, loss of employment is the real story for the media. They are already printing a tidal wave of stories with headlines like "Computer Cover-Up Leaves Workers High and Dry" and "AT Software Sends Workers Packing."

By the following morning, negative media coverage has not abated. Although the news media now have the right statistics, emphasis is on the 10 percent of workers allegedly to be put out of work by the software. To top it off, a newly formed activist group, WACS (Workers Against Computer Software), is picketing outside of the main offices of AT Software with signs proclaiming "AT Software Trades in People for Programs." The local TV stations are all present to cover the protest and give up-to-the-minute reports.

In addition, the media is out in full force and has gone to the local congressman Bill Zealot for reaction. His last election campaign was focused on creating jobs for America. Zealot, up for reelection in the fall, pledges his loyalty to the hard-working American public and vows to fight "big business pushing aside the little guy and trying to make him obsolete in the name of progress." It looks as if there may be legislative reaction against MER.

Later that afternoon you receive a call from the Computer Software Programmers Association (CSPA). Initially, they were behind this program, but with all the bad press they're getting a bit nervous. They don't want to endorse a program that will cause so much flak. Without the backing of CSPA, the future of this product is going to be difficult.

It is now 9:00 P.M. and things look a bit bleak for MER and AT Software. Clearly what should have been a great announcement has become garbled by the gatekeepers. You are wondering how to get the real message out to the audiences that matter. You ask yourself:

- Which groups are garbling my message?
- What other groups are likely to become involved?
- What are the likely behaviors of each group?
- How can I minimize the garbled messages and maximize my messages to the publics I would like to reach?
- Can I reach those publics without using the usual venues, in order to avoid media, political, and activist gatekeepers?

1. With those questions in mind, how would you go about creating a plan to reach key publics in order to stay some of the immediate damage caused by the negative reactions of those groups that have been most vocal?
2. What use would you make of social media, if any, in this situation?
3. Could AT Software have avoided this negative uproar to MER? What actions should have been taken before presenting this product to the public through the media?

# 8

# Public Issue Campaigns and Debates

The backbone of Jeffersonian democracy is an intelligent, well-informed public and electorate.

The handling of public issues makes evident the link between public relations and the idea of democracy. For the people to be able to participate in decisions that affect their lives, those decisions must be put before them in a thorough, forceful manner. The ramifications of potential decisions need to be debated fully. *In the Court of Public Opinion, public relations practitioners are the attorneys.*

In this setting, an *issue* is a subject on which there are (1) two or more strongly opposing arguments, (2) emotional involvement of a large number of people, and (3) concern that the decision will have an impact on people's lives or the smooth functioning of society. Gun control, abortion, smoking policies, and the other topics in this chapter clearly meet these criteria.

When issues get out of hand—that is, cannot be settled before they become huge and threatening—they move to the category of *crisis.* A crisis is a public or organizational issue that has grown to such proportions that its ultimate resolution appears to mark a turning point. Depending on the decision, things may not be the same afterward. Chapter 9 presents several crisis cases.

Although businesses, schools, hospitals, and other established organizations with sophisticated public relations policies devote substantial effort to anticipating or avoiding issues that might have a negative effect, they also raise issues when they believe that public discussion might be beneficial. In contrast, the major activity of many special interest groups is to raise issues—in the American democratic tradition in which the people ultimately decide. Because of the number of variables at play and the societal importance of public debate, dealing with issues is one of the most challenging segments of public relations.

## TYPES OF ISSUES

An issue can be assigned to one of four categories:

- *Latent.* Just being formulated by far-thinking scholars or social activists but with sufficient apparent validity that it could become an issue sooner or later.

- *Emerging.* Starting to be written about in scholarly journals or specialty media; perhaps a special interest organization adopts the idea or a new group forms around it. Early adopter opinion leaders begin to be aware of it; it starts to spill over to wider publics, but no coherent action plan or broad support is yet evident.
- *Hot.* It is currently being debated.
- *Fallout.* Remnants from the settlement of hot issues that can come back onto the public agenda because they have already attained visibility.

Elements of all four types of issues are evident in many of the cases in this chapter.

## TARGET AUDIENCES

Most of the time, practitioners work with specified target audiences such as employees, neighbors, stockholders, members, donors, and customers, who are perceived to have self-interest reasons to support the organization. These audiences make up the organization's constituency. Contacts with them seek to reinforce, broaden, or deepen the two-way commitment.

## THEN THERE'S THE GENERAL PUBLIC

When the term *general public* is used, it usually describes the uncommitted, often uninterested bystanders whose support or opposition might ultimately have a bearing on the outcome of a situation or issue. Because they are unaware or uninterested, members of the general public do not have much of a stake in the outcome or a depth of conviction.

If a matter eventually will be on the ballot, voted on by a legislative body, or decided in the marketplace, where people "vote with their dollars," involvement of the general public can be vital. If social policy is being set, it is the general public that will decide what it will be—with or without laws to enforce it. At other times, interest in an issue will be so specialized that the general public will forgo its right to participate and leave the decision to the special interest groups who do care about the subject.

Therefore, the first problem faced by practitioners is to get people interested. Sometimes individuals or organizations do this by attempting to speak for the general public. When consumer advocates began questioning the quality and price of various products or services, they took on a task that most people had often done themselves—so people were happy to have this leadership. But when religious fundamentalists claimed to speak for average citizens in demanding the removal of certain books and magazines from libraries and newsstands, the public rejected them. In both cases, these spokespersons were not elected or otherwise appointed by those for whom they undertook to speak. They were accepted or rejected by public consent. This principle is key to understanding issue debate.

Persons or organizations that take stands on issues, pro or con, or neglect to do so, exercise a privilege and a prerogative in the democratic process. It is fundamental to effective public relations that this freedom of expression prevail. Without it, the individual or the organization is totally subject to the point of view of the state or of the noisy and the militant. Experience suggests that freedom of expression as a basic underpinning of public relations practice is a concept that is balanced and weighted by many adjustments. For example, the theoretical democratic process suggests that the majority rules. In reality, this does not always hold true. Quite often, a minority prevails. Less than half of eligible voters register to vote, and an even larger percentage of those who register do not vote. In almost all elections, it is a vocal, motivated, active minority who votes and therefore rules. Within most organizations, to use another setting, a relative few almost always hold the decision-making power for the whole body politic or membership.

Two cases in particular in this chapter illustrate the concept that a general public does exist, available to be influenced, but that the perceived will of that unorganized body is carried out through groups focusing on a particular issue or concern. One such group became an advocate for nonsmokers. Another wanted drunken drivers off the road.

In a slightly different context, Planned Parenthood claims to speak for the rights of women, and across the aisle the Right-to-Life movement offers its position on moral issues as one that has precedence over personal choice.

The uncommitted general public provides an arena (via public relations campaigns, the news media, and sometimes the courts) in which the motivations of special interest groups can be challenged by those who openly represent viewpoints or programs claiming to deserve a higher priority or to embody a higher moral purpose.

The general public and its elected representatives hold the key in the continuing controversy between the business sector and government agencies over how much and what kind of regulation there should be and by whom.

## PUBLIC SERVICE AS PREVENTIVE PUBLIC RELATIONS

Public service programs are expressions of an organization's concern for societal problems and needs. The public relations responsibility for organizations engaged in public service programs is normally that of creator and implementer. This role calls for the handling of:

- Strategy, planning, and research
- Program design
- Civic participation
- Government and educational liaisoning
- Meetings and events
- Media placement and relations
- Preparation of print, audio, and visual materials
- Interviews and news conferences

Some public service programs spring out of a crisis or an emergency, from criticism of an organization's doings, or from public clamor, as in the conservation of endangered species.

Increasingly, public service programs have not waited for problems to arise. They have been devised to head off the difficulties posed by protests, confrontations, or increased governmental regulations. Public service programs are seen as practical means of demonstrating socially responsible behavior, gaining trust for good deeds, building customer or clientele goodwill, or building working relationships with a constituency of public officials, investors, members, donors, or voters. For most successful enterprises and institutions, the attitude is that public service programs and expenditures are important to earn public approval. As a practical matter, management normally places two requisites on public service programs:

1. A program must fit logically into the mission, objectives, timetable, and field of endeavor in which the organization has expertise.
2. There must be an identifiable, measurable benefit to the organization as well as to the public groups or noble purpose involved and affected.

Such strategic public service programs often call for cooperation between public relations or public affairs, human resources, marketing, and other departments.

## SPECIAL INTERESTS

Citizens in a democratic society tend to band together in polarized common interest groups such as labor unions or manufacturers' associations, meat eaters or vegetarians, hunters or conservationists. People feel that collectively, on a given issue, their voices and their votes can get the attention needed to favorably influence decisions.

The United States, more than any other free nation, has become the world's prime example of what happens, both good and bad, when the democratic process is carried to an extreme. The nation has become factionalized to a point where the decision process is hobbled by a host of single-issue champions, protesters, and crusaders. On many public issues, factionalization has generated such a severe confrontation that reconciliation becomes impossible.

The practice of public relations, historically and now, is deeply involved in helping factions to have their voices heard and their influences felt on behalf of their particular special interests.

In representing competing or opposing factions, practitioners face off against each other much as lawyers do in lawsuits or courts. The justification, if any is needed, is simply that each faction, in the eyes of its sponsors and its beneficiaries, holds that its view or needs do, in fact, serve the best interest of all. This freewheeling debate in the court of public opinion, or the marketplace of ideas, is exactly what Jefferson and the Founding Fathers had in mind when they created the United States as the first true democracy.

## IMPORTANCE OF COMPROMISE

Given factionalization and confrontation, elected government in a free society must assume the roles of *referee* among contestants and *interpreter* of the greater public good.

*When powerful and determined factions or special interests meet head on, the outcome is generally a reconciliation, with both sides compromising a bit.* For example, in the matter of environmental protection, the upper atmospheric layer, or ozone, high above the earth filters out some of the sun's ultraviolet rays, helping assure that humans can live above ground and expose themselves to the sun. Chlorofluorocarbons (as in spray deodorant, insecticide, and detergent cans) have been identified as damaging to the ozone layer. The government, acting in the public interest and spurred by environmentalists, considered a ban on certain chlorofluorocarbons. Makers of products using them said, in effect, "Give us some time to switch over without loss of the market." Granted time, manufacturers set about providing nonpressurized containers for their products and advertising and promoting the desirable features of roll-ons, pump-can devices, and wipe-ons.

Because so much of this kind of compromise has occurred in areas of social concern, from integration to equal employment opportunity, from atmospheric pollution to metropolitan area blight and roadside litter, and even sexuality, the phrase *an era of tradeoffs* has come into popular use.

## THE UNFORGIVING DECADE

However, there is a tendency today toward emphasizing those issues that have become so emotional, or are so deep-seated, that they evoke almost (or actual) religious fervor in their adherents. These divisive issues seem to tear at the social fabric and raise doubts about the future of the democratic process. Among them are abortion, assisted or legalized suicide, medical triage, sex education in schools, other areas of educational curricula, gun control, smoking, gay marriage, and civil rights for animals.

Overzealous "believers" among activists have resorted to violence—the murder of physicians at women's health clinics. They have also participated in angry protests against organizations, such as picketing or boycotting companies that have, or don't have, medical coverage for gay partners. These zealots can make an organization swerve far off course unless public relations practitioners are sufficiently knowledgeable and influential to prevent overreaction. Because a few zealots put you in the headlines is no reason to panic, or to pander to what are often their very undemocratic, minority-opinion demands.

One result of this social warfare is what public relations consultant Ann Barkelew terms "The Unforgiving Decade." She notes that no matter what actions you take or which policies you adopt, *someone* is going to be angry enough to denounce you—loudly and publicly.

Target Corporation discovered this principle when pickets ringed a company department store unexpectedly one day—protesting an activity the company had taken for granted. The "pro-life" picketers were angry that Target contributed (as it had for years) to Planned Parenthood, who the picketers considered to be promoting abortion. (Planned Parenthood says this is not true; they counsel on abortion as well as all other choices available to pregnant women who seek their advice.)

Because the contributions had continued for years, a way out, thought one company official, seemed to be to discontinue them—with the rationale that under any circumstance contributions should shift among various causes. But when this "solution" was announced, an even *larger* number of pro-choice picketers surrounded the store.

No matter how the issue was to be resolved, the company was going to make enemies and probably lose some customers.

One resolution would be to count heads; which group has the most supporters and so could do the most damage? But what organization wants to be in such a losing situation? An alternative

## Issue Anticipation Teams[*]

Issue anticipation (IA) teams are working well for many organizations that wish to identify issues before they become a problem. In many organizations, setting up IA teams both meets the need *and* deals with the middle management "wall." Teams usually involve managers from all ranks and departments. To keep interest high, teams report every so often to a formal "issues board" composed of senior officers. Some organizations have one team that looks at the realm of issues. Others have several teams concentrating on specific areas of concern. At its simplest, the team answers two questions: (1) What's happening out there and in here? (2) Could it affect us or become an issue for us?

## Benefits of Teams

- Serving on a team is an honor, which motivates the members.
- It forces team members to read and observe things they previously didn't.
- Members interact with people they might not come in contact with otherwise.
- Members learn to build consensus and to work as a team.
- Supervising managers start to think broadly about the implications of what the organization does and are sensitized to public relationships.
- They help identify and train the company's rising stars.

[*] *pr reporter,* April 27, 1987.

strategy is to work with the "side" that will be favored in order to gain pledges of extra business and support to make up for the lost customers. Neither is ideal, and both keep the organization on the hot seat of being identified with a divisive issue.

## ISSUE ANTICIPATION

The way to avoid issues is to see them coming and to find ways to reach accommodation before they become public and "hot" (see box above "Issue Anticipation Teams"). Some say, indeed, that the real value of public relations is what *doesn't* happen! Jim Grunig's paradigm (see also Chapter 2) is a superb tool for anticipating issues and making appropriate plans.

The most striking element of this paradigm is that publics are subsidiaries of stakeholder groups—not vice versa:

- Stakeholder groups are people who should care and be involved because the issue could or will affect them.
- Nevertheless, they contain large contingents who don't get the message, can't be bothered, just plain don't care, or because of barriers won't do anything about the issue. *These segments together can be as high as 90 percent of a stakeholder group.*

The viable term for those who *do get excited* about the issue is, therefore, publics. Grunig identifies three types who together are often limited to the 10 percent plus who will engage in the issue:

1. *Long haul*—those interested in the full ramifications of the topic
2. *Special interest*—those concerned only about certain elements of the topic
3. *Hot button*—those aroused only by emotionally debated elements

This useful way of managing issue anticipation involves (1) focusing on which stakeholders are known to be skittish about which potential decisions, and then (2) modeling how the three types of publics will fall out and what their response will likely be.

## SCENARIO TECHNIQUE

The way to foresee how an issue might affect your company is to create multiscenario possibilities,[1] advocates Kerry Tucker, CEO of the San Diego public relations firm Nuffer, Smith, Tucker. This means "creating stories of equally plausible futures," and then planning for them. Highlights of the advantages of this approach:

- Putting trends in some kind of logical story form creates a fresh sense of understanding.
- Scenarios are "what if" stories, taking the most pressing forces on your organization and putting them together in a useful narrative.
- Once you know the alternative futures, you can plan for them; otherwise, strategic planning is "scratching at the surface."

As you review the cases in this chapter, see whether there were early warnings that might have enabled public relations practitioners to help their organizations take action to steer around the public debate that ensued.

---

[1] Kerry Tucker, "Scenario Planning," *Association Management,* April 1999.

# References and Additional Readings

Alinsky, Saul. *Rules for Radicals: A Practical Primer for Realistic Radicals.* Vancouver, WA: Vintage Books, 1989.

Baskin, Otis. *Public Relations: The Profession and the Practice.* 4th ed. Columbus, OH: McGraw-Hill Higher Education, 1996.

Baus, Herbert. "Working with Influential Groups," in *Lesly's Handbook of Public Relations and Communications.* 5th ed. Chicago, IL: NTC Business Books, 1997, Ch. 32: 475–481.

Broide, Mace. "Having a Voice in Politics," in *Lesly's Handbook of Public Relations and Communications.* 5th ed. Chicago, IL: NTC Business Books, 1997. Chapter 7: 103–112.

Buchholz, Rogene. *Business Environment and Public Policy: Implications for Management and Strategy Formulation.* Upper Saddle River, NJ: Prentice Hall, 1989.

Coleman, Cynthia-Lou. "What Policy Makers Can Learn from Public Relations Practitioners." *Public Relations Quarterly* 34 (Winter 1989–90): 26–31.

*Corporate Public Issues and Their Management* offers a variety of information regarding public policy formation and issue management. For more information, contact: Issue Action Publications, Inc., 207 Loudoun Street S.E., Leesburg, Virginia 22075, 703-777-8450, www.issuemanagement.org.

Cutlip, Scott, Allen Center, and Glen Broom. *Effective Public Relations,* 8th ed. Upper Saddle River, NJ: Prentice Hall, 1999.

Ewing, Raymond. *Managing the New Bottom Line; Issues Management for Senior Executives.* Homewood, IL: Business One Irwin, 1987.

Foundation for Public Affairs. *Public Interest Profiles 2001–2002.* Washington, DC: Congressional Quarterly, 2000.

Fox, J. F., "Communicating on Public Issues: A Changing Role for the CEO." *Public Relations Quarterly* 27 (Summer 1982).

Hammack, David. *Making the Nonprofit Sector in the United States: A Reader.* Bloomington, IN: Indiana University Press, 1998.

Heath, Robert. *Strategic Issues Management: Organizations and Public Policy Challenges.* Thousand Oaks, CA: Sage Publications, 1997.

Jones, Barrie, and Howard Chase. "Managing Public Policy Issues." *Public Relations Review,* Vol. 5, No. 2 (Summer 1979). A classic.

Kelley, Stanley, Jr. *Professional Public Relations and Public Power.* Baltimore, MD: Johns Hopkins University Press, 1966. Classic study of a perennial question.

Lesly, Philip. "Policy Issues, Crises, and Opportunities" in *Lesly's Handbook of Public Relations and Communications.* 5th ed. Chicago, IL: NTC Business Books, 1998. Chapter 2: 19–37.

Mathews, David. *Politics for the People: Finding a Responsible Public Voice.* 2nd ed. Champaign, IL: University of Illinois Press, 1999.

National Rifle Association. For pamphlets explaining the organization and its objectives and programs, 1600 Rhode Island Avenue, N.W., Washington, DC 20036, www.nra.org.

Newsom, Doug, Judy Van Slyke Turk, and Dean Kruckeberg. *This Is PR: The Realities of Public Relations.* 6th ed. Belmont, CA: Wadsworth Publishing Company, 1996. Chapter 9, "Laws Affecting PR Practice."

Olasky, Marvin, "Engineering Social Change: Triumphs of Abortion Public Relations from the Thirties through the Sixties." *Public Relations Quarterly* 33 (Winter 1988–89): 21.

*pr reporter,* Vol. 37, No. 14 (April 4, 1994). Lead article concerns the value of public relations in grassroots organizing and coalition building.

Public Relations Body of Knowledge. New York: PRSA. See abstracts dealing with "Ethics and Social Responsibility."

Scheel, Randall. *Maxims for the Issues Manager.* Stamford, CT: Issue Action Publications, 1991.

Sopow, Eli. *The Critical Issues Audit.* Leesburg, VA: Issue Action Publications, 1995.

Stoltz, V. "Conflict PR in the Formation of Public Opinion." *Public Relations Quarterly* 28 (Spring 1983).

*The Futurist,* six-times-yearly magazine on significant trends and where those trends are leading, from the World Future Society, 7910 Woodmont Ave, Suite 450, Bethesda, MD 20814, www.wfs.org.

Public service programs are regularly reported in the following periodicals:

*pr reporter,* PR Publishing Co., P.O. Box 600, Exeter, NH 03833, or contact ssmith@jjwpr.com.

*PR News,* 201 Seven Locks Road 300, Potomac, MD 20854.

*Public Relations Quarterly,* P.O. Box 311, Rhinebeck, NY 12572–0311.

# Case 8-1 Rights and Choices—For Whom?

*I have met thousands and thousands of pro-choice men and women. I have never met anyone who is pro-abortion. Being pro-choice is not being pro-abortion. Being pro-choice is trusting the individual to make the right decision for herself and her family, and not entrusting that decision to anyone wearing the authority of government in any regard.*

—*Hillary Clinton*

*The greatest destroyer of love and peace is abortion, which is war against the child. The mother doesn't learn to love, but kills to solve her own problems. Any country that accepts abortion is not teaching its people to love, but to use any violence to get what they want.*

—*Mother Teresa*

*The U. S. Supreme Court ruled in* Roe v. Wade *in 1973 that a Texas law criminalizing most abortions violated a woman's constitutional right of privacy, which the court said was implicit in the due-process clause of the 14th Amendment.*

*Jane Roe was an alias used to shield the identity of Norma McCorvey, who sued Dallas County District Attorney Henry Wade.*

*In the 7–2 decision, the court sought to balance a woman's right to privacy with a state's interest in regulating abortion . . . .*

—*USA Today, April 17, 2006, p. 2A*

The 1973 Supreme Court case of *Roe v. Wade* brought abortion to the forefront. The landmark case, legalizing abortion in the United States, came under fire in the early 1990s, and in the summer of 1992 the nine Supreme Court justices were faced with a decision that could have severely limited abortion rights or even have overturned *Roe v. Wade* altogether, again making abortion illegal. The justices ruled in favor of *Roe v. Wade,* however, allowing abortion to remain legal in the states.[2]

The beginning of the new millennium seemed to bring with it little hope for any kind of agreement on the abortion issue. New concerns surrounding the abortion debate emerged, and Congress was charged with developing new legislation. As in years past, right-to-life and pro-choice groups increased their efforts to sway public opinion.

Groups on both sides have tried different strategies over the years to get the behaviors they prefer from society. The pro-lifers have worked hard to elect officials responsible for appointing Supreme Court justices who might limit or reverse *Roe v. Wade.* They have joined politically with other conservative causes to boost their power and influence on this issue. In recent years, they have shifted strategies and focused on changing legislation at the individual state level.

Although the likelihood of a resolution of this issue is far from being reached, each side hopes to sway public opinion through the use of classic public relations strategies and tactics. Zealots, however, have resorted to both illegal and immoral tactics—and this has influenced the debate as well.

## Where It All Started: Margaret Sanger's Crusade

Abortion as a political issue emerged nearly a century ago, in 1912, when Margaret Sanger launched a personal crusade in the form of two radical articles, "What Every Woman

---

[2] *Planned Parenthood v. Casey.*

Should Know" and "What Every Girl Should Know," with the goal of emancipating women, via contraception, from sexual servitude. Sanger named her proposition "birth control," believing that *every child born should be wanted by parents who are prepared to care for that child.* Otherwise, conception should be prevented.

Her crusade continued with the establishment of the journal *The Woman Rebel,* in which she attacked the Comstock Law. *Her strategy was to test the law by breaking it.* *The Woman Rebel* was promptly banned from the mails, and Sanger was threatened with a prison term and a $5,000 fine. The magazine became a best seller overnight. This was the first planned event in this debate—breaking the law in order to get attention.[3]

Next Sanger published a pamphlet, *Family Limitation,* which she stored in a variety of cities *for release at a strategically right time.* When she was arraigned for *The Woman Rebel,* she fled to England, wiring her associates to release *Family Limitation* three days after she left.

Sanger returned from Europe to face charges for violating the Comstock Law after visiting the world's first birth control clinic in Amsterdam and conducting birth control research of her own in Europe. Sanger found that public attitude had shifted in her favor. The government was no longer pursuing the Comstock Law. It was then that she established the first birth control clinic in the United States.

Birth control leagues were started in several cities and joined together in what came to be known as the American Birth Control League (later becoming the Planned Parenthood Federation of America). The Clinical Research Bureau opened, as did scores of other birth control clinics. Distinguished professionals and citizens alike began enthusiastically supporting the movement. Events from the 1930s to the present have strengthened the movement.

## Strategies and Tactics on Both Sides

Although the two sides have very different views on abortion, they present and communicate in a variety of ways—some that are similar (e.g., publications, rallies, general publicity, social media) and others that are quite different (e.g., focusing on elected officials, controlling or not controlling zealots).

Traditionally, **pro-life groups** have used techniques such as publishing a special edition of the *National Right-to-Life News* reproducing a series of articles from the *Chicago Sun-Times* on "Abortion Profiteers." One of the pro-life events has been an annual March for Life in Washington, D.C., that has been duplicated in several major cities. Another event is the annual National Right-to-Life convention. Other vehicles for pro-life views include counseling hotlines, speakers bureaus, informational videotapes, slide shows, and annual banquets. The pro-life groups also train volunteers, publish pamphlets and brochures, provide information on the rhythm method of birth control, organize protests at abortion clinics, and use Facebook and other social media to focus awareness on the subject.

In the 1990s, the radical fringe of the pro-life movement undertook more violent actions. Radical groups bombed and burned abortion clinics. Radical groups such as Operation Rescue orchestrated violent protests outside abortion clinics. A pro-life zealot killed a Florida abortionist on his way into the clinic where he worked. Pro-lifers engaged in shocking tactics, including displaying traveling billboards showing the graphic results of an abortion; displaying aborted fetuses; and convening emotional demonstrations adjacent to abortion clinics and Planned Parenthood offices.

These extreme acts backfired in swaying public opinion and drowned out the more sensible voices of the pro-life movement for a time. Through this time, legislation continued to be passed that protected a women's right to choose.

*(Continued)*

---

[3] The Comstock Law, enacted in 1873, banned the mailing of "obscene" literature. Contraception materials were among the materials deemed obscene.

---

## Legislation

Federal abortion laws show the breadth of legislation on this issue:

- **Freedom of Access to Clinic Entrances (FACE).** This federal statute provides criminal and civil sanctions for obstructing or interfering with a woman's access to a clinic where abortions are performed. (Pro-life oppose, pro-choice support.)
- **Child Custody Protection Act.** Prohibits the transport of minors across state lines, in order to circumvent laws requiring the involvement of parents in abortion decisions. (Pro-life support, pro-choice oppose.)
- **Informed Choice Act.** Allows the Secretary of Health and Human Services to make grants to free, community-based medical clinics for pregnant women for the purchase of ultrasound equipment, which would be used to provide free ultrasound examinations for those women. Each grant recipient must, in return, (1) provide each woman receiving services a visual image of the fetus from the ultrasound and a general anatomical and physiological description of the characteristics of the fetus, and (2) provide information on abortion and alternatives to abortion, such as childbirth and adoption, and information concerning public and private agencies that assist in those alternatives. (Pro-choice oppose, pro-life support.)
- **Partial-Birth Abortion Ban Act.** A bill designed to prohibit the performance of late-term abortion procedures, such as partial-birth abortion, dilation and extraction, and intact dilation and evacuation. This bill was vetoed. (Pro-life support, Pro-choice oppose.)
- **Abortion Non-Discrimination Act (ANDA).** This act is supposed to help clarify the 1996 Coats-Snowe Amendment, which was enacted to "protect the right of health-care providers to decline to participate in the killing of unborn children." The National Right-to-Life Committee believes that some have read the 1996 law narrowly, protecting only medical residents and residency programs and only in the training context, and that the ANDA would clarify that the term *health-care entity* includes the full range of participants involved in providing health care. (Pro-life support, pro-choice oppose.)

---

Recently the pro-life movement changed strategies. Working in states where conservative beliefs are in the majority, they have sought to pass a slew of legislation designed to make getting an abortion difficult. By controlling their zealots and presenting a more rationale, thoughtful argument, they have been successful in passing many restrictive laws across the country. For instance:

- Requiring that only licensed physicians perform the abortions
- Prohibiting the use of federal funding
- Laws involving parents of pregnant minors in abortion decision making.
- Waiting periods requiring counseling, ultrasounds, listening to the fetus heartbeat, and so on.

**Pro-choice groups** such as Planned Parenthood and NARAL are also well organized and have been in existence for decades. The pro-choice movement works from a different strategic perspective. Instead of trying to change a law, they are trying to protect it. Therefore, their strategies and tactics are slightly different.

Pro-choice groups continue to work a great deal in the legal system and with Congress to defend the gains they have won, so they spend a lot of time in the public-policy arena. They defend against any and all attempts to limit access to abortion, whether it comes in the form of a legal challenge to *Roe v. Wade* or in conditions imposed on family planning funds in overseas programs.

However, with the rising sophistication and influence of the pro-life movement, the pro-choice side has had to make inroads at the local, state, and national levels simultaneously. The pro-life side has made Planned Parenthood the face of abortion in the country even though the majority (over 90%) of the services it offers are not abortion related.

Increasingly, the sides and strategies have become more polarized while becoming more sophisticated. Pro-choice activists, so long as *Roe v. Wade* is in effect, have the advantage of being on the "winning side." With that advantage goes the so-called "moral high ground" of offering a "choice" to those affected by an unwanted pregnancy.

## Is There an Upside?

With all the talk and controversy around abortions, awareness has increased and the rate of abortions is down. This is good if women are taking greater precautions not to have unwanted pregnancies. It is not good if it is because abortions are just harder to get. In 2010, the National Center for Health Statistics reported that teen births were at their lowest level in almost 70 years. This was attributed to strong pregnancy prevention messages and contraceptive use. Maybe the ever-present controversy over abortion and its limits has contributed as well.

## Where Is the Debate Now?

With the more toned-down approach by the pro-life contingent, public opinion has swayed slightly in their direction. A 2009 Gallup Poll reported for the first time that 51% of Americans consider themselves "pro-life," whereas 42% are "pro-choice." Both sides still spend a great deal of time "preaching to the choir" in an effort to keep the troops mobilized and motivated. And it seems that opinion will continue to be in flux for some time to come.

So, the question remains, where do we go from here? Is there a "correct" answer? With all the controversy surrounding the issue, it is likely that there will never be a definitive answer—even when the Supreme Court gets to weigh in.

| Important Events in the Abortion Controversy | |
|---|---|
| 1935 | Radio censorship of birth control topics was ended by NBC. |
| 1936 | The U.S. Circuit Court of Appeals ruled that physicians could distribute through the mails material "for the purpose of saving life or promoting the well-being of their patients." |
| 1937 | The American Medical Association endorsed birth control. |
| 1942 | The U.S. Public Health Service adopted a policy of giving requests from state health offices for financial support of birth control the same consideration and support given other state medical programs. |
| 1950 | President Eisenhower became honorary chairman of Planned Parenthood and the first of many presidents, including John Kennedy, a Catholic, to endorse the aid program. |
| 1960 | The first contraceptive pill was introduced. One of its three developers is a Catholic, Dr. John Rock showing how far public and professional attitudes had moved. |
| 1966 | The American Nurses Association recognized family planning education as part of a nurse's professional responsibility. |
| 1967 | Social Security amendments created a family planning project grants program and mandated state welfare departments to service those with extremely low incomes. |
| 1967 | The United Nations Fund for Population Activities was established in response to resolutions in the UN General Assembly and the Economic and Social Council. |

*(Continued)*

| | |
|---|---|
| **1970** | Congress adopted the Family Planning Services and Population Research Act. |
| **1973** | The Supreme Court ruled that abortion is a matter to be decided between a woman and her doctor in *Roe v. Wade*. |
| **1976** | Congress enacted the Hyde Amendment, cutting off federal (Medicaid) funding for abortions for poor women. |
| **1981** | President Reagan opposed abortion and asked that the 1973 ruling be overturned. |
| **1992** | President Bush comes under fire during the election for his endorsement of the "gag rule," which prohibited staff and doctors in clinics receiving public funds from even discussing the abortion option. (Bill Clinton was elected president on a pro-choice platform, among other issues.) |
| **2005** | President Bush appoints two "conservative" justices to the Supreme Court. |
| **2006** | South Dakota Governor Mike Rounds signs into law a bill banning abortion in that state. |
| **2010–2011** | Many states continue to chip away at access to abortion. Mississippi passes restrictive legislation that it makes it nearly impossible for the last abortion clinic in the state to operate. Other states are following suit. |

### Questions for Discussion

1. Breaking the law as a tactic to gain awareness and build public support has had a role in this debate, as well as in others (e.g., Boston Tea Party, environmental movement, civil disobedience during the Civil Rights movement). Should this tactic be part of a public relations strategy? If so, to what extent can it be used and be effective?

2. With *Roe v. Wade* in place, the "behaviors" needed by the pro-choice movement are significantly different from those needed by the pro-life movement. How do you feel the strategic decisions made by each side have helped or hurt in achieving these behaviors?

3. How might you see a resolution to this issue coming about? What public relations techniques might others, outside the core activists groups, take to help resolve the issue? What other issues now on the national agenda may become insurmountable?

4. What do you think Planned Parenthood should do to protect its position and funding?

## References

http://www.guttmacher.org/pubs/fb_induced_abortion.html

http://www.npr.org/2011/04/13/135354952/planned-parenthood-makes-abortion-foes-see-red

http://www.gallup.com/poll/118399/more-americans-pro-life-than-pro-choice-first-time.aspx

http://www.guttmacher.org/statecenter/spibs/spib_OAL.pdf

http://www.nrlc.org/index.html

# Case 8-2 Take Your Choice—Tobacco or Health

## Introduction

The so-called "tobacco war" is just about over, and the health of Americans is the clear winner. The tobacco industry, buffeted by a relentless barrage of medical and legal setbacks, has abandoned its strategy of denial. In its place, industry leaders such as Philip Morris and R. J. Reynolds are trying to make peace with the American public while fighting over dwindling market share. Overseas markets and diversification into nontobacco ventures seem to be the future for a 400-year-old industry that once claimed some 50 percent of the American public as customers.

## History

Tobacco has been part of the American landscape and economy since there has been an America. Legend has it that when Columbus waded ashore in 1492 he discovered Native Americans smoking tobacco. The explorers took the habit back to Europe, and thus began the long intertwined history of tobacco and the American economy.

Two centuries later, the United States was exporting some 23 million pounds of tobacco to Europe, which helped finance the Revolutionary War. Among the early tobacco producers were George Washington and Thomas Jefferson, both Virginia farmers when not busy creating and establishing "a new nation, conceived in liberty and dedicated to the proposition that all men are created equal."[4]

Tobacco remained at the forefront of American culture and deeply embedded in the economy until 1964 when the Surgeon General of the United States officially declared for the first time that smoking was hazardous to the health of the smoker. At that time, more than half the male population of the United States regularly smoked, as did more than one-third of women. Estimates at the time placed regular and casual smokers at some 51 percent of the adult population.[5]

As of 2012, 19.3 percent of Americans smoked, less than half of the number that smoked in 1964.[6] Although this represents approximately 45 million smokers, the number of cigarettes sold hit a low of 360 billion in 2007 (down 12 billion from 2006) as a result of changing mores, tougher laws, and a landmark settlement with the tobacco industry that limits advertising of its products. Most important to the future of the issue, nearly 70 percent of young adults (aged 18–24) had never smoked cigarettes.[7]

Worldwide the picture isn't so clear. More than 1.1 billion people smoke, including some 622 million in Asia, where nearly 55 percent of the population smokes. Not surprisingly, the largest tobacco companies are in China.[8]

## The Situation

When Surgeon General Luther Terry issued his landmark announcement in 1964, he kicked off what would be a public relations war of epic proportions. On one side was the tobacco industry with its deep pockets, lobbyists, public relations and advertising experts, and nearly half of the country regularly using its products. On the other side was a growing

(*Continued*)

---

[4] Declaration of Independence, 1776.
[5] "Smoking Prevalence Among U.S. Adults." CDC, August 6, 2002.
[6] CDC report. http://www.cdc.gov/tobacco (accessed July 23, 2007).
[7] "Smoking and Tobacco Use." CDC, November 2006.
[8] "Tobacco in China." *Far East Economic Review,* December 13, 1998.

## Tobacco Timeline

| | |
|---|---|
| **1492** | Columbus discovers America and Native Americans smoking tobacco. |
| **1703** | Tobacco exports to Europe exceed 23 million pounds. |
| **1881** | The cigarette-rolling machine is invented, creating the modern tobacco industry. |
| **1920s** | American women are socialized to smoke by public relations icons Edward L. Bernays and Ivy L. Lee. |
| **1964** | U.S. Surgeon General declares tobacco and cigarettes harmful to public health and linked to various types of cancer. |
| **1971** | Tobacco ads are removed from U.S. television. |
| **1981** | Secondhand smoke is declared a carcinogen by the Environmental Protection Agency. |
| **1984** | Congress mandates stronger warnings on U.S. tobacco packages. |
| **1989–1993** | RJR Nabisco introduces the "Joe Camel" ad campaign, which increases youth market share by 50 percent. |
| **1997** | Liggett Group breaks ranks with the industry, admitting that cigarettes cause cancer, nicotine is addictive, and that the tobacco industry has historically targeted teens. |
| **1998** | The tobacco industry reaches a landmark accord with the U.S. attorneys general that requires reparations to 46 states and bans much traditional tobacco advertising. |
| **2003** | Lowe's (a national hardware and building supplies retailer) bans smoking in its stores or on its premises. The ban applies to employees and customers alike. |
| **2005** | Weyco, Inc., (a Michigan-based health-care administration company) bans its 200 employees from smoking on or off the job. Four employees lose jobs. |
| **2006** | Scott's (an Ohio-based fertilizer company) follows suit, banning smoking by its 5,300 workers on or off the job. Employees are given 10 months to stop smoking or find another job. About one third of employees are affected. |
| **2009** | The University of Kentucky bans cigarettes campuswide. Some 500 universities have taken similar steps. |
| **2010** | Michigan became the 38th state to go "smoke free," banning smoking in nearly all public places. Tobacco companies' sponsorship of NASCAR ends. |
| **2012** | The Federal Drug Administration (FDA) requires cigarette companies to report on the amounts of 20 chemicals in their cigarettes that are associated with cancer and other health problems. |

army of health professionals armed with an increasing array of facts and figures destined to become part of the national agenda. In between were media companies conflicted by the need to discuss vital public issues such as this one and the billions of advertising dollars annually offered up by the tobacco industry.

Although Terry's report was the first shot, it certainly was not fatal to tobacco. The industry fought back with the thinly disguised Tobacco Institute, firing off facts about smokers' rights and tobacco's economic impact and denying that tobacco smoke was a major source of pollution. The Tobacco Institute also debated the legitimacy of the health issue and claimed that common courtesy should govern smoking, not state or federal law.

Health advocates, while lacking competitive budgets, were nonetheless active and effective. Study after study increasingly linked smoking to a variety of health woes, including lung cancer, heart disease, emphysema, breast cancer, and high blood pressure. Researchers isolated 69 cancer-causing chemicals in common cigarette smoke, 43 of which remain in secondhand smoke.

## The Facts

Tobacco is the leading cause of preventable death in the United States and probably the world. According to the 11th World Conference on Tobacco, more than 1.1 billion people smoke worldwide, 500 million of whom will die from tobacco-related causes. It is expected that tobacco smoking will soon result in more deaths than those from AIDS, murder, suicide, and auto accidents combined.

In the United States, about 20 percent of all deaths can be attributed to smoking and tobacco products. According to the Centers for Disease Control and Prevention, approximately 12 million Americans currently are afflicted with a tobacco-related disease, nearly half of whom continue to smoke. Tobacco-related fatalities in the United States number about 440,000 each year, with secondhand smoke estimated to cause some 50,000 deaths annually. "There is no such thing as a safe level of smoking," says Thomas Glynn of the American Cancer Society.

All the while, tobacco remains a legal product. Although the U.S. Department of Agriculture is phasing out tobacco subsidies, the economic impact of tobacco as an industry cannot be denied.

According to an industry publication "Tobacco. . . . Working for America," tobacco is America's seventh-largest cash crop behind wheat, hay, soybeans, corn, cotton, and peanuts. On a revenue-per-acre basis, tobacco—at $4,000 yield per acre—is the most valuable of these crops. North Carolina and Kentucky account for two-thirds of U.S. tobacco production.

Tobacco wages contribute some $3.8 billion to the national economy. Seventy percent of finished tobacco products are sold via grocery and convenience stores, adding another $2.7 billion in impact. The entire tobacco enterprise, judging from direct and indirect measures, contributes nearly $55 billion to the U.S. economy, according to "Tobacco . . . Working for America."

Taxes are a second high-dollar factor in tobacco's economic impact. The latest figures show that state and federal taxes from tobacco sales amount to more than $35 billion, according to the American Economics Group. Of these levies, more than $14 billion was collected by state governments in 2006, "Tobacco . . . Working for America" says.

A look at the industry leader Philip Morris USA (a division of Altria Group, Inc.) gives a clear picture of the economic realities of tobacco. In its annual report for 2011, cigarette sales topped $21 billion, and profits from tobacco were more than $5.5 billion.

## The Problem

For those trying to shut down smoking, the problem was twofold. First, most people who smoked were doing so because they enjoyed it or they were addicted. Second, the tobacco industry presented a well-financed and united front that conceded not one point in the discussion over health issues.

With the surgeon general's 1964 report, most casual smokers quickly dropped the practice, but that still left more than 40 percent of all Americans who regularly smoked. This was the group that became the target of health-care efforts. To win substantive behavioral change, however, is tough. Smokers have to be convinced that their existing behavior (smoking) is wrong, and that not smoking is a suitable substitute. The benefits of not smoking and negative consequences of continuing to smoke must be obvious, and smokers must be able to see a brighter future before they will consider changing their behavior.

Further, communication alone usually isn't sufficient to get the desired behavioral change. Knowledge does not equal behavior, which means that steps beyond communication need to be taken to facilitate real behavioral change.

*(Continued)*

Sociologists have identified a three-step pattern leading to changes in societal behavior:

1. **Folkways** are feelings, perceptions, and actions common to a social group that when adopted by a wider audience become
2. **Mores** (Mawr-eyz), which are folkways that are conducive to the welfare of society and which become patterns that govern societal behavior. Sometimes these mores are codified into
3. **Laws,** either on the local, state, or national level.

It was this pattern that the health-care industry followed to effect a reduction in smoking. Communication was directed toward smokers and nonsmokers alike, pointing out the dangers to everyone—not just smokers. The goal was to make smoking socially unacceptable, creating an environment in which nonsmokers would be justified in protesting the actions of smokers.

Just as effective public relations tactics had made smoking acceptable to the masses in the 1920s, so would good public relations be used to reverse the trend. Shaping negative perceptions about smoking would be a strategy that was effective and affordable. The "truth" in the form of health-related facts would be the backbone of the campaign. The central message would be that smoking is harmful to your health, but it would be wrapped in a tongue-in-cheek message that smoking isn't "cool" either.

One well-known antismoking poster showed pictures of the posteriors of various animals—row after row of rear ends—concluding with an ashtray full of cigarette butts. The message? "Butts are ugly." Another ad showed a similar ashtray with the notation, "Kissing a smoker is like licking an ashtray." No subtlety there.

Slowly, the tide of public opinion began to turn. Smoking in public became problematic.

In one high-profile situation, television star Larry Hagman was spotted carrying a handheld fan. If someone lit up in his presence, he would activate the fan to blow the smoke back toward the smoker.

Research showing smokers to be at the lower end of various social scales further emphasized the bad choice that smoking presented. "Today . . . smokers are typically the least-advantaged low-income minorities in the nation's cities and low-income whites," says Dr. Cheryl Healton, president and CEO of American Legacy Foundation, a public health foundation devoted to tobacco issues. "Americans below the poverty level are 33 percent more likely to smoke than are those above the poverty line, and people without high school diplomas are also more likely to smoke."[9]

## Tobacco's Side

In 1967, New York Senator Robert Kennedy said when addressing the first World Conference on Smoking and Health, "The cigarette industry is peddling a deadly weapon," advising that it was up to Congress to regulate smoking and tobacco.

The tobacco industry countered with a strategy initially designed to maintain the status quo. Included in the strategy is what the International Development Research Centre (a public corporation created by the Canadian government to monitor and address public issues) calls "The Nine $D$s."[10]

- **Deny** the health consequences of smoking.
- **Deceive** consumers about the true nature of cigarettes through marketing and public relations.
- **Damage** the credibility of industry opponents.
- **Direct** advertising to women and youth, in addition to men.
- **Defeat** attempts to regulate the industry or control smoking.

---

[9] "Adult Cigarette Smoking in the U.S." CDC report. http://www.cdc.gov/tobacco (accessed February 28, 2007).
[10] http://www.irdc.ca.

- **Delay** legislation that can't be defeated.
- **Destroy** legislation once it passes, either through legal challenges, exploiting loopholes, or simply ignoring the laws.
- **Defend** lawsuits against the industry.
- **Develop** new markets around the world.

At the forefront of this strategy was the use of front groups, such as the Tobacco Institute, to represent protobacco arguments. While trying to maintain the appearance of grassroots organizations, most were in reality organized and financed to a large degree by protobacco interests.

These groups focused their communication on a few key points:

1. Tobacco smoke is not a major source of air pollution.
2. People are not allergic to tobacco smoke.
3. Nonsmokers in a smoke-filled room don't inhale significant amounts of smoke.
4. Even though a surgeon general's report says that carbon monoxide in a smoke-filled room exceeds permissible levels, such conditions are only rarely found.
5. Antismoking efforts notwithstanding, hard evidence against smoking is not increasing.
6. Thorough review of the world's scientific literature indicates that smoke is not a significant health hazard to the nonsmoker.
7. Common courtesy, rather than laws, should determine nonsmokers' rights.
8. Tobacco is a legal product, available to adults who chose to consume it.

## Evidence Mounts and Momentum Shifts

In 1981, the effect of secondhand smoke was magnified by research showing increased risk to nonsmokers exposed to it. The EPA was moved to declare that secondhand smoke causes cancer. Assistant Surgeon General John Duffy said, "There is no such thing as a nonsmoker in America today."

With these declarations, the tobacco lobby saw several key arguments slipping away.

In 1984, Congress passed legislation requiring stronger warnings on cigarette packs. With antismoking groups keeping up the pressure, Americans became more socialized against tobacco. Media events such as the Great American Smokeout and Kick Butts Day drew continuing attention to the fact that smoking was no longer fashionable. Restrictive laws would soon follow.

While this controversy rages on, some of the major tobacco companies have taken steps to protect their shareholders, and perhaps other stakeholders, by diversifying their product mix.

On the antismoking side, the Coalition on Smoking or Health (an alliance of the American Heart Association, the American Lung Association, and the American Cancer Society) has increased its efforts, encouraged, no doubt, when Congress passed a law banning smoking on all domestic commercial airline flights. It didn't hurt matters, either, when the EPA issued its warning against secondhand smoke. The Coalition has taken this new evidence and used it to emphasize that smoking is not just an event that affects the smoker. "As long as we have to live and work around smokers, we must accept some of the risks of smoking."[11]

The prime source of programmed antismoking activity continues to be the American Cancer Society. It directs the annual Great American Smokeout, a national event in which smokers all quit on the same day (see Problem 8-A). The Society offers a guide promoting the event. It also has available a news media handbook, *Smoke Signals,* with a variety of ideas and instructions for groups wanting to tell the Smokeout story in news outlets.

*(Continued)*

---

[11] "The Need for a Safe, Healthy, and Smoke Free Workplace." *World Smoking and Health,* American Cancer Society, Summer 1990, p. 3.

## A Legal History of the Tobacco Debate

Long-time smokers (and their survivors) have had success in legal battles with tobacco companies by claiming that the companies hid health hazards associated with their products. In 1992, the Supreme Court ruled for Rose Cipollone's family (Ms. Cipollone died in 1984). (See box, p. 229.) It has been an uphill battle for the tobacco industry because health issues, legal comments, and public opinion have all turned against it. The war is just about over, and the health forces are prevailing. Tobacco companies are left to fight over the 20 percent of the American public still smoking while pushing diversification and overseas expansion. The following is a summary of the principal disputes faced by the major tobacco companies in recent years.

The courts have made huge monetary judgments against the major tobacco companies. Additionally, the companies are facing a lawsuit filed against them in 1999 by the U.S. Department of Justice.

- In June 2001, a Los Angeles jury, in *Richard Boeken v. Philip Morris, Inc.,* found the Philip Morris Company liable for the lung cancer killing the plaintiff in the case and ordered the company to pay $3 billion in punitive damages. As in most cases when the industry loses, it will appeal the verdict. According to the Web site of the Tobacco Control Resource Center and the Tobacco Products Liability Project of Northeastern University School of Law (www.tobacco.neu.edu), this verdict was the seventh defeat for the tobacco industry over the last 23 jury verdicts on individual claims dating back to February 1999.

- In July 2000, in the first class action suit brought on behalf of smokers (the *Engle* case) the five major cigarette makers—Philip Morris, Lorillard, the Liggett Group, R.J. Reynolds Tobacco Company, and Brown & Williamson Tobacco Corporation—were ordered by a Florida jury to pay a record $145 billion in compensatory and punitive damages.

- A lawsuit filed by the Justice Department in 1999 alleges that "tobacco companies engaged in a 45-year pattern of false and misleading statements about the health effects of their products and tried to cover up information that contradicted their marketing."[12] The suit sought more than $100 billion in damages.

---

### Cipollone V. Liggett

In one of the most famous liability suits, Rose Cipollone brought suit against three different cigarette companies, citing them as liable for her smoking-related illness. After her case was brought before the Supreme Court in 1992, it paved the way for many more liability lawsuits against cigarette makers. The court's ruling stated that cigarette manufacturers may be sued if they have allegedly deceived the public about the dangers of smoking. The industry was claiming that the warning labels on the packages were enough to shield them against any personal injury suits.

The ruling, however, does not make it easy for a smoker to prove the liability of the cigarette manufacturer. The plaintiff must "convince juries that smokers were not primarily at fault for starting and continuing their habit because they relied on industry misrepresentations."[1] The depiction of healthy people in cigarette advertisements is not enough to prove that the industry has been deceptive.

---

[1] James H. Rubin, "Cigarette Makers Can be Sued," *The Boston Globe,* June 25, 1992, pp. 1–4.

---

[12] *The Washington Post,* April 26, 2001, p. A2.

The Master Settlement Agreement (MSA), reached in November 1998 between the tobacco companies and the state attorneys general of 46 states, puts numerous restrictions on the tobacco industry. The regulations in the MSA have these and other effects:

- Outdoor advertising, including billboards, is restricted.
- Beginning in May 1999, the types of cartoons that can be used in the marketing of tobacco are restricted; as a result, the use of the Joe Camel image was discontinued.
- The tobacco industry is prohibited from directing its advertising at the youth market.
- The Tobacco Institute and the Council on Tobacco Research is dissolved.

The apparent cooperation of the tobacco industry in the MSA was actually part of a resolution of a lawsuit brought by the state of Minnesota against the cigarette producers. However, according to an article in *Advertising Age* magazine, the tobacco industry has already violated the agreement by continuing to spend millions of dollars targeting the youth market.[13]

In July 1998, President Clinton issued an executive memorandum requiring the tobacco industry to release documents that had historically been concealed from the public. There are now numerous Web sites providing tobacco industry documents. The increase of governmental intervention in the operations of tobacco companies is likely a result, in part, of the release of information to the public about the industry's practices.

One of the few places the tobacco companies can still present their explanation of the issues—outside of the courtroom—is on their corporate Web sites. Some of the points that are advocated on most of the company Web sites are:

- Smoking is a matter of choice.
- Cigarettes are a legal product.

- Through continued production and research, a safer cigarette may be created.
- Stopping the production of tobacco products would have a great economic impact on the industry's employees and their families and others in tobacco-related jobs.

The corporate Web sites also include tips for quitting smoking, descriptions of their youth smoking prevention programs, and information on their social responsibility programs. With continued governmental regulation, court-ordered damage payments, and general bad press, the tobacco companies are most likely grateful they have this one outlet for presenting their side of the story and highlighting their image as responsible corporate citizens.

Although the war is mostly over, skirmishes continue. One major battlefield is the college campus. Recognizing that some 90 percent of all smokers started smoking by their 19th birthday, tobacco companies have developed a sophisticated approach to college markets.

A 1994 internal memo from Young & Rubicam—the advertising consultant to Philip Morris USA—released as part of the tobacco settlement, describes college students as "an ideal market because of the stress they may feel in response to all the changes happening in their lives." Such students, away from the boundaries of home and high school, are likely to take up the habit or smoke more frequently.

To increase this likelihood, tobacco companies have aimed much of their marketing efforts at campuses. The *Chronicle of Higher Education* detailed such efforts in the 2005 article "The Battle for Hearts and Lungs."[14] One study cited was from the *American Journal of Public Health* (2004), which showed that tobacco companies had sponsored at least one social event at 118 of 119 colleges surveyed. Such promotions seem to be working.

*(Continued)*

[13] *Advertising Age,* February 5, 2001, p. 18.
[14] *Chronicle of Higher Education,* March 18, 2005.

A Harvard School of Public Health survey of 10,000 college students showed that nearly 33 percent had smoked during the last month.

Tobacco company representatives deny they are creating new smokers. "We're not soliciting new smokers," one Camel promoter is quoted in the *Chronicle* article. "We're just trying to get existing smokers to switch brands."

Smoking is banned in bars and clubs in California, and all tobacco company promotions—a number that exceeds 35,000 annually—must be registered with the attorney general. This gives California some of the most serious smoking regulations in the nation, yet at UCLA student smokers represent some 25 percent of the campus, compared with 17.8 percent of the general population aged 18 to 29. "We don't think it's a huge priority," says a UCLA health administrator, pointing out that students are far more likely to drop dead from alcohol abuse or eating disorders than lung cancer. "It's not a big health issue we need to address."

Such attitudes are music to the ears of the tobacco industry, which is spending more than $15 billion on marketing cigarettes, a figure that has increased more than 120 percent since the industry settlement that included limits on advertising.

Included in those expenditures are some programs designed to win back some of the ground lost over the past decades. Philip Morris is the industry leader—both in sales and in communication designed to put smoking in context. A visitor to the Philip Morris Web site will find a consistent message that there is no safe cigarette and that the best way to avoid the dangers of smoking is to not smoke. In support of this position, Philip Morris has volunteered to not advertise in college newspapers.

R. J. Reynolds, Philip Morris's closest U.S. competitor, has a partnership with the Miss America pageant under which state titleholders visit schools to promote healthful choices. The Campaign for Tobacco-Free Kids (CBFK), among others, is not impressed.

Citing R. J. Reynolds's connection to Joe Camel, candy-flavored cigarettes, and other programs directed toward youth markets, CBFK president Matthew L. Myers called on Miss America organizers to eschew such a relationship: "Surely state Miss America pageant winners do not want to represent that kind of irresponsible corporate behavior or take it into America's classrooms."

So, the battles continue. Anecdotal evidence indicates the tobacco industry is falling further behind:

- Leading companies such as Weyco, Inc. and Scott's (fertilizer) have banned employee smoking—at work or at home. Smokers will lose their jobs if they won't or can't quit.
- In Virginia, a smoker mom was arrested for smoking around her two children.
- The American Legacy Foundation's "truth" campaign reduced teen smoking by some 300,000 between 2000 and 2002.
- Nearly 700 localities restrict outdoor smoking, including the city of San Francisco.
- The Westin Group of hotels banned smoking in all of its 77 United States, Canadian, and Caribbean hotels. Nearly 75 percent of all hotel rooms in the United States are now smoke free.

Still, millions continue to smoke, making billions of dollars for domestic tobacco companies. Will it ever end?

A number of potential solutions loom on the horizon. Most likely is what sociologists call an "engineered solution." For tobacco users, this means a scientific approach to smoking. Today, patches and nicotine-laced gums are available to help curb the smoker's craving for nicotine.

Another proposed alternative to smoking would be a ceramic "cigarette" containing a nicotine element that releases small amounts of the narcotic to the "smoker." This addresses the problem of secondhand smoke while allowing the addicted smoker to satisfy the body's demand for nicotine. It can be purchased for about $100.

Another solution would be for the FDA to be given jurisdiction over nicotine. The FDA made an attempt in 2000 to declare nicotine a pharmaceutical, but failed. The Supreme Court, in *FDA v. Brown & Williamson,* ruled that nicotine had no medicinal properties.

However, this might change with new studies showing that nicotine has a medicinal effect in the treatment of depression. If the FDA is successful in gaining control of nicotine, then it would be available only by prescription, lessening its availability to new users while permitting those currently using nicotine to get it as a prescribed drug. Then, perhaps, the cigarette war will finally be over.

# Case 8-3 Guns—For Whom? For What?

An emotionally charged controversy has long swirled around the availability, ownership, and use of rifles and handguns. On one side are those who are shocked by crime rates and feel that violent behavior is encouraged by gun ownership. On the opposing side are the constitutional rights to keep arms and to be secure in one's home. There are legal provisions for game hunting and target shooting as sport, recreation, and employment. Somewhere in between are the wildlife conservationists, the millions who must walk dark streets at night, and the millions who, by nature, abhor violence and killing in any form.

## Fact Finding

The Second Amendment to the Constitution of the United States (Article 2 of the Bill of Rights) stipulates "a well-regulated militia, being necessary to the security of a free State, the right of the people to keep and bear arms shall not be infringed." The interpretation and the ongoing applicability of this amendment constitute the basis for the controversy involving the personal and private ownership of guns.

Key words in the constitutional amendment appear to be *militia* and *keep and bear arms*. One dictionary defines *militia* as "all able-bodied male citizens from eighteen to forty-five, not members of the regular military forces, and legally subject to call for military duty." That is clear enough as applied to colonial times. But what is a "militia" in modern times when the United States has a trained standing army, large Reserve and National Guard units, a Pentagon brain center, and a worldwide intelligence network, all of which are backed by an enormous nuclear capability that could be unleashed by a word of command and the pressing of a few buttons?

As for the right to bear arms, did our nation's founders intend that one needed to be a *member* of the "militia," or might he or she be *any able-bodied man or woman?* And do "arms" apply only to the flintlock weapons of 1776, or should they include the automatic pistols, AK-47s, and other weapons of today? Such questions of definition make up only one small part of a long and many-sided debate.

Since those pioneer days, the conversion of gun usage from protection to criminal ends has unfortunately attained disturbing proportions. According to the Web site of the Brady Campaign to Prevent Gun Violence, in 2010, firearms were used to kill 9,484 people in the United States, and this country is fourth in the world in gun deaths, behind South Africa (31,981), Columbia (21,898), and Thailand (20,032). According to the FBI Uniform Crime Reports for 2010, guns were used to kill nearly 65 percent of the 14,748 people murdered that year.

Americans, meanwhile, are divided over the issue.

"The latest national survey by the Pew Research Center for the People & the Press, conducted in 2010 among 1,500 adults, finds the public is evenly split over whether it is more important to protect the rights of gun owners (46%) or to control gun ownership (46%). That is largely unchanged from April 2009 (49% control gun ownership vs. 45% protect gun rights). But from 1993 to 2008, majorities had consistently said it was more important to control gun ownership than to protect the right to own guns" (pewresearch.org).

## The Legal Controls

The old cliché, "There ought to be a law against it," seems appropriate. Four significant federal laws support different forms of gun control. The first one, the National Firearms Act of 1934, is aimed at control of special weapons. This statute covers such firearms as sawed-off shotguns, but does not involve the pistols, revolvers, regular shotguns, and rifles commonly displayed in gun shops.

The second federal statute—The Federal Firearms Act—came four years later, in 1938. It prohibited the interstate shipment of all firearms to or by convicted felons, persons under criminal indictment, and fugitives from justice. In addition, it required manufacturers, dealers, and importers doing firearms business across state lines to have a federally issued license.

Twenty-five years later, in 1963, just a few months before President John F. Kennedy was assassinated, a third federal statute was introduced in the Senate (S.B. 1975). It was known as the Gun Control Act. Its purposes were to ban mail-order and interstate shipment of firearms to individuals, to stop over-the-counter sales of guns to minors, to prohibit possession of guns by convicted criminals, and to bar the importation of concealable foreign handguns. This act, with some modifications to its original form, was passed in 1968.

Then, after years of often acrimonious debate, the Brady Bill was enacted in 1993. The Brady Handgun Violence Prevention Act established a national system of background checks and waiting periods for people buying handguns from federally licensed firearms dealers. The act is named after James Brady, a former press secretary who was wounded in the 1981 assassination attempt on President Ronald Reagan. The Supreme Court ruled in 1997 that it was unconstitutional for the federal government to require states to perform the background checks specified by the Brady Bill.

In 1998, Congress replaced the five-day-waiting-period clause in the Brady Bill with a "national instant felon ID system" that requires gun dealers to perform background checks on all gun purchasers. From 1994 to 2005, some 70 million permits were processed; of those, 1.4 million (two percent) were denied.

In 2008, the U.S. Supreme Court decided by a 5–4 vote that individuals have the right to own and bear arms, overturning a Washington, D.C., local ordinance banning handgun ownership. A year later, the same court, by the same vote, overturned a Chicago law that banned handguns. It is clear at this point that the Court considers gun ownership a right, an opinion with which a growing percentage of Americans agree. Between 2004 and 2009, the percentage of Americans approving of a ban on handguns has fallen from 36 percent to 28 percent (Gallup Poll, *USA Today,* April 19, 2010, p A1).

This whole matter is complex and emotional. There are strong personal convictions and frequent flare-ups of public controversy. Hunters, hobbyists, competitive range shooters, law enforcement personnel, wildlife conservationists, gun and ammunition makers, and frightened nightshift workers, among others, hold strong convictions. The victims of armed robbery, rape at gunpoint, kidnapping, and hijacking, and the families and friends of those killed or maimed by gunshot, harbor deep emotional feelings. At times, a whole nation has been shocked with guilt.

Numerous school shootings—from Virginia Tech to Bethel, Alaska, from Conyers, Georgia, to Johnston, Rhode Island, to Jacksboro, Tennessee—have focused national attention on the horrors wrought by guns and elicited emotional outcries for more gun control, longer waiting periods, mandated gun locks, stricter licensing, and restricted sales. In 2011, a deranged shooter in Tucson, Arizona, killed six and wounded 13, including Congresswoman Gabrielle Giffords. A year later, a neighborhood watch officer in Sanford, Florida, shot and killed a 17-year-old black male in a case that raised national furor and brought attention to the so-called "Stand Your Ground" self-defense law that Florida and other states have adopted.

On the flip side, National Rifle Association (NRA) advocates point their fingers at people, not guns, and ask, "How do you legislate sanity?" In the court of public opinion, both sides are strong participants.

*(Continued)*

## Representing Gun Owners

The NRA, founded in 1871, boasts some four million members. It marshals and sustains resistance to restrictive firearms measures that its members feel might infringe on the Second Amendment. At the same time, it supports mandatory sentences for the misuse of a firearm in the commission of a crime.

The objectives of the NRA extend to supporting legislation that continues to permit the use of firearms by law-abiding citizens for pleasure and for protection. The NRA describes itself as an independent, nonprofit organization. In its literature, the NRA asserts that law-abiding Americans are constitutionally entitled to the ownership and legal use of firearms. Some programs of the NRA, as it has described them, include:

- Guardianship of the Second Amendment right. Through its Institute for Legislative Action and Political Victory Fund, the NRA continually monitors, tracks, and systematically combats all threats to the right to keep and bear arms at the federal, state, and local level, and supports lawmakers who uphold that constitutional right. For more information, visit www.nra.org.

- Sponsorship of various shooting clubs and marksmanship programs. It initiated civilian marksmanship programs more than 100 years ago and youth training more than 70 years ago.

- Participation on a national board to promote rifle practice and to operate national rifle and pistol matches.

- Assignment by the U.S. Olympic Committee as the national governing body for competitive shooting in the United States and membership in the International Shooting Union.

- Creation of a code of ethics for hunters and the nationwide "Sighting-In Day."

- Donation of various trophy awards.

- Origination of safety training for hunters and safety courses for firearms in the home.

- Functioning as a certifying agency for instructors, counselors, and referees.

- Total financial support for all expenses of U.S. shooting teams in international competitions.

## How the NRA Is Financed

The NRA has three affiliated organizations that qualify as 501(c)(3) tax-exempt, nonprofit charitable organizations, for which donations are tax deductible for federal income tax purposes. These are (1) the NRA Special Contribution Fund (Whittington Center), (2) the Firearms Civil Rights Legal Defense Fund, and (3) the NRA Foundation. Through membership dues, contributions, and the sale of items related to membership or gun ownership, the NRA has an annual budget of more than $300 million.

The NRA publishes *American Rifleman*, *American Hunter*, and *America's First Freedom* magazines for members. *Shooting Sports USA* is available to members and nonmembers by subscription only. Advertising in these publications is another source of income. The NRA also publishes *InSights* for its junior members and publishes firing range plans and instructions, handbooks, instruction manuals, and a wide variety of pamphlets.

## An Active Constituency

Despite strong public support among Americans for federal gun legislation, the NRA claimed, as far back as the 1960s, that it had the ability to produce "within 72 hours more than half a million letters, postcards, and telegrams to members of Congress on any gun bill issue."[15] Its target constituency includes owners of some 192 million firearms,

---

[15] Richard Harris. "Annals of Legislation: If You Love Your Guns." *New Yorker,* April 20, 1968.

comprising 39 percent of American house-holds; veterans of all wars; licensed hunters; gun club members; gun collectors; gun deal-ers; and manufacturers of equipment for hunt-ing and target shooting.

## The NRA Strategy and Tactics at Points of Controversy

When shocking incidents such as assassina-tions, school shootings, and gang-related violence seize the front page, public opinion swings suddenly and widely. The public often sympathizes with the families and friends of the victims, deploring the senselessness of violence and demanding the apprehension of the perpetrator, swift and stern justice, and stricter controls of firearm ownership. Concerned citizens write letters to editors. Law enforcement officials speak up for gun registration and regulation, and other controls.

- In the immediate aftermath of tragic episodes and public outrage, the NRA has not often taken a stance of overt rebuttal. Its strategy seems to be to lie low, knowing that the pendulum of opinion will in time return to positions held before the shocking event.

In its dealings at the political and legisla-tive level, however, the NRA has not wavered or gone silent. Its lobbying strategy for many years has emphasized that "guns don't kill peo-ple: people kill people," implying that people rather than guns require more control—sterner penalties for criminal use of a gun are what is really needed. Its lobbying tactics, with an amazing track record of successful opposition to restrictive legislation, have been assertive, not defensive. Its opposition to the Brady Bill, which was first proposed in 1985, helped to delay the passage of this bill for seven years.

In its public information and education, the NRA has emphasized these points:

1. Firearms legislation would disarm the law-abiding citizen without affecting the

criminal, who would ignore the legislation.
2. If firearms were not available, some other weapon would be used by the criminal.
3. Most weapons found in criminal hands have been stolen.
4. Registration of arms might leave law-abiding citizens at the mercy of criminals, of a subversive power if it hacked gov-ernment files or of the nation's enemies if they occupied the country.

## The Role of Public Relations

Within the structure of the NRA, its Institute for Legislative Action includes a governmen-tal affairs office, field services, information services, member services, and fiscal services. This is where the organization's expertise lies. Since 1997, the NRA has been steadily ascending *Fortune* magazine's "Power 25"— the magazine's listing of the most influen-tial lobbying groups in America. In 1997, the NRA ranked sixth. In 1998, it moved to fourth. In 1999, it made second place. *Fortune* did not do the rankings in 2000. In 2001, the NRA reached the number-one spot, displac-ing the AARP, which held the spot for years.[16] Although *Fortune* no longer rates lobbying firms, the NRA retired on top.

## On the Other Side of the Issue

The persuasive power of the NRA has given the impression in the past that those on the other side, the gun control advocates, are invisible and silent, perhaps overwhelmed or intimidated. To many peole who are neutral or fence sitters, it might seem that the success of the NRA reflects popular public sentiment. Neither impression is complete or valid.

Gun control advocates have made these points:

1. There are as many firearms in the United States as there are people.
2. In most states, no license is required to purchase a handgun.

*(Continued)*

---

[16]"The NRA Goes Global." Jason Vest, *Salon Politics 2000*, April 3, 2000.

3. The United States is the only civilized nation in the world that does not regulate the ownership of firearms.
4. According to a 2011 *Time Magazine* report, 31,224 people in the United States died from firearm-related incidents including murders, suicides, accidents, and justified homicides (Time, January 24, 2011, pp. 36–37).
5. Guns should be treated like cars—they should be registered, and the people who use them should be licensed.

Statistical information backing up the gun control advocates is impressive. The U.S. General Accounting Office (GAO), in a survey of crime for one full year, found that 63.8 percent of all murders, 24.6 percent of all aggravated assaults, and 42.7 percent of all robberies were committed by persons using guns. The GAO asked Congress to consider specifically the denial of a gun to a person with a criminal record and the regulation of transfers of guns from one person to another.

## There Are Grassroots Citizens Groups

For years, the most vocal national citizens' lobby was Handgun Control, Inc. James and Sarah Brady joined this group, as well as its sister organization, the Center to Prevent Handgun Violence (CPHV), after the attack on President Ronald Reagan during which James Brady was wounded. Sarah Brady became the chair of CPHV in 1991. In 2001, Handgun Control was renamed the Brady Campaign to Prevent Gun Violence, and CPHV became the Brady Center to Prevent Handgun Violence. Later that same year, these sister organizations merged with the Million Mom March—another gun control group with 230 chapters across the country. The three combined are the largest national, nonpartisan grassroots organization leading the fight to prevent gun violence.

This merged organization seeks to attract enough contributing members to face off with the NRA in lobbying Congress for legislation, to alert its constituents to those candidates up for election who favor gun controls, to report the voting records of members of Congress on gun issues and the amount of financial support each gets from the NRA, and to provide a continuous rallying point.

## Bringing Things Up-to-Date

In legislative confrontations, the NRA is a single-issue organization. Its strategy is to take an inflexible posture. Officials are convinced that to make one concession would establish a precedent and invite a nibbling away at the Second Amendment right.

However, this ironclad stance received several blows in the 1990s because of the turning tide of public opinion and the lobbying efforts of the Brady Campaign and other gun control advocates, including police organizations. Specifically:

- **1994:** President Clinton signed into law the Violent Crime Control and Law Enforcement Act, which includes the first-ever federal assault weapons ban, banning the future manufacture and importation of military-style assault weapons.
- **1995:** In the wake of the Oklahoma City bombing, the NRA faced intense public scrutiny and widespread criticism for its views. NRA membership dropped and President George Bush resigned his life membership after it was revealed that the NRA called the Bureau of Alcohol, Tobacco, and Firearms agents "jack-booted thugs" in a fund-raising letter.
- **1996:** Congress passed legislation to prohibit anyone convicted of a misdemeanor domestic violence offense from buying or owning a gun.
- **1997:** The Supreme Court struck down the background check requirement of the Brady Law. Still, the waiting period and other provisions of that law survived an NRA-financed challenge. Law enforcement officers continued to

conduct background checks voluntarily until the National Instant Check System went into effect in 1998.

- **1998:** New Orleans became the first public entity to sue the gun industry.
- **1999:** In the wake of Columbine High School shooting, the U.S. Senate passed legislation to close the gun show loophole, which allows unregulated private sales. Similar legislation in the House was defeated, and the Senate bill stalled in conference committee.
- **1999:** *Merrill v. Navegar* resulted in the first appeals court ruling that a gun maker can be held liable for negligence leading to the criminal use of a gun.
- **2000:** Smith & Wesson became the first gun manufacturer to settle with cities and counties suing the gun industry, agreeing to make sweeping changes in its manufacturing and distribution practices.
- **2000:** After two years of court battles, the Attorney General of Massachusetts became the first in the nation to use consumer protection powers to regulate guns.

The pendulum began to swing in the other direction in the new millennium.

- **2005:** Congress passed the Protection of Lawful Commerce in Arms Act, which protects gun manufacturers from civil law suits related to "criminal or unlawful misuse of a firearm."
- **2008:** The U.S. Supreme Court ruled that the Second Amendment right to bear arms is an individual right, overturning a Washington, D.C., law banning handguns.
- **2009:** Congress voted to allow people to carry guns in national parks. "The NRA is taking over the House and Senate," groused Rep. Carolyn McCarthy (D/NY) after the vote (Associated Press, May 21, 2009).
- **2010:** The U.S. Supreme Court ruled gun owners are not bound by local laws, overturning a Chicago ban on handguns.

As a societal issue and as a legislative issue, gun control is a subject that is not going to go away. An online search of "gun control legislation" yields 5,490,000 mentions. During the final years the George W. Bush administration, two conservative judges were added to the Supreme Court, to the complete delight of the NRA. Among the NRA's top legislative goals was a law to permit employees to bring guns to work so long as they are left in personal vehicles. As of 2009, ten states enacted such laws.

No major gun control legislation has been passed since the Brady Bill in 1994. Many of its provisions expired in 2004. Further, major bills favorable to the gun industry and its lobby have been passed.

## Questions for Discussion

1. The strategy of the NRA has been to oppose any legal measures that might tighten controls. The grounds are that any of these would be a foot in the door leading to demands for more such laws. As an

With the 2008 election of President Obama, the pro-gun community went into overdrive convincing their members that the President's aim was to take away their guns. Nothing brings in support—monetary or otherwise—than a potential threat to a cause. Pro-gun legislators in many states introduced a variety of legislation designed to loosen gun laws further. "Stand Your Ground" laws that allow an individual to shoot someone in self-defense have been passed in some form in at least 32 states. Given the 2012 Trayvon Martin case in Florida, the tide may be about to turn on this law and others. But the NRA is very effective at all levels of government in protecting that which they have worked hard to put in place.

*(Continued)*

objective communications professional, how do you feel about this "no exceptions," "no compromise," "not one inch" attitude? Has your attitude changed at all by your studies of the ultimate purpose of public relations? If so, how and why?

2. What similarities and differences do you find in the foundations of the convictions of those who hold to a hard line on the gun issue (on either side) and those who hold to a hard line on abortion (on either side)? In their strategies and tactics?

3. Using the definitions of a public issue and of a crisis given in the introduction to this chapter, which of the following would you consider issues and which crises, and which are neither?
   a. Abortion rights
   b. Gun control
   c. Integrity in public office
   d. Insurance rates
   e. Crime rates
   f. Drug usage

4. Can you think of a strategy that the NRA could take to influence the public to agree with its actions and goals? What strategies is it using that soften its position? That strengthen it?

5. Was this case presented in a biased manner? Give evidence for your position. This type of analysis is a regular task of public relations practitioners preparing plans and strategies.

6. How can a group with only 10 to 15 percent of the public supporting its views—which has historically been the case with the NRA—be so powerful? Why would officeholders listen to its views? What strategies do you feel enable such a minority view to prevail for so long? What must the Brady Campaign and other groups opposed to unregulated gun ownership do to successfully make their case?

# ★Case 8-4 United Way and the Boy Scouts of America: A Question of Funding

Neither the United Way nor the Boy Scouts of America (BSA) wanted the social and political standoff that materialized after numerous local United Way chapters instituted and enforced a "nondiscrimination" policy that excluded from United Way funding any organization that excluded anyone because of sexual orientation, including the BSA. This case examines the fallout from the dilemma and how both organizations met the inherent public relations challenges.

In June 2000, the U.S. Supreme Court ruled that the BSA, as a private organization, has the right to establish its own membership and leadership standards and that this right is protected under the Constitution's First Amendment right of expressive association. This protection allows the BSA to exclude homosexuals, who the BSA believes are not appropriate role models, from serving as Boy Scout troop leaders. Although the BSA has adopted a policy of "don't ask, don't tell," some troop leaders whose sexual orientation has become known are now no longer allowed to be leaders.[17]

The laws of the land, it seems, were in conflict, and so were the Boy Scouts and the United Way.

In 2009, United Way of America and United Way International came together to create United Way Worldwide [UWW]. It is the largest privately supported non-profit in the world. In 2010, UWW raised $5.09 billion through nearly 1,800 local United Ways in 41 countries and territories.

Since the merger, UWW's focus has shifted from being a fundraising organization to one focused on community impact in the areas of education, income, and health—the building blocks for a good quality of life. More than 90% of local United Ways focus on these core areas. (A)

The BSA, founded in 1910, currently comprises more than 2.7 million scouts, and one million adult volunteers serving through some 300 local councils and some 111,000 packs and troops. Membership has been problematic. Scouting officials say the decline is more related to America's busy family agendas than any knock on scouting. "We conducted focus groups," says Gregg Shields, APR, former BSA spokesperson now in private practice, "and parents told us they were 'just too busy' to participate. Americans are just not joining organizations the way they used to."

United Way organizations have a long history of funding Boy Scout councils across the country. However, because each of the local United Way agencies is autonomous, local offices can individually decide how they will handle the funding of regional Boy Scout councils in light of the Supreme Court ruling. A variety of methods have been developed by the independent United Way chapters, which include:

- Funding only those organizations that are willing to sign a member agency agreement that contains a nondiscrimination clause.

  (A) Del Galloway, vice-president, communications, UWW
- Giving donors the opportunity to designate which organizations, including the BSA, will receive their contributions.

*(Continued)*

---

[17] *Boy Scouts of America v. Dale.*

- Abiding by the BSA membership policies and continuing funding.

Because each United Way chapter is unique, an individual office might use one of these methods or a combination of them, or create its own policy.

Numerous local United Way offices chose to withdraw their funding of the BSA, and *USA Today* reported, "In September 2000 alone, 'the Scouts lost nearly $530,000 in public money and charitable aid as one local government after another voted to end relations with the group because it excludes gay people.'"[18]

BSA representatives are quick to point out that funds from the United Way have been declining for years. "As a percent of overall funding for BSA, money from the various United Way chapters has been declining for the last 20 years or so," says Shields. "However, more than 90 percent of these United Way chapters are still funding Boy Scout councils in their communities." For example, the Circle Ten Council, comprising a dozen counties around Dallas, Texas, received $256,000 for 2012 from its United Way—2.2 percent of its overall budget. Other councils have been cut out entirely.

Unfortunately for the BSA, that money now has to be made up via other fundraising activities or compensated for in loss of services. Neither is a desirable option. In 2006, BSA president Rick Cronk told *USA Today* that his goal for the organization was to double the size of the population served, not cut back in any way.[19] By 2012, however, the number of young men involved in scouting had declined to 2.7 million, down from 2.9 million in 2006. The number of packs and dens fell 2.9 percent between 2010 and 2011, although the number of Boy Scouts grew 1.3 percent to 848,291, according to the BSA 2011 annual report. Meanwhile, scouting looks for answers to its declining numbers.

Specifically, BSA is looking to non-traditional audiences—urban, ethnic, and underrepresented in scouting. Three Cub Scout manuals are printed in Spanish, Shields says, and other materials are offered in nearly 15 languages besides English. One program, aimed specifically at Hispanic youth, is called "Soccer in Scouting," playing on the popularity of the sport for Hispanic kids. In African-American communities, BSA is sponsoring college-aged leaders to organize and promote scouting among populations currently underrepresented.

Such activities seem to be working. Shields says research shows external audiences have "overwhelmingly" positive perceptions of scouting—"similar to [their impressions of] the Girl Scouts." Meanwhile, internal behavior, as measured by participation and activities, is on an upward trend. Eagle Scout awards are trending upward (51,473 awarded in 2011), and everything from merit badges earned to days in camp show positive trends, even in the face of declining membership.

But the pressure continues to mount. The New Jersey Supreme Court has ruled that the BSA cannot ban homosexuals from leadership posts, even though several other states (California, Oregon, Connecticut, and Kansas) have ruled otherwise (*The Washington Post*, August 5, 1999). In 2012, one BSA member submitted a resolution calling on the BSA to reconsider its policy, and in May, 2012, a lesbian den leader, dismissed from her scouting post, responded by filing a petition on Change.org. That petition quickly collected nearly 300,000 signatures, and a representative of Change.org was able to present the petition to BSA leaders at the organization's national convention. Scouting leaders, however, said the petition was accepted only as an act of courtesy, and that nothing in its policy was changing.

---

[18] Laura Parker, *USA Today,* October 10, 2000, p. 1-A
[19] *USA Today,* May 23, 2006.

## The Boy Scouts of America Clarifies Membership Policy

June 7, 2012

"Contrary to media reports, the Boy Scouts of America has no plans to change its membership policy. The introduction of a resolution does not indicate the organization is "reviewing" a policy or signal a change in direction.

### Resolution:

In April, a single individual submitted a resolution asking the Boy Scouts to consider amending its policy on not granting membership to open or avowed homosexuals. The resolution asked that the policy be amended to allow local units to determine their own standards. . . .

Resolutions and petitions on this subject are not unique and go back as far as 2000, when the U.S. Supreme Court reviewed this matter, and have been widely covered in the media since that time. In addition, in the past individuals have submitted resolutions asking the BSA to reaffirm its current policy. Those resolutions were handled in the same manner.

The introduction of a resolution is procedural and handled with respect but does not indicate the organization is "reviewing a policy" or signal a change in direction.

### Petition:

Completely unrelated to the introduction of this resolution, on May 27, an online petition asked the Boy Scouts to meet with a spokesperson from the group circulating the petition and accept signatures generated from the online petition, which asked the BSA to change its policy.

While it was not on the Boy Scouts' national business meeting agenda, out of courtesy and respect for differing viewpoints, the BSA accepted the petition during a private meeting. This meeting to accept the petition was not related in any way to the introduction of the resolution.

### BSA Policy:

The BSA policy is: "While the BSA does not proactively inquire about the sexual orientation of employees, volunteers, or members, we do not grant membership to individuals who are open or avowed homosexuals or who engage in behavior that would become a distraction to the mission of the BSA."

Scouting believes same-sex attraction should be introduced and discussed outside of its program with parents, caregivers, or spiritual advisers, at the appropriate time and in the right setting. The vast majority of parents we serve value this right and do not sign their children up for Scouting for it to introduce or discuss, in any way, these topics.

The BSA is a voluntary, private organization that sets policies that are best for the organization. The BSA welcomes all who share its beliefs but does not criticize or condemn those who wish to follow a different path."

(scouting.org Web site 2012)

Unfortunately for the United Way, no matter which policy a local chapter uses in connection with the BSA, it is sure to offend people on one side of the issue or the other, which can result in a substantial drop in funding. If donations are withheld because of a chapter's funding policies, the loss of donations also affects all the other programs that a chapter supports in its community. Both the United Way and BSA appear to be faced with a no-win situation on this issue.

In 1992, then United Way President William J. Aramony was accused of misusing funds and was fired. The United Way of America took a nationwide and very proactive approach in responding to the news of its president's illegal dealings. The actions taken were aimed at regaining credibility with both the public and the local chapters. Some local chapters, however, used this situation to distance themselves from the national United

*(Continued)*

Way by emphasizing the distinction between the national office and the autonomous local chapters.

In the case of the BSA and the Supreme Court ruling of June 2000, the national United Way office has employed the "distance" strategy used by the local offices previously. Because the United Way of America does not dictate policy or funding decisions to the local offices, and the issue of funding the BSA rests solely with the local chapters, this was an opportunity for the national office to recuse itself from the controversy.

When the issue first arose, the United Way of America Web site (national.unitedway.org) had a section, "United Way Funding Boy Scouts," in which it emphasized in a variety of ways that the national office does not dictate policy to the local chapters and that each local chapter is a separately incorporated, independent organization that sets its own funding policies. At the time (2000), about 30 local United Way chapters decided to implement the nondiscrimination policy, according to Brian Quail, then-executive director of the Heart of Florida United Way in Orlando, Florida, itself one of the 30. Later that number would grow to more than 50. However, in 2005–2006, at least two high-profile chapters—in Atlanta, Georgia, and Fox River, Wisconsin—decided to reinstate funding to BSA.

A possible solution for the UWW might lie in the new "education, finance, and health" focus. By directing funds to these specific areas, UWW might find it easier to change its funding mix while at the same time remaining true to its mission.

## Public Relations Implications

Although the problem can be addressed in the near term via one of the options described earlier, long-term consequences have to be considered. Public relations must take the long-term perspective, looking at the big picture before making plans, offering advice, or deciding on a course of action.

What are the social trends? What does an environmental scan show? More important, should public opinion or social mores determine what an organization should do? Is there an ultimate "right" posture? Is there even an ultimate correct social moral law? Is it possible that the answer differs from situation to situation?

Nowhere is the news good. For whatever reason, membership in BSA is down— 6 percent from 2010 to 2011. For United Way chapters across the country, another cloud is on the horizon. Competitive agencies are springing up, promising "open giving" for all donors. If these become established, the obvious loss of organizations funding the United Way would curtail its ability to meet its mission. Charitable organizations have to be cognizant of future funding.

Competitive fundraisers are eating into what had been a corporate monopoly for the United Way. For example, City of Orlando employees pledged $332,000 to local charities in 2001, about 30 percent more than in 2000. But the local United Way received less than half of that amount. The other half went to the competing charities. In terms of net dollars, the United Way received all of the city's pledges of $247,000 in 2000. In 2001, pledges to the United Way dropped to $121,735. Similar scenarios were played out with Universal (Studios) Orlando and Seminole County employees.

The *Orlando Sentinel,* in an editorial following the fall campaign, said:

> United Way agencies face an additional challenge that is likely here to stay: increased competition. More workplace donors have options now about where to direct their donations. Other organizations, such as America's Charities, are aggressively pushing into the workplace.

## What Is United Way's Position on the Boy Scouts?

"United Way Worldwide, the leadership organization for the almost 1,800 member United Ways in 40 countries around the globe, does not dictate policy or funding decisions to its member organizations, except to the extent that funding decisions must be consistent with applicable law. As such, the responses to the 2000 Supreme Court's ruling on the Boy Scouts by these volunteer-driven local United Way organizations have been and will continue to be decided community by community, with each United Way community assessing its own needs and setting its own funding priorities.

The success of the United Way system is the autonomy of its membership and the spirit of local volunteerism as a means of accomplishing its goals. Local United Way funding decisions have always been decided using an inclusive community process—a process that involves the community in a broad dialogue with donors, volunteers, and other concerned citizens dedicated to building a stronger community.

United Way Worldwide embraces inclusiveness, diversity, and equal opportunity as part of our core values, Code of Ethics, and human resource policies. We understand that the nation is stronger when all segments of the community and the gifts of all people with their diversity of viewpoints are respected and embraced. . . .

We also respect and value the diversity of opinion and process in community building efforts undertaken by our member United Ways as they assess their relationship with the Boy Scouts. United Way's work in advancing the common good through our focus on education, income, and health as the basic building blocks of a good quality of life has changed many funding policies. Partners funded by United Ways that have committed to this community impact model have to demonstrate outcomes in reaching goals in that area. At the national level, our three main ten-year goals are:

- Cut by half the number of young people who drop out of high school.
- Cut by half the number of working families that lack financial stability.
- Increase by one third the percentage of healthy young people and adults.

The values of United Way are embodied in our **LIVE UNITED**® campaign. This is a call to action—and invitation for everyone to join us, regardless of their stance on various issues—to move forward on these goals. It's going to take everyone working together—giving, advocating and volunteering—to make progress on these goals across the country. Meanwhile, we invite varying points of view and voices to all come together so we can move forward.

In the end, we hope the millions of individuals, organizations, and corporations who comprise the United Way and represent many differing opinions will continue to embrace the local autonomy that has always been the hallmark of the United Way system."

(United Way Web site 2012)

That the United Way of America does not take a firm stand on such issues seems to be a plus, because any stand could potentially jeopardize future donations for an array of local organizations. The uncommitted stance taken by the national office may help to retain the public's trust and therefore also protect the interest of the local offices. In addition, the United Way has no problem funding the BSA with contributions specifically earmarked for the organization.

*(Continued)*

United Way organizations must be prepared to compete in that new marketplace.

That's especially urgent for Heart of Florida United Way [HOFUW], which fell $2.6 million short of its $20.6 million goal in its recent campaign. In addition to the factors listed above, the local organization also fell short because of its antidiscrimination policy, which banned discrimination against all groups, including gays. After the Boy Scouts refused to endorse that policy, United Way compromised, upsetting people on both sides of the issue.[20]

The editorial continued to say that the HOFUW should maintain its antidiscrimination stance, first because it is the right thing to do, but also because altering this stance "might prompt an even larger number of people who support the policy to withhold their donations."

Donations to HOFUW continued to drop for four years. Finally, in 2011, the Orlando-based agency was able to raise more than $19 million, a recent high, but still below the $21 million level from before the BSA problem emerged.

With a fragmented marketplace, a divided giving public, and difficult economic times, the United Way, the BSA, and all those trying to help create a healthy community have a daunting challenge—building (and rebuilding) positive relationships that lead to positive behavior. Shields believes the solution is to continue to work together. "It is not an 'us-versus-them' situation," he says. "In most communities, often it is the same people working with both organizations, or at least people closely connected—close personal friends who don't want either side to suffer."

It is in these tight situations that a legitimate public relations counselor can make a major difference. Wise counsel can help establish how the organization wants to be perceived by its stakeholders and can suggest programs and decisions to bring those perceptions to reality.

### Questions for Discussion

1. When laws conflict with mores, how can one decide what is right?
2. Are the positions of the BSA and the United Way really mutually exclusive?
3. Discuss the strategy of United Way America pushing decisions down to the local-chapter level.
4. If you were public relations counsel to the BSA, what advice would you offer?
5. If you were public relations counsel to UWW, what advice would you offer?

---

### The Scout Oath

On my honor, I will do my best to do my duty to God and my Country, and to obey the Scout Law; to help other people at all times; to keep myself physically strong, mentally awake and morally straight.

---

[20] "Less United," *Orlando Sentinel*, December 10, 2001, p. A-14.

# ⭐ Case 8-5 Mothers Against Drunk Driving—MADD

In response to tragedy, people often reach out to others for support. Many find comfort in doing what they can to right a terrible wrong or prevent others from going through what they have gone through. Often these support groups can become a powerful and compelling voice for social change. One of the most successful and accomplished of these coalitions is Mothers Against Drunk Driving (MADD). MADD's mission is twofold: (1) to provide support for those who have experienced the tragedy of a drunk driving accident and (2) to advocate, both socially and legislatively, against the act of operating a vehicle under the influence of drugs and alcohol.

MADD was established by Candy Lightner in 1980 in response to the loss of her daughter in a drunk driving accident. The organization currently has some 400 chapters across the United States. Membership is about two million. Funding raised and spent in support of education, public awareness, victims' assistance, and other programs has increased four times over. Donations to MADD total nearly $43 million annually.

MADD's efforts, combined with overall efforts to increase highway safety, are working. In 2010, traffic fatalities totaled 32,885, the lowest number since 1949, and only 1.10 deaths per 100 million miles driven. Of those fatalities, 10,228 (31%) were alcohol related, a decrease of about five percent over 2009, according to the National Highway Traffic Safety Administration (NHTSA).

Despite MADD's positive influence, much needs to be done to change people's behavior relative to drinking and driving. According to NHTSA, eight percent of all drivers (17 million) admitted to drinking and driving in 2009.

## The Publics

MADD targets several audiences, which are on different sides of a drunk driving accident.

- Along with its sister organization, Students Against Drunk Driving (SADD), MADD educates *teens* (a group with a high incidence of alcohol-related accidents) against the dangers of drunk driving.
- Another focus is the *adult driver* who may become impaired after a social night out.
- The *repeat and reckless drunk driver*—the cause of many alcohol-related deaths—is targeted in MADD's legislative efforts for harsher penalties.
- MADD also supports *public service professionals,* such as police, paramedics, and physicians, who must deal with the daily consequences of one person's carelessness.
- Finally, MADD maintains programs aiding family and friends who have experienced the trauma of a drunk driving accident.

## Goals and Objectives

MADD works at the grassroots level to end the senseless deaths and crippling physical and emotional injuries caused by drunk drivers. MADD supports programs that:

1. Achieve *voluntary* liquor and beer industry support to curb alcohol advertising when television or live audiences include large percentages of watchers under age 21. One goal is to find alternate advertisers.
2. Encourage sponsors of sporting events to limit alcohol sales later in the event, thereby increasing the probability that fans will arrive home safely.
3. Convince Congress to add a victim's rights amendment to the U.S. Constitution—similar to the Victim's

(*Continued*)

Bill of Rights in the Michigan, Florida, and Rhode Island state constitutions.

## Activities and Tactics

*Project Red Ribbon* has become one of MADD's most successful campaigns. During the holiday season, red ribbons are distributed to drivers to be tied on to car antennas and mirrors.[21] The ribbon acts as a *reminder* not to drive if the driver becomes impaired and as a *sign of solidarity* against drunk driving. The act of tying the ribbon also reminds the individuals of other preventive behaviors as well, such as calling a cab for a friend or holding his or her car keys to prevent drunk driving. The program is successful because it links a specific behavior (tying the ribbon) to a commitment against drunk driving *before* the first

toast is raised, and it does this at the *point of behavior.*

More than 30 million red ribbons are distributed each year by volunteers, MADD chapters, and supporting organizations, such as 7-Eleven stores, across the country. In addition to grassroots support, several companies have tied marketing efforts to the program. Welch's promoted its nonalcoholic cider in conjunction with the program. This action may or may not have boosted Welch's sales, but it did give more exposure to the MADD program—and the anti-drunk-driving ideal.

MADD's ultimate goal is to get year-long commitment against drunk driving, not just one for the holidays. There is evidence that Project Red Ribbon helps reach this goal—MADD receives requests throughout the year for replacements for worn-out ribbons.

---

### One-Way and Two-Way Communication Tools that Helped Madd Build Support for its Mission

1. *Support for the MADD message in television programming.* In 1988 to 1989, millions of Americans tuned in to their favorite television show and got a clear warning about drinking and driving—"The two don't mix." A portion of the credit goes to the Harvard School of Medicine Alcohol Project campaign, which encourages producers and writers to promote responsible drinking and designated-driver programs. MADD's national office served as script advisers.
2. *National poster contest.* More than 45,000 young people have participated in annual nationwide poster and essay contests aimed at preventing drunk driving. Cultural barriers were breached by including Spanish-language entries.
3. A *toll-free victim's assistance crisis hotline* was established by MADD to provide support to those affected by a drunk driver's actions.
4. *Formation of victim impact panels.* One hundred victim impact panels were formed to serve as forums for voicing grief, pain, and frustration associated with drunk driving accidents. These can send a powerful *emotion-laden* message to the public. Convicted drunk drivers are occasionally required to attend one of these panels as part of their sentence.
5. *Candlelight vigils* have been held to honor drunk driving victims and serve as a reminder.
6. *Crisis response teams* were formed to assist families and friends of victims.
7. MADD *lobbied strongly for legislation for stiffer penalties* to keep the drunk driver off the road and to curb underage drinking.
8. MADD published *MADDvocate*, a magazine for victims and advocates.

---

[21] Originally, they were tied on to door handles to keep drunks from getting into their cars—but most present-day handles have no place to attach them.

## The Outcome

Coalition efforts paid off. In addition to the 7.7 percent decrease in fatalities over 10 years, the Omnibus Anti-Drug Act was passed in 1988. It is a significant victory in federal anti-driving-while-intoxicated legislation. The enactment of the federally sponsored national minimum drinking age of 21 is another significant gain.

## Legislation: Another Form of Persuasion

Years of scholarly research on public relations programming have established a four-step method for effecting mass behavior change—which is MADD's goal, of course (See box, page 260). Step two is enforcement, and this is where restrictive and punitive laws play their part. Thus, MADD's program has included enforcement (including punishment) to preserve the whole agenda of behavior change.

MADD deserves much of the credit for one of the most remarkable behavior-change efforts in recent times. Only a decade ago it was still acceptable to talk about the "drunken party" you went to over the weekend. Today, in most circles, anyone who mentions such behavior would be scolded and possibly shunned. In large measure, this change can be traced to the catalytic leadership of MADD. Here are some of the laws that MADD—along with a host of coalition partners, often brought together by MADD—has successfully enacted:

1. *Drunk Driving Prevention Act of 1988.* States were offered incentives in the form of highway-safety-fund grants for passing legislation aimed at reducing alcohol-related offenses and deaths, including a minimum drinking age of 21—up from 18 in most states. The act was controversial, but eventually most states adopted the age to avoid losing federal funds.
2. *Victim's Crime Act of 1984.* This act provides compensation rights and grants for the survivors of drunk driving accidents.
3. *Alcoholic Beverage Labeling Act of 1988.* This act states that all alcoholic beverage containers bear a warning about the dangers of driving after drinking.
4. 40 states now require ignition interlocks for those convicted of various degrees of drunk driving. All 50 states and the District of Columbia have enacted some sort of ignition interlock legislation. Sixteen states (and four California counties) have made ignition interlocks mandatory or highly incentivized for all convicted drunk drivers, *even first-time offenders.*

The laws that have been passed are a good example of using "enforcement" to change behaviors. "Social reinforcement" will continue with the red ribbons and public service ads. (See box, page 260).

### Questions for Discussion

1. MADD was an organization established by someone who had suffered a great tragedy because of the carelessness of a drunk driver. Today the organization has been extremely successful in exacting changes in societal attitudes about drunk driving. What does its success indicate about relationships formed when people who have suffered the same tragedy band together?
2. Can you think of another organization that was formed because of an emotion-laden circumstance? Has it been as successful as MADD? Explain your answer.
3. What other communication vehicles could MADD utilize to spread its message?
4. As society begins to "forget" as drunk driving fatalities decrease, romanticizing drinking has returned. Shows such as "Mad Men" glorify the drinking culture. Liquor ads are once again allowed on television. What would you recommend MADD to do going forward to counteract these mixed messages?

*(Continued)*

---

### Four Steps to Public Behavior Change through Public Relations Campaigns

The work of Jim Grunig, Harold Mendelsohn, Brenda Darvin, Maxwell McCombs, and many others suggests this approach:

1. **Coalition campaign,** so that the target audience gets the feeling that everyone who counts is trying to persuade them, that it is obviously the thing to do socially. Appeals in such a campaign must follow three phases:
   - *Problem (or opportunity) recognition.* Gaining widespread understanding that the issue is an opportunity or a problem.
   - *Problem (or opportunity) personalization.* Making target audience realize it involves them, they could be affected.
   - *Constraint removal.* Letting the audience know they can do something about it.
2. **Enforcement.** Establishing rules and laws mandating or outlawing the behavior.
3. **Engineering.** Enacting a structural change to work around the situation, for example, raising the drinking age to reduce drunk driving accidents by young drivers.
4. **Social reinforcement.** When the behavior becomes the societally accepted norm, and social rewards and punishments take over the job of enforcing it.

---

## PROBLEM 8-A   A SMOKEOUT CAN BE A HOT POTATO

You are a first-year employee at W. L. Fixit Associates, a public relations firm in Piedmont, North Carolina, a city of 40,000 people that has long thrived on tobacco growing and manufacturing. Mr. Fixit started the agency 10 years earlier after handling communications for the local Chamber of Commerce. He is well known and knows everybody important in the region.

You're doing well. You've just been advanced to associate account executive and assigned the Piedmont General Hospital as your very own client. Among other clients of the agency are a nearby college, a large resort hotel, a new downtown shopping mall, and the United Way.

At the hospital, you're helping deal with complaints about the high costs of health care, as well as promoting a new day-care adjunct and an annual fund-raising campaign and raising employee morale.

One day in August, the Fixit senior account executive comes into your office and says, "You're about to get your first sticky wicket to handle." He tells you that the United Way has committed to implement the "Great American Smokeout" annual event of the American Cancer Society and has asked the Fixit agency to implement it with all its clients. Mr. Fixit thinks that the agency could duck out by pleading a conflict of interest, but with a public health issue like this that would do the agency more

harm than coming up with a plan that has a chance of keeping everybody happy.

Your supervisor tells you, "It will be your job to come up with a catchy, contagious one-day event at Piedmont General." He hands you a packet that explains the Smokeout concept of affecting smokers' behavior, suggests ways to get the cooperation of various organizations, tie in local public health officials and other community leaders, attract the media, instruct those in the facilities how to prepare, make it a fun event, recognize and reward those who abstain for a day, and measure the success of the event. The packet includes examples such as one about an organization that gave out survival kits including chewing gum and candy, another that put baskets of apples all around its offices, another that set up smoke eaters in designated smoking areas, another that removed cigarette vending machines on Smokeout day, and another that sent a congratulatory letter from the president to each smoker employee who reported successfully abstaining on Smokeout day. Then the account supervisor threw the curve.

"This is no piece of cake," he said. "Your hospital's largest contributor is the tobacco company over in Winston. There's a wing named for its founder, Colonel Piedmont. Also, have you noticed that the Piedmont's administrator is a chain smoker? That's why all the major committee meetings are held out on the penthouse roof in good weather. You've got to come up with an event that makes us look good enough to nonsmokers and the United Way without doing damage to our relationship with the hospital administration. Maybe you can persuade them there is a tradeoff for them. As for smokers and the tobacco industry around here, don't do anything that could cause permanent alienation. Mr. Fixit wouldn't mind landing a tobacco account someday, and tobacco companies are branching out more and more into food products."

He added, "Mull it over. If you can't get both sides to work with each other, at least figure out a project in which neither's ox is gored so badly they have to fight back. Put your ideas down on paper with a reasonable objective; keep in mind that United Way isn't a big-spending account; list what's new and newsworthy about your event, and explain what you have built into the plan to protect against seriously riling the tobacco people, including Colonel Piedmont's family, who made their millions on tobacco. Give me a call in 10 days and we'll take a look together at what you've come up with."

As you start thinking about a solution to this situation, you remember that a successful message strategy

- Emphasizes the benefit statement
- Avoids stiffening the resistance
- Asks for a willing suspension of disbelief

With this in mind, what further background research will you do before you start defining the objectives and activities of your program? Who will you talk to, what concerns do you anticipate, and how will you deal with them?

Using the feedback from this research, define the objectives of your program and explain how the proposed activities will support your communications strategy. Include some means of measuring your success in obtaining your objectives.

Do you see any ethical issues that might arise in handling this situation? If you do, how would you deal with them?

## PROBLEM 8-B    REFEREEING A NEW KIND OF GAME

After earning three letters for sports at Louisiana State University, you were sidelined by a knee injury that kept you out of the professional draft. Fortunately, your journalism/public relations major helped you land a good job with the Dorino, Marion public relations agency. The firm does some work for professional sports teams and suppliers and has good connections in the state capital. They also have a reputation for public service assistance to nonprofit organizations. You like it at Dorino, Marion. They like you.

The main account you personally handle is the subcommittee of the Mardi Gras celebration, which brings in celebrities for the annual event. Your work tends to be seasonal except for periodic planning meetings, some out-of-town contacts, and some correspondence. Thus you have considerable spare time.

That situation changed suddenly one day, when the agency was approached to take on the public relations problems arising from the actions of Brother Omans, the charismatic, activist minister of the local Bible-for-Everybody Church. It seems that Omans, with the active support of a doctor who wrote an antiabortion book, has challenged the activities of the local Birth Control Institute Inc., an affiliate of Planned Parenthood International. It is known to perform and arrange abortions.

Brother Omans has notified the institute by mail that it is "committing murders" and that it risks "harsh judgment" in which "proper penalties can be imposed." He has led a picketing group, some of whose members went beyond passing out pamphlets to shouting at clients heading into the institute.

Mrs. Safeway, head of the institute, has gone to the police for protection. The police say that the picketers are not trespassing as long as they stay on the sidewalk, and that they have rights of assembly and freedom of speech. If and when Brother Omans or his constituents break any law, they will be apprehended.

Mrs. Safeway is concerned that this reactive attitude may allow further escalation and potentially lead to violence. She therefore approaches Dorino, Marion to ask for advice in seeking a more proactive approach to the situation.

You are assigned the task of analyzing the situation and coming up with a pro-active approach as a public service of your agency. You know that Louisiana favors restricting abortion rights and probably would, if it were legal, forbid any abortions except in very narrow circumstances.

To get your facts straight, even before you go to see Mrs. Safeway, you talk to a member of the local media with whom you went to school. He tells you that Brother Omans set up shop locally about eight years ago. A profile the newspaper did on him shows that he has had quite a career. Hailing originally from San Antonio, Texas, he was at one time a circus barker, traveled through the southern Bible Belt, became a minister, and then moved to New Orleans. If he had anything in his background of moral turpitude, or arrests, there is nothing about it in the newspaper morgue.

*(Continued)*

From other sources, you find that in the past eight years, Brother Omans, from the pulpit, has taken on or opposed witches, homosexuals, pornography, X-rated movies, the "mercy death" of a 93-year old comatose man, Mormon missionaries in general, and any woman who has gone into politics.

Armed with this information, you go to see Mrs. Safeway at the Birth Control Institute. She's scared. Because of the many instances of bombing or arson at Planned Parenthood clinics, she can envision some of Brother Omans's constituents making her place a target. She has notified the Planned Parenthood national office. She has read their Clinic Defense Manual and notified the appropriate offices in New Orleans of her concern. She hopes you can do something that would calm the situation down but that would not antagonize Brother Omans, his doctor supporter, or his followers. She appreciates that your agency has agreed to take on this project as a public service. You respect her professionalism but recognize that some of her actions have themselves been adversarial.

## Time to Fish or Cut Bait

Back at your office, you talk it over with your boss. You agree that there are such strong feelings on both sides that it would be tough to marshal enough neutral public opinion to induce reconciliation and that it would be hard to not move special interests with strong biases toward a confrontation or worse.

"This looks like one of those situations calling for a brainstorming session at the agency, bringing together representatives of groups with a stake in peaceful coexistence, and no ax to grind, on abortion," your boss says. "Maybe we can get a strategic plan out of the session. If not, it will put Brother Omans on notice that some important people are watching him, and it may reassure Mrs. Safeway she isn't about to be bombed."

Your boss instructs you to make up an invitation list of about 15 organizations, starting with city hall, the police department, and the county medical society; write a brief statement of the meeting's purpose; and plan a tentative agenda for the meeting. "When you get those done, let me have a look," your boss says.

1. Before you start on this project, what issues affecting other members of the firm and the firm's reputation in the community might you want to discuss with your supervisor? How would you suggest dealing with them?

2. Do you agree with the suggestion that the invitations list should include city hall and the police department? If so, why? If not, on what basis would you suggest omitting them?

3. Would you include Mrs. Safeway or Brother Omans or both in this initial meeting? What could be the positive and negative results of having them there?

4. What would be your list, the statement to invitees, and the agenda?

5. What would be your recommendation about alerting or not alerting the media and dealing with the possibility of a premature leak?

## PROBLEM 8-C   ANTICIPATING EMERGING ISSUES

You are in a one-person public relations department for a large public school in the Midwest. You've done everything from writing newsletters to campaigning to passing a referendum for a school addition. The school is doing well, no big problems to contend with, just the day-to-day communications. But your antenna is always up, listening to your publics—students, teachers, administrators, community members, parent-teacher organization, elected officials, etc.

Last week you had a call from a parent complaining about the school's mascot—the Brave. You also noticed an article in the local paper about a group called Find Another Name dealing with the issue of using American Indian names and mascots. An emerging issue? Or just a coincidence? A staff meeting with the principal is coming up on Friday. You decide to look into the issue and make a recommendation.

Currently, the school doesn't have an issue anticipation team, and it crosses your mind that it would be beneficial for the school to have one, but everyone is so overworked you wonder how it could happen. Even so, you decide to recommend that an issue anticipation team be formed and that the subject of the school's mascot be considered.

For the upcoming meeting, put together a report about the school's mascot and make a recommendation for the school. Consider the ramifications of changing or not changing the name. Also, make recommendations for forming an issue anticipation team, where members would come from (school, parents, community, etc.), how often they would meet, what work they need to do between meetings, and how such work would help the school and the community.

# 9

Crisis Management

Because a true crisis is a turning point, after which things may change drastically, an organization not prepared to deal with crisis is constantly at risk. Even sudden emergencies of crisis proportion can be anticipated—if not avoided—so risk management, issue anticipation, and crisis communication programs have become an important part of public relations practice.

Despite the many connotations of the term, *crisis management* does not imply that an organization or its public relations staff can *manage* external influences. What can—and must—be managed is *response*. This depends on the practitioners' thorough understanding of three things:

1. The **public and political environment** in which the crisis is occurring.
2. The **culture and inner workings of the organization** facing the crisis.
3. **Human nature**—how will the persons and groups involved most likely react to the crisis itself, to attempts to alleviate it, and to various communications, events, or activities?

## UNDERSTAND HOW PEOPLE TYPICALLY RESPOND TO ISSUES

Philip Lesly, a veteran public relations counselor and philosopher/critic of the field, developed the following model. On any given issue dividing public opinion, people will fall into one of these groups:

Zealots will be the first to take firm stands on the issue—for and against. The majority, however, will watch to see which way the opinion leaders go before they are firm enough in their views to speak or act.

Public relations efforts must focus on the opinion leaders—the 8 percent who can influence the 90 percent. Resist the temptation to capitalize on the zealots who support your view. They anger people on both sides of the issue, including those inclined to agree with them.

Keep in mind that opinion leaders are rarely the visible leaders (elected officials or organization officers). Look for them at all levels and in all segments of society. The opinion leaders are not necessarily the educated and articulate, but are always the familiar and trustworthy. Most of us are inclined to seek reinforcement for our choices from people who are in the same situation we are, not from people who are "different."

## HUMAN NATURE

When people are subjected to great emotional stress, their normally self-controlled behavior tends to become irrational and unpredictable. Their motivation regresses down the hierarchy of human needs developed by Abraham Maslow. Maslow was a psychologist known for his theory of human motivation. At the bottom, of course, are a person's physical needs. One step above are a person's safety needs. When people feel that their physical needs and safety needs are threatened, they are prone to panic. In panic, people's baser instincts for survival take command. This "survival" might be physical, financial, social, or something else vital to a person's life, but you can count on self-interest or self-preservation to take command of a person's emotions and actions.

These phenomena become immediately apparent in such catastrophic circumstances as fires, floods, explosions, and tornadoes (see Case 9-5). The same pattern emerges, with less severity, in noncatastrophic situations such as a scarcity of gasoline or coffee, a spate of crime in a community, or even a standing-room-only crowd at a public event. The symptoms of potential panic and the concern for self are there. Similarly, sensations approaching panic may invade us when it appears that we may miss a departing airplane flight, lose a dear friend, find ourselves unexpectedly deprived of light in our home at night, or walk down a dark street to our parked car.

## THE ROLE OF COMMUNICATIONS

People tend to get reassurance concerning their physical well-being and safety largely from believable information that pierces through the uncertainty, rumors, and gossip. Human nature, fortunately, has a toughness about it, enabling most people to handle substantially bad news or physical danger by making adjustments. Knowing the alternatives, we make the best of even a bad deal. But we find it very difficult to cope for long periods with the uncertainties that come from not being informed or not trusting the information, whether the threat to us is as vital and near as a local rumor of a toxic chemical leak or as remote and impersonal as a drop in the Dow Jones stock market average.

Not every crisis is of the "instant" variety. Some crises develop over a period of time—days, weeks, or even months. Nevertheless, these events are crises just as much as those that are fast-breaking. But the consequences for managing a crisis, for keeping credible communication flowing, are intensified when the situation drags out. In any case, the public expects the leaders of trusted organizations to act with total honesty and sensitivity during and after a crisis.

## TYPES OF CRISES

The Institute for Crisis Management (ICM) defines a crisis as "a significant business disruption that stimulates extensive news media coverage. The resulting public scrutiny will affect the organization's normal operations and also could have a political, legal, financial, and governmental impact on its business." ICM identifies four basic *causes* of a crisis:

1. **Acts of God** (storms, earthquakes, volcanic action, etc.)
2. **Mechanical problems** (ruptured pipes, metal fatigue, etc.)
3. **Human error** (the wrong valve was opened, miscommunication about what to do, etc.)
4. **Management decisions, actions, or inaction** (the problem is not serious, nobody will find out)

Most fall in the last category and are the result of management not taking action when they were informed about a problem that eventually would grow into a crisis.

There are two basic types of crises, depending on the amount of warning time: (1) a **sudden crisis,** which comes without warning (employee injury, death of a key executive, oil spills, product tampering, etc.) and (2) a **smoldering crisis,** which is generally not known of internally or externally until it goes public and generates negative news coverage. These problems are representative of operational or organizational weaknesses, bad practices, and other discoverable or predictable bombs waiting to explode. Issue anticipation teams (see Chapter 8) can expose and eliminate these crises. ICM's analysis of business crises since 1990 indicates that the sudden crises are the minority. The majority are smoldering crises.

## NEWS MEDIA INFLUENCE

The interpretation of public events affecting our lives falls heavily on the media—traditional and social. News prerogatives and privileges are legally assured by the First Amendment to the U.S. Constitution. Abuses of these rights surface most often when fierce competition among the media makes a competitive advantage more important or urgent than simple truth and accuracy in protecting the public interest. The Internet, especially, is vulnerable to abuse because of the unedited and unfiltered nature of its content. Just about anyone can post just about anything with impunity.

Few would argue that in recent years the news media have been responsible carriers of information needed by citizens; most would say they have concentrated on scandals and titillating trivialities that provided public entertainment. Jon Stewart and Stephen Colbert are considered by many to be legitimate sources of news and information. This perception must be taken clearly into account when planning crisis strategy.

Similarly, the obligation of public relations toward the public interest is sometimes submerged or subverted by the responsibility to represent the interests of employers or clients.

The ability to communicate trustworthy information, whether directly or via the news media, is a measure of a practitioner's effectiveness or ineffectiveness. In unexpected situations of disaster, crisis, or emergency, the news media and the practice of public relations have demonstrated both the highest quality of public service and the most severe episodes of failure and ineptitude. The cases in this chapter illustrate this point.

## FUNDAMENTAL GUIDELINES

The following are some of the guidelines that help organizations prepare for and manage crisis situations:

1. **Anticipate the unexpected.** Most crisis events can be anticipated. You might not know when they will happen, but an organization can anticipate a fire, a flood, a strike, a fatal accident on the job, a robbery, and many other unexpected events. Unfortunately, *the greatest single obstacle to effective crisis preparation is management denial that one will occur,* notes ICM.
2. **Institute and practice a crisis communications plan** for those events that may affect your organization.
3. **Train employees** in what to do in these circumstances.
4. Have **one spokesperson** communicating to the public and media during the crisis.
5. If it is a crisis affecting the public, rather than just the organization, **another spokesperson** or persons will also be required to directly advise elected officials and opinion leaders.
6. **Do not speculate** on the cause, the cost, or anything else. Provide information about only what is known.
7. **Remember,** how an organization communicates through a crisis will determine, in the minds of most people, how it actually *handled* the crisis.

# Case 9-1 Trouble in the Pews:
# The Catholic Church and Child Molestation

The sexual abuse of minors by some priests in the Roman Catholic Church looms as one of the saddest situations in recent history and led to one of the most aggressively covered stories in recent history. One diocese learned that the "traditional wisdom" on handling crises did not always work. The challenge became one of keeping an eye on the final destination while changing course, taking different tacks, and sailing under full sail while trimming back to navigate some rocky sections.

Before this crisis is described, it must be stated clearly here that the abuse of minors by priests—or by anyone—is wrong and deplorable. The harm done to those who were abused has lasted for decades and will continue to have a profound effect on their lives. No one in the Church ever excused this terrible behavior. The Church people involved in this situation wanted to first help those who had been harmed and then to be sure they did everything in their power to prevent future occurrences. At the same time, the leaders in the diocese needed to manage a crisis of unprecedented scope and intensity.

## The Crisis Didn't Break—It Erupted

On January 6, 2002, *The Boston Globe* published the first of two parts of a *Globe* Spotlight Team story on the Rev. John J. Geoghan, who was about to stand trial for the criminal abuse of minors. The story raised questions about the Catholic Church's policies and practices regarding the assignment of priests who had had allegations of abuse made against them.

If this article was the first rumble, then the following two and a half years were full-force eruptions for the Roman Catholic Church in Boston and other dioceses around the country. The neighboring Diocese of Manchester in New Hampshire was the first to feel the effects of the explosion in Boston.

The Diocese of Manchester encompasses the state of New Hampshire. The Manchester bishop served in the cabinet of Cardinal Bernard F. Law in Boston for 10 years. His final two years in the cabinet included responsibilities as the cardinal's delegate for sexual misconduct. His name began to be mentioned in the context of the archdiocese's practices regarding sexual abuse of minors by priests.

As the *Globe* stories continued, more individuals came forward stating that they had also been abused by priests, and not just Geoghan. The story grew in force, and its effects were now spreading quickly to other dioceses.

## If All Politics Is Local, Then All News Has a Local Angle

The southern part of New Hampshire—the part where the bulk of the population lives—is influenced by Boston media. As the *Globe*'s coverage of the sexual abuse story increased, so, too, did the *Boston Herald*'s and that of the network and independent television stations. New Hampshire was abuzz with the details coming from Boston. Soon, the New Hampshire media were devoting space and time to this story.

Lay people, clergy, and the state's top law enforcement officer all asked the same question: "Is there a similar problem here?"

The bishop and diocesan officials reviewed the records of priests who were in the ministry, retired, or on leave. They developed a list of priests who had had allegations of sexual abuse of a minor made against them. Only one such priest was still in the ministry, and he was immediately removed.

The media and the state's attorney general were asking the diocese for information. After considering the right of the public to know what the situation was—as well as considering the rights of priests who had never been charged or tried—the bishop decided to send the attorney general a letter describing what the diocese's policy was for removing priests and to append a list of 14 priests who had been accused of sexual abuse and what their current status was. Simultaneously, the bishop opted to hold a news conference and release the names to the public. The diocese knew that the names would eventually be made public and wanted to demonstrate that it was not trying to hide anything.

Following the tried-and-tested crisis management technique of getting bad news out quickly and completely, the diocese released this information barely a month after the first story appeared in the *Globe*. The diocese hoped that this painful revelation would mark the end of the problem in New Hampshire. It soon found out that was wishful thinking.

## Issue Consolidation

After the release of the names of priests with allegations of abuse against them, the diocese hoped it could concentrate on moving forward. A number of related—but distinct—issues, however, soon made that impossible:

- The attorney general decided he wanted to conduct an investigation into the past practices of the diocese, to determine if any laws were broken and if there were sufficient safeguards in place to prevent any priest from being in the active ministry if he had abused a minor.
- Many—eventually hundreds—of individuals came forward to state that they had been abused in the past. Many of the priests named in these allegations had no previous allegations against them. Those who were still alive were placed on what most would recognize as administrative leave. This meant they could not be

in the ministry, they could not present themselves publicly as priest, and they could not wear clerical garb.

- Activist groups quickly became vocal in their condemnation of the Church and their calls for action. The groups became convenient sources of comment for the media as the story became solidly framed.
- The attorney general in Massachusetts announced he would begin an investigation of the archdiocese and would be calling the bishop of Manchester to testify.
- Numerous civil lawsuits were initiated, with wide media attention.

## Media Sets the Agenda and Frames the Story

To be certain, the media did not create the situation, but they certainly gave it shape and propelled it to the forefront of the nation's consciousness. This is not an attempt to "blame" the media. However, in order to learn some lessons on how to manage crises in the future, one must understand how the media behaved in this situation.

The horrible and salacious nature of sexual abuse makes it an issue the media love. Like every good story, however, there needs to be a framework, good guys and bad guys, and a simple resolution. The media are not equipped to handle numerous subplots, subtle distinctions, and multiple shades and nuances regarding actions taken and decisions made.

On a regular basis, sometimes daily, *The New York Times* and *The Washington Post* called the diocese for information and interviews. The national news shows and news magazines all expressed interest in the story. On a particularly active day, as many as 25–35 calls might come from local, regional, and national media. It was not unusual to have two or three television microwave broadcast vans outside the diocese offices with reporters giving stand-up reports.

*(Continued)*

*Reinvented History* has become a way of describing the behavior of our society when judging past actions based on today's values. Decades ago, Church officials tended to address sexual abuse problems in the priesthood by moving the priest to a new parish. Sometimes the priest was sent for "treatment" before being reassigned to a new parish. **Stakeholders look at the actions the Church took 50 years ago in response to sexual molestation and, with today's views and opinions, find it appallingly lacking**. In those days, that is how such things were typically handled. Other organizations have been in similar situations. For instance, environmental dumping was perfectly legal and acceptable 20 years back, but not today. Consider the lawsuits suffered by Hooker Chemical (Love Canal), John's-Manville (asbestos), Dow-Corning (breast implants), and the entire tobacco industry.

It is the practitioner's responsibility to look at his or her organization's actions and reactions not only through the eyes of today's stakeholders, but also through the eyes of the stakeholders who will judge those actions in the future.

## Setting Goals, Managing Expectations

After the initial disclosure of names did not establish a point at which the diocese could begin to separate the past from the present and move forward, it was clear that a more sophisticated crisis management strategy was needed. The diocese realized that it was not going to be successful in communicating to its critical publics through the media. The media had framed the story in such a way that everything the diocese said appeared to be defensive.

The diocese developed a crisis management plan with clear goals and identified its core constituencies. The diocese also developed a crisis management team. The bishop delegated management of the crisis to a priest in his cabinet. The team included communications, legal, and support members. From time to time, the team called on the expertise of canon (in-house) lawyers, accountants, ministry personnel, and others.

The goals of the diocese's plan were:

- To respond pastorally to those who had been harmed
- To concentrate on Catholics to help them retain their faith in the Church
- To act with as much transparency as possible to help restore public confidence in the Church

The diocese's main audiences were:

- Those who brought forth claims of abuse by a priest
- The "people in the pews"
- Clergy
- Employees and volunteers in the diocese and parishes

## Strategies and Tactics

The main strategy the diocese employed was to *go direct*. It wanted to find ways to communicate to its key constituencies without the filter of the media. From past research, the diocese knew that the most trusted source of information for Catholics was their own parish priest. Catholics preferred to receive information in Church through the bulletins and handouts. Using this knowledge, the diocese developed some key action steps:

- **E-mail to priests.** The crisis team decided that no information should go out to the media before it was available to the priests. The diocese set up an e-mail distribution system, supplemented by a fax system for those priests without e-mail. Every time a news release or announcement was being made public, the priests received a copy first.
- **A live TV address.** The crisis team was able to convince the only network affiliate

television station in the area to dedicate a half hour of programming to the bishop. Taped live and shown later in the day, the bishop was able to make a 15-minute statement that covered his regret over the past, offered an assurance that there was no priest in the ministry who was credibly accused of sexual abuse of a minor, and described what the diocese was doing to prevent any further abuse. The remainder of the program was devoted to questions to the bishop from two reporters. Because the program was taped live, the message was unfiltered.

- **Taking it to the people.** The team knew that the pastors and parish leaders needed to hear directly from the bishop. In February 2003, one year after the initial release of the names, the bishop invited the pastor and two to five lay leaders from every parish in the state to Concord for a meeting. At the meeting, held in a parish church, the bishop laid out a clear and direct plan for how the Church was going to move forward. He recognized his own failings in the past and reaffirmed that he was not planning to resign, but planned to continue to dedicate his ministry to making the Church safe for all. The media were invited to attend and cover this event.

- **Regular bulletin announcements and information.** The diocese used parish bulletins to inform the faithful about programs to protect children and to describe other steps it was taking.

In order to be transparent, the diocese established several practices:

- **Return all media calls.** The spokesperson for the diocese returned every media call on the day it was received—if possible. The spokesperson would try to respond to all inquires and provide information, although some information was not made available due to its confidential

nature. The diocese gave the local media consideration before the regional and national media. In most cases, requests from the national news and entertainment programs were politely declined. The diocese kept its focus on its local audience, which followed local media.

- **Announcements of a priest's removal.** When a new complaint was received about a priest still in the ministry, the diocese would conduct an immediate review to confirm that the complaint was at least probable. After that, the bishop would remove the priest from active ministry pending a complete investigation of the claim. The bishop, auxiliary bishop, or the delegate for ministerial conduct would go to the parish where the priest was serving and announce the allegation, the fact that the priest would be on leave, and that there would be a priest appointed to serve as administrator of the parish. The bishop would also meet with parishioners after each Mass.

- **Public notice of priests on leave.** After notifying the parishes and the other priests, the diocese would send out news releases to inform the public that the priest was on leave because of a credible allegation of sexual abuse of a minor.

- **Meeting with activist groups.** The bishop met with the members of a protest group who appeared at the cathedral. After Mass, the bishop invited the 20 or more individuals to the church hall and listened to their issues. He later met with leaders of other groups and established a liaison between the diocese and the Voice of the Faithful group in New Hampshire.

- **Financial disclosure.** In 2004, the diocese published the results of the first-ever outside audit of its central administration. Although in the works for a couple years, this audit was seen as a response to calls for more transparency. The diocese

*(Continued)*

disclosed the total dollars in settlements reached with victims of past abuse.

- **Parish visits.** The bishop decided that his time was best served meeting directly with parishioners. He was in a parish almost every weekend that he did not have another commitment. He would say Mass, meet with parish leadership, and go to the church hall to meet with any parishioner who wanted to speak with him. He found that while many had questions, most parishioners were focused on moving forward and making sure that no such scandal would ever recur.

## Managing an Extended Crisis

Most crises deal with an incident and the aftermath of the incident. Each one has a flash point, a high point, and a resolution.

The sexual abuse crisis in the Church kept unfolding, taking new turns, and extending over time because of lawsuits and government investigations. The Church was in active crisis mode for two and a half years. It eventually was able to move out of crisis mode and begin to rebuild trust with members. At the time of the crisis, some parishes experienced a drop in contributions, attendance, or both; others didn't. Those who suffered a loss are estimated by officials to have recovered within five years of the scandal. The diocese has moved on, with many of the leadership who were active at the time of the problem coming to the end of their service and retiring. Since these individuals have left, the few critics that remained vocal have subsided as well.

Recently, the Church in Philadelphia has been in court over similar types of sexual issues. But the impact in New Hampshire has been minimal because the New Hampshire diocese continues to be as open

and transparent as possible. It publishes an annual audit online and issues an annual report on any new claims of sexual abuse. It now provides mandatory training for volunteers and paid staff, including clergy, and has volunteer safe-environment coordinators in all parishes and schools. Whereas from 2002 to 2004 it received written complaints or comments daily, today it receives none. The Church in New Hampshire made a solid effort not only to deal with the issue of clergy sexual abuse when the problem was first uncovered, but to continue to make changes when necessary and provide communication that informs parishioners and supports those changes.

### Questions for Discussion

1. Some critics of the Catholic Church wouldn't accept the Church's position that crimes that occurred years ago should be judged by the standards of the day. What should the Church have said to those people?

2. Most crisis communication strategies recommend gaining or setting the "agenda" and establishing reasonable expectations. In this case, the media and the critics seemed to have jumped on both the agenda and expectations. What could the Church have done to get control of the issue?

3. This case focuses on New Hampshire and the Boston area, but the problem is much more widespread than New England. Shouldn't the Church lead some national or international effort? What would you recommend?

4. How does the diocese handling of this crisis compare with the handling of the sexual molestation case at Penn State (see Case 10-2)?

# Case 9-2 The West Virginia Mine Disaster:
# An Emotional Roller Coaster and Public Relations
# Train Wreck

In the wee hours of a cold January morning, an underground explosion in the Sago mine in West Virginia left the fate of 13 miners in serious jeopardy. Although rescue efforts began immediately, it was 22 hours later before a fresh-air tunnel could be drilled into the mine shaft and workers could make their way to the trapped miners. There were no signs of life, even though the miners were veterans and each had been issued survival equipment. Monday, January 2, 2006, was a long day for family and friends.

Late the next day, rescue workers were able to penetrate deeply enough into the mine to reach an area near where the trapped miners were thought to be. Initial reports were that one miner's body was found; then, around midnight, reports that the other 12 miners were alive began circulating among friends and family gathered at the site. Joyous pandemonium erupted. Families hugged and danced. The governor of West Virginia, Joe Manchin, made an "official announcement" of the good news.

All across America, morning newspapers went to press carrying the banner headline "They're Alive!"

But, they weren't.

## Miscommunication Causes Second Catastrophe

Through some dreadful miscommunication, the message was reversed. One miner, Randal McCloy, Jr., was alive. The other 12 were dead. It was West Virginia's worst mining accident in 28 years.

So, early Wednesday morning, Ben Hatfield, president and CEO of International Coal Group (ICG), which operated the mine, told the families that the news—now about three hours old—was wrong and that their loved ones were not coming out alive. About 45 minutes later Hatfield made a general announcement that the initial reports were wrong and that the news was bad, not good.

Many Americans awoke on Wednesday to read the "good news" in their morning papers. Like the families, they later learned the truth. The broadcast media and online news services, of course, were able to more easily correct the misinformation. But nearly everyone was asking, How could this have happened? Why was everyone misinformed?

The answer is probably never going to be known for sure, but among the contributing factors could be:

- Rescue workers were wearing full-face oxygen masks, making clear communication difficult.
- The rescue crews were exhausted.
- Some communication was encoded.
- Poor connections and conditions made static-free transmissions impossible.
- The command center lines were "open," which meant that anyone standing near could hear (and possibly misunderstand) communication between rescue workers and those at the base.

It is important to note that Hatfield and ICG didn't make an official announcement about the miners' safety. Governor Manchin was apparently repeating what he heard at the scene, and even ICG officials were deceived for a while by the unconfirmed reports. Of course, everyone wanted to believe the best.

*(Continued)*

**FIGURE 9.1**    West Virginia Then-Governor Joe Manchin addresses the media

(Courtesy of Steven Wayne Rotsch)

The misinformation likely came from well-intentioned bystanders who thought they heard good news. Cell phones were prominent among those present, making it easy to spread what was thought to be good news.

## The Company Takes Extreme Criticism for Poor Communication

With the truth came a firestorm of emotional criticism, much of it directed at Hatfield and ICG. Family members believed the initial reports came from ICG. "He strictly told us they was alive," said one relative. "Three hours later, he comes back and said they was dead." Others promised to sue. Just who and on what grounds wasn't clear, but emotions were raw. Police stood by to restore order if necessary.

Once the truth was known, Hatfield and ICG followed textbook procedures in communicating the hard facts. "We prayed for miracles," he said. "Despite our grief and despair at the loss of our 12 coworkers, we want to celebrate the one miracle that was delivered." People in the crowd screamed, "He lied to us."

Hatfield would later say that he deeply regretted "allowing the jubilation to go on longer than it should have." He understood what people were going through, even those who were critical of him. "They certainly have some basis for their frustration, having been put through this emotional roller coaster. I wouldn't wish that on anyone. I regret that it happened. I would do anything if it had not happened."

Those thoughts were small consolation to a nation seeking answers. One online poll taken on Wednesday, January 4, showed 61 percent of the respondents felt ICG had done a poor job of communicating. Another 20 percent thought the company was right in withholding any news until all the facts were in, and 19 percent just didn't know.

As might be expected, law firms in Charleston, Morgantown, Bluefield, and other West Virginia cities cranked up the advertising, one claiming to be specialists in "West Virginia coal mine accident" lawsuits.

## Seeking to Lay Blame, All Became a Target

In the aftermath, one Democratic blog suggested President George W. Bush was to blame for the accident because "he didn't do anything to prevent the accident" (MyDD.com). The AFL–CIO accused Congress of doing too little, too late to improve mine safety.

There was plenty of blame to go around.

Mine officials and politicians were not the only ones on the hot seat. Media critics were quick to point out that reporters, editors, and correspondents passed along the unfounded information, often without attribution. Others could see how the problem evolved. Alex Jones of the Harvard University's Shorenstein Center on the Press, Politics, and Public Policy speaking the day after on PBS observed:

> This is a huge public interest story, the kind of story that grips a country like ours. Everybody was watching it. The news media were there; of course the families were gathered there.

And a miscommunication happens when someone overheard or misoverheard a statement that they had found the miners, interpreted that to mean that they were alive, and started cell phone calls to family members, giving them the idea that their loved ones had been saved.

The bells started ringing, the governor spoke; everyone was clamoring. And it was very, very clear that something wonderful had happened, except it didn't happen to be true.

This was not, of course, an official piece of information. But it's very hard for me to fault the press in reporting that the families were saying they had gotten word that this had happened because that was literally the truth.

Rachel Smolkin, managing editor of the *American Journalism Review*, offers other considerations:

> Well, a lot of it is deadline-driven. And this is a story that happened right on deadline for many papers, particularly papers on the East Coast. Then you have your deadline looming, you're hearing news that appears to be wonderful news, certainly news you want to get out to your readers; this is a miraculous ending to what seemed like it could be a very sad story, that these miners had been found.

---

"After the 2006 Sago mine disaster in West Virginia, Congress passed the Mine Improvement and New Emergency Response Act. Its provisions included a requirement for emergency response plans and a mandate for breathable air underground that could be accessible in the event of an accident. Civil and criminal penalties were also increased for violations of safety standards, and the Mine Safety and Health Administration was given the authority to temporarily shut a facility for nonpayment."

---

*The Washington Post* editorial, April 7, 2010.

*(Continued)*

I think the problem, if there is one, what the media maybe can be faulted for to some degree, is not being a little more careful with their qualifiers. You have to be very careful about attributing information.

Dave Byron, APR, Volusia County, Florida, community information director, puts the controversy into perspective for public relations practitioners:

The coal mine tragedy in West Virginia brings to light some immediate public information lessons that we need to remember:

- It is absolutely essential only factual, confirmed information be released. This especially is true when it comes to injuries and fatalities and the numbers of them.
- We must always remember the impact information has (good or bad) on family members and others close to a situation.
- We again learn the lesson that affected family members want to be given straightforward, unfiltered information as quickly as possible, again either good or bad news. They do not want their emotions to be toyed with.
- We learn that a governor's office may or may not have all the straight information. Local public information officers (or corporate spokespersons) must take control and rise and fall with their own abilities. We cannot rely on outside agencies.
- We learn . . . that being defensive about a bad situation only creates the perception that there's something to hide.
- We again confirm the fact that speaking with one voice during a tragedy is essential.
- We also learn that if we are an agency with inspection/oversight responsibility, we will be held accountable if we

do not follow through with corrective action before a tragedy occurs. Burying the head in the sand hardly ever brings good.
- We also learn that once a tragedy occurs, we cannot knee jerk react from emotion. Investigation will take months. It's important to allow the authorities/agencies the time it takes to get to the bottom of the cause/solution, and so on.

In the beginning, everyone feared the worst. Mine accidents, many times, have no happy endings.

In the end, everyone's fears were realized. That one escaped was a miracle. The victims even understood their plight. Some used their dying moments to pen letters to their families.

It is the middle that is troublesome. There should have never been a middle. The concept of "One Clear Voice" has never been more important.

Better communication systems, better communication techniques, and better control of the communication command base would have eliminated the false hope that miscommunication brought. This is a lesson for all practitioners. Be prepared. Once disaster strikes, it's too late to write a crisis plan or develop a legacy of trust.

### Questions for Discussion

1. What preparations might ICG have made to (1) anticipate the incident at the Sago mine and (2) avert the communication fiasco? Is it possible to "expect the unexpected"?
2. Did you detect a public relations presence during this case? Explain.
3. What role did the governor's pronouncement play in the scenario? Was this a good idea? Why or why not?

# Case 9-3 Crisis Communication Lessons Learned: The Crash of Continental Connection Flight 3407

Passengers aboard Continental Connection Flight 3407 were probably anticipating a routine landing as the turboprop plane approached Buffalo Niagara International Airport on the evening of Feb. 12, 2009.

The commuter flight, operated by Colgan Air, Inc., had departed from Newark Liberty International Airport at 9:20 P.M., two hours behind schedule due to Newark's high winds. The aircraft, a Bombardier Dash-8 Q400, had encountered wintry weather en route—a mix of rain and light snow. But no one was prepared for the worst possible outcome: the flight's fiery crash at 10:17 P.M. into a home in suburban Clarence Center, New York, that killed 50 people, including all 44 passengers, all four crew members, one off-duty crew member, and one person in the home.

In an instant, the quiet Long Street neighborhood where the crash occurred became the focus of intense activity. Emergency personnel, airline and government officials, journalists, public relations practitioners, and investigators from the National Transportation Safety Board (NTSB) quickly descended on the scene, which would be featured for many days on broadcast newscasts, on news Web sites, and in print publications around the world.

## Quick Response

Fire and police responders immediately swung into action, having conducted a mock emergency drill only months earlier, based on Erie County's existing emergency management plan. Among the first at the crash scene were two neighborhood residents, Erie County

Executive Christopher Collins, who became one of a handful of official spokespersons during the crisis, and C. Douglas Hartmayer, director of public affairs for the Niagara Frontier Transportation Authority (NFTA), which operates Buffalo Niagara International Airport.

"I live two streets from Long Street and I heard the explosion," said Hartmayer. "So not knowing completely what it was, I was ready. I got a phone call, heard it was Long Street, and dressed in warm clothing because I figured I'd be out there awhile. It helped that it was in my community because I knew the emergency coordinator and the fire chief. My assistant director was also a Clarence resident and was there. So we got there pretty quickly and saw some things that we didn't like to see. But we reacted—we went down to the fire hall, and we established the central information center at Clarence Town Hall."

Within 45 minutes of the crash, local news media began reporting on the tragedy, with nearly all reporters reassigned to the crash story. TV stations quickly scrapped their planned 11 P.M. newscasts to report live from the scene, initially featuring phone reports from journalists on the scene until the stations' live trucks could start sending video.

Buffalo radio and newspaper reporters also began filing stories. For Buffalo's only daily newspaper, *The Buffalo News,* it was the first major story in which the *News* functioned as a multimedia information center. "We weren't just putting out our print version, which was already on the printing presses by 12:30 or 1 A.M.," said reporter Brian Meyer. "We also were gathering photographs for our photo

*(Continued)*

---

Contributed by Dr. Deborah Silverman, Associate Professor & Associate Chair, Buffalo State, SUNY

galleries, we had video from our photographers, I was helping to produce and narrate some of those, and of course, we were doing constant Web updates. So the crash was a really historic time for our newspaper."

The plane crash quickly became international news, with CNN International and other networks simulcasting local TV stations' coverage starting at midnight. Buffalo public relations practitioners and journalists found themselves doing dozens of interviews with media outlets around the world.

One local radio reporter noted that he spoke to approximately 20 different international news media outlets, including radio and TV stations in Bogota, New York City, Charlotte, Montreal, and Ireland, providing them with frequent updates.

Public relations specialists such as Grant Loomis, the county executive's communication director, fielded dozens of calls as well, prioritizing them so that he responded first to local media and then national and international media.

## Factors for Communication Success

Loomis, other public relations practitioners, and journalists who communicated about the crash noted that a number of factors accounted for effective communication during the crisis.

- **A crisis communication plan was in place.** Organizations such as Erie County government and the NFTA were ready to go when the crash occurred. "Obviously, you have to adapt as the situation changes, but when you have something as startling, sad, and unexpected as a plane crash in Clarence, it is nice to know that you don't have to look to your left and right and say, 'What do we do now?'" said Loomis. "There is a plan in place for the county. It not only involves communication, but it reflects a host of our departments—the health department, emergency services, public works, budget and purchasing." Doug Hartmayer of the NFTA added,

"The airport has a crisis manual, and we go through a couple of tabletop exercises per year. They're generally held at the airport, and all of the emergency folks from Erie County, the first responders from the hospitals and the morgue participate. That's why everything seemed to flow in an orderly, succinct manner. Everybody went about their job in a professional way."

- **A central information center was quickly established to ensure accessibility for the media.** Clarence Town Hall and later an incident command center adjacent to the senior citizens center in nearby Cheektowaga were designated as the official information centers. "The PR practitioners did an excellent job, by putting together the various people wearing different hats, so that we (reporters) didn't have to run around to 20 different places," said reporter Brian Meyer. "We had folks from the NTSB sitting with County Executive Collins, the town's emergency services person, environmental people, the local agent in charge of the FBI. All of these people were sitting at one long table many times, and it made our job as reporters a lot easier."

- **Organizations spoke with One Clear Voice.** Less than four hours after the crash, communicators planned their strategy. "Around 2 in the morning on Friday, we had a brief meeting about how to set up the command center," said Grant Loomis. "That's where we sat and mapped out everything, leaving room for change, but we all agreed upon when our next press briefing would be, how long it would go, what sort of information we thought we'd have to release at that point, who was going to be the public information officer, and who was going to run the command center."

- **Never say "No Comment" to the media.** "I took every media phone call," said former TV reporter Mary Murray, public information officer for the county sheriff's office. "If I didn't know the information they were looking for, I told them, 'I do not have that information now, but I will get back to you if you're still interested in it.'"

- **Quick response time, within one hour of the tragedy.** Initial information was given to the media within 45 minutes of the crash.

- **Familiarity with media needs and deadlines.** "As a PR person, you need the news people," said Mary Murray of the sheriff's office. "So you always want to treat them with respect and know their deadlines. But by the same token, you may need to hold back information for whatever reason. And the media were very respectful."

- **Providing a constant flow of information.** Local reporters felt that they didn't have to press any of the public relations practitioners for details, because fresh information was being provided on a regular basis.

- **Presence of top officials on the scene immediately, taking charge and expressing their concern.** Erie County Executive Christopher Collins and Town of Clarence Supervisor Scott Bylewski were among the first on the scene and quickly became official spokespersons. Philip Trenary, president and CEO of Pinnacle Airlines, parent company of Colgan Air, flew to Buffalo for a 6 A.M. media briefing the day after the crash, and New York State Governor David Paterson arrived later that morning to meet with families and the media.

- **Effective use of news media, the Internet, and face-to-face communication.** Colgan Air posted news releases, a media advisory, and a list of frequently asked questions on its Web site, and Continental Airlines issued a news release expressing its "profound sadness" over the crash. Airlines and airport representatives, the Red Cross, and local clergy members regularly met with, assisted, and answered questions from family members in the days following the crash.

## A Crisis Communication Model

Within days, families held memorial services for the victims, whose life stories were recounted in the local media. Continental Airlines renamed Flight 3407 as Flight 3411, and Governor Paterson established a scholarship fund to aid the children of crash victims. In June 2012, a memorial was dedicated at the site of the crash, funded by a nonprofit organization, Remember Flight 3407, Inc.

Lawsuits have been filed by the victims' families, and an airline safety advocate group is suing the Federal Aviation Administration (FAA) for failing to act on suggested improvements to the runway and in airplane deicing procedures, as previously recommended by the NTSB.

The Buffalo crash drew national attention because regional airplane flights, such as Flight 3407, comprise half of all U.S. flights and carry 23 percent of passengers. Nearly 75 percent of U.S. airports are now served exclusively by regional flights, according to the Regional Airline Association. So in May 2009, when the NTSB conducted three days of hearings into the crash, there was national media coverage. The hearings revealed:

- A lack of training in the plane's stall recovery system. In the final minute before the crash, as it prepared to land, the plane slowed down dangerously to 130 knots, causing it to stall. In response, the pilot, Captain Marvin D. Renslow, 47, incorrectly jerked the plane upward, causing it to spin out of control, rather than lowering the nose of the aircraft, increasing power, and leveling the plane's wings. Copilot Rebecca L. Shaw,

*(Continued)*

24, incorrectly put the plane's flaps up. Earlier in the flight, Shaw said she had never flown before on an icy night, according to a transcript of the flight's cockpit voice recorder.

- Renslow and Shaw's lack of "situational awareness" of the plane's dangerous drop in speed as they prepared for landing. They also engaged in cockpit chatter below 10,000 feet, a violation of FAA regulations, apparently ignoring crucial flight information.

- Colgan Air was not aware, when it hired Renslow in 2005, that he had failed three FAA "check ride" flying tests. Colgan never double-checked with federal officials to see whether his application, which listed only one failed check ride, had revealed his complete test record.

- Low pay for pilots and copilots is common in the commuter airline industry, in contrast to the major airlines. Copilot Rebecca Shaw earned only $16,000 per year at Colgan Air, so she initially held a second job at a coffee shop. Pilots on Colgan's largest planes earn $67,000. Shaw couldn't afford an apartment in Newark, where she was based, so she commuted from Seattle and slept during cross-country commutes and in the crew room at the Newark airport. Renslow commuted from his home near Tampa, and no record showed that he had rented an apartment or hotel room in Newark.

After the crash, Colgan Air improved its pilot training and raised its minimum number of flight hours required for employment from 600 to 1,000. Renslow had 625 hours at the beginning of his employment at Colgan.

In February 2010, the NTSB released its final report on the crash. It determined that Captain Renslow inappropriately responded to the activation of the stick shaker, which led to an aerodynamic stall that resulted in the crash. Copilot Shaw incorrectly set the plane's speed and put the wing flaps in the wrong position.

The report also cited contributing factors, including the crew's failure to recognize the position of the low-speed cue on their flight displays, which indicated the stick shaker was about to activate, and the crew's failure to adhere to "sterile cockpit" procedures that ban pilot conversation about anything except the flight at hand.

Other contributing factors were the captain's failure to effectively manage the flight and Colgan Air's inadequate procedures for selecting and managing airspeed during approaches in icy conditions.

As a result of its accident investigation, the NTSB made recommendations to the FAA on strategies to prevent flight crew monitoring failures, increasing pilot professionalism, reducing pilot fatigue, improving remedial training, maintaining pilot records, providing stall training, and revamping air-speed selection procedures. The NTSB also announced plans for forums about what are considered high standards for pilots and air-traffic controllers. They will also discuss code sharing—the practice of large airlines marketing their services to the flying public while using other companies, such as Colgan Air, to actually provide the transportation.

Even before the NTSB's final report, the Obama administration and Congressional leaders were taking actions to prevent a similar tragedy in the future. In June 2009, the day before the first of three Congressional hearings resulting from the Flight 3407 crash, the Obama administration ordered government inspectors to immediately review the pilot training programs of regional airlines to ensure compliance with federal regulations.

In July 2009, members of the House of Representatives and the U.S. Senate introduced a bipartisan bill to improve airline safety, spurred by the crash of Flight 3407. It was approved by both houses one year later and immediately signed into law by President Obama. The new law increases the amount of flight time required for new pilots to begin work, from 250 hours to 1,500 hours. It also establishes a pilot records database to make it easier for airlines to obtain pilots' flight records before they are hired, requires airlines to develop fatigue risk-management systems for pilots, and mandates strict training to ensure that pilots know how to operate stall recovery systems.

The legislation was welcomed by the families of Flight 3407 victims. After the crash, leaders of the group, Families of Continental Flight 3407, lobbied numerous times in Washington, D.C., for improvements in airline safety, and they were present when the House and Senate approved the bill.

Continental Connection Flight 3407 ranks as the 22nd most deadly crash of a commercial flight in the U.S. during the past 30 years, according to FAA data. Not only did this crash prompt long-needed improvements in airline safety, it also was a model for media relations efforts during a crisis as everyone worked together to deliver timely information about the crash to audiences around the world. "The information flow between the public relations practitioners and reporters was extremely effective," said *The Buffalo News* reporter Brian Meyer. "There were numerous updates, and the PR people let reporters know when they could expect such updates. While there were still many unanswered questions in the days following the crash, the communication model that was used helped to keep reporters abreast of any new information that surfaced."

## About the Author

Deborah A. Silverman, Ph.D., APR, is an associate professor of communication at Buffalo State College, where she teaches public relations courses and serves as faculty advisor to a chapter of the Public Relations Student Society of America. A past member of the national Public Relations Society of America board of directors, she previously was a public relations practitioner and journalist for more than 20 years.

# Case 9-4 Realist Sense-Making in Crisis Public Relations: The Case of BP

On April 20, 2010, a major explosion ripped through the Deepwater Horizon oil rig at the Macondo well in the Gulf of Mexico, killing 11 workers, injuring 17 others, and triggering the worst environmental disaster in America's history.

The oil rig, owned by Transocean of Switzerland, was being leased by BP (formerly British Petroleum), one of the world's largest oil companies and a leader in deepwater drilling efforts. Although the blast was Transocean's responsibility, BP, as owner of the oil, was liable for the clean-up. An estimated 500,000 to 800,000 gallons of oil leaked into the Gulf of Mexico each day until the leak was plugged (NBC *Today* interview with BP CEO Tony Hayward, 2010).

In May 2010, BP installed marine protection booms along the coast of Louisiana, Mississippi, Alabama, and Florida to keep the oil at bay. The company also sent submarine robots to the seabed to attempt to activate a shut-off switch on the well, coordinated four Hercules aircraft to spray oil dispersants, placed sand-filled barricades along shorelines, and brought in 530 ocean-going skimmers (Pagnamenta, 2010, p. 33).

The leak was stopped on July 15, when the gushing wellhead was finally capped after it had released 205.8 million gallons of oil into the Gulf. This far surpassed the environmental damage caused by America's worst disaster until then, the 1989 oil spill caused by the Exxon Valdez oil tanker, which dumped 11 million gallons of oil into the waters along Alaska's coast.

The Gulf oil spill has caused extensive damage to wildlife and marine habitats along the Gulf coast, in addition to the region's tourism and fishing industries. It also resulted in a temporary government-imposed moratorium on deepwater oil drilling, which was lifted in October 2010 (Banerjee, 2010). The U.S. federal government, holding BP accountable for the spill, required BP to create a $20 billion compensation fund for individuals and businesses impacted by the spill. Approximately 91,000 people and businesses have filed claims ("91,000 Gulf Oil Spill Claims," 2011).

## Public Relations Gets to Work

While BP's geologists and environmental experts focused on capping the gushing well and trying to contain damage to the environment, the company's public relations department was communicating about the disaster, with advice from the U.K.-based public relations firm Brunswick ("BP Boss Sails into New Public Relations Disaster," 2010). A content analysis of BP's online newsroom revealed 127 news releases, dated April 21, 2010, to October 1, 2010, under the title, "Gulf of Mexico Response." The first release, on April 21st, was entitled "BP Offers Full Support to Transocean After Drilling Rig Fire." Subsequent news releases followed classic crisis communication advice, talking about BP's response to the oil spill, offering BP's sympathy to the families of the employees killed in the explosion, pledging BP's full support for government probes into the explosion, and providing updates on efforts to stop the oil spill.

In addition to the news releases, BP's public relations department created four "state response" micro sites on its Web site, one each

Contributed by Dr. Deborah Silverman, assistant professor, Buffalo State College and Dr. Jonathan Slater, associate professor, SUNY Plattsburgh for the states of Alabama, Florida, Louisiana, and Mississippi, containing updates on clean-up efforts in each state. The BP Web site also featured a series of videos documenting the company's efforts to stop the leak, protect the Gulf shoreline, and support the local community. BP also used social media including Facebook, Twitter, YouTube, and Flickr to communicate about the crisis.[1]

BP supplemented its public relations strategy with a controversial advertising campaign, launched in June 2010, that featured apologetic CEO Tony Hayward in a coastal setting, sea birds chirping in the background. The $50 million ad campaign, which appeared on national cable and broadcast networks in the United States, had the same tagline as BP's newspaper ads in *The New York Times, The Wall Street Journal, USA Today,* and *The Washington Post*: "We will get this done. We will make this right." The TV commercial was produced by a Washington-based, bipartisan political consulting firm, Purple Strategies, but it was lambasted by advertising and marketing specialists as ineffective because of social media and a live video feed of the underwater leak that was all over the Internet and television (Smith, 2010). President Obama joined in the criticism, questioning BP's spending on its image.

## Tony Hayward's Public Relations Gaffes

Crisis communication experts advise their public relations clients to speak with One Clear Voice during a crisis. For BP, that task fell to the company's CEO and self-described "lightning rod," Tony Hayward. Unlike Exxon CEO Lawrence Rawl following the Exxon Valdez oil spill, Hayward immediately flew to the disaster site to coordinate the company's clean-up efforts. A prophetic newspaper story in *The Times* of London noted on April 23, "The main worry is, of course, limiting the damage to the environment. But Mr. Hayward will also be hoping to minimize the damage to BP's reputation. . . . A great deal is riding on Mr. Hayward's handling of the crisis" (Wighton, 2010, p. 57).

Since replacing CEO John Browne in 2007, Hayward had worked hard to rehabilitate BP's reputation as a badly run, accident-prone company. Those accidents, on Browne's watch, included a deadly 2005 explosion at BP's Texas City refinery, which killed 15 workers. Hayward was credited with turning BP around, boosting production, cutting costs, significantly reducing on-the-job injuries, and talking about a "change of culture" at BP just one month before the Deepwater Horizon rig explosion (Chazan, 2010, p. 22).

Hayward, 53, had joined BP as a 22-year-old geologist with a Ph.D. ("Center of the Storm: Who Is Tony Hayward," 2010). He soon came to the attention of John Browne, who groomed Hayward as his successor. However, unlike the outgoing Browne, Hayward was not media savvy, admitting in June 2010 to *The Sunday Telegraph* of London, "One of the things you learn is not to read a newspaper or watch television. Others read them but I don't bother" (Mason, 2010, p. 5).

Hayward made a series of verbal gaffes that lacked empathy, harming BP's efforts to repair its image and leading the *New York Daily News* to dub him "the most hated and clueless man in America" (Mason, 2010, p. 5). Hayward initially upset Gulf residents in May 2010 by commenting that the spill was just a tiny drop in a "very big ocean," and that "the environmental impact of this disaster is likely to have been very, very modest." Then in June 2010, he uttered another remark that deeply angered Americans. While apologizing for

*(Continued)*

---

[1] See BP's "Gulf of Mexico Response" Web page at http://www.bp.com/extendedsectiongenericarticle.do?categoryId=40 &contentId=7061813 for details about the videos, micro sites, and links to social media.

the "massive disruption" to the lives of Gulf coast residents, he added, "There's no one who wants this thing over more than I do. You know, I'd like my life back" ("New BP Ads Don't Make Things Right with Locals," 2010). President Obama blasted Hayward, telling NBC's *Today Show* that if Hayward were his employee, he'd fire him for those statements ("Obama Says He Would Fire BP CEO Hayward," 2010). Leading U.S. media, including *The New York Times,* were calling for Hayward's resignation as early as June 9th (Hughes and Currie, 2010, p. 2).

Hayward and BP Chairman Carl-Henric Svanberg met on June 16th at the White House with President Obama to discuss the creation of a compensation fund for the Gulf oil spill victims, and the following day Hayward testified before the House of Representatives Energy and Commerce Committee. Although Hayward formally apologized for the disaster, he angered members of the House panel by evasive answers to many questions, such as "I can't answer that question because I wasn't there," and "I don't know" (Bolstad, 2010; Chaddock, 2010). British public relations professionals and media were split over Hayward's testimony to the Congressional committee. Public relations professional Mark Borkowski noted in *The Daily Telegraph* that Hayward "looked like a tired undertaker who was rather bored with having to look mournful," and *The Daily Mail* was sharply critical of Congressional investigators, saying that Hayward "was treated like Public Enemy No. 1 by American politicians" ("'Tired' Tony Hayward 'Savaged' by Congress, Say U.K. Media," 2010). London's *Daily Telegraph* charged that Hayward was "subjected to a sustained attack by U.S. Congressmen" (Spillius, 2010, p. 4). One Canadian newspaper, *The Globe and Mail,* suggested BP's lawyers advised Hayward to be evasive during his Congressional testimony, rather than admitting negligence, to avoid even greater liabilities that could financially cripple the company (McKenna, 2010, p. B1).

## Hayward Goes Yachting

The dust from Hayward's Congressional testimony had scarcely settled before the American and international media reported on a new Hayward misstep: a weekend yachting trip June 19th around Britain's Isle of Wight. President Obama's chief of staff, Rahm Emmanuel, called the trip another "in a long line of PR gaffes" ("White House Chief: Yacht Trip Another Gaffe by BP," 2010). British public relations professionals were baffled by Hayward's yachting trip; Ian Monk, a crisis control expert, called the trip "death wish stuff," while British celebrity publicist Max Clifford commented, "Either he's being deliberately steered into becoming the most demonized man in the world, or the man has got absolutely no clue about public relations and public perception" (Foster, 2010, pp. 4–5). Britain's *PR Week* called the yachting trip an "unforgiveable gaffe," noting that "Hayward has now become a case studying how poor comms [*sic*] skills will only magnify a corporate crisis" (Rogers, 2010, p. 14).

By early July, Hayward's future as BP CEO looked dim. Media on both sides of the Atlantic began speculating on his replacement, noting that his public relations errors had seriously damaged the company's reputation. On July 27, less than two weeks after BP capped the Gulf oil leak, BP announced that Hayward would be replaced as CEO by Mississippi native Robert Dudley, effective October 1, 2010.

Hayward was offered a severance package worth up to $20 million and a new job as a nonexecutive director at BP's Russian venture, TNK-BP (Vasilyeva, 2010). In November 2010, a month after his departure as CEO, Hayward told the BBC that the company was unprepared for the disastrous Gulf oil spill and the resulting media frenzy, noting that BP came close to financial disaster as its credit sources disappeared (Lawless, 2010).

The massive $32.3 billion cost of the cleanup led BP to a record loss of nearly $17 billion for the second quarter of 2010, forcing it to sell

$30 billion of assets in order to return to profitability ("BP's Hayward Ignites Fresh U.S. Anger As He Heads for the Exit," 2010; Watt, 2010, p. 7).

## Mixed Response Creates Muddled Reputation

In terms of its crisis communication during the Gulf oil spill, BP's record is mixed. The company's public relations department followed the generally accepted rule of "Tell it all and tell it fast!" (Seitel, 2004, p. 498) as evidenced by the number and content of news releases following the spill, the creation of micro Web sites for the four states most affected by the oil spill, videos showing BP's cleanup, and its use of social media. BP also provided a constant flow of information and it designated a single spokesperson (Tony Hayward), thus upholding two additional tenets of crisis communication (Wilcox, Cameron, Ault, and Agee, 2003, p. 183).

However, Hayward's frequent and insensitive verbal gaffes, whether due to his lack of media training, his personality, or sheer exhaustion, combined with his behavior (the yachting trip) seriously damaged BP's reputation at a critical time—when it needed to rebuild goodwill among its key publics. Moreover, Hayward's evasiveness in front of a Congressional committee, whether the result of coaching by BP's lawyers or an innate reluctance to speak for fear of incurring liability for BP, was perceived by important key publics (Congress and American citizens) as deception. His frequent comment, "I don't know," during his Congressional testimony was akin to "No comment," a statement that public relations practitioners tell their clients to avoid (Wilcox, Cameron, Ault, and Agee, 2003, p. 183).

In addition to Tony Hayward's performance as CEO, however, BP's leadership also could be faulted for its ignorance of possible safety problems at the Macondo well, as acknowledged by Hayward at the Congressional hearing (Bolsta, 2010). They also failed to apologize immediately for mistakes and attempted to downplay the magnitude of the environmental disaster.

Leading industry publication *PR Week* deemed the BP public relations crisis "a wake-up call," and a "fundamental landmark in crisis communication" (Daniels, 2011, p. 43). Indeed, contends the magazine, firms that merely developed crisis plans based on probability scenarios will now be developing those plans with their very organizational survival in mind (Daniels, 2011, p. 43). Will this truly be the case or will corporations such as BP continue to navigate crises while relying heavily on a realist approach to their public communication?

Organizations routinely feel that they need to keep up appearances and give the impression that its leaders know what they are doing. Organizations remain under pressure to reinforce the image their publics hold in their minds—definitions that stakeholders take to be the accurate organizational reality. Despite their best intentions to do the right thing during a crisis, corporate leaders and their public relations advisors need to be alert to the ways their own communication can subvert their ability to make sense of what is happening.

## References

Banerjee, N. (October 13, 2010). "U.S. Lifts Moratorium on Deep-Water Drilling in Gulf of Mexico." *Los Angeles Times.* Accessed February 22, 2011, at http://articles.latimes.com/print/2010/oct/13/nation/la-na-oil-moratorium-20101013.

Bolstad, E. (June 17, 2010). "An Angry Congress Lambasts BP Chief Hayward over Safety." *McClatchy's Washington Bureau.* Retrieved February 4, 2011, from LexisNexis Academic database.

"BP Boss Sails into New Public Relations Disaster" (June 22, 2010). *International Oil Daily.*

*(Continued)*

Retrieved February 4, 2011, from LexisNexis Academic database.

"BP's Hayward Ignites Fresh U.S. Anger As He Heads for the Exit." (July 28, 2010). *Agence France-Presse—English.* Retrieved February 4, 2011, from LexisNexis Academic database.

"Center of the Storm: Who Is Tony Hayward." (June 4, 2010). *ABC News* transcript. Retrieved February 4, 2011, from LexisNexis Academic database.

Chaddock, G.R. (June 17, 2010). "BP Oil Spill: Tony Hayward's Stonewalling Approach Before Congress." *The Christian Science Monitor.* Retrieved February 4, 2011, from LexisNexis Academic database.

Chazan, G. (May 4, 2010). "BP's Credibility Slips on Gulf Oil Spill." *The Australian,* p. 22. Retrieved February 4, 2011, from LexisNexis Academic database.

Daniels, C. (February 2011). "BP: A Year Later." *PR Week,* pp. 41–43.

Foster, P. (June 21, 2010). "It's As If He Is Being Left to Sink, say PR experts." *The Times (London),* pp. 4–5. Retrieved February 4, 2011, from LexisNexis Academic database.

"Hayward and Obama Outings Send Bad Message." (June 22, 2010). *Bowling Green Daily News (Kentucky).* Retrieved February 4, 2011, from LexisNexis Academic database.

Hines, N. (June 21, 2010). "BP Chief Sails into Storm at White House After Day Off on His Yacht." *The Times (London),* pp. 4–5. Retrieved February 4, 2011, from LexisNexis Academic database.

Hughes, C., and Currie, A. (June 9, 2010). "A Slip Too Many for BP's Chief." *The New York Times,* p. 2. Retrieved February 4, 2011, from LexisNexis Academic database.

Jonsson, P. (June 17, 2010). "America's 'Small People' and BP's Gaffe-Prone Gulf Oil Spill Response." *The Christian Science Monitor.* Retrieved February 4, 2011, from LexisNexis Academic database.

Lawless, J. (November 9, 2010). "Ex-CEO Says BP Was Unprepared for Oil Spill." *The Associated Press.* Retrieved February 4, 2011, from LexisNexis Academic database.

Mason, R. (June 6, 2010). "BP chief Tony Hayward has been called 'the most hated man in America'." *The Sunday Telegraph (London),* p. 5. Retrieved February 4, 2011, from LexisNexis Academic database.

McKenna, B. (June 18, 2010). "Hayward derided for stonewalling, ducking questions before Congressional panel." *The Globe and Mail (Canada),* p. B1. Retrieved February 4, 2011, from LexisNexis Academic database.

Mendick, R. (September 12, 2010). "The Beleaguered BP Chief and the Wife Trying to Clean Up His Reputation." *The Sunday Telegraph (London),* p. 3. Retrieved February 4, 2011, from LexisNexis Academic database.

NBC *Today* interview with BP CEO Tony Hayward. Subject: Update on top-kill procedure; BP's estimate of the daily amount of oil spilled. Interviewer: Matt Lauer. (May 28, 2010). *Federal News Service.* Retrieved February 4, 2011, from LexisNexis Academic database.

"New BP Ads Don't Make Things Right with Locals." (June 5, 2010). *National Public Radio.* Retrieved February 4, 2011, from LexisNexis Academic database.

"91,000 Gulf Oil Spill Claims, Just 1 Final Payment." (January 31, 2011). *Associated Press.* Accessed January 31, 2011, at http://www.yahoo.com.

"Obama Says He Would Fire BP CEO Hayward." (June 8, 2010). *UPI.* Retrieved February 4, 2011, from LexisNexis Academic database.

Pagnamenta, R. (May 14, 2010). "BP chief admits his job may slip away; Tony Hayward tells of hate mail and the pressure from the U.S. government. *The Times (London),* p. 33. Retrieved February 4, 2011, from LexisNexis Academic database.

Rogers, D. (June 25, 2010). "From the Editor: Poor Comms Skills Just Magnify a Crisis." *PR Week,* p. 14. Retrieved February 4, 2011, from LexisNexis Academic database.

Seitel, F. (2004). *The Practice of Public Relations,* 9th ed. Upper Saddle River, NJ: Pearson.

Smith, A. (June 3, 2010). "BP's Television Ad blitz." *CNNMoney.com.* Retrieved February 4, 2011, from LexisNexis Academic database.

Spillius, A. (June 18, 2010). "BP Chief Endures American Inquisition." *The Daily Telegraph (London),* p. 4. Retrieved February 4, 2011, from LexisNexis Academic database.

"'Tired' Tony Hayward 'Savaged' by Congress, Say U.K. Media." (June 18, 2010). *CNN.com.*

Retrieved February 4, 2011, from LexisNexis Academic database.

Vasilyeva, N. (July 27, 2010). "Hayward to Get New Job at BP's Russian Venture." *Associated Press Online*. Retrieved February 4, 2011, from LexisNexis Academic database.

Watt, C. (July 28, 2010). "U.S. Public Demonised Me over Oil Spill, Says Axed BP Chief." *The Herald (Glasgow)*, p. 7. Retrieved February 4, 2011, from LexisNexis Academic database.

"White House Chief: Yacht Trip Another Gaffe by BP." (June 19, 2010). *Associated Press Online*. Retrieved February 4, 2011, from LexisNexis Academic database.

"White House Scorns BP CEO's Complaint He Was 'Demonized.'" (July 27, 2010). *Agence France-Presse—English*. Retrieved February 4, 2011, from LexisNexis Academic database.

Wighton, D. (April 23, 2010). "BP's Reputation on the Line." *The Times (London)*, p. 57. Retrieved February 4, 2011, from LexisNexis Academic database.

Wilcox, D.L., Cameron, G.T., Ault, P.H., Agee, W.K. (2003). *Public Relations Strategies and Tactics*, 7th ed. Boston, MA: Pearson.

**Questions for Discussion**

1. Could BP have "passed the buck" to its drilling partner, Transocean? Would this have been a good strategy? Why? Why not?

2. Was putting Tony Hayward "out front" as spokesman for the crisis effort a good idea? Why? Why not?

3. Hayward was CEO of the company. How might the public relations staff have better prepared him for his role in the crisis?

4. BP followed most of the traditional steps in dealing with a difficult situation. What went wrong? What steps did BP's public relations people miss?

5. Was the U.S. Congress trying to help the situation or posturing for political gain?

6. Now that the spill is over, the cleanup pretty well wrapped up, and the public agenda focused elsewhere, what will the lasting impact of this crisis be?

# Case 9-5 Hurricane Katrina: A Disaster from Beginning to End

*One of the most shocking disclosures after Katrina and Rita was how little prepared the local and state governments were not only in handling the hurricanes but also their aftermath.*
—*Jonathan Turley,*
*Professor of Public Interest Law*
*at George Washington University*

## The Situation

The morning of August 29, 2005, Hurricane Katrina first struck the lower Louisiana coast and then the Mississippi Gulf coast with a 20-to-30-foot storm surge and winds in excess of 165 miles per hour. By late morning, the levees protecting New Orleans at the Industrial Canal and the 17th Street Canal were breached, allowing eight to 13 feet of water to rush into New Orleans. In the meantime, Katrina's power swept away 74 miles of Mississippi coastline.

In its wake, Katrina left thousands stranded and homeless. The devastated area looked like a flooded war zone. Now the recovery began. However, in Louisiana, the "gumbo pot" would face many obstacles before help arrived.

## Political Turmoil and Communication Breakdowns

Perception and fact merged in the toxic sludge of Louisiana. From the beginning, Louisiana Governor Kathleen Blanco, a Democrat, clashed with President George W. Bush, a Republican, over whether to federalize the Louisiana National Guard. Thousands of Louisianans were suffering in New Orleans while all three levels of government support— city, state, and federal—crumbled.

Former White House Press Secretary Mike McCurry sent a memo to Bob Mann, Blanco's communications director, saying, "By the weekend (September 2–4) the Bush administration will have a full-blown public relations disaster/scandal on its hands because of the late response to needs in New Orleans." The Louisiana blame game had begun, and the Blanco officials were becoming concerned about who would get the blame for the slow response, them or the president's team.

Like the officials in most states dealing with a disaster, after Hurricane Katrina Louisiana officials first looked to National Guard units under the control of the governor and then drew additional guardsmen from other states to assist under the same command. The President also provided federal ground troops under his command. During the week after the storm, tensions rose between Governor Blanco and the White House over when President Bush would deploy his troops and whether Bush would "federalize" the National Guard forces, which would have moved them from Blanco's to Bush's control.

## The Facts

The facts about Hurricane Katrina are well known: hundreds of thousands of people displaced; hundreds of lives lost; property damage in the billions of dollars; confusion, consternation, and complacency coming together to leave a landmark American city in shambles.

The devastation in New Orleans was real. Only the famous French Quarter escaped destruction. The rest of the city and outlying parishes were flooded and destroyed, along with the lives of those who lived there. People had nowhere to go. Many fled the city. Others tried for makeshift shelters. Many perished.

There was no plan in place for dealing with the 165-mile-per-hour winds, the storm surges, the breached levies, and the thousands of gallons of seawater pouring throughout the city. No one was ready: not the people of New Orleans, not the Federal Emergency Management Agency (FEMA), not the State of Louisiana, not the City of New Orleans. All seemed equally surprised at the developments that brought a once-proud city to its knees.

No one was ready for the hurricane. No one was ready for its aftermath of displaced citizens, lost services, disease, death, and destruction. Many people failed to evacuate, despite more than 48 hours of advance warnings. No shelters were in place for those who stayed. No transportation was established for those who wanted to leave. No destinations were established for those who had transportation.

One telling image from the aftermath of Hurricane Katrina is that of Interstate 10 out of New Orleans crammed with cars—all lanes backed up—with completely empty lanes coming into the city. No one thought to open the inbound lanes to outbound traffic.

One problem, possibly, was that many affected people were unable to prepare for or respond to a disaster of this magnitude. Most didn't fully understand the potential danger of a Category 5 hurricane. Considering that nearly two-thirds of those involved were living below the poverty line at the time, many had no other option than to wait it out and hope for the best.

Perhaps most telling, however, was the fact that no one was prepared to communicate through the crisis. One axiom of crisis communication is that how one communicates through the crisis fixes in most people's minds how the crisis was addressed. The general public, for the most part, isn't able to fully evaluate

how well a crisis is handled. However, people know what they hear and see, and communication helps them form opinions about how the crisis was handled.

The makers of Tylenol, for example, communicated well through their well-known crisis, and even though no one has ever been arrested and no one knows why or how the tampering occurred, Tylenol and Johnson & Johnson generally got high marks for how they handled the crisis.

No one in New Orleans approached the problem the way Johnson & Johnson did. There seemed to be no one setting a realistic agenda—telling people what was going on. There was no attempt to set expectations—how long and how bad or how soon before it gets better. Those who knew what to do either were not heard or were ignored. Politics seemed more important than the people.

## Perceptions

During most crisis events, facts and perceptions are seldom congruent. Things are seldom as they seem. In the aftermath of Katrina, however, the perceptions seemed pretty much in line with reality.

The vast majority of Americans watching this horrible story unfold were of the opinion that no one knew what to do. That there was no plan in place was obvious. No one seemed to be in charge. Avoiding responsibility and affixing blame on someone of another political party seemed the top priority.

In reality, that was fact as well as perception. Veteran public relations practitioner Art Stevens once defined public relations as "the shaping of perceptions through communication. . . ." By Stevens's definition, no one was practicing public relations in New Orleans that fateful August.[2]

*(Continued)*

---

[2]"PR All-Stars," *Reputation Management,* Fall 1992.

**FIGURE 9.2**   Editorial cartoon

(Copyright 2005, "KAL" Cartoonists and Writers Syndicate and Cartoon Arts International)

One perception that lingers is that the recovery might have been more expeditious if those affected had been attractive, affluent people of Anglo-Saxon ancestry. Most of the misery was centered in the minority communities, and the images of people in the Superdome, wading down streets in water up to their waists, and in Walmarts pushing carts of "reclaimed" goods reinforced this fact. The mayor's "Chocolate City" comment only added to this perception, but it did help him get re-elected.

Regardless, perception is reality, facts notwithstanding. And the perception around the globe was that Katrina was awful, but those in charge of cleaning up the mess were worse.

## The Problem

The problem in New Orleans was a bifurcated one—half operations and half communication. On the operational side, the cleanup suffered from:

- Poor planning
- Poor anticipation
- Poor execution

On the communication side, the story was similar. Communication efforts suffered from:

- Poor planning
- Poor anticipation

- Poor execution
- Lack of anything to communicate

No one knew what needed to be done or said. There was little compassion from FEMA or state or city officials. The people of New Orleans were suffering from the hurricane, but they were also suffering from neglect. No one was able or willing to meet the needs of those most affected by Katrina.

Elected and appointed leaders had nothing to tell their publics. There was little good news. There was no rainbow, let alone any pot of gold. With no operational plans in place, no one could accurately predict what relief might appear or when it would arrive. Communicators were left with little or nothing to communicate.

One great truth of public relations is that "communication must follow performance." In New Orleans, performance didn't happen. Little was getting done. There was no performance for communication to follow.

That left public officials pointing fingers at each other, posturing for votes and decrying the lack of others' contributions. Said former FEMA Director Michael Brown, "If I had an opportunity to re-do what happened after Katrina, I'd communicate more often." But what could he have said? Unless the facts could have been different, nothing he could have said would have made much difference. People were still homeless and helpless. Without performance, communication is hollow, and even disingenuous.

## The Public Relations Impact

There was no consideration prior to, during, or after of how a coordinated public relations plan would help in the aftermath of Katrina. There was no One Clear Voice. No one was able to set a positive agenda. No reasonable expectations were established. No one seemed to have "expected the unexpected" and made any preparations. If there was competent public relations counsel available, it was difficult to see amid the confusion that was New Orleans in August 2005.

Decision makers were equally impaired. The mayor, the governor, the director of FEMA, no one was able to make sense of what was going on. Rumors thrive in the vacuum of no information, and rumors ran rampant after Katrina. It is likely that the finest public relations counsel would not have made much difference, but, then again, it might have.

Planning and preparation are invaluable. When disaster strikes, it's too late to write a crisis plan or develop a legacy of trust with key publics. What might some good public relations planning and preparation have added to the situation in New Orleans?

First, **One Clear Voice could have been established**. In a disaster of this magnitude, having one spokesperson is not practical, but speaking with One Clear Voice is. Establishment of a chain of command, having a coordinated communication effort, and making trained communicators available might have helped shape perceptions away from the ego-driven images that America saw.

**Regular news alerts could have been scheduled** to report on what was known at the time. All the media need from those in public relations is access and accuracy. This can be provided, even under the most difficult of circumstances. Believable communicators speaking through trusted channels of communication will drive out rumors every time.

With a **good crisis communication plan in place,** perhaps there would have been more to communicate. Such a plan would have an operational component, of course, and the implementation of that component would give the communicators something to say. Even if the news wasn't "good," it would at least be news—accurate information of interest to those affected by, and those attracted to, the story.

*(Continued)*

Good public relations **could have antici-pated the conditions,** at least to a certain extent. An environmental scan of pre–Katrina New Orleans would have told a wise counselor that some New Orleans residents wouldn't get the message and many wouldn't be able to respond. That information, alone, would have helped New Orleans prepare for what was to come.

In addition, **opinion leaders trusted by disenfranchised publics could be lined up,** providing effective intervening publics for those who might not hear or believe main-stream media.

**Messages could be pretested** to be sure that what is being said is being heard and understood by those to whom it is being said. The traditional communication model actually does work. Governmental jargon is deadly enough without the chaos of ris-ing water and diminishing hope. Pretested messages can smooth the path to better understanding.

Good public relations planning could, and should, spill over to operational departments as well. In lining up dependable communi-cation tools, the public relations counselors would have **anticipated traditional media being out of operation**. Phone lines, cell towers, and broadcast media won't survive 165-mile-an-hour winds. So the savvy prac-titioner will look for short-wave/ham opera-tors, satellite communication, and other ways to keep in touch with key audiences. This type of planning would have served FEMA and the others well.

None of this is meant to imply that good public relations planning is the answer to a Category 5 hurricane. It's not. However, in the mess that was Katrina, any planning and preparation would have lessened the hard-ships that followed. Michael Brown was partly right when he said he should have communicated more. What he also should have said was that he needed to communicate better.

## Hurricane Katrina Strikes Louisiana

*Day 1:*    The majority of Louisiana National Guardsmen are in Iraq, but 5,671 members are deployed in the storm-impact areas in Louisiana. The U.S. Coast Guard is positioned to respond. Support from the U.S. Navy, Air Force, and Army is put into action, including medical, supply, and rescue missions, but no federal ground troops are deployed.

Joint Task Force Katrina Commander Lieutenant General Russell Honoré, in charge of federal forces responding in the Gulf region, sets up headquarters in Mississippi. State officials oversee the response from the Office of Emergency Preparedness Center in Baton Rouge, Louisiana.

Governor Blanco calls President Bush and says, "We need everything you've got." The White House later says it heard no request on August 29 for federal troops.

*Day 2:*    6,124 National Guard members are deployed, with numbers increasing as guards-men arrive from other states. Blanco visits New Orleans and the Superdome, a shelter for thousands with short supplies, twice during the day. Evacuation is a priority.

That evening, responding to a request by Blanco, Adjutant General for the Louisiana National Guard Major General Bennett Landreneau asks Honoré for federal troops; their main mission would be to help with the evacuation.

*Day 3:*    6,137 National Guard members deployed.

In a comment recorded off air while awaiting a television interview, Blanco whispers to an aide that she should have requested troops earlier. The incident is cited as evidence that she was tardy in calling for federal military relief, but Blanco discounts that.

Blanco visits the Superdome again and sees increased suffering. Only Louisiana National Guard members are on duty. Thousands take refuge at the city's Convention Center, but it has few supplies because it is not an official shelter. Blanco places calls to the White House to ask when the federal forces are coming, but her question does not reach a top official until later in the day, according to the governor's timeline.

Later, Honoré arrives at state emergency office and greets Blanco, who asks why he has not shown up with federal troops.

Talking with Blanco chief counsel Terry Ryder at the state emergency center, Senator David Vitter says he spoke with Bush strategist Karl Rove, who said the White House wants to federalize the storm response operation.

Blanco officials and the military discuss a proposal for federalization.

Still later, learning of Vitter's conversation, Blanco calls Bush to say she wants U.S. troops but does not want to federalize them, according to administration notes of that conversation. She pushes for federal troop mobilization "today" and asks to be informed when troops will arrive. Blanco asks for 40,000 additional troops, but does not specify what kind.

*Day 4:*   7,403 National Guard members deployed.

National media focuses heavily on the slow relief and evacuation efforts and the suffering at the Superdome and the Convention Center.

The White House, Pentagon, and U.S. Department of Justice discuss legal options for sending in federal active-duty troops, including resorting to the Insurrection Act, which would give federal authorities extraordinary powers for the response effort. Blanco people later say the Insurrection Act was never discussed with them.

At the state emergency center, U.S. District Attorney Jim Letten, on the phone with the U.S. attorney general's office, asks a Blanco aide for specifics about what troop deployments the governor wants. Blanco officials interpret this as further evidence that the White House wants to federalize the operation.

Later, Blanco communications director Bob Mann, attributing an observation to former President Clinton press secretary Mike McCurry, writes a memo saying, "By the weekend, the Bush administration will have a full-blown public relations disaster/scandal on their hands because of the late response to needs in New Orleans." It is one of several memos among Blanco officials indicating their concern about who will get the blame—the White House or Baton Rouge.

That evening, Rear Admiral Robert Duncan, commander of the 8th Coast Guard District in New Orleans, returning from a day of rescue operations, tells Ryder that law and order must be restored and recommends federalization of troops.

Speaking with the governor at the state emergency center, Lieutenant General H. Steven Blum, chief of the National Guard Bureau, says that if the state agrees to federalize it will

*(Continued)*

lose control of the response operation and not gain any additional troops. He says National Guard units from around the nation are flowing in fast, and he will get more military police to assist.

Late that night, Michael Fleming, an assistant adjutant general for the Florida Army National Guard, who is in Louisiana assisting the state's response effort, gives similar advice as Blum's not to federalize.

*Day 5:*    8,417 National Guard members deployed.

Bush and Blanco meet on Air Force One in New Orleans, and the President offers to put Honoré in charge of the combined state and federal operation. The President, his chief of staff, and the governor talk privately for about half an hour.

Later that morning, Blanco sends a letter to Bush repeating her request for 40,000 additional troops and other military and relief support and requests the "expeditious return" of the Louisiana-based 256th Brigade Combat Team from Iraq to help with the storm relief effort.

By end of day, the Superdome evacuation is complete and the Convention Center is secured. But many people are still being evacuated from the overpass departure point.

Late that night, a fax from the Bush administration arrives at the state emergency center with a draft letter for Blanco to sign and a memorandum of understanding that would put Honoré in charge of all Guard and federal troops and relief operations. Blanco is awakened by a call informing her of Bush's memo, which Blanco officials say was unexpected. They work through the night forming a response to Bush memo.

*Day 6:*    9,328 National Guard members deployed.

Before dawn, Landreneau relates his phone conversation with Blum, who had flown to Washington for a meeting at the White House. Blum now recommends that Blanco sign the memo putting Honoré in charge. Landreneau advises the governor to reject the offer.

Blanco Chief of Staff Andy Kopplin sends memos to fellow staff members indicating that he thinks the memo is a maneuver by Rove to gain the upper hand, and comments, "Rove is on the prowl."

Midmorning, Blanco talks on the phone with White House Chief of Staff Andy Card, who says the President is about to make a Rose Garden announcement that he will send U.S. troops. He will not federalize the National Guard or require a change in the governor's role. About this time, Blanco faxes letter to Bush saying it's okay with her if Honoré takes charge of all federal forces in the Gulf region, but not inviting Honoré to take over the National Guard.

Bush announces he will sign the troop deployment order.

That evening the Convention Center evacuation is mostly complete.

*Day 7:*    11,145 National Guard members deployed.

An advance team of federal Army and Marine forces arrives in New Orleans.

On CNN and on later TV appearances, New Orleans Mayor Ray Nagin, who was with Blanco and Bush on Friday, says Blanco dropped the ball by delaying a decision for 24 hours on Bush's federal troops offer. "It didn't happen, and more people died," he said.

*Day 8:*    19,708 National Guard members deployed.

Thousands of federal active-duty soldiers and hundreds of vehicles with the 82nd Airborne and 1st Cavalry divisions begin arriving at the Belle Chasse Naval Air Station and Hammond. During another Louisiana visit with Blanco and a Congressional delegation, Bush says he is satisfied with the command structure.

*Day 9:*    27,065 National Guard members are now deployed in Louisiana. In total, more than 18,000 federal active-duty personnel and 42,990 Army and Air Force National Guard members are at work supporting relief operations in the Gulf area.

## Questions for Discussion

1. If you were responsible for your community's crisis plan, what three areas would you focus on primarily and why?
2. What do you believe was unique about the New Orleans culture that should have been taken into consideration by practitioners?
3. What might local public relations professionals have done on behalf of the city to assist in the days following the disaster? Do you believe the political stranglehold was too strong to make a difference?

## PROBLEM 9-A    WHEN ASSOCIATES DISAGREE ON HANDLING AN EMERGENCY

Three months ago, you were hired to start a public relations department at Reliable Steel Products Company. This is a young company with big ambitions. It is located in a medium-sized city in an area where industrial and residential building are predicted to boom. Reliable manufactures pipes, beams, rods, and other heavy parts for just about any kind of building.

After three months, your "department" consists of you and a secretary. Your outlook is bright, however. You report directly to the president, and she wants to be publicly known and highly regarded in the community and in the industry. To be of maximum help, you have done your homework by checking on the reputation of Reliable around town and in the industry. In the home community, Reliable and its president are not universally known, but employees, neighbors, and the people at the Chamber of Commerce feel that Reliable is well-managed, makes good products, and is a civic-minded neighbor. A few people did say that there have been a few accidents involving employees; it seems a rather dangerous place to work.

One morning, when the president is on her flight to the state capital, you get a call from a reporter at the local daily newspaper. He says that an ambulance driver told him a Reliable employee had been killed a few minutes earlier, when some pipes rolled off a pile while a truck was being loaded in the shipping yard. The reporter asks for details.

You tell him you will check it out at once and get back to him. You call the safety supervisor. He blows up and insists that no details be released to any outsider until all the facts can be determined, the employee's family notified, the insurance company alerted, and the company lawyers informed. He says for you to hold off until the president can be reached. The crisis plan in place leaves the safety supervisor in charge in this type of crisis. You agree on the priority of notifying the employee's family, but explain that you cannot prevent the newspaper from publishing anything it has gotten elsewhere, whether it is accurate or not.

The safety supervisor says to take it up with the personnel director. You call her. She says the company has someone out at the employee's home now, but she agrees with the safety supervisor that situations like this can lead to all sorts of possible problems, with a chance of backlash. She thinks an unplanned response without the president's knowledge would be dangerous. She wants no part in it.

A number of alternatives are open to you, but you have little time to choose among them. What would be the best course to follow now? Everything considered, what immediate initiatives—if any—would you take?

*(Continued)*

What further issues can be anticipated as a result of the crisis? How would you recommend dealing with them?

## PROBLEM 9-B    WHAT TO DO WHEN AN EMPLOYEE'S PROBLEMS AFFECT THE COMPANY

You have been called in to offer public relations advice to an appliance service company involved in a crisis. ABC Appliance Repair, a local company with 10 employees, has become enmeshed in an employee's legal problems. One of the employees was accused of raping a young woman on the local college campus. The owner of ABC Appliance Repair is a boss who treats his employees like family. He didn't think twice about putting up bail to get his employee out of jail. Unfortunately the media got wind of the circumstances, and the story made the front page of the next morning's newspaper: "ABC Appliance Repair Pays to Free Alleged Rapist Employee."

The owner calls you, angry at the way the newspaper presented the case and afraid he will lose customers. He doesn't know what to do: Should he call the media and fight back? Take out an ad and plead his case? He believes in his employee and would pay the bail again if he had to. Maybe, though, he wouldn't have talked so freely with the reporter.

The case will be going to court in about a month. The employee, in the meantime, is coming to work. Already, however, the company is receiving calls from irate members of the community complaining about the owner's actions. He's afraid of what this might do to his business. Two scheduled clients have called to cancel. It may get worse when his employee goes to court—especially if the media continues to follow the story.

To whom does he need to communicate? Prioritize his publics and identify how to reach each one. Then put together a plan (strategy and tactics) that will deal with the current crisis ABC Appliance Repair is facing.

What would you recommend the owner do about the media? Should he respond? If he does, what might happen? If he doesn't, how else can he communicate his message?

# 10

## Standards, Ethics, and Values

Regulation of human conduct by standards rather than brute force or basic biological drive is the definition of civilization. Social conduct is regulated by five factors:

- **Tradition.** How has the situation been viewed or handled in the past?
- **Public opinion.** What is currently acceptable behavior to the majority of one's peers?
- **Law.** What is permissible and what is prohibited by legislation?
- **Morality.** Generally connotes a spiritual or religious prohibition; immorality is a charge usually leveled in issues on which religious teachings have concentrated.
- **Ethics.** Standards set by a profession, an organization, or oneself, based on conscience—what is right or fair to others as well as to oneself?

Admittedly, these factors, as described, are attempts at pragmatic definitions. It would not be hard to get into an argument over the differences or the details. The point is that, however we use the words, there are forces that keep society functioning despite the strong pull of self-interest, ego, competitiveness, antisocial behavior, criminality, and other ills that could destroy it.

### THE ROLE OF CONSCIENCE

Corporations and other formal organizations exist only on paper, and therefore have no conscience. Those who manage and make decisions for organizations may be guided by codes of ethics, but they are also influenced by their personal ethics.

The difficulty in trying to pin down ethics in terms of standards or principles of conduct is that there is so little uniformity. Short of what is legal or illegal, the determination of what kinds of conduct are acceptable, in various kinds of circumstances, comes down to the individual or the group conscience. And among individuals or groups having differing functional roles, the threshold of conscience can be high or low, near or far.

Consider the range of conscience that exists between a clergyman, prostitute, used-car dealer, illiterate, doctor of medicine, judge, or addicted derelict, to name but a few. Also, there are wide variations within each functional role, based on the personal makeup of the individual. The range varies from the person who feels that "anything in my own interest is right as long as I don't go to jail," to "anything that pricks my conscience is wrong, no matter what anyone else says or does."

## Ethics Programs Are Big Business

As evidenced by the cases you are about to read in this section, organizations today are finding it imperative to establish codes of ethics—and then to educate their members about them: two jobs for public relations.

Ethics training and education have become hot topics as centers such as the Josephson Institute of Ethics in California, the Ethics Resource Center in Washington, D.C., and the Center for Business Ethics at Bentley College in Massachusetts, among many others, offer assistance to organizations to create ethics programs.

In 1991, the Center for Business Ethics established the Ethics Officer Association. An ethics officer is in charge of creating and maintaining an organization's ethics program. Currently the Association has 250 individual members representing more than 200 companies. Today 35–40 percent of major U.S. companies have an ethics officer, up from 15 to 20 percent 10 years ago.

The 2000 National Business Ethics Survey conducted by the Ethics Resource Center shows that companies today are doing more in terms of their ethics programs, compared to 1994. More companies have written ethics standards, ethics training programs, and means for employees to get ethics advice. A majority of employees are positive about ethical standards in their organizations. As a result, employees say they are more satisfied with their organizations overall. Concern for ethics is an important reason, they say, for continuing to work there.

What does this new emphasis on ethics mean for the practice of public relations? What many esteemed practitioners have been saying all along—without ethical behavior there is no credibility. And without credibility there is no business.

An already distrustful public is wary of the motives of business, government, and even non-profit agencies, as scandal after scandal surfaces about improprieties and mismanagement. A solid commitment to an ethics program by management and employees can help to gain, regain, or hold public trust and credibility, both internally and externally.

Transparency and accountability are going to be matters of rising public concern around the world in the years ahead, according to Frank Vogl, a senior ethics advisor with the Ethics Resource Center and a communication professional.

Then, too, most people tend to prescribe for others ethical standards of conduct that they do not practice themselves.

Customs and changing times are significantly involved in ethics and standards. Gifts and favors of various kinds are accepted in many countries as part of the cost of doing, or expediting, business. U.S. businesses that are international in scope claim they must comply to compete. In this country, public attitude in general frowns on gifts and favors as thinly disguised forms of bribery or payoff.

As another example, the dogma and ways of groups committed to strict standards and stern discipline are under assault. Consider the pressure on the Amish people as they see the luxuries and laxity of their neighbors. Or the differing practices of orthodox and reform Jews. Or the Catholic dogma, or the "Protestant work ethic" opposing a wave of permissiveness, liberation of the young, and psychiatric forgiveness for lapses in self-discipline.

## APPLICATION TO THE PRACTICE OF PUBLIC RELATIONS

Any effort to bring these considerations down to the practical world of public relations finds generalizations fraught with exceptions. The practice of public relations has been codified for the 20,000 members of the Public Relations Society of American (PRSA) since 1950. In 2000, PRSA adopted a member code of ethics www.prsa.org/AboutPRSA/Ethics/CodeEnglish/. But more than 200,000 persons are engaged in activities identifiable as public relations, most without equivalent standards or discipline.

That the public relations calling has been able to outgrow such labels as "flackery" and to rise above recurrent instances of news manipulation, cover-up, sugar coating, and some cases of deliberate deceit testifies eloquently to the potential power and promise of two-way communications and positive relationship building when the skills are turned to noble purposes.

For most practitioners, the Golden Rule is seen as an ethical guide—even as a definition of public relations. *If we do unto others as we would have them do unto us, harmonious public relationships will result.*

## THE ASPIRATIONS AND CONCEPT ARE PURE

Consider the following concept. If people would communicate more—and better—in a spirit of compromise and reconciliation, most problems in human relations would be solved. There would be understanding and peace. Lifestyles would include self-discipline and acceptance of responsibility, affluence with charity, possession without greed or avarice, and personal integrity under rules of law and mutual respect.

It is in this area that the public relations function has sought to fulfill its aspirations by exerting an ethical and moral force as well as technical skill and, by doing so, developing an identity and a professional discipline of its own.

It has been a long road to travel, but the destination is getting closer: The body of knowledge has been codified; there is an accepted academic curriculum leading to a distinct, recognized public relations doctorate. Today, approximately 70 schools offer master's degrees or a graduate emphasis in public relation. Four universities offer doctoral programs specifically in public relations. There is still no *licensing* of practitioners, but there is a Universal Accreditation Program formed in January 1998 by the PRSA and nine other public relations organizations. Members with at least five years of full-time paid professional PR experience must pass a written and oral exam to be accredited APR.

In the past, practitioners have functioned generally as skilled communicators and persuaders on behalf of the organizations that employ them. Ethical standards have tended to be the reflections of the employers and clients served. Putting it another way, the public relations voice has generally emerged publicly more as an echo of an employer's standards and interests than that of a professional discipline applied to the employer's problems.

The practitioner still may come on as narrowly organizational rather than broadly professional, but this situation is changing as both employers and the profession embrace a new wave of ethics. Today, public relations continues its struggle for broad recognition as advocates of understanding and public interest, qualified by academic discipline and professional accreditation.

## WHAT IS ACCEPTABLE ETHICALLY?

- Is it acceptable for food companies, in the name of nutrition and education, to provide elementary schools with educational kits prominently featuring their labels, product photographs, slogans, and product recipes?

- Is it acceptable for a county agency supported by taxpayers to spend money for a public relations firm to put out its news and promote its work?
- Is it acceptable for a utility to include in the rates to customers the cost of donations it makes to charity, for which it gets credit as being generous?
- Is it acceptable for soft drink, cereal, and other product manufacturers to shower television and movie prop people with free merchandise so that their products appear to be "standard" on television and in motion pictures?
- Is it acceptable for big businesses to preach that their growth creates jobs, when many of them have doubled in sales over a 10-year period while their employment numbers remain what they were 10 years ago?
- Is it acceptable for a corporation to hand out a news release at the outset of its annual meeting saying that its presentation was accorded a standing ovation?
- Is it acceptable for television networks to tie in a tire-company blimp with their newscasts at sports events, giving the blimp owner free publicity?
- Is it acceptable for a public relations counselor to send a client a flattering clipping with a note, "I knew you'd like to see this as soon as we got it," as if the counselor had something to do with generating the publicity, though actually he or she had not?
- Is it acceptable for an incumbent member of Congress to use perks of office such as staff paid by taxpayers, free mailings, pork barrel (including $25 million for grasshopper control back home), and PAC money to clobber any opposition and remain in office?
- Is it acceptable for a public relations director to tell the public a lie on a matter of no real significance if the intent is to protect the privacy or reputation of his or her boss?
- Is it acceptable to use fear in advertising to raise funds for poor people flooded out of their homes? To help cut down on the sale of tobacco? To sell a fire detection device? Insurance?
- Is it acceptable for a Congressperson to accept a box of oranges from a grateful fruit grower in his district? An envelope with $20 in it? Season tickets to the Washington Redskins games? A television set? A new automobile?
- Is it acceptable to announce publicly that an official has resigned "for personal reasons" when in fact he or she was fired for the good of the organization, or at the whim of a more powerful, jealous individual?

"So what?" is often the reaction to such questions about ethics. This type of comment is the result of two different trains of thought: (1) I'd never do any of those things, or (2) I'd have to wait until I saw what else was involved before I decided what I would do.[1]

---

[1] For an interesting classroom exercise in professional ethics, see Lynne Masel-Walters, "Playing the Game: Ethics Situations for Public Relations Courses," *Public Relations Research and Education Journal* 1, Winter, 1984, pp. 47–54.

# Case 10-1 The Danger of Organizational Culture Neglecting Ethics: Forest Laboratories and Celexa

Contributed by Shannon A. Bowen, Ph.D., University of South Carolina

It is not an overstatement to say that life and death decisions are made inside pharmaceutical firms every day. Pharmaceutical firms have a unique responsibility to engage in ethical public relations because their products help many people but also carry dangerous risks and side effects. Issues management, the process of problem solving and assessing risk in order to help communication managers prevent crises before they occur, is essential in a pharmaceutical company. Most of those types of issues include an ethical component. The products researched, developed, approved by the Food and Drug Administration (FDA), manufactured, and marketed are subject to intense issues management and ethical scrutiny. Marketing of these products is then subject to the highest ethical standards, based on honest and accurate information, so that consumers and their health-care providers can make informed decisions.

Although many pharmaceutical companies recognize this enormous ethical responsibility and seek to adhere to the highest ethical standards, there are lapses. There are many pharmaceutical cases with settlements in the billions of dollars, such as those at Pfizer or Lilly, arising from bad marketing practices or exaggerated claims. However, Forest Laboratories provides what is perhaps one of the most illustrative cases in recent decades of a lack of consideration for the ethics of their decisions and a corporate culture that seems to disregard ethics. As discussed in the foreword of this chapter, a culture inside of an organization that values and discusses ethics is essential. This case highlights the importance of an organizational culture that values ethics, the importance of the involvement of public relations in the ultimate decisions of the organization, the need to build trust and credibility with stakeholders—as well as the importance of ethics to the financial bottom line.

## Prescriptions and FDA Regulation

All prescription drugs marketed in the United States are required to gain approval from the FDA for use in treating a specific illness, and that illness then becomes the labeled use for the drug. Forest Laboratories got into the most trouble because it used a practice called "off-label marketing" in addition to providing illegal gifts to prescribers of its drug Celexa. Off-label use occurs when physicians use a drug for something other than what the FDA approved it for, and is legal when the drug is used at the discretion of the health-care provider. Marketing the drug for off-label uses is *not* legal, and most observers believe it is not ethical because it can lead to dangerous conditions of which the patient is not aware or informed about.

Prescription medications are required to go through extensive testing and clinical trials to gain approval from the FDA for their on-label use. Any potential side effects or drug interactions are then documented and can be described to prescribers and patients. Using drugs off-label needs to be closely monitored by the health-care provider because the potential risks and side effects related to the

*(Continued)*

off-label use have not been studied. Pediatric uses of medications must specifically be studied among children to gain FDA approval.

The FDA guidelines indicate that only a physician can prescribe medication for a condition that is not "on the label." It also indicates that it is illegal for pharmaceutical companies to promote prescriptions for off-label uses. The FDA also places gift bans on pharmaceutical company sales representatives so that health-care providers are not offered personal incentives to prescribe certain drugs.

## Who Is Forest Laboratories?

Forest Laboratories, Inc., is a publicly traded pharmaceutical company based in New York City that researches, manufactures, and distributes prescription medications. The company's annual sales are $4.4 billion (Hoover's 2012), and it has subsidiaries in other countries that also report revenue individually. Forest ranks number 513 in the Fortune 1000. It is a large firm but not global on the scale of some others such as Johnson & Johnson.

There are 108 executives in Forest's New York headquarters, led by Chairman, President, and CEO Howard Solomon. Solomon's annual salary is on file as $1,277,500, plus a $900,000 annual bonus. The CEO is the top leader of the day-to-day operations in an organization; when a person is also chairman and president, that individual is responsible for the entire organization. That responsibility is often said to be *fiduciary*, meaning bound to act in trust of others, especially in public policy and financial matters.

Forest researchers invented the drug Celexa as a treatment for major depression, in the class of antidepressants called selective serotonin reuptake inhibitors (SSRIs). The FDA approved Celexa to treat major depression in adults as its on-label use in 1998. The drug was heralded as a breakthrough and set to break records in sales for Forest.

In 2010, Celexa was among the most commonly prescribed SSRI in the United States, at roughly 28,000,000 prescriptions (Wikipedia). Celexa, whose chemical name is citalopram, is used throughout most of the world under various other brand names, promoted by Forest's subsidiary firms.

## Impending Ethical Issues

Although Forest did not conduct pediatric tests or clinical trials for Celexa in children or young adults, accusations began to circulate that it was promoting the drug off-label. Those reports indicated that Celexa was being marketed as an effective antidepressant for use in children and young adults in sales representatives' meetings with health-care providers. Such an off-label use would be at the discretion of the health-care provider, but it is illegal for the pharmaceutical firm to promote it. If Forest was promoting the drug for pediatric use, was that deceptive? Was it ethical?

Further, complaints to the FDA began to surface that Celexa representatives were also giving kickbacks to physicians who prescribed the drug, including tickets to sporting events, lavish dining, expensive entertainment-event tickets, and even vacations for high prescribers of Celexa. These physicians and health-care providers clearly violated their medical codes of ethics. But where were the ethics at Forest? Where was public relations —the part of an organization that many scholars conclude should be responsible for driving and implementing ethics in these situations?

At this point, one would expect Forest to engage in issues management, to investigate and resolve these complaints. If no issues management took place, one would expect the public relations department to eventually implement a crisis-management plan to effectively and ethically handle the impending and widening crisis.

No such actions were taken with regard to public relations. In fact, Forest only issued one news release related to the entire matter, and that release was compelled speech as part of a settlement with the government.

## Ethical Crisis

The FDA took note of the rising number of complaints it received and began an investigation into Forest. The United States Department of Justice (DOJ) and Carmen Ortiz, the U.S. Attorney General for the District of Massachusetts (not the state only, but the federal judicial district), began civil and criminal proceedings against Forest for the off-label marketing charges, violations of gift bans and "anti-kickback laws," and various other charges of deceptive practices.

The investigations revealed that Forest was engaging in unethical and illegal practices. Findings revealed that Celexa was promoted off-label as a pediatric antidepressant. Its use in children or young adults had never been studied, documented, or approved by the FDA. Further, the investigation revealed that kickbacks were given to physicians who prescribed Celexa.

The lack of ethics inside Forest was so severe that, according to news media reports, it was not able to mount a credible defense for the case. Some might ask at this point: What were the ethical and moral responsibilities of the Chairman, President, and CEO, Mr. Solomon? Was his fiduciary duty not only to stockholders but also to health-care providers and consumers? Where were ethics training and supervision for the pharmaceutical representatives who met with health-care providers? Who was responsible for endangering the pediatric patients who received Celexa, thinking it was a safe drug for them? Who authorized expenditures on entertainment and vacations as kickbacks for physicians? Who was responsible for the deceptions that took place?

Perhaps most importantly from a public relations standpoint, where was the internal organizational culture of valuing ethics that should not have allowed these events to occur?

Here is a summary of the events and their financial impact.

### Forest Case Timeline

| Date | Event |
|------|-------|
| 1997 | Forest filed a new drug application with FDA for Celexa |
| 1998 | Celexa approved by FDA as antidepressant medication in the United States and Puerto Rico |
| 1999 | Celexa sales of $90 million, 16.8% of Forest's yearly sales |
| 2003 | Celexa sales peaked at $1.42 billion, 69.4% of Forest's yearly sales. Exclusive Celexa marketing rights extended by FDA |
| 2004 | Subpoena issued for documents related to Celexa marketing |
| 2005 | Release of generic forms of Celexa into the market |
| 2006 | FDA began investigation of anti-kickback and off-label promotion violation |
| 2007 | Celexa accounted for 0.8% of Forest's yearly sales |
| 2010 | Forest pleads guilty to criminal and civil charges |

Media coverage of the Forest case was dense. More than 20 major media outlets covered the story, including *The Wall Street Journal, BusinessWeek,* the Fox news channel, *The New York Times,* NPR, *Bloomberg,* and *Forbes.* The national-level case quickly generated a media agenda focused primarily on the deceptive organizational culture at Forest, geared toward marketing above all else. The media widely quoted Ortiz, for the prosecution, who said, "Forest deliberately chose to pursue corporate profits over its obligations to the FDA and the American public." It is hard to imagine an organization's reputation being more damaged.

Forest settled the cases with the DOJ and U.S. Attorney for the District of Massachusetts,

*(Continued)*

pleading guilty and paying extensive financial penalties. The $313 million settlement included $88 million paid to the U.S. government; $66 million for civil settlements; $14 million in assets; and, a $150 million fine, no doubt for punitive purposes. Other penalties included entering into a corporate integrity agreement with the Department of Health and Human Services with a five-year agreement to have annual reviews of Forest's ethics and marketing practices, and to notify health-care providers about the guilty plea. Forest did not issue any comments on all of the investigations other than stating that the CEO was relieved that the long-running investigation was over. The organization did nothing to accept responsibility or rebuild trust with publics.

Forest Laboratories is an excellent case study for understanding the role of public relations within the top-level, strategic management of an organization. If Forest had been engaging in issues management, these problems could have been solved long before federal investigations, lawsuits, and millions of dollars in penalties ensued.

The role of an ethical organizational culture is also highlighted in this case because the government investigation shows that Forest clearly did not understand the importance of ethics, training employees on ethics, or adhering to any particular ethical values system in its business practices. A large $313 million dollar fine paid for these ethical infractions seems to have not been enough to create a new culture of ethical behavior inside the organization.

Was public relations counseling the CEO on the ethics of the Celexa situation? Doubtful. Although many CEOs caught in this type of corporate scandal claimed they were not aware that certain practices were taking place in their organizations, it is the ultimate responsibility of the CEO to be in control of the operations of the organization. Deceptive marketing practices clearly fall within the purview of the CEO. Even if there is no ethics officer at the helm and no public relations counsel to advise on ethics, the CEO is ultimately responsible

for the behavior of the company. In this case, the investigation and fines show that Solomon failed in his fiduciary responsibility not only to the stockholders but also to all of the other stakeholders and publics of Forest, including employees, regulators, health-care providers, and patients. Although everyone in an organization should play the role of an ethics agent, an official ethics officer should advise the CEO on ethics. Even so, the final voice of ethical responsibility is that of the CEO.

Finally, what is the role of public relations in this type of catastrophe? Should PR advise the CEO on ethical behavior as many scholars argue? In this case, it appears that public relations took a very limited role in supporting the marketing function and engaging in deceptive promotions. These activities clearly run counter to the ideal type of public relations in which relationships are based on trust and credibility with stakeholders and publics. That type of organizational culture would be supportive of being guided by ethics, and allow discussion of the ethical dilemmas in a way that supported resolving issues before they became crises.

## Questions for Discussion

1. To what extent did Forest consider its stakeholders when marketing Celexa?
2. If you had been the public relations officer at Forest when this crisis began to unfold, how could you have responded?
3. What would you identify as problematic within Forest's organizational structure? Specifically, what was the role of the public relations function, and was that an effective use of public relations? Was there an ethics officer, or who was in charge of ethics at all? What was the "safety net" in case of problems?
4. If you were hired as a consultant to work with Forest on creating an issues management plan for the future, what types of things would you recommend?

5. What recommendations would you make to Forest to "institutionalize a corporate conscience" and ingrain the importance of ethics within its organization?

6. Who is ultimately responsible for the ethics of an organization? What role does the CEO play in both ethical and fiduciary responsibilities?

## References and Further Reading

Bowen, S. A. (2008). "A State of Neglect: Public Relations as Corporate Conscience or Ethics Counsel." *Journal of Public Relations Research,* 20(3), 271–296.

Bowen, S. A. (2009). "What Communication Professionals Tell Us Regarding Dominant Coalition Access and Gaining Membership." *Journal of Applied Communication Research,* 37(4), 427–452.

Bowen, S. A. (2010). "Almost a Decade Later: Have We Learned Lessons from Inside the Crooked E, Enron?" *Ethical Space: The International Journal of Communication Ethics,* 7(1), 28–35.

Bowen, S. A. (2010). "An Examination of Applied Ethics and Stakeholder Management on Top Corporate Web Sites." *Public Relations Journal,* 4(1) Retrieved from: http://www.prsa.org/Intelligence/PRJournal/Vol4/No1/.

Bowen, S. A., and Heath, R. L. (2005). "Issues Management, Systems, and Rhetoric: Exploring the Distinction Between Ethical and Legal Guidelines at Enron." *Journal of Public Affairs,* 5, 84–98.

Grunig, J. E. (2001). "Two-Way Symmetrical Public Relations: Past, Present, and Future." In R. L. Heath (Ed.), *Handbook of Public Relations* (pp. 11–30). Thousand Oaks, CA: Sage.

Grunig, J. E., and Grunig, L. A. (1996, May). "Implications of Symmetry for a Theory of Ethics and Social Responsibility in Public Relations." Paper presented at the meeting of the International Communication Association, Chicago.

Grunig, J. E., and Repper, F. C. (1992). "Strategic Management, Publics, and Issues." In J. E. Grunig (Ed.), *Excellence in Public Relations and Communication Management* (pp. 117–157). Hillsdale, NJ: Lawrence Erlbaum Associates.

Grunig, L. A., Grunig, J. E., and Dozier, D. M. (2002). *Excellent Public Relations and Effective Organizations: A Study of Communication Management in Three Countries.* Mahwah, NJ: Lawrence Erlbaum.

*Hoover's Online Handbook of Business.* (2012). Forest Laboratories, Inc., Entry retrieved from: http://www.hoovers.com/company/Forest_Laboratories_Inc/rrshri-1.html

Kendall, B. (2010). "Forest Labs to Pay $313 Million Penalty." *The Wall Street Journal,* online business section. Retrieved from: http://online.wsj.com/article/SB10001424052748703743504575494190717156422.html

Wikipedia. (2012). Antidepressant entry. Retrieved from: http://en.wikipedia.org/wiki/Antidepressant#cite_note-165

# Case 10-2 Penn State University: Sandusky Matter Sullies School Reputation

Ethical behavior has frequently been defined as "doing the right thing for the right reason." The philosophy behind this definition is that doing the "right thing" is good, but to be truly ethical, one must do the right thing for the right reason.

Thus, unethical actions can result from both behavior and motive. If one does "the right thing" for personal gain, has that person behaved in an ethical manner? If one does something unethical, yet attains a beneficial result, does that justify the action?

Or, should everyone just follow Kant's categorical imperative, "I am never to act otherwise than to will that my maxim should become universal law."

Those (and many other) questions began to surface in State College, Pennsylvania, in 2011 when a man who had been a popular assistant coach at Penn State was accused of multiple counts of abuse of young boys.

Not only was the coach under attack from critics, so was the university, its iconic football coach, its president, and just about everyone connected with the situation. The primary question was, did PSU and its leaders do enough to (1) stop the abuses and (2) punish the accused coach?

Or, in ethical terms, did PSU do the right thing? For the right reason? Or did it hide its head in the sand to protect its vaunted football program, and by extension, the university itself?

The situation certainly looked bad.

The grand jury report cited "52 counts related to alleged sexual abuse of 10 boys over 15 years."[1] Jerry Sandusky, Hall of Fame assistant coach at PSU for years, was led off to jail. A few months later, Sandusky would be convicted of 45 counts of child sex abuse. Sandusky is expected to appeal the verdict.

The Penn State board of trustees fired iconic football coach Joe Paterno (winner of 409 games, more than any other Division I football coach) and PSU President Graham Spanier. (Paterno would die of cancer shortly thereafter, January 22, 2012.)[2]

Students and alumni were appalled and furious that Paterno was cashiered (via telephone call) on November 9, 2011, unwilling to believe he was guilty of a "failure of leadership."[3]

The serene campus in Happy Valley would never be the same.

## The Situation

The storm that would sink Paterno and PSU began forming in 1998 when PSU police, along with State College, Pennsylvania, law enforcement, were notified of possible misconduct by Sandusky related to a minor boy in the PSU football team showers. A long report was filed, but no prosecution was forthcoming. The case was closed, at the request of PSU's campus police commander.

Sandusky, who admitted showering naked with and hugging one victim, was told to quit showering with little boys, and he said he would not do it again.[4]

Could Penn State have acted differently at this juncture? Might it have made a difference? Sandusky, who was widely considered a successor to Paterno, should the coach ever retire, was told by Paterno (in May 1999) that he (Sandusky) would not be his successor. Sandusky "retired" from coaching and began devoting most of his time to a nonprofit organization he had helped establish.

The Second Mile (TSM) was a charity founded by Sandusky in 1977 to reach out to "children who need additional support and who would benefit from positive human contact....[5] "Through The Second Mile," the grand jury report said, "Sandusky had access to hundreds of boys, many of whom were vulnerable because of their social situation."[6] (Sandusky would resign from TSM in September 2010. The agency would close its doors in 2012.)

With Sandusky as its primary fundraiser, TSM would grow to a statewide organization, with some 100,000 children involved. All that would crumble with his arrest. Funding dried up; staff and clients withdrew. The grand jury report was damning and damaging. On November 11, 2011, TSM issued a statement:

> Although the allegations against Jerry Sandusky and the alleged incidents occurred outside Second Mile programs and events, this does not change the fact that the alleged sexual abuse involved Second Mile program children, nor does it lessen the terrible impact of sexual abuse on its victims.[5]

The abuse situation came to a full boil in March 2002, when a graduate assistant football coach walked in on Sandusky allegedly engaging in intercourse with a preteen boy in a shower. The assistant left, and the next day told Paterno what he had seen. Paterno later told his superior, athletics director Tim Curley, who had been a PSU quarterback for Paterno in the 1970s. Neither Curley nor Paterno called police. A week and a half later, Curley called the assistant coach, who repeated his story for the athletics director and for Gary Schultz, the PSU vice-president who oversaw the PSU campus police. Two weeks later, Curley called the assistant coach to tell him that Sandusky's keys had been confiscated and the incident had been reported to The Second Mile.[7]

Curley told Sandusky that he could no longer bring little boys to campus, even though Sandusky was allowed continued access to facilities via his "emeritus" status, granted on his retirement in 1999.[7] Had Penn State missed an opportunity to bring the situation under control?

## Several Opportunities Missed

It is clear that no one wanted to confront (1) the likelihood that children were being abused on the PSU campus, (2) Jerry Sandusky, or especially (3) Joe Paterno.

Several opportunities arose for someone to have stepped up and taken action between the first incident reported in 1998 and the final straw which fell in 2011.

- In 1998, Sandusky brought an 11-year-old boy home from a "workout" at PSU. The boy's mother noticed his wet hair and became suspicious. The mother persuaded PSU police to "eavesdrop" on conversations she had with Sandusky about her son. She confronted Sandusky, and he responded, "I was wrong...I wish I were dead." A detailed investigation of this incident ended with the county district attorney deciding there were no criminal charges to file. The PSU campus police closed the case at the direction of its director.[11]

A psychologist reported in 1998 that Sandusky's actions fit the profile of a pedophile, "but the university seemed to do nothing about Sandusky in the wake of that report in 1998."[8] Paterno and Spanier both said they knew nothing of the incident. State welfare department investigator Gerald Lauro said later that he thought the 1998 allegation fell into "boundary" issues, not sexual assault. He theorized that the victim, at that point much older, told the 2009 grand jury "a much more explicit account."[9]

- In the fall of 2000, a PSU janitor observed Sandusky allegedly performing oral sex on a preteen boy in an assistant coach's shower. The janitor told his fellow workers and his boss. One worker had seen Sandusky and a preteen boy leaving

*(Continued)*

the showers, and the janitorial supervisor saw Sandusky and the boy in the parking lot around midnight. The janitor, new in his job, feared losing his position if he reported Sandusky, so no report was made.[10]

Questions abound.

1. Why was Sandusky allowed to remain in society for three years while the grand jury completed its investigation? "The way (Corbett's?) office handled the investigation raises inevitable and legitimate questions about why an alleged sexual predator was allowed to remain at large for nearly three years while the grand jury investigated. The question of politics cannot be avoided. It should also be noted that Corbett was running for governor in 2009 and 2010. Was he inclined to go the route of a lengthy grand-jury probe...because he didn't want to alienate potential donors with Penn State ties?"[12]

2. What happened to the Centre County district attorney who dismissed the original 1998 case against Sandusky? He disappeared without a trace in 2005, eight months prior to his planned retirement. A district attorney for 20 years, he didn't return from a road trip. His car was found beside a river. His laptop was recovered from the river. He was declared officially dead six years later.

3. Why didn't Joe Paterno address Sandusky's problems when they became known in 1998? Paterno, says Maureen Dowd, "must have decided that his reputation was more important than justice."[7]

   Others agree. "The great JoePa (Paterno), . . . did nothing to stop Sandusky's alleged depravity but kick it upstairs to superiors, when everyone knew Paterno had no superiors...."[12]

4. Was Paterno doing the right thing? For the right reason?

Mitch Albom, a supporter of Paterno, said: "Sexual abuse was not a secret in 2002. A more concerned Paterno would have gone beyond telling his athletic director—even though Sandusky, at the time, was no longer on the Penn State staff. Do I believe Paterno could have been so wrapped up in football that he didn't know much more? Maybe. Or maybe he didn't want to know."

Paterno, himself, said after he was fired, "This is a tragedy. It is one of the great sorrows of my life. With the benefit of hindsight, I wish I had done more."[14]

## The Problem for Penn State

Jerry Sandusky's problem is obvious: He was convicted of molesting young boys. He will likely go to prison for a long time.

Penn State's problem isn't so cut and dried. Its history is part of the problem.

The university's top administrators kept allowing Sandusky to invite some of those boys into campus sports buildings—locker rooms, showers, a sauna, and a swimming pool—where prosecutors now say he fondled, molested, and sexually assaulted some of the most vulnerable in the place known as Happy Valley.

Too many, from the university president to department heads to janitors, knew of troubling behavior by this revered, longtime coach who founded a charity for children with hardscrabble backgrounds. But at this school whose sports programs vow "success with honor," the circle of knowledge was kept very limited and very private.

Year after year, Penn State missed opportunity after opportunity to stop Sandusky. Secrecy ruled, and the reaction to complaints of improper sexual behavior was to remain silent, minimize the complaints, or explain them away—all part of a deep-rooted reflex to protect the sacred football program.[15]

Some of that attitude was reflected by students and alumni following Sandusky's arrest and Paterno's firing. At the first opportunity to elect new members of the Board of Trustees, the alumni (who elect trustees) selected a former Paterno player and a wealthy donor who was critical of the decision to fire Paterno, as two of the three new trustees.[16] "The alumni sent a message that they were dissatisfied with the Board's decisions," said the newly elected trustee.

On the night of Paterno's dismissal, students rioted, massing in front of his house near campus, in a show of support. Six months later, PSU trustees were moved to issue a statement underscoring its rationale for letting the long-time coach go. "The board decided to issue another statement now," said trustee Keith Eckel, "because alumni had continued to ask questions."[17]

## Going Forward

Overcoming that culture is going to be the gist of PSU's problem going forth.

It won't be easy, even with a commitment from new President Rodney Erickson to restore confidence and "rebuild our community." Too much damage has been done. The U.S. Department of Education is investigating whether the university violated federal law by failing to report the alleged sexual assaults. Some donors are expected to pull back, at least in the short term. One football recruit has already changed his mind about attending Penn State next year. Moody's Investors Service, Inc., warned that it might downgrade Penn State's bond rating as it gauges the impact of possible lawsuits.[18]

But there are some positive signs.

The university was expecting its largest incoming class in six years in 2012, with a six-percent increase in acceptances, Erickson said. Applications for admissions increased more than two percent, another record.[19]

President Erickson and the Board are also committed to more transparency.

"I accepted this presidency with the intention that I would lead Penn State with a commitment to openness and communication," Erickson said.

That is the type of communication some said the board did not exhibit when it was needed most. Governor Corbett, who sits on the board, agrees. "Transparency is a big thing for me, and I think moving forward the board will have to sit down and face some difficult decisions."[20]

Perhaps the best sign is the hiring of two professional public relations firms. Penn State announced in April 2012 the hiring of Edelman and La Torre Communications, to help plan and execute the next step in Penn State's recovery. It won't be cheap. The college has committed $2.5 million for the first year, after already having spent $7.5 million on crisis communication related to Sandusky.

Penn State says the firms will communicate with current and prospective students, alumni, faculty, staff, parents, and media as well as "support the university throughout upcoming litigation."[21]

## The Public Relations Impact

It is too early to predict what impact the public relations agencies can have on the PSU problem. The 46-year history with Paterno, the culture of secrecy, the lack of outrage by students and alumni over sexual abuse running rampant, are going to be difficult to change.

Football put Penn State on the map. The college takes in some $70 million annually from its football program. Allowing it to drive moral decisions is a mistake. "Like the Roman Catholic Church," says Maureen Dowd, "Penn State is an arrogant institution hiding behind its mystique."

*(Continued)*

## "The Emperor Wears No Clothes"

The familiar nursery story of the little boy who voices what no one else will drives at the core of why this scandal and others like it continue to occur. When organizations adopt a sycophantic worship of, in this case, a coach, or, in other cases, a CEO, telling on them is practically impossible. An employee will fear for his or her job and being cast out socially, and will speculate that maybe nothing wrong is going on if no one else is speaking out either. Whistle-blowers, though protected by federal law, know how difficult it can be to reintegrate in the same or even another organization afterwards. One of our most important jobs as public relations practitioners is to have our ear to the ground, to know what is going on that could harm the reputation of our organization and, if necessary, as the Quaker's say, "speak truth to power" and do the right thing.

The new leadership recognizes the value of transparency. It had the good judgment to bring in outside counsel. Time will tell if anyone listens to them. Will PSU be able to do the right thing? For the right reason?

### Questions for Discussion

1. How could this situation have been defused earlier or avoided?
2. What role did politics play in the many critical decisions made along the way?
3. Could Joe Paterno have stopped what was happening in 1998? How?
4. Why did PSU "kick the problem down the road" for so long?
5. What might The Second Mile have done to mitigate this mess?
6. After reading the grand jury presentation, what do you think of Penn State's response?
7. Did anyone do the right thing? For any reason?

### Citations

1. Grand Jury-Pennsylvania Attorney General (www.attorneygeneral.gov/sandusky-grand-jury-presentment.pdf) 5/8/12 via ABC *News*.
2. Wikipedia, 2012 "Joe Paterno."
3. *USA Today*. USA Today "Penn State Board: Paterno Fired for 'Failure of Leadership' " March 13, 2012, p 2A.
4. *The New York Times*, Investigation of Sandusky in 1998 Raises Questions No. 13-Mitch Albom "Paterno's Legacy is not the real issue today," November 9, 2011.
5. TheSecondMile.org.
6. Grand Jury presentment, p. 1.
7. *The New York Times*, Maureen Dowd, "Personal Foul at Penn State," November 8, 2011.
8. *The New York Times*, "Sandusky Investigation…," March 24, 2012.
9. *The New York Times*, "Investigation of Sandusky in 1998…," November 9, 2011.
10. Grand Jury report, p. 21.
11. Grand Jury report, p. 18.
12. *The Daily Beast*, November 21, 2011.
13. Mitch Albom, *Detroit Free Press*. November 10, 2011.
14. Mlive.com/sports. "Paterno Issues Statement…"
15. CBSSports.com. "Penn State Culture…"
16. *Associated Press*. USA Today "Debate Over Paterno's Firing Not Over Yet" May 4, 2012.
17. *USA Today*. "Sandusky Defense to Seek Dismissal of Charges," March 13, 2012, p. 2A.
18. *Columbia Missourian*, November 13, 2011. "Penn State Students, Alumni…"
19. *The Boston Globe* (Boston.com), "PSU President Says Admissions, Acceptances Up," May 4, 2012.
20. ABC27.com, "Penn State Board of Trustees Moves Forward…," January 20, 2012.
21. *Fox Sports*, April 25, 2012.

# Case 10-3 Corporate Social Responsibility and Ethics: Nike and Apple Face Similar Challenges a Decade Apart

Corporations are no longer accountable to only their investors, nor can they base their success solely on high sales figures. A legacy of the social movements of the 1960s and a demand for political correctness now compels organizations to have practices in place that demonstrate their commitment to social responsibility.[2] Corporate social responsibility can include embracing the issues of environmentalism, prohibiting testing of products on animals, human rights, or other social or political concerns affected or perceived to be affected by an organization's policies. Corporations are now finding that stakeholders expect them to have an ethical, and not necessarily financial, interest in their policies and how those policies affect the rest of the world.

It has become important to organizations to cultivate their socially responsible image. Socially responsible corporate practices and ethical standards are a reflection of each organization. Corporations have learned that being socially responsible is good for business, that their beneficence also benefits the company.

Although some companies are following through on their commitments, others only project the appearance of being socially responsible. This discrepancy between a company's environmental image and actions has been referred to as *greenwashing*. This term has earned an entry in the 10th edition of the *Concise Oxford English Dictionary* and is defined as "disinformation disseminated by an organization so as to present an environmentally responsible public image." Mark Twain must have experienced early versions of greenwashing in his time when he said, "The secret of success is honesty and fair dealing—if you can fake these, you've got it made."

If an organization is accused of social irresponsibility or demonstrating unethical practices, it may not necessarily be doing anything illegal. Violating an Environmental Protection Agency regulation and discriminating against an employee are illegal acts. Selling fur products or making a corporate donation to Planned Parenthood are not illegal, but some may see these acts as unethical. Many companies have been boycotted based on their actions that are legal but perceived to be unethical by groups that disagree with specific actions.

The German philosopher Immanuel Kant (1724–1804), in his works on ethics, wrote, "Act only on that maxim through which you can at the same time will that it should become a universal law." Before a company advances a policy or produces a new product, it may want to address the issue of business ethics by asking the following questions:

- Will anyone be damaged or compromised by our actions?
- Will anyone gain an unfair advantage?
- Is there anything inherently wrong with these actions?
- If these practices reach the media, will we look bad?
- Are we able to feel good about following these practices? Would we be happy applying the practices or policies to ourselves?

*(Continued)*

---

[2] Betsy Reed, "The Business of Social Responsibility," May 1998; Jon Entube, "Corporate Ethics and Accountability." Corporate Governance Web site (www.corpgov.net).

In other words, should the Golden Rule also apply to business practices? Does there have to be a tradeoff between corporate social responsibility and making a profit?

Finally, actions that an organization may take today—even when they are approved, supported, and welcomed by laws and mores of the day—can be interpreted in the future as bad behavior worthy of boycotts, lawsuits, and negative reputational chatter in the future. Our role as practitioners expands not only to interpret organizational behavior through the eyes of our stakeholders today but to how we will be perceived and treated in the future.

## Nike's Problems Foreshadowed— Nike Forewarned

Today Nike, Inc., is the world's number-one shoe company and controls almost 19 percent of the U.S. shoe market. Nike employs approximately 35,000 worldwide corporate employees and about 950,000 people in Nike-contracted factories around the world. Revenues worldwide in 2011 were almost 21 billion dollars

## 1992 and an Early Code of Conduct

In 1992, Nike was much like it is today—the biggest player in the market (with a 20 percent market share) and a half million people working in Nike-contracted factories around the world.

To deal with contracted labor and bulletproof themselves against possible negative public opinion, Nike established its own code of conduct in 1992 to ensure that specific guidelines on wages and working conditions were followed at all of its facilities, including those under the supervision of subcontractors overseas.

Nike began to receive negative coverage concerning its labor practices in the early 1990s. In 1992, Jeff Ballinger, who had spent four years in Indonesia helping workers to organize unions, returned to the United States with information on abusive labor practices in Nike factories in Indonesia. In 1993, CBS flew Ballinger back to Indonesia to narrate a story

on the workers' struggle for a living wage in those facilities.

After the CBS report, Nike received a flurry of negative media coverage from the press in both the United States and the United Kingdom over the next two years. During this time, the company issued various press releases and statements asserting its commitment to the welfare of its workers and to improving factory conditions. Nike seemed to successfully endure the reactions to the bad press. After its stock price fell slightly at the end of 1993, it began a steady upswing starting in 1995. Between 1996 and 2006, Nike stock rose from about $55 to $80 per share, reaching more than $90 at one point. Nike shares gained 17 percent from 2005 to 2006.

## Someone Blows the Whistle on Nike

In November 1997, a disgruntled Nike employee leaked a secret internal report to the Transnational Resource and Action Center, a San Francisco–based organization now known as Corporate Watch. Nike had hired the Ernst & Young accounting firm to audit the working conditions at one of its shoe manufacturing plants in Vietnam. The inspection report stated that workers were exposed to harmful levels of carcinogens because of poor air ventilation in the plant and that 77 percent of the employees had respiratory problems. The report also stated that employees were forced to work 65 hours a week, yet did not receive a living wage. This information seemed to contradict Nike's earlier statements of commitment to the welfare of its workers.

The Ernst & Young report was supplied to *The New York Times,* which then printed a story on it on November 8, 1997. Nike responded by pointing out that, soon after it had received the report, the problems were addressed and steps had been taken to improve the working conditions.

However, this time, with the release of the Ernst & Young report, the damage was done.

The problem of Nike's apparent exploitation of its overseas employees, based on long hours and low pay, was now compounded by the issue of the unhealthy environmental condition of the factories. Six months later, Nike was presented with another hurdle.

In April 1998, a lawsuit was filed by labor activist Marc Kasky against Nike in a California Superior Court alleging that Nike's statements of protection of its workers amounted to false advertising under California's consumer-protection laws.[3] Under California's broad consumer-protection laws, a plaintiff is not required to prove he or she has suffered personal injury—only that there was a likelihood of deception.

The main question of the lawsuit was whether Nike's public statements were considered advertising for the company and therefore subject to truth-in-advertising laws, or if they were simply public statements that are protected by the First Amendment.

The California Court of Appeal agreed with Nike that the information in question was "corporate speech" and therefore protected by the First Amendment, saying, in effect, that Kasky could not proceed with a lawsuit on the merits of the case. The California Supreme Court, however, sided with Kasky, ruling that the intent of Nike's speech was to advance its commercial interests and therefore was not protected by the First Amendment. Under this ruling, Kasky was permitted to proceed with his legal actions.

Nike appealed to the U.S. Supreme Court, which initially agreed to hear the case. However, in June 2003, the Court decided to dismiss the "writ of certiorari, thereby refusing to decide the questions presented, at least for now" (*Nike v. Kasky,* U.S. Supreme Court). In September 2003, Nike and Kasky buried the legal hatchet. Nike agreed to donate $1.5 million to the Fair Labor Association, settling the legal battle without ever having the facts of the case go to trial (see the box "*Nike v. Kasky:* More at Stake Than Labor Issues").

## Nike Puts Its Best Foot Forward

Nike was now experiencing some financial repercussions—drops in stock prices and sales—from the coverage of their labor practices, which were viewed by many as exploitive and unethical. Nike was finally facing the fact that its policies *did* make it look bad in the press, were inherently wrong, and engendered a feeling of ill will. This time, the company took a more proactive approach.

In May 1998, at the National Press Club in Washington, D.C., Chairman and CEO Philip Knight announced Nike's new labor initiatives aimed at improving factory working conditions worldwide. The main elements of the initiatives are:

- Increase the minimum age of new employees in the shoe factories to 18 years of age
- Improve the air quality by using the standards enforced by the Occupational Safety and Health Administration (OSHA)
- A commitment to a policy of open communications on corporate responsibility issues
- A pledge to allow independent monitoring of its factories by nongovernmental organizations

However, the initiatives do not address the issues of forced overtime and increasing earnings to a living wage. (*Editor's Note: Just what constitutes a "living wage" is at the heart of the debate over Nike's business practices. Many U.S.-based manufacturing operations are moving jobs to countries such as China, Indonesia, and Singapore because the workers earn much less than those in similar jobs in the United States. Such countries often have nothing like the EPA, OSHA, and*
(*Continued*)

---

[3] Josh Richman, "Greenwashing on Trial," MoJo Wire (*Mother Jones Magazine* online), February 23, 2001.

*similar workplace watchdogs that can add to manufacturing costs. Union representation is much less likely in offshore factories as well. Although wages paid in these countries might be "normal" for the area, they frequently pale in comparison to wages in the United States.)* In his speech, Philip Knight said, "These moves do more than just set industry standards. They reflect who we are as a company."

## Both Sides Use the Internet

As the Internet has become an everyday resource for more and more people, companies of all sizes now use it as a worldwide marketing and public relations tool. If a company wants to let people know what it has to offer by promoting itself globally, the Internet provides that outlet.

The Internet is also an outlet for activism against corporations.[4] The online attacks can take place on specific Web sites, in chat rooms, or on Web bulletin boards. Negative postings on the Internet are considered a serious public relations problem by companies because millions of people could potentially see those messages. Controversial information about a company, whether factual or not, can result in a public relations nightmare that could take years to resolve.

Personal journals or Weblogs (blogs) also are of increasing concern to companies. A technorati.com search of "Nike" yielded 413,964 blog posts in 2007 with some reference to the company or its namesake brand.

Nike's Web site (www.nikebiz.com) became operational in 1996. The site contained a great range of information on the company, including a section entitled "Responsibility." Within that section, Nike addressed the issues of global community, the environment, and diversity. In the section on labor, the company provided information on factory monitoring results and updates on working conditions at various factory locations. Today, the section still exists though an interested party would have to dig deep to find it on the Web site.

## 2001—The Three-Year Anniversary of Nike's Labor Initiatives

In May 2001, Nike, Inc., on the three-year anniversary of its new labor initiatives, issued a press release that reviewed the successes and challenges of its corporate responsibility. It noted that Nike was "working collaboratively alongside human rights groups and various NGOs" and that it had "increased wages more than 100 percent over the past several years for entry-level Indonesian footwear factory workers." Despite these and other successes, the release also stated that "there is still progress to be made." As Dusty Kidd, vice-president of corporate responsibility, put it, "As in every area of Nike's business, there is no finish line, and improving the lives and working conditions of the workers who make Nike products is no exception."

Within 24 hours of the release of Nike's statement, *The Wall Street Journal* reported, on May 16, 2001, that Global Exchange, a human-rights organization, had accused Nike of failing to follow through on many of its 1998 initiatives. In addition to other criticisms, Global Exchange said that the living-wage issue had still not been fully addressed and that Nike's factory-monitoring resources were not truly independent of the company.

Nike suspended releasing its "Corporate Responsibility Report" for three years, reintroducing it in 2005.

In recent years, Nike has continued to be a target of boycotts, media investigations, and international protest. A frequent complaint is that the company treats the labor problems as a public relations issue and not as a human rights issue in that it *presents* itself as a socially responsible corporation. Most any company would want to be viewed as doing the right thing, but how much should good

---

[4] Jamie Carrington, "Answering to the Internet," *The World Paper,* October 2000.

intentions alone be rewarded? Nike contends it is improving conditions in its many plants, but acknowledges "there is no finish line" when it comes to human rights and humane working conditions. So the question remains: Who determines if the socially responsible steps a corporation has taken are enough?

## Déjà Vu Apple? Why Not?

So, Apple computer, the darling of Silicon Valley and consumers everywhere, knew they had to deal with the ethical liability of working with contract employers overseas and their management styles and culture. Apple

---

### *Nike v. Kasky:* More at Stake than Labor Issues

When Nike decided to settle the *Nike v. Kasky* lawsuit by donating $1.5 million to the Fair Labor Association (a labor-conditions watchdog group), it was the official end to a case that had (and has) immense ramifications for the public relations industry.

Still unsettled, however, are the issues that brought the case to the U.S. Supreme Court in the first place: Can a company defend itself in the court of public opinion and have that speech fall under the Freedom-of-Speech clause of the First Amendment? The companion question is: Can anything (and everything) said by a profit-making company be construed as commercial speech (and unprotected), because of the assumption that everything a profit-making organization does is focused on a commercial purpose?

In the *Nike v. Kasky* suit, the Supreme Court first decided to hear the case and determine if Nike was protected by the First Amendment when it mailed news releases; letters to the editors of papers, including *The New York Times*; brochures to retail customers; and letters to key colleges and others who had a stake in Nike's business. After accepting briefs and hearing oral arguments, the Court "took the highly unusual step of deciding that the appeal had come to them prematurely and sent the case back to California" (Ken Paulson, executive director, First Amendment Center, September 28, 2003). That left the California Supreme Court decision intact, but did nothing to address the larger question that Paulson said "could have forever altered the free-speech rights of corporations...."

Nike's mailings—standard public relations tools—were based, in part, on a study of working conditions in Third World nations completed by Dr. Andrew Young in 1997. Dr. Young, a close associate of Dr. Martin Luther King during the 1960s civil rights movement, later served as U.S. Ambassador to the United Nations under President Jimmy Carter and was elected to two terms as mayor of Atlanta. It was this pedigree that made his report so credible—and worthy of broad distribution by Nike. Essentially, he found Nike's contract shops to be at least up to standards in their countries and, in many cases, above standard. The report didn't address wages, but rather focused on working conditions.

Kasky's 1998 suit was based on these actions and similar efforts by Nike to offer the public a different look at the so-called "sweatshop" issue. Nike, naturally, wanted a rosier view of its practices, but Kasky, a veteran activist with environmental and community-service groups, protested that Nike's statements were misleading and, therefore, constituted false advertising. The California court agreed, and the U.S. Supreme Court did not disagree.

"The clear winner here was Kasky and workers' rights organizations," said Paulson. "The list of losers is not limited to Nike. Every corporation doing business in California now has to think long and hard about any public statements concerning its company."

This is a major hurdle for the public relations profession, because perhaps the primary function of public relations is advocacy. We are supposed to be strong, ethical advocates for our employers and clients. If robbed of that function, then public relations, as a profession, loses one

---

*(Continued)*

of its major strengths. Nike's defense was bolstered by more than 40 briefs filed by such strange bedfellows as media corporations, chambers of commerce, and the American Civil Liberties Union. None wanted corporate speech to lose its First Amendment protection.

The good news surrounding *Nike v. Kasky* is that the decision now in effect in that case applies only to California. California is well known for its interesting legal and political climate. At the time of the Kasky suit, the State of California permitted a private citizen to act as a de facto attorney general suing on behalf of people with whom no relationship was established and on matters in which the citizen had no personal standing. Those were the conditions of Kasky's suit against Nike. He needed to show no personal loss or damage to bring action against Nike.

Since that time, that avenue has been closed in California, but the state is still known for liberal interpretation of laws, especially those related to advertising and commercial speech. For example, the book *The Beardstown Ladies' Common-Sense Investment Guide* claimed on a cover blurb that the amateur-investor ladies had realized investment gains exceeding 23 percent over a 10-year period. However, some independent math put the gains at less than 10 percent. In 1988, a class-action lawsuit was filed on behalf of all book buyers (some 800,000), but a New York court decided the cover-blurb copy was a summary of information contained in the book—and therefore protected by the First Amendment.

A similar suit was filed in California, where the court decided the blurb constituted "commercial speech" and was therefore "false advertising." The publisher settled the suit by offering a free book to those affected, but it spent more than $1 million in its defense.[5]

This *Beardstown* example illustrates that legal interpretations differ from state to state, which is why a California decision applies only to California. That is also why there is a U.S. Supreme Court. Laws of the land that apply generally need to be consistent. The same suit shouldn't get polar opposite rulings in two states.

The real danger of allowing *Nike v. Kasky* to stand lies in the "chilling effect" of such a lawsuit. Paulson quotes Quentin Riegel, vice-president of litigation for the National Association of Manufacturers, who said, "Companies will be pressured into cutting back their participation in and dialogues on important issues."

So-called "corporate speech" (also known as "political speech") has been around since landmark cases such as *First National Bank of Boston v. Bellotti* (1978) and *Bolger v. Young's Drug Products* (1983). In these cases, the Supreme Court ruled that corporations have First Amendment rights to free speech on issues of importance to society. The content of the speech, not the nature of the "speaker," was determined to be paramount.

Nike was looking to the courts to declare its defense part of the public debate on important issues. For now, that's not happening. With the financial settlement, no determination as to the accuracy or validity of Nike's statements will be made. Constitutional issues and financial expediency took that determination off the table.

---

[5] Available at writ.news.findlaw.com/ramasastry/20060202.html.

---

earned $12 billion in the second quarter of 2011 alone, selling 35.1 million iPhones, 11.8 million iPads, 4 million Macs, and 7.7 million iPods. Multiple Apple products populate most houses in America. The company was successful everywhere. One of the best known companies in the world, Apple had much to lose

if human rights abuses occurred as a result of manufacturing their products.

Learning from other companies' mistakes and having a corporate commitment to doing the right thing, Apple established contracts that delineated how its foreign workers would be treated. Contract employers would have to abide by the contract or not continue as Apple suppliers. According to the supplier contracts, "all of our suppliers [must] provide safe working conditions, treat workers with dignity and respect, and use environmentally responsible manufacturing processes. Our actions—from thorough site audits to industry-leading training programs—demonstrate this commitment."

Apple laid out an audit process that included regular and surprise inspections and a series of policies that, they claimed, were the toughest in the industry. Not relying just on their own standards, Apple adopted standards put in place by others, including the Electronic Industry Citizenship Coalition (EICC), an organization established in 2004 to promote common codes of conduct for the electronics and information and communications technology industry. The EICC code was developed using internationally recognized standards from the International Labor Organization and the United Nations. Apple said these standards in fact "go beyond in the areas of ending involuntary labor practices, eliminating underage labor, and preventing excessive working hours."

In January 2012, a blogger and theatrical performer of monologues by the name of Mike Daisey went on NPR's *This American Life* and told "embellished or fabricated" stories of worker abuses at the plants of Apple contractors in China. Soon after, a reporter who questioned some of Daisey's stories dug deep and found that his stories were false.

Apple's response was muted since the media that had reported the story actually did the work to refute it once it was out there. Most likely good relationships between Apple and the news media prompted a closer look at the Daisey reports. The uproar over Daisey's fabrications by the media who reported it in the first place did more to vindicate Apple than all the protestations and facts that Apple could ever have produced.

*Forbes* magazine blogger, Josh Barro, asked the obvious question, "Why didn't Apple sue Daisey?" He answered his own question by surmising that Apple knew it wouldn't serve its interests and would only be a rehash of the details already published. As it was, Daisey's fans continued to support him and his shows regardless. And though the actual stories Daisey told were fabricated, it would not have stopped some from questioning the Chinese business practices that Apple tacitly supports by doing business in China, regardless of its honorable contracts with suppliers.

## Questions for Discussion
### Nike

1. Does Nike have a responsibility to monitor working conditions in plants owned and operated by contractors? Why?
2. Is "a low wage is better than no wage" a sound public relations strategy for Nike? Why?
3. What role did falling stock prices and dwindling sales play in Nike's strategy and actions?
4. Is the working environment in a contract work site an operational or a public relations problem?

### Apple

1. What purpose would it have served for Apple to sue Mr. Daisey?
2. How do you believe the outcome might have been different if Apple did not have its contract in place prior to the controversy?
3. What are the ethical considerations of doing business in a country that treats its employees significantly differently from how we do in the United States, even if that treatment is in keeping with the culture of that country?
4. What pros and cons about suing Mr. Daisey would you have presented to Apple's management?

*(Continued)*

http://investors.nikeinc.com/Theme/Nike/files/
    doc_financials/AnnualReports/2011/index.
    html#select_financials

http://nikeinc.com/pages/about-nike-inc

http://www.statista.com/statistics/216821/forecast-
    for-nikes-global-market-share-in-athletic-foot-
    wear-until-2017/

http://www.dailyfinance.com/2011/04/08/growth-
    potential-for-nike-may-hinge-on-sports-apparel-
    market/

http://www.nikeresponsibility.com/report/content/
    chapter/labor

http://www.apple.com/supplierresponsibility/audit-
    ing.html

http://www.apple.com/supplierresponsibility/
    code-of-conduct

http://www.forbes.com/sites/joshbarro/2012/03/17/
    why-didnt-apple-sue-mike-daisey/

http://news.cnet.com/8301-13579_3-57426193-37/
    apple-critic-mike-daisey-is-as-hot-as-ever/

# Case 10-4 Dow Corning and Breast Implants: Dealing with the Perception of Deception

The most popular cosmetic surgery of 2011 was breast augmentation, with 307,180 women getting saline or silicone implants. Those numbers clearly exceeded the runners up: nose jobs (243,772) and liposuction (204,782).

The number of breast augmentations represents a marked turnaround for a procedure that once generated 19,000 lawsuits and bankrupted a major manufacturer: Dow Corning. After banning silicone implants for 14 years, the Food and Drug Administration (FDA) in 2006 gave the green light to silicone, based on long-term studies that showed no causal relationship between implants and the several medical problems prompting the law suits.

Breast implants never really went away. In the midst of the FDA ban, women continued to receive implants—just not silicone. In 2000, for example, six years before the FDA reapproved silicone, women received 212,500 augmentations, according to statistics from the American Society of Plastic Surgeons. As recently as June 2011, the FDA was confirming the "relative safety" of silicone.

For Dow Corning, the FDA approvals and confirmations represent too little too late.

One of the biggest headaches for manufacturers continues to be the proliferation of product liability suits. Some companies are taking products off the market because of the risk of these suits, yet a number of the cases are filed with reason. What would be the responsible and ethical thing to do if a product has been implicated as defective or harmful, even if research may indicate the opposite? What can be done to make it up to those who may have been harmed or to allay the fears of those who *perceive* the product as harmful?

In the early 1990s, Dow Corning was faced with a great number of angry women when silicone-gel breast implants (manufactured by Dow Corning and several others) were indicated as a possible cause of health problems the women were experiencing. This case examines how public *perception* of Dow Corning's behavior evolved into a question of credibility for the organization.

The company *did* have an ethics policy in place since 1976 that was guiding decision making, but the public perceived that it was making business and legal decisions without addressing the ethical issues around the continued use of its breast implants.

## History

The history of breast implantation in the United States is a long one. Since 1962, women have been paying to have doctors surgically enhance their breast size, for various reasons, through the use of silicone-gel or saline solution implants encased in silicone envelopes. Many do it for self-esteem reasons (about 80 percent), and others want reconstructive surgery after having a mastectomy due to breast cancer (about 20 percent). Almost 2 million women have had breast implants to date.

Silicone gel was the choice for many women because it seemed more "lifelike" after implantation. Saline solution implants (made of salt and water) were considered less risky for the body, but women chose them less often because they did not feel as natural and sometimes made "sloshing sounds."

Until 1991, the highest perceived risk from breast implantation was in the surgical procedure itself. (Like any device implanted into the body, it may have adverse effects in a small number of patients.) However, silicone's effects on the human body's autoimmune

*(Continued)*

system were not known. An enormous amount of breast-implant testing had been done beginning in the 1950s, but when the issue arose in the 1990s there was a perception that there was little, if any, product testing completed. Despite the amount of research that had been done, breast implants were alleged to be the possible cause of serious medical problems, including immunological disorders, arthritis, infections, reduced mammogram effectiveness, and cancer.

The possible risks of breast implants fall into two basic categories: those related directly to the breast (easy to observe) and those that may involve distant parts of the body (much harder to observe and difficult to measure).

Some of the possible breast-related risks are:

- Difficulty in detecting abnormalities in the breast when mammographic X-rays are taken
- Breasts may harden—as a result of fibrous tissue growing around the implant—possibly causing discomfort and pain
- Breakage of the envelope, causing the gel filling to be released

Other risks are:

- Migration of the gel filling throughout the body (with possible unpleasant cosmetic effects)
- The perception that breast implants may cause autoimmune diseases

## Dow Corning's Role

Dow Corning Corporation, jointly owned by the Dow Chemical Company and Corning, Inc., had been one of the most visible manufacturers of silicone-gel breast implants, although implants represented less than one percent of the company's sales prior to and at the start of the legal actions. Dow Corning came under fire in 1991 when Marianne Hopkins, who had received silicone-gel breast implants in 1976, brought suit—claiming the product was responsible for damage to her immune system. The alleged cause was silicone leakage. With this case, many questions began to surface about implants.

One contributing factor to the uproar is that all medical devices were unregulated until 1976, 14 years after breast implantations had begun, so there was no standard of testing and regulation to follow. Devices in use before the regulations were considered "grandfathered," which meant the manufacturers of those products were not required to provide the FDA with scientific evidence of safety and effectiveness. That stipulation in the law was based on the premise that more was known about the safety of a device that has been in use for some time than about one that had been newly developed. However, if questions arose over time that cast any doubt about a grandfathered device's safety, the law gave the FDA the authority to go back and require that its manufacturer provide evidence to demonstrate that the device was safe and effective.[6]

In the 1980s, the FDA devices division did not have the budget or personnel to regulate medical devices adequately, and had adopted a lax attitude in testing and regulating new medical devices put on the market. Finally, in April 1991, with intensified publicity and court cases, implant manufacturers were ordered to prove that their silicone implants were safe. This regulatory action had been recommended by an FDA advisory panel a decade earlier, although it had not been enforced—a fact that damaged public perceptions.

## Credibility Problems

In June 1991, Dow Corning documents surfaced in a *Business Week* article that implied

---

om "Background Information on the Possible Health Risks of Silicone Breast Implants," released by the FDA
ber 1990 and revised February 1991.

that the implants might have been rushed to market without proper medical testing. Top management was reassuring the general public of the relative safety of its product, but internal memos (created by those not aware of research taking place or past research that had been conducted) were being passed around that seemed to indicate an awareness of animal studies that linked the implants to cancer and other illnesses. In addition, investigative reports dating back 25 years were brought to light indicating that implants could break or leak into patient's bodies. (Those reports had been a matter of public record, but now received attention with this new public scrutiny.) The company *appeared* as if it had been covering up the reports and hiding the true facts.

At first, Dow Corning attacked investigators. This action was interpreted as a lack of concern for the public interest and prompted many to criticize the company as lacking any code of corporate ethics, concerned only with covering itself legally. The reality was that the company did have a code of ethics in place.[7] Some of the initial communication actions that it implemented to allay public misconceptions were:

- Developing a packet of information that physicians could share with their patients that was user friendly and explained the research conducted by Dow Corning and others about the implants. It outlined the possible risks associated with silicone breast implants.

- Company physicians and scientists scheduling technical presentations at medical meetings to discuss the scientific implications of implants.

- Making public all proprietary information available to competitors by publicly releasing all the scientific studies used to support its premarket approval application for the implant.

- Meeting directly with breast cancer support groups and representatives of other consumer groups, both for and against breast implants.

## Company Is Dealt Painful Legal Blow

Judgment in the Marianne Hopkins case was handed down in December 1991. She was awarded $7.3 million in compensatory and punitive damages, and Dow Corning was found to have committed fraud and malice by failing to disclose evidence from its research on the implants. With this damaging judgment, public scrutiny intensified, and many questions were brought up in the media about the implants and what other information Dow Corning may have withheld.

The company was taking the hard line in dealing with this issue in the media. Dow Corning was finding it difficult to appear sympathetic to the women who did have problems without undermining its legal strategy and admitting fault. It appeared to be a classic case of legal versus public relations. And it was not helped by CEO Lawrence A. Reed, who unfortunately was not adept in media situations. This deficiency reduced his ability to take command of this crisis or to stay ahead of the critics. Reed's invisibility as a spokesperson confirmed the prevalent perception in the court of public opinion that the company was not concerned with the welfare of those who had received the implants.[8]

The task of presenting the Dow Corning "voice" to the public was passed around to many people until it rested on the shoulders of the vice-president in charge of health care, Robert

*(Continued)*

---

[7] Lee W. Baker, *The Credibility Factor,* Homewood, IL: Business One Irwin, 1992, p. 35. An informative book that emphasizes the importance of ethics in the practice of public relations by examining the mistakes and successes of organizations in varying ethical situations.

[8] Kevin McCauley, "Dow Corning Fumbles PR in Breast Implant Crisis," *O'Dwyer's PR Services Report* 6 (March 1992), p. 1.

T. Rylee, and others on his staff. There was no One Clear Voice responding to the public.

Reed's failure as a leader in the public eye was compared in the news media to the fumbling responses and lack of reaction from Exxon CEO Lawrence Rawl in handling the Exxon Valdez oil spill in 1989. At Dow Corning, spokespeople were taking a reactive stance and focusing on the fact that there was little or no *scientific* evidence proving that the implants caused these health problems—ignoring the fact that women had gotten the implants for *emotional and cosmetic* reasons and would predictably respond on an emotional plane.

To deal with the barrage of questions from the public, Dow Corning set up an "implant information hotline" in July 1991. By the end of the year, that, too, was receiving criticism from the FDA and high-profile news media coverage. Callers to the hotline were being reassured by the operators about the safety of the implants, and Dow Corning was accused of overselling their safety. The company then agreed to send only printed information to callers. However, the operators of the hotlines were ultimately retrained to offer only factual information in order to allay any public misconceptions. More than 50,000 women called the hotline to obtain information.

## The FDA Takes Action

On January 6, 1992, as public scrutiny intensified, FDA Commissioner David Kessler proposed a voluntary moratorium on the sale and use of silicone implants pending further investigation. Most all silicone-gel implant manufacturers complied.

Dow Corning complied with the request, still claiming that the implants did not have a damaging effect on the body. However, public and media scrutiny did not abate; instead, it intensified. *The Wall Street Journal* and *The New York Times* ran articles giving Dow Corning failing marks for its handling of the crisis. The rising tide of lawsuits was threatening the corporation and further diminishing its already waning credibility.

*The New York Times* stated that Dow Corning failed in the court of public opinion because it was ignoring how consumers respond to health threats:

1. Even a small number of people who feel they have been mistreated by a company or received a poor product can rally enough friends and allies to have a great negative impact on the company involved.

2. The number of defective or dangerous products often turns out to be higher than the company that manufactures them originally projects. With the publicity that the implants were receiving, many more complaints, both valid and invalid, were bound to surface.

3. Consumers who feel they have been deceived often become extremely upset. The information that leaked out over the years of litigation about the implants suggested that Dow Corning was trying to cover up information that may be damaging to its product without concern for the consumer.[9]

## Media Coverage Intensifies Problem

As the issue unfolded, Dow Corning began to track the media coverage of the controversy. While the news media were widely reporting on the situation as it developed, most of the coverage was incomplete and unbalanced. Women were clamoring for information because of the intense media scrutiny. To respond to the need for information, Dow Corning reached out to those concerned by taking the following communications actions:

- Became more responsive to the news media by distributing an 800-page book compiling memos, scientific studies, and related issues.

---

y J. Feder, "Dow Corning's Failure in Public Opinion Test," *The New York Times,* January 29, 1992, pp. D1–D2.

- Gave a grant to the American Society for Plastic and Reconstructive Surgical Nurses to distribute educational materials to patients.
- Proposed a national communications registry, a collaborative effort between the FDA, consumers, health professionals, and current and former breast-implant manufacturers to provide periodic newsletters to breast-implant recipients.[10]

## Dow Corning Responds

On February 10, 1992, Dow Corning began to take steps to repair its battered reputation. Lawrence Reed was replaced by Keith McKennon, a former Dow Chemical executive well known for his conciliatory abilities. McKennon had helped Dow steer itself out of potentially damaging public relations situations that involved the Agent Orange defoliant used in Vietnam. McKennon's attitude was much more take-charge and less defensive, and from the start of his appointment he was the company voice on the issue. In the spirit of this new openness, McKennon gave almost 100 interviews on the controversy.

In keeping with this new attitude, Dow Corning announced in March 1992 its plans to get out of the breast-implant-manufacturing business. In addition, it promised to spend $10 million on research into the safety of the implants and would contribute up to $1,200 per patient (depending on financial need) to remove the silicone-gel implants. While Dow Corning still maintained that the implants were safe, it was finally taking conciliatory actions that recognized the need for further research to satisfy the concerns of the FDA and those women possibly at risk.

Dow Corning succeeded in removing some of the damaging attention from the information that had suddenly been brought into public view. Now the company focused on the *positive* actions it would take to make restitution to those women who felt they had been wronged.

## Rebuilding Its Credibility

Dow Corning has succeeded in making small gains to win back public opinion. It is funding 30 laboratory and clinical safety tests and epidemiological studies on a global basis to establish the risks of the implants in the human body. Some women have been allowed to have the silicone implants if they agree to become part of a long-term study on the implants' effects. Also, the International Breast Implant Registry was founded in 2002 under the auspices of the International Plastic, Reconstructive and Aesthetic Surgery Foundation to help monitor the women's health.

In September 1993, the company announced that a global settlement had been proposed, a $4.75 billion fund for breast-implant recipients, funded by the manufacturers, suppliers, doctors, and insurance companies involved in the implant industry. It would give women the opportunity to recover money for their injuries over the course of 30 years. Dow Corning would contribute up to $2 billion to the fund over that time period. The fund would pay for checkups for women with implants, removal of the devices, and treatment of varied illnesses. Other terms of the agreement were:

- Recipients of any brand of breast implant would be included.
- Claimants would not be required to prove that their breast implants caused their injuries.

*(Continued)*

[10] Ralph C. Cook, Myron C. Harrison, and Robert R. LeVier, "The Breast Implant Controversy," *Arthritis and Rheumatism* 37, February 1994, pp.1–14. A thoughtful article examining the medical issues and communication problems of the breast implant controversy, written by three Dow Corning scientists (available from the company, Midland, Michigan).

- Those who claimed the breast implants had caused damage to their health would be able to exclude themselves from the general settlement and then sue individually.
- A recipient of breast implants who had sued a financially unstable company would be able to submit a claim to the fund.[11]

## Continued Controversy

In the wake of this financial settlement, the effects of silicone implants continue to be greatly disputed. The FDA has engaged in heated debates with the American Medical Association (AMA) about the level of risk posed by silicone breast implants. To date, the AMA has supported allowing all women the right to have breast implants once they have been informed of the risks. Former FDA Commissioner Kessler disagreed because he felt physicians were not being responsible about informing women of risks, in spite of the fact that the FDA panel that looked at the breast implant studies recommended the implants be kept on the market. He faulted physicians for using implants for 30 years without adequately discussing the risks with patients.[12]

---

In November 2006, the FDA removed its 14-year ban on silicone breast implants. Dow Corning is no longer in that business, but two companies—Mentor and Allergan—are expected to enter the market. The hometown paper of Dow Corning, the *Midland Daily News,* wrote the following on the day the announcement was made.

### Our View: Who's Sorry Now?

Something was missing in Friday's announcement by the Food and Drug Administration that it was lifting a 14-year ban on silicone-gel breast implants: an apology to Midland's Dow Corning Corp.

That's the least the agency could do, since it was the FDA's ban on the implants in 1992 that sparked an onslaught of lawsuits—19,000 of them—and forced Dow Corning into Chapter 11 bankruptcy to keep the company afloat.

Billions of dollars later, Dow Corning emerged from bankruptcy. Perhaps along with an apology, the FDA should have offered some help in paying those billions the company had to shell out to settle its legal claims. Isn't that the least the FDA could do, since it played such a huge role in casting doubt about the silicone-gel implants the agency now is saying are safe?

Dow Corning officials, in their response to the FDA announcement, took the high road, simply pointing out that this case shows "the critical need for science literacy and its importance in making informed decisions, as individuals, as government agencies, and as a society."

We'll take it one step further. This case shows the problems that occur when a government agency becomes a pawn for a class-action-eager civil lawsuit system willing to take down an innocent company for the sake of the almighty buck.

The FDA's announcement Friday was welcome, but it was more than a decade overdue.

*Source:* "FDA," *Midland Daily News,* Midland, MI, November 21, 2006.

---

"Dow Corning Nears Implant Settlement," *Associated Press* story, as it appeared in *Bangor Daily News,* September ?3.

?her Connell, "Doctors Protest Curb on Breast Implants," *Associated Press* story as it appeared in *Bangor* ), December 1, 1993.

One irony is that, as the multibillion-dollar settlement was established by the other implant manufacturers, and Dow Corning filed for Chapter 11 to avoid the onslaught of more than 19,000 lawsuits, new evidence has emerged that shows no causal link between the implants and the autoimmune diseases allegedly caused by them. Since no link was found between the implants and the diseases they have been accused of causing, should Dow Corning still have to pay close to $5 billion to emerge from Chapter 11? Should women still be allowed to file lawsuits against Dow Corning? What would be the ethical thing for Dow Corning to do in the future? These questions pose some interesting public relations problems.

## Questions for Discussion

1. Dow Corning fumbled this crisis because it found it difficult to initially show concern for the recipients of breast implants while still maintaining a legal stance that endorsed the safety of the product. What could the company have done differently to keep this issue from rising to the epic proportions it did in the public arena? Could the entire issue have been avoided through appropriate communications?

2. Can a company act unethically and maintain credibility? Why or why not? Can you think of examples one way or the other? Is it unethical to withdraw a product from the public when there is no proof of a problem, thus denying the public access to the product?

3. Several companies manufacture implants. It is surgeons who suggest them to women and perform the operations. Yet only Dow Corning drew unfavorable public reaction. Why?

4. Whose responsibility is it to inform women who are interested in having breast implants of the risks of the procedure? Why do you believe this?

5. What are the ethical implications now that scientific study has shown that the implants have not caused negative health effects? What are the implications for Dow Corning?

6. Does the ultimate vindication of Dow Corning and silicone implants change your perspective on this case?

## PROBLEM 10-A   WHETHER TO BLOW THE WHISTLE

You are nearing the end of your second year of employment as editor of the main publication for employees in one of the three largest nonprofit hospitals in the county. You have a good deal. Your boss, the director of public relations, a woman of about 35, listens to your ideas about the publication. You have converted it from a tabloid appearing once a month to a weekly newsletter with online headline updates as needed for need-to-know information. An audit shows that readers, including staff doctors and donors as well as employees, find the newsletter combined with the online information to be more dynamic than the earlier publication. They like it. The only intervention you have had from your boss was near the end of your first year. At that time, she told you to follow the hospital's policy of getting three competitive printing bids annually and then to award the contract for the next year to one of the three. You noted that the current supplier's bid was not the lowest. Your boss explained that she preferred the quality of the selected supplier and added that the printing firm had made generous financial contributions to the hospital. At that time, you followed the directions of your boss.

The future looks bright to you. And why not? You are aware that your boss has her eyes on the next job up, as director of development, a position now occupied by a woman scheduled to retire in a few years. You can see yourself succeeding your boss at that time.

Looking back, you consider your first two years to have been a period of learning the ropes and how the game goes in the hospital. During this period, the owner of the printing firm doing the newsletter has established a social relationship with you and your spouse, including taking you to dinner at their country club.

*(Continued)*

You have also noticed that the printer has a close personal relationship with your boss and the hospital's director of development. You know that they receive free tickets to entertainments and other gifts. When the director of development decided to buy a new car, the printer sent her to a dealer who gave her a fantastic discount. As for the public relations director, your boss, she was sponsored for membership in the printer's "Executives Only" tennis club.

Here you are, finishing up your second year. A few days ago, quite by coincidence, you overheard some disconcerting comments during a cocktail party. The comments indicated that your boss's husband is the brother of the printer's wife—this you didn't know. Also, your boss apparently has had some sort of financial interest in the printing firm. Your director of development's daughter, you heard, has worked at the printing firm as a typist-receptionist. Someone at the party said that she earned more than other clerical employees there, including those with greater skills and experience.

Naturally, this information is upsetting to you, and, to make matters worse, this is the week the three competitive printing bids for next year's contract have come in. You have looked at them. The present printer, whom you have again been told to favor, has submitted a bid 20 percent higher than the lowest of the three.

You have every right to be upset and in a quandary. If you grant the business for the coming year, amounting to $60,000, to the highest bidder, and someone in the treasurer's office questions it, you could be in big trouble. If you tell the present printer he has to submit a second bid at a figure 50 percent lower, you will be unethical in conduct and in contravention of the hospital's stated policy. Beyond that, what if one of the other bidders found out and turned in a complaint to the consumer advocate in the state's attorney general's office? If you take the matter to your boss, you may have to confront her with what you have heard about an apparent conflict of interest on her part.

Of course, an alternative would be to go over the boss's head to the director of development. She, too, has accepted favors from the printer on a social basis. Maybe she would just as soon not get involved. On the other hand, perhaps she has been involved in helping the printer get work from other departments in the hospital. If so, where would that leave you?

Then there is the hospital administrator. If you bypass both of your superiors in the structure, you will almost surely wind up with an unhappy working situation—or be out looking for a new position.

Finally, if you do nothing, are you committed to a standard of honesty or business ethics that you cannot live with?

Everything considered, what are you going to do—specifically, in what sequence, with what goals, and what personal strategy and tactics?

## PROBLEM 10-B    WRITE THE TRUTH OR "MAKE US LOOK GOOD"?

You've just been hired by a prestigious philanthropic organization that donates a lot of money to help the poor and the undereducated. You are joining a well-oiled public relations department where you report to the vice-president. You are excited by the chance to "serve," to do something "meaningful" with your expertise.

At the first all-departments meeting, you notice some derogatory comments being made about the people the organization serves. You overlook them and think that people are just being people. But then, as discussion comes up about where to focus the organization's money, you notice the direction isn't where the money is most needed but where the organization can get the most "bang for the buck" in terms of building its image.

You're beginning to have a dilemma. The organization does good deeds by giving out its money and helping others. But, inside, the culture stinks in the way it talks about its clients and how it aims to use its money. No one else there seems to share your view—or at least no one acknowledges that they do.

Now your boss is asking you to write the news release announcing the organization's newest funding project and wants you to "make us look good. The folks getting the money won't mind if you make some of it up." You want to just write the truth and let that speak for itself, but you're afraid your boss might question your ability. You don't want to get fired. What will you do?

# INDEX